A History of the Renaissance Picture

Ground work

David Young Kim

Princeton University Press
Princeton and Oxford

Published by Princeton University Press, 41 William Street, Princeton, New Jersey 08540

In the United Kingdom: Princeton University Press, 99 Banbury Road, Oxford OX2 6JX

press.princeton.edu

Jacket image: Detail from Giovanni Bellini, *St. Francis in the Desert*, ca. 1480

Library of Congress Cataloging-in-Publication Data

Names: Kim, David Young, author.
Title: Groundwork : a history of the Renaissance picture / David Young Kim.
Description: Princeton : Princeton University Press, [2022] | Includes bibliographical references and index.
Identifiers: LCCN 2021050075 (print) | LCCN 2021050076 (ebook) | ISBN 9780691231174 (hardcover) | ISBN 9780691238470 (ebook)
Subjects: LCSH: Painting, Renaissance—Italy. | Painting, Italian. | Background (Art) | Ground (Coatings)
Classification: LCC ND615 .K54 2022 (print) | LCC ND615 (ebook) | DDC 759.5—dc23/eng/20220423
LC record available at https://lccn.loc.gov/2021050075
LC ebook record available at https://lccn.loc.gov/2021050076

British Library Cataloging-in-Publication Data is available

Designed by Jeff Wincapaw

This book has been composed in Dante MT Std

Printed on acid-free paper. ∞

Printed in Italy

10 9 8 7 6 5 4 3 2 1

Contents

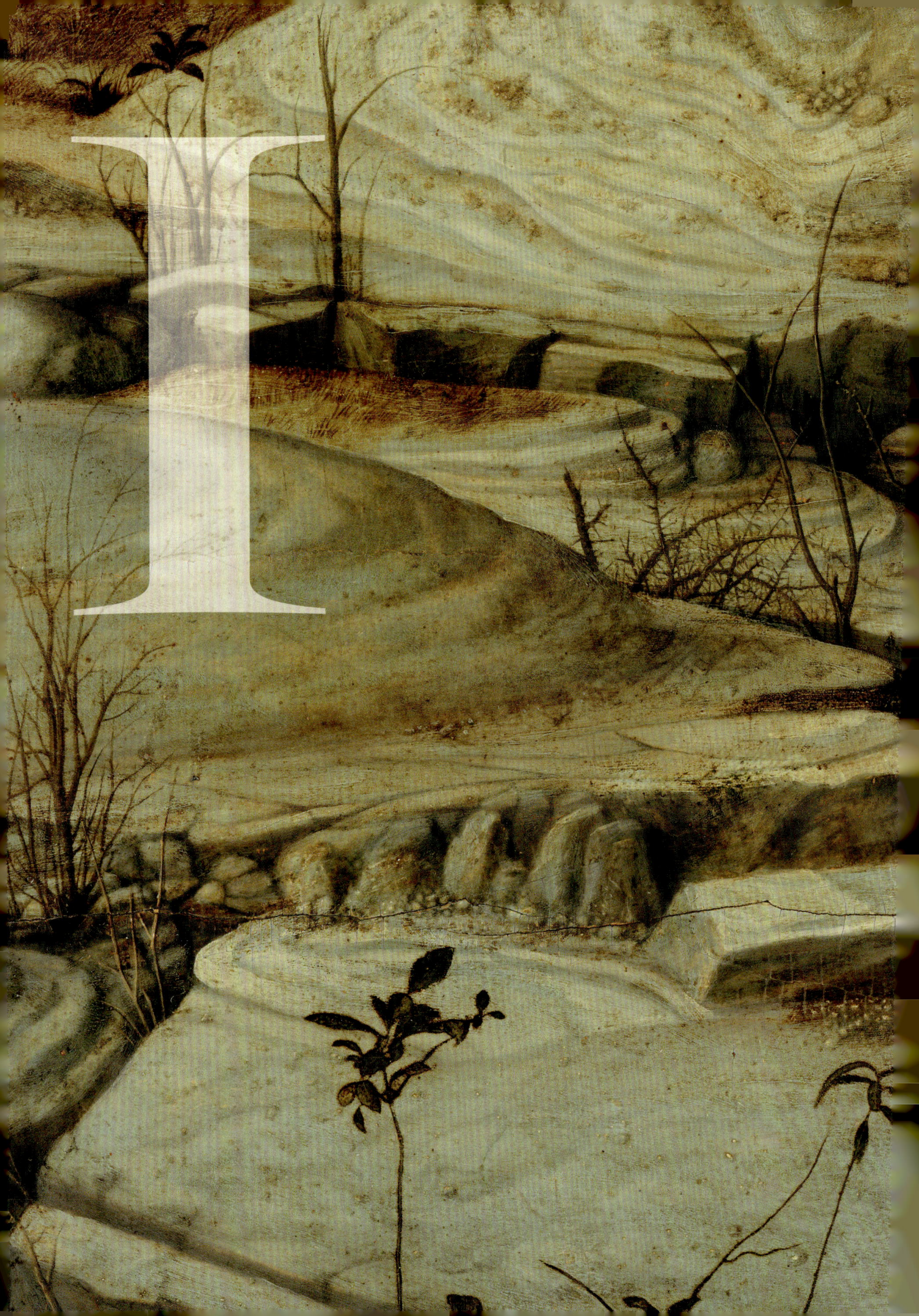
I

Introduction: Beyond Figuration

"THERE IS THE FIGURE—AND YET."

We owe the Italian Renaissance picture more than the idealized human figure. To be sure, Giotto, Donatello, Raphael, Michelangelo, and Titian, just to unfurl a triumphalist banner of some of the protagonists in this era, are cer-tainly preoccupied with the body—be it Christ suffering on the cross, a heroine enacting a mythological narrative, or, in a more secular vein, a portrait of a pope, princess, or duke. Renaissance writers on art, too, devoted much of their critical thinking toward describing and prescribing how artists portrayed the figure. Giorgio Vasari, author of the germinal *Lives of the Most Excellent Painters, Sculptors, and Architects* (1550/1568), articulated one of his most significant art theoretical concepts—*maniera*, which we might translate loosely as "style"—in relation to the portrayal of the human body. Seeking to explain the characteristics of the third age of art—the climax in his history—Vasari declares that "*maniera* reached the greatest beauty from the practice of incessantly imitating the most beautiful objects, and joining together, and joining these most beautiful things, hands, bodies, and legs." This practice, Vasari continues, was carried out "in *every* work for *all* figures, and for that reason it is called the beautiful manner." It is no accident, then, that the human figure has been identified by Michael Cole, in his perceptive volume on the subject, as "the single most continuous feature of Italian Renaissance art." And as he points out—not without a note of irony—the body's ubiquity "demonstrates its banality."[1]

The Renaissance picture *is* the figure—and yet.[2] I have chosen this qualifying epigraph to make an obvious yet often overlooked point: there is no figure without ground. It is painting's sine qua non, without which the picture cannot exist and convey meaning. But what do we mean when we refer to the "ground" of painting? What aspects of the Renaissance picture do we group under this category?

The dyad figure/ground that features in art historical writing presumably refers to ground as the field around and against which figuration occurs. More fundamentally, ground can be defined as "any material surface, natural

Detail, Figure 3.1

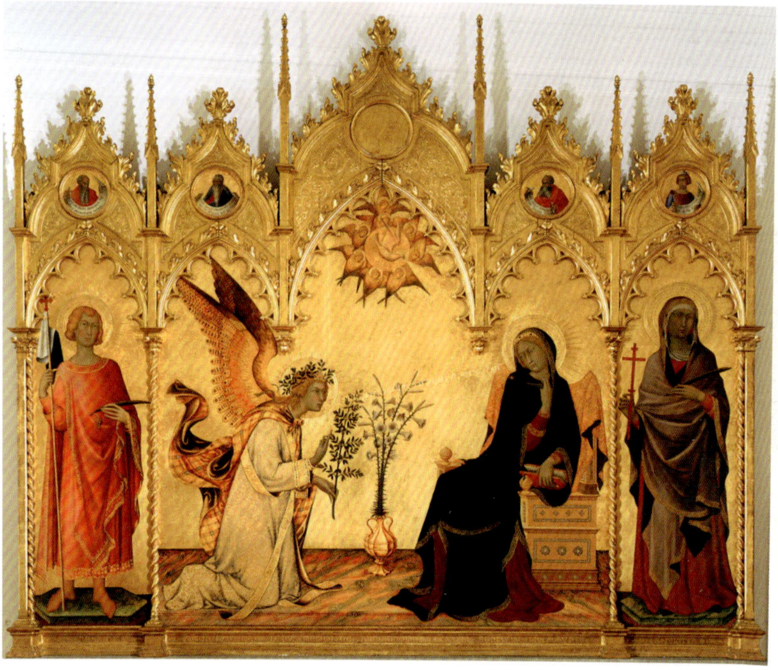

Fig. I.1. Simone Martini, *Annunciation with Saints Ansano and Margaret, and Four Medallions of Prophets Jeremiah, Ezechiel, Isaiah, and Daniel*, 1333. Tempera on panel. (184 × 210 cm). Galleria degli Uffizi, Florence.

or prepared, which is taken as a basis for working upon." A dictionary entry might further elaborate that ground is "a main surface or first coating of color, serving as a support for other colors or a background for designs." These preliminary definitions of ground—ground as material support and ground as field—are certainly implied when art historians write of, or more properly, write over the empty ground that surrounds Michelangelo's figures in his *Last Judgment*, or else when they speak of tenebrist painters, whom they often describe as working up layers of paint from a reddish-brown ground layer.[3]

How ground has been defined in and of itself may account for why it has been overlooked in favor of other elements, such as figure and perspective. While I will return to these issues in more depth in chapter 1, for now let us consider the dominance of the figure, which is often understood as self-constituting and self-sufficient. Projecting out into space by means of foreshortening and coloring, the human body becomes the primary focus of the viewer's attention, the site where meaning purports to be located and contained. By contrast, ground is what we might call *prepositional*: it only exists when couched in territorial relation to the autonomous substantive. In the Renaissance, ground appears above, against, along, around, behind, below, beneath, and with the figure—rarely without it.

Meanwhile, backgrounds also register shifts in Renaissance painting. Over the course of the fifteenth century, gold grounds give way to perspectival and landscape views; in turn, backgrounds darken and disappear in the chiaroscuro painting of the late sixteenth century. Grounds also often stage

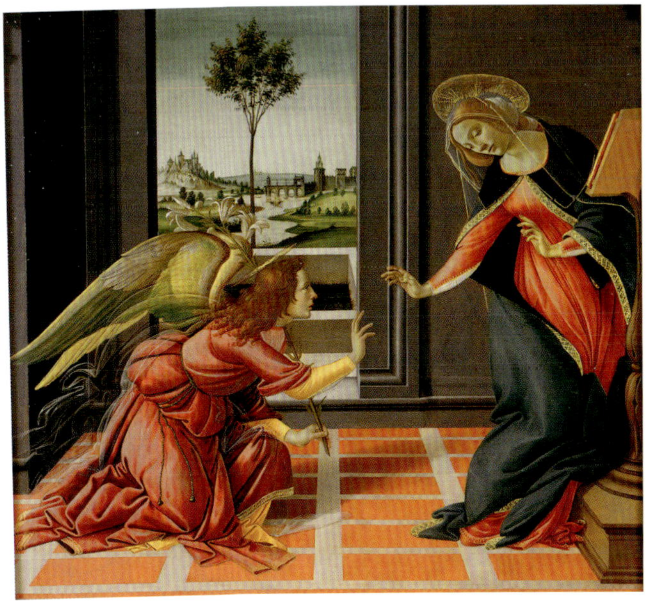

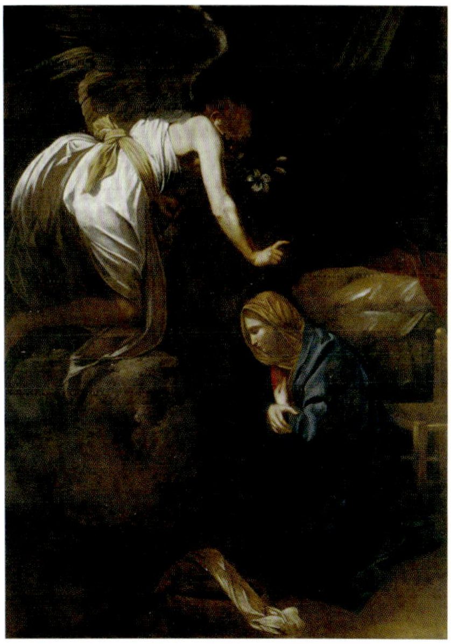

the tension between the picture's status as an object, which is associated with a tradition of craftsmanship, and the picture's status as an illusionistic representation, which is associated with the new category of "art." Three works from the fourteenth to the seventeenth century depicting the Annunciation—when the Archangel Gabriel informs the Virgin Mary that she is "blessed among women," will conceive in her womb and bring forth Christ in the world (Luke 1:26)—demonstrate the breadth of difference in the uses of ground.

In these cases, grounds are more than featureless, meaningless planes hidden beneath, below, or behind the figure. They spring out, calling for our attention. Grounds impinge on figuration and therefore function as a material, perceptual, and semantic variable in the Renaissance picture. In the first example (fig. I.1), a gold background unifies the Archangel Gabriel and the Virgin in an otherworldly space. The cracks on the surface reveal the seams where the rectangular gold leaves overlap. Gold ground is a "prepared surface" but sits on top and proclaims itself rather than lying underneath.

Gold grounds give way over the course of the fifteenth century to perspectival planes and landscape backgrounds, but the physicality of ground remains operative. While the background in Botticelli's *Annunciation* offers an illusionistic view outdoors (fig. I.2), this background is a crafted surface. The vertical orientation of the panel support guides and accentuates the crisp lines of the chiseled doorway. In opposition to the curving bodily contours of the figures, the background puts forward a concept of the line as a sharp edge. The white gesso ground is more than a mere preparatory layer; it contributes to the illusion of the white inlay below, perceived as near, and the clear sky above, perceived as far from, the viewer.

(LEFT)
Fig. I.2. Botticelli, *The Cestello Annunciation*, 1489–90. Tempera on panel (150 × 156 cm). Galleria degli Uffizi, Florence.

(RIGHT)
Fig. I.3. Caravaggio, *The Annunciation*, c. 1610. Oil on canvas (285 × 205 cm). Musée des Beaux-Arts, Nancy.

Finally, a feature of Baroque tenebrism is the darkened background (fig. I.3). In Caravaggio's *Annunciation*, the background "fades to black." The dark ground merges with the shadows, seeming to absorb the Virgin's bed, chair, and basket. The viewer's attention, instead of being drawn toward a single vanishing point inside the picture, is now pulled into the whole picture as if it were a vacuum. We could even say that the tenebrist background distributes the focus of perspective from a single point to the entire picture plane.

When confronted with this range of artworks, one wonders whether the conception of figure/ground as characterized above is capacious enough to grasp the numerous ways painters deployed the ground in their compositions. A question arises: is the terminology and method currently in use in art history able to account for the complexity of this fundamental pictorial element?[4] Let us consider the word "ground" itself, whose multiple meanings Matteo Burioni has mapped in his fundamental work on the concept. As a word with roots deep in the Anglo-Saxon and Germanic lexical past (*grundus*, *grunt*, *krunt*) and as part of our everyday vocabulary, "ground" bears a host of connotations that are adjacent and complementary to the word's art historical usage. In a physical sense, "ground" can mean "the lowest part or downward limit of anything," a foundation, substratum, or more simply, floor. Then, "ground" in a territorial sense indicates an enclosed portion of land, a delimited extent of property legally belonging to an owner. When traveling, "to cover a lot of ground" means to go far—and this traverse can also apply metaphorically to subject matter in a discussion. In theological contexts, fourteenth-century medieval mystics used "ground" to refer to the divine essence of being or the focal point of the soul where union with God transpires. "Ground" was also understood as the vernacular equivalent to classical terms that referred to the causes, reasons, and origins of things, such as *logos* (reason or word) and *archē* in Greek; *ratio*, *fundamentum*, and *principium* in Latin. Hence the appearance of "ground" in philosophical and literary contexts as "a circumstance on which an opinion, inference, statement, or claim is founded."[5] Ground has a broad horizon, traversing many domains, among them the pictorial, geological, legal, theological, and philosophical. But in art history our models of interpretation tend to be figurally driven, so that grounds often escape our attention. What would we discover if we displaced our customary focus to the area around, beneath, below, and behind the figure?

THREE GROUNDS

Having surveyed some uses of "ground" in the history of English, I would like to return to the two senses of "ground" as an art historical term and introduce a third element. As stated previously, the first "ground" is the material preparation of a planar support. We speak, for example, of "gesso ground," the layer of gypsum mixed with water that when applied to a panel, transforms it into a hard and smooth working surface. Such grounds become substrata as successive layers of paint bring the picture to completion. They are therefore often only readily visible in unfinished or damaged works of art. Yet this type of ground is primary, in that it primes or readies the support. Ground also participates in bounding the picture and, in doing so, prepares it to become a protagonist in cultural history. "Through the closure and smoothness of the prepared picture surface," Meyer Schapiro claimed, "the image acquired a definite space of its own," in contrast to prehistoric wall paintings, which had to "compete with the noise-like accidents and irregularities of a ground."[6]

"Ground" also refers to the platform or irregular terrain where figures place their feet in the world of the picture (as in our own). Bodies and objects in a picture need to be located somewhere, on a certain point on a plane—to speak in mathematical language—or in a particular setting or context that establishes their role in the world or in narrative.[7] Ground as plane is also fundamental for viewership: the viewer looking at the picture stands, most often, on a squared-off architectural ground. A painting's foreground mediates our entry into the picture, leading us to the middle ground, which contains the principal point or points of action in a composition. Ground as ground plane guides the viewer into the imaginative space of the picture; it is commonly asserted that it does this by "receding" into depth of space according to the laws of perspective. Yet there are ground surfaces, such as cracked, rocky, geological earth or meandering pools of water, which do not lend themselves to perspectival representation and which merit our attention. In Italian Renaissance art criticism, the ground plane in a picture is often referred to as *piano,* which also appears in musical terminology as a dynamic indication meaning "soft." In talking about what is inconspicuous, we must tread lightly and exercise acute looking and listening.[8]

Then, "ground" also designates the background, the field in and against which a picture's chief object of contemplation stands. In this sense, "ground" can refer to anything ranging from views in the distance to a darkened plane. Images that are more schematic reduce pictures to a dialogue between figure and ground. In the first decades of the twentieth century, Edgar Rubin and other psychologists explored the distinctions between the two in their experiments on human perception. Do we see, for instance, a face in profile or a vase?[9] This Gestalt example comes into use in the early twentieth century at the same time as experiments in painting by Henri Matisse or Pablo Picasso start to produce situations in which the figure/ground relation is reversed'. Yet the face/vase visual test can also be brought into connection with gold ground paintings, in which the background is often conceived as a flat monochrome, or with tenebrist paintings, in which the dark ground functions as a gap between forms. Even so, in Renaissance art literature, terms that will be discussed in chapter 1, such as *campo* (field) or *lontani* (views in the distance), denote a background that is understood as opposing or setting off the figure.

GROUNDWORK

These grounds constitute sites in the Renaissance picture where artists engage in what I propose to call *groundwork*. Conventionally, groundwork is understood as a base-level preparation or foundation, superseded in interest (though not significance) by that which is built on top; groundwork can also refer to the work entailed in constructing this foundation. I favor this second sense of the term. If work is an action that unfolds over time, then groundwork is best described as a process whereby materials are deposited in layers, figuration is disclosed or withdrawn, and meaning accrues, obtrudes, or dissipates. This multilateral and durational process of making and viewing implicates, in the sense of "folding in," the artist who paints and the beholder who sees, whereby the artist often doubles as the first viewer. Artists initially engage in the process of groundwork when they lay down the picture's material foundation and construct the represented plane and field on and against which figuration occurs. As the painting continues to develop, groundwork establishes the horizon of "the possible," a term I anchor in its two humanist senses, which will be explicated in further detail in chapter 2: first, the possible as *potere*, or power, the artist's capacity to handle and exploit the behavior and characteristics of the picture's inherent materiality; second, the possible as *potentia*, or potential, the capacity of the ground itself to erupt from the material substrate or from its subsidiary role to shape the terms of pictorial representation. Groundwork was one of the fundamental means by which artists conceptualized the stakes of the Renaissance picture, what it purported to do—as an object justifying itself and its conditions of possibility in relation to other media; and as a visual experience that enables deviating modes of thinking, imagining, and feeling. The picture offers implications that prepare its viewers to follow chains of metaphor in their own minds. Characteristic of groundwork is ultimately its capacity to subvert the very foundation that it purports to be, especially in those moments when it erupts to the surface. That which is oblique, latent, and suppressed can paradoxically become a driving factor behind what is portrayed, even when the artist's portrayal at first glance seems to disclose itself in a self-evident manner.

Artists' groundwork, therefore, *works* on the viewer, transferring a sense of semantic possibility from the multiple grounds of the picture to the self. Groundwork not only becomes an object of visual contemplation or historical inquiry but also forms the basis for a deeper hermeunetic engagement in the power and potential, as well as the limits and contingencies, of representation. Groundwork is what artists do. Groundwork is what art historians should take the time to see. This book therefore attempts to offer a critical language about ground's functions, definitions, permeable boundaries, and shades of meaning. This way of speaking about ground unlocks a deeper understanding of the Renaissance picture that seriously attends to its degrees of sedimentation: in other words, its profundity. I also propose, in deploying groundwork as a category worthy of historical investigation and theorization, that art history make more of an effort to recognize that which seems missing, removed, or depleted in its own field of study. While as an approach it is ostensibly formalist, groundwork agitates for a politics of visibility, a mode of attentive looking that, in the act of unearthing, recognizes the desire for that which is underfoot, often hidden in plain sight. The pressure of figuration (and therefore meaning) is released from the restrictive confines of the human body, allowing the currency of significance to be transferred and distributed throughout the picture.

This study, then, does not only undertake a historically contingent ontological hypothesis of painting, to define what it *is* in the period from 1400 to 1600, especially in Italy. I also want to ask how the ground dramatizes what painting aimed to be and to become. The ground marks the moment where the picture *begins*, by serving as painting's generating medium and point of departure. The beginning, as Aristotle claimed, is "the first thing from which something either exists or comes into being or becomes known" (*Metaphysics* 5.1013a). The ground as point of origin, then, establishes the principles of what can be or what can be known. In the case of art study, the ground must be recognized through close looking and not through intellection alone. This book indeed investigates the questions, "What is ground?" and "What does ground do?"; but beyond them, it aims to understand what the ground *wants* of the picture, in respect to its status as physical object, site of representation, and focus of critical reflection. Groundwork might additionally be defined as expressing itself in moments when the ground as material preparation, plane, and field makes its desire to assign its place in the picture both visible and known, felt, remembered.

Thinking about groundwork generates insight that passes through the procedures of making and the ambitions of artistic representation to arrive at the critical issues of viewership and subjectivity. Erwin Panofsky famously claimed that the Renaissance perspectival picture, rather than showing an objective vision of reality, instead posited the viewing subject in a posture of reflexive self-awareness. As Margaret Iversen observes in her reading of Panofsky and his interlocutors, the perspectival picture signals "the relation of mind to things and [. . .] the nature of art as being essentially about that relation."[10] The beholder discovers a version of the self in and through the picture. The idea of groundwork advanced in this book pertains to the viewer's work of interpretation in pictures that are not strictly perspectival, and thereby posits a specific model of subjectivity that is neither authoritative, integral, and totalizing, on the one hand, nor fractured and discontinuous, on the other. Groundwork offers a model of viewership that begins at degree zero, starting from "that which lies beneath or behind," to understand narrative action and meaning. The beholder thinks in ablative terms, asking of the picture not only "Who?" or "When?" but also "Whence, where, under what circumstances, and by what means?" That is, in looking at the picture, the viewer as subject internalizes a sense of possibility. True, the picture is physically present. It is *there*. But the endeavors of looking and interpreting find something more. This excess is provided by the picture's viewers, who in finding that surplus in the image also find surplus in themselves.

PERSPECTIVE VERSUS GROUND

How can we bring the ground into view—especially given that it is covered, to borrow a phrase from Leo Steinberg, by the "Cloud of Unseeing"? In addition to figure, another core art historical concept to which I have just alluded has also deflected our attention from the ground: namely, perspective. Far from disputing the significance of figure and perspective, my intention is to point out how consistently they have guided and, at times, distorted our understanding of the Renaissance picture and have encouraged us to focus on certain elements at the expense of others. We tend to look through, though not necessarily at, the Renaissance picture through the lens of perspective. Take the classic example of Masaccio's *Trinity*, once covered by an altarpiece by Vasari, and which itself covered previous fresco campaigns on a rough masonry wall (fig. I.4, 5). As the spiel goes, the ground, like the figures themselves, submits to a perspective with the effect that the flat planar wall dissolves, opening a view onto the chapel's interior. Never mind the inconvenient details that emphasize the fresco's material presence: the crisply delineated architectural ornament, the sweeping brushwork in Christ's shroud, or the haloes composed of gold leaf applied to gilt tin. The schematic diagrams we employ in teaching subsume the physical ground to the paradigm of perspective, in accordance with the analogy between the picture and "open window" that Leon Battista Alberti described in his treatise *On Painting* (1435).[11]

The so-called Albertian window itself is a gross generalization; Alberti's original "window" metaphor refers to the picture frame and does not intend to understand the image itself as extending beyond an invisible surface like a transparent glass pane. And yet, the metaphor of the Albertian window has behaved, as Joseph Masheck pointed out in a memorable observation, like an invasive species. "Clichés, like weeds, prove difficult to uproot," is the essay's first line. Erwin Panofsky's essay on perspective nourished this organism. Perspective, as he stated, transforms the picture into a window through which we look, so that "the material surface of the painting or relief is negated." To modernist painters who sought to emphasize the picture plane, the Albertian window represented the hegemony of the Renaissance and the failure of nineteenth-century historicism.[12] But the overly general equation of perspective with the Renaissance also had the effect of suppressing the multiple, varied, and evolving treatments of ground in the period under consideration in this book.[13]

There may be deeper reasons for this art historical occlusion. In the title to an essay, the literary critic Barbara Johnson asked, "Is Female to Male as Ground Is to Figure?" In the works of fiction that she analyzes, Johnson argues that women become represented as ground to the male figure, a relationship that culminates in the annihilation of the woman as

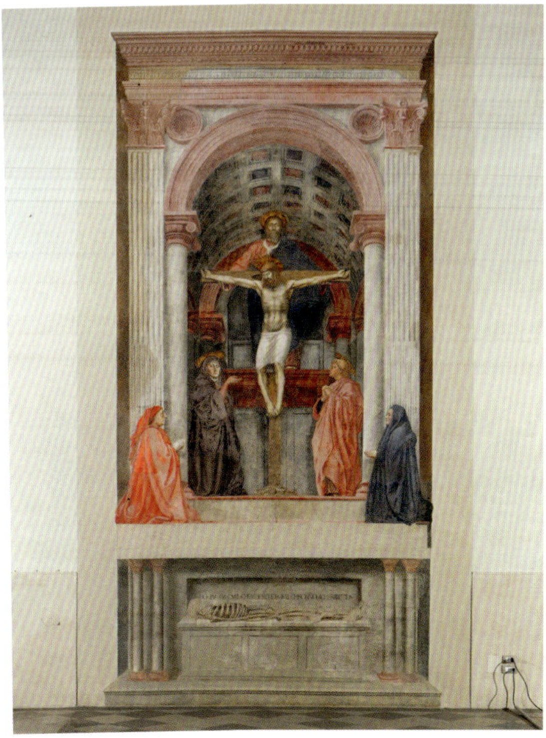

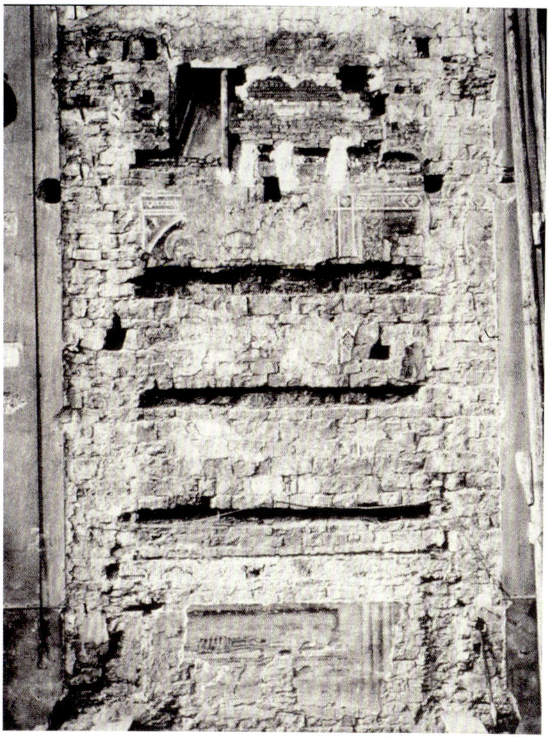

blank ground—she is erased, made to vanish, institutionalized. Johnson cites Douglas Hofstadter's notion of "recursive figuration," according to which the positions of figure and ground are mutable and dialogic. As Johnson quotes Hofstadter, a "cursively drawn figure is one whose ground is merely an accidental by-product of the drawing act," a negative space or "dead page." A "recursive figure," on the other hand, is "one whose ground can be seen as a figure in its own right." A ground can be seen as a figure; by the same token, every figure can also be perceived as a ground. Addressing issues of class and race, Johnson also acknowledges that there are "other figures trapped in the ground," unobserved within interpretive norms, while figure itself can be an internally differentiated and mutable category. Johnson is of course addressing a context radically different from ours. Her essay nonetheless calls attention to the practice by which oppositional binaries—be they male / female, figure / ground, white / black—structure and underline the systems of power at work in scholarly engagement with any topic.[14]

How can recursive figuration inform how we look at the Renaissance picture? The sources themselves challenge us to confront this question. In a well-known passage from Francisco de Holanda's *Da pintura antiga* (1548), Michelangelo is famously portrayed as giving priority to certain pictorial elements and regional styles over others. The painter declares that women, especially very old and very young women, naively appreciate Flemish painting with its interest in background elements such as "stuffs and masonry, the

(LEFT)
Fig. I.4. Masaccio, *Holy Trinity*, c. 1425. Fresco, postrestoration. Santa Maria Novella, Florence.

(RIGHT)
Fig. I.5. Detail view of the wall behind the *Holy Trinity* fresco, with fragment of Memento Mori. Santa Maria Novella, Florence.

green grass of the fields, the shadow of trees and rivers and bridges." These women, in his view, fail to appreciate the substance and vigor of the figure. In this recounted conversation, the divine master is portrayed as establishing a hierarchical relationship between figure and ground. He supports his views through recourse to analogies operating within a gendered, stylistic, regional framework. To formulate a rejoinder to "Michelangelo" is to reconfigure, disorient, and destabilize the set of asymmetrical and hierarchical relations between ground and figure. The result is a more holistic and complex account of the Renaissance picture, especially in Italy, in the tradition where the figure achieved the greatest prominence.[15]

ITALIAN BACKGROUNDS

While the prominence of figure and perspective have impeded a more integrated understanding of the picture as a whole, it is not the case that the ground has entirely eluded discussion. Not surprisingly, attention to the subject has come from unlikely quarters. For instance, one of the most perceptive comments was voiced by the American novelist Edith Wharton, who, though a friend of Bernard Berenson and well acquainted with the Old Masters, was by no means a professional art historian. In her travelogue *Italian Backgrounds* (1905), Wharton writes, "In the Italian devotional pictures of the early Renaissance, there are usually two quite unrelated parts: the foreground and background." The foreground, she says, is the place of the conventional, where we encounter the usual "saints, angels, and Holy Family." By contrast, "relegated to the middle distance, and reduced to insignificant size, is the real picture, the picture which had its birth in the artist's brain." Wharton ultimately employs the metaphor of foreground and background to make a distinction between the tourist site and the hidden destination, the casual sightseer and the informed traveler. Nonetheless, her observation that the background is where originality resides shows how the hierarchy that places figure over ground might be reversed and makes us rethink where we locate artistic individuality.[16]

Another not particularly well-known publication is a 1959 dissertation on the landscapes in the backgrounds of Leonardo's paintings, which was written by Eva Beuys-Wurmbach and published in 1974 with drawings executed by her husband, Joseph Beuys (fig. I.6). The purpose of the dissertation, as Beuys-Wurmbach put it, was to examine Leonardo's landscape backgrounds as a distinct entity in his paintings, and by so doing to provide an essential insight into his thinking as an artist. She suggests that in the *Mona Lisa*, for example, Leonardo strove to connect the figure and landscape, to create what she called a "living circuit inside the natural world." Backgrounds reinforce figural groupings and amplify their resonance in a larger spatial, or even spiritual, dimension. While this connection between figure and ground, microcosm and macrocosm, features prominently in the Leonardo literature, Beuys-Wurmbach's publication is noteworthy in illustrating it with graphic means. Beuys's drawings recall the illustrations in previous

→

Fig. I.6. Joseph Beuys, drawing after the *Mona Lisa*. From Eva Beuys-Wurmbach, *Die Landschaften in den Hintergründen der Gamälde Leonardos*, 1977.

ander fort zum Bildrand strebenden Motive von Fluss und Weg. Im See des Hintergrundes und in der Frau findet der zwiespältige Mittelgrund sein Gleichgewicht. Und dabei scheint das Wasser, das nach vorne strömt in dem Flussbett, und das sich ja zu verwandeln vermag "in der Natur des Ortes, an dem es vorbeifliesst", in den Händen der Frau die Verwandlung vollzogen zu haben in die seltsame Form, die auch ein Blutstropfen sein könnte, der zurückfliesst in den See: Wasser, das nun rot und dickflüssig geworden ist.

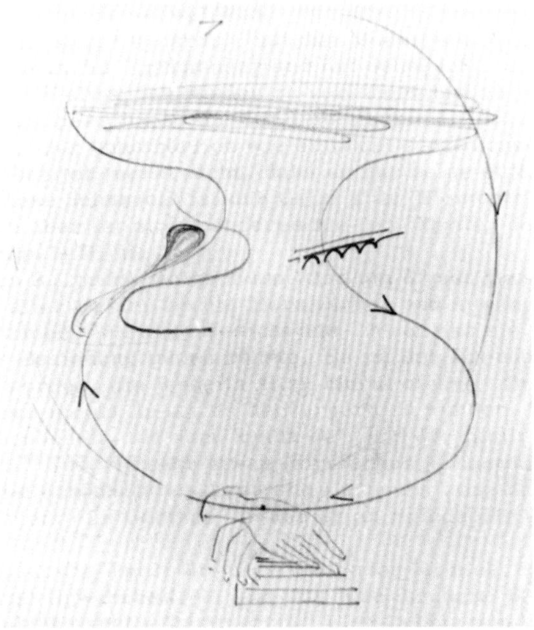

In dieser Landschaft sind die Formen des Makrokosmos offene Zeichen für das Geschehen, das im menschlichen Mikrokosmos wirkt. Die Bewegung, die in den Organen der Welt geschieht, ist auch Bewegung der inneren Organe des Menschen und seiner Seelentätigkeit. Die Landschaft ist der Ausdruck des Psychischen, das in der Welt und in der Mona Lisa wirkt. Sie ist der Ausdruck der triebhaften Kräfte. Über den aufgerissenen Bergen liegt ein schwefliger Dunst. Leonardo sagt: "Der Sitz des triebhaften Lebens ist in der Glut, die an verschiedenen Stellen der Erde ausströmt, nämlich in Schwefelgruben und anderen Orten." (Leic. 34r.)

Das Porträt und die Landschaft gehen über alles Individuelle hinaus, sie sind Symbol geworden. Über Beiden liegt die Unwirklichkeit des Traumhaften. Und will man den Traum endlich als eine Wirkung tiefster Organfunktionen annehmen, so sind beide der Ausdruck

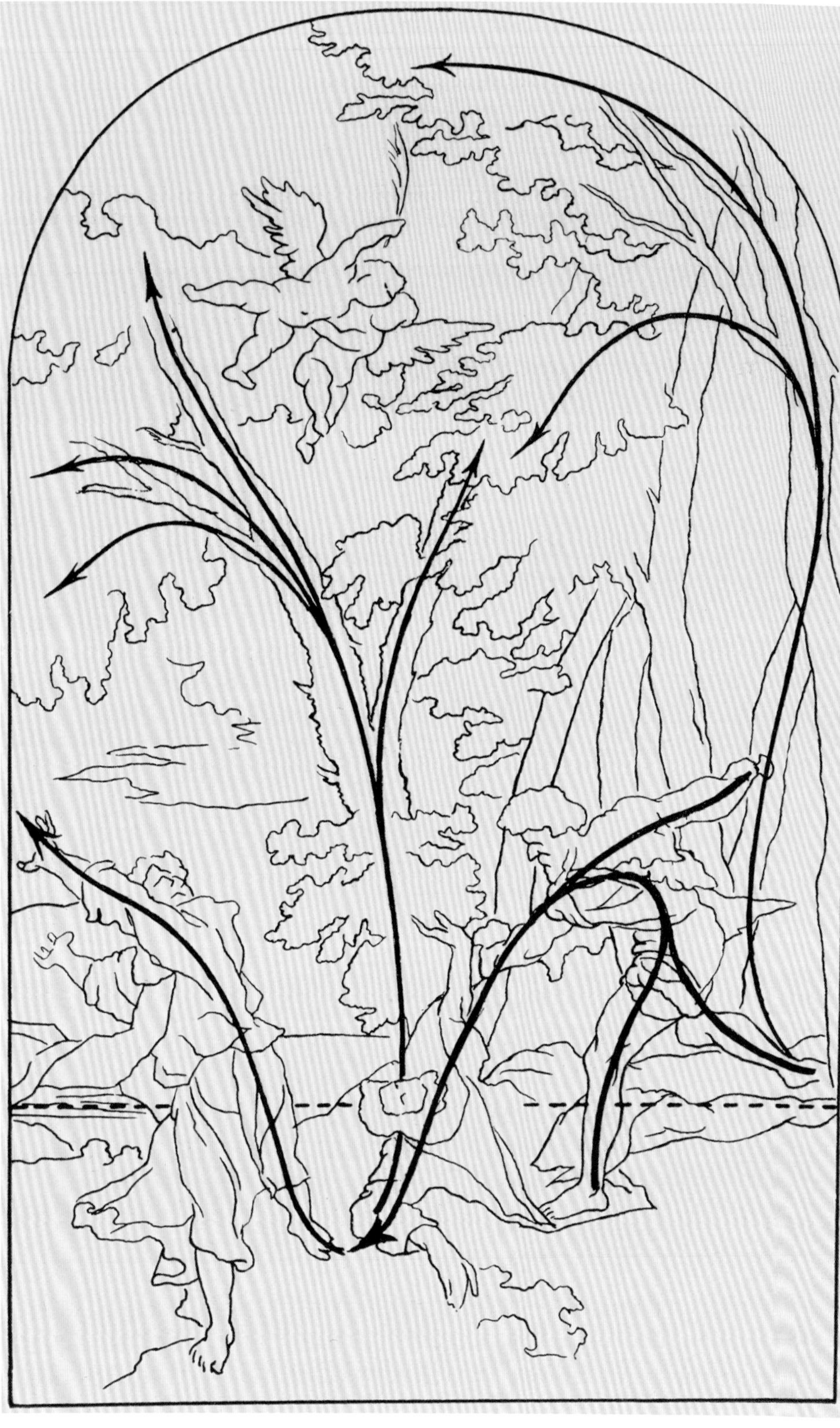

Germanophone art scholarship, such as Joseph Gramm's *Die ideale Landschaft* (fig. I.7). These diagrams make explicit through arrows and dotted lines how figures extend their action beyond the body into the landscape, and vice versa: how landscape shapes figural composition.[17]

The ground as a focus of inquiry has also received attention in recent art historical scholarship on the early modern period. While I engage with their specific points of argument throughout the book, several key contributions deserve brief mention here, if only to expose the historiographic foundation on which this project aims to build. Given that this examination considers ground as a discursive bridge linking art practice and art theory, Jeroen Stumpel's 1998 essay "On Grounds and Backgrounds: Some Remarks about Composition in Renaissance Painting" is germinal. There, he demonstrates that what we in English call the "ground" or "background" appears in sources as a different term, namely *campo* (field or open plane), whose period meanings and connotations I discuss in chapter 1. Stumpel's philological approach was taken up by Thomas Puttfarken in *The Discovery of Pictorial Composition* (2000), where he sees the Renaissance picture as primarily interested in *rilievo* (relief), the projection of the figure from the surrounding ground in service to intelligible narrative. Complicating this dyadic notion of figure/ground is *Der Grund. Das Feld des Sichtbaren* (2012), a landmark publication edited by Gottfried Boehm and Matteo Burioni. Although beginning from an art historical perspective (and specifically Stumpel's essay on campo), the editors bring together contributions that explore how ground works as an operative concept in literature, philosophy, theater, geography, and calligraphy. What allows the volume to embrace such a diverse range of fields, the editors acknowledge, is the particular *Sprachzauber* (literally, "word-magic") the word *Grund* carries in the German language. As previously mentioned, "ground" was the English vernacular equivalent of classical philosophical terms for reasoning, foundation, and beginning. Hence there are also numerous German words based on the lexical unit *Grund* that refer to justifying (*begruenden*), fathoming (*ergruenden*), substantiating claims (*zugruenden legen*). Without ground (*grundlos*), you fall into an abyss (*Abgrund*). It is fitting that one of the foundational texts of art history, by Heinrich Wölfflin is entitled *Kunstgeschichtliche Grundbegriffe*, specifying literally the "ground concepts" of art history.[18]

As Boehm and Burioni see it, this panoply of cognates invites consideration of the ground as a dynamic entity, as both physical substrate and process. The availability of terms in a given language underscores interpretive possibilities and limitations. In his essay, Lothar Ledderose notes that in French, English, or German one might speak of the "ground becoming background" in a landscape by Cézanne, to describe how the canvas becomes part of the view through a forest (fig. I.8). Ledderose argues, however, that this notion of ground as background would be questionable in Chinese art theory. To be sure, *Six Persimmons* by the thirteenth-century painter Muxi may seem to exemplify an interest in ground as background (fig. I.9); but

←

Fig. I.7. Karl Hofner, diagram of Titian's *Death of Saint Peter Martyr*. From Josef Gramm, *Die ideale Landschaft: ihre Entstehung und Entwicklung*, 1912.

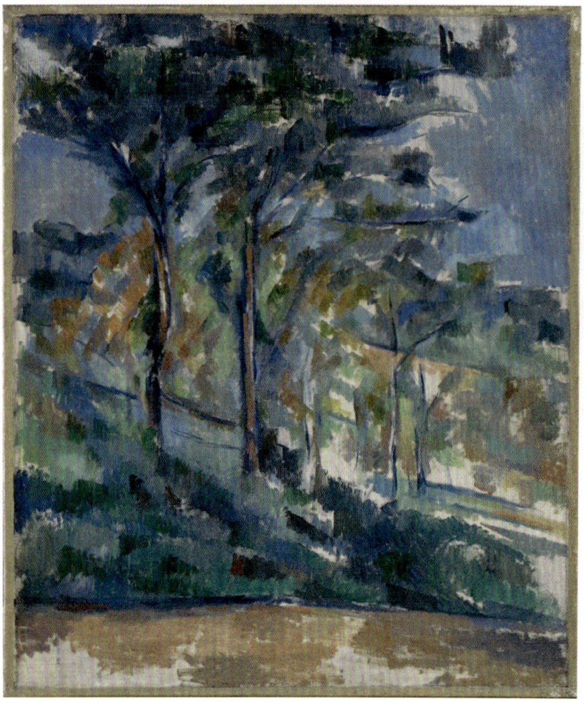

Fig. I.8. Paul Cézanne, *Landscape: The Forest Clearing*, c. 1900–1904. Oil on canvas (62.2 × 51.5 cm). Fitzwilliam Museum, Cambridge.

it is doubtful whether contemporary viewers would have described the areas where the ground comes through the body of the fruit as a deliberate conflation. Instead, discussions would emphasize the subtle gradations of ink tonalities, the brushwork delineating the stems, and spatial intervals.[19]

Beyond the particularities of a given idiom, the larger issue is that of how words relate to pictures. Pictures fade when words end. We see what we say. Or put more accurately, we see what has already been said: it is harder to see that for which no words yet exist. Therefore, we need more than the lexicon of present-day art history to conjure the ground. We also need to dig through the historical bedrock of campo to extract and lay bare the assumptions implicit in the term's use. As we might expect, these assumptions shape our expectations for how the Renaissance picture ought to look, and even more intriguingly, how the Renaissance picture can look.

CHAPTER OVERVIEWS

This book narrates and explains how the picture works through the ground, or how art is *groundwrought*, to restitute a now obsolete form of the word, in a broad sweep of the early modern period with especial focus on Italy. Even though grounds are largely taken for granted, we intuitively use them, just below the surface of observation, to register shifts in Renaissance painting. Over the course of the fifteenth century, gold grounds give way to perspectival and landscape views; in turn, these grounds darken and disappear in the chiar-

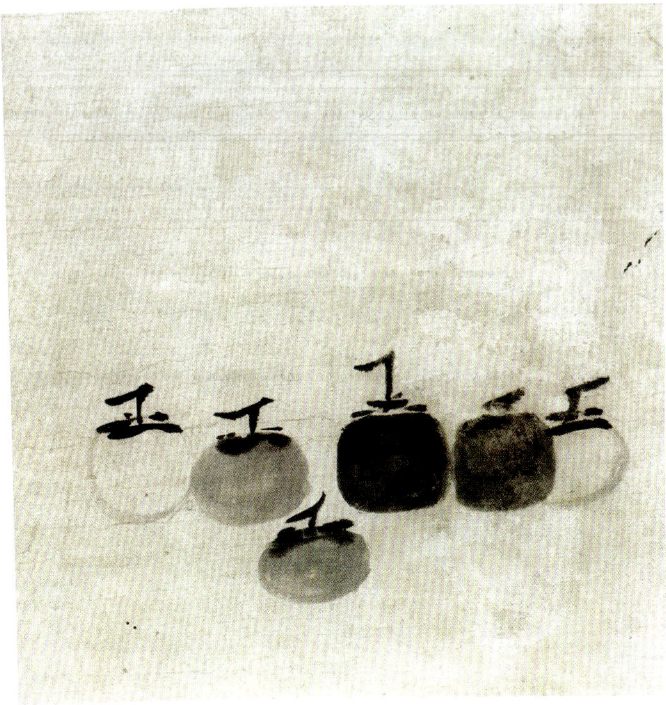

oscuro painting of the late sixteenth century. This book broadly interrogates these shifts and attends to the divergences, inversions, and interruptions in art theory and art historiography proper.

Chapter 1 ("Words for Grounds") elaborates on the three semantic fields pertaining to the word "ground": ground as material support; ground as terrain or platform; and ground as background. In addition to conducting a philological examination of the early modern terms for these grounds as described in primary sources, I examine a series of paintings for how grounds inform their coloration and compositional structure and shape their meaning. Here I take into account what Stephen Campbell has described as "the relationship between representation and physical reality"—how paintings function as "objects in the world as well as evocations of the world." Indeed, as Jodi Cranston observes in relation to the materiality of Titian's late paintings, "the unprecedented role given to the depicted ground, the actual canvas ground, and the compromised figure contributes to and challenges the self-sufficient status of the figure and artist."[20] The set of material and conceptual tensions embodied by the ground can be located in origin myths of painting that discover figuration in murky clay, the surface of water, patterns in rocks, and shadows on walls. Following the philosopher Hans Blumenberg, I draw upon these and other myths especially for the way that they engage with "absolute reality," forces in nature that are felt to be beyond human control, resistance, or articulation. Myths, as archives of that which remains hidden or unknown, seem particularly well suited as analytic

Fig. I.9. Muxi, *Six Persimmons*, mid-thirteenth century. Ink on paper (36.2 × 38.1 cm). Daitoku-ji, Kyoto.

implements in approaching the ground as a field inhabited by unspoken or unacknowledged forces.

The remaining four parts of the book explore how artists posited differing conceptions of ground, often in meaningful dialogue with one another. Chapter 2 ("Possibility") discusses the process and meaning of gold ground in Cennino Cennini's *Libro dell'arte* (c. 1390) and Gentile da Fabriano's *Madonna and Child with Angels* (c. 1405), with focus placed on the technique of granulation (*opus punctorium*). Gold ground functions not simply as a structural analogy with divine line and expansive space, as art historians in the early twentieth century often reiterated. Artists exploited the malleability of gold, its capacity to be hammered into thin sheets, so as to render gold ground an area in the picture that demands the work of detailed and focused looking, ultimately placing figure and ground in complementary, even competing, positions. In its two modalities as a chromatically varied, illuminated plane that, according to the viewer's standpoint, can be seen to contain delineated forms, gold ground demonstrates a basic condition of ground in general.

Chapter 3 ("Metamorphosis") explores the transition from gold ground to landscape views in early Renaissance painting. Focus is placed on Giovanni Bellini's *Saint Francis in the Desert* (c. 1480), in particular the use of geological forms to structure the relationship between the figure of the saint, his withdrawal to the hermetic retreat in the wilderness, and the view of the city beyond. Bellini dramatizes different properties of ground through the geological forms of mountain, rock face, cave, and liquefied rock, which shift between background, stratified plane, and unstable foundation. These forms are associated with painting itself as stratified, fissured, liquid, and solid. Just as Francis's stigmata serve as a primordial imprint, the crack in the rock face can be thought of as the original line as it is spontaneously found in nature. Given its formal and semantic import, the crack might even be considered the *Pathosformel* of the earth—the expression of the ground's dynamic movement. In thus alluding to an earthquake, the panel connects La Verna with the Holy Land and characterizes Francis as Adam, the primordial human figure fashioned from the ground. Bellini's depiction of Francis's open mouth, about to speak or sing, bears analogy with the cave, an aperture in the rock face that opens up the possibility of descent into the earth.

In chapter 4 ("Articulation,") the discussion moves indoors toward examining the condition of painting's background as wall, the elevation of an architectural interior. The chapter examines the portraiture of Giovanni Battista Moroni through his sitters' relationship with chromatic fields of gray that function as backdrops. Rather than seeing his portraits as unmediated, naturalistic depictions of their subjects, as art historians previously have done, I argue that Moroni's figures and their gray walls enter into an exchange that moves between articulation and concealment of affect. While Moroni's sitters appear stoic and inscrutable, the artist displaces attributes of their inner life to the wall, such that the portraits constitute images of figured walls or walled figures. Meanwhile, the contrast between pink flesh and gray stone in these portraits alludes to the polychromy in landmarks local to Moroni's sitters, a relation that transforms these portraits into painted monuments. It can be concluded that Moroni's figures are products of their grounds and exist in an (interrupted) exchange with these grounds.

From the gray ground of the wall and the backdrop of the sixteenth-century city-state, the discussion returns, in chapter 5 ("Transumption"), to the darkened chambers of the primordial cave, while advancing to the tenebrism of late Renaissance painting. In works by Caravaggio, the scene appears to be set in a darkened interior so that figures and objects can only be identified by their illuminated fragments. The correlation of obscurity with a hidden though tangible presence is central to the critical reception of Caravaggio. Therefore, the chapter opens with close readings of ancient and early modern texts that associate the mythological figure of Echo with the primal site of the cave and its darkness. As Baroque poet Giambattista Marino phrased it, Echo is an "invisible image," continually present despite being obscured. The criticism of blackness, which appears as a lexical echo in period accounts of Caravaggio's paintings, alludes to the artist's emendation of the Renaissance idealized figure, a breaking apart of form reminiscent of Echo's fragmentation of utterance. Following the poet and critic John Hollander's understanding of transumption as an echo that occurs in spite of, or because of, repression, I also argue that Caravaggio's darkened grounds allude to the previous grounds that they obscure.

This study works through the force of critical examples, seeing how they bear strategic importance for the larger representational issues the ground implicates. The case studies invite readers to participate in intense observation and to generate a different narrative of the Italian Renaissance picture for themselves. An entire book devoted to the ground—to that which stands below, behind, or tangential to the chief object of contemplation—may seem nugatory. At the same time, a *complete* history of the ground in Renaissance art would require attention to areas beyond the Italian peninsula, especially in regions north of the Alps where painters such as Jan van Eyck or Pieter Bruegel the Elder made thorough investigations of ground.[21] Even so, as Daniel Arasse said of the detail, the ground likewise "constitutes an efficient touchstone to perceive the stakes of much larger historical links and aesthetic choices." Or as Friedrich Nietzsche aphoristically stated, for the scholar, "not that which glitters, shines, excites but often insignificant seeming truth is the fruit which he knows how to shake down from the tree of knowledge."[22]

A NOTE ON METHOD: FORMALISM AND HISTORY

Groundwork undoes the hierarchical binary of figure/ground by showing how each passes into and imparts characteristics to the other, making visible what Nicola Suthor has called "anomalies of depiction, the so-called language of the painter."[23] As a method, groundwork oscillates among different areas of art historical inquiry: the artist's workshop practice, material processes, and technique as can be gleaned from conservation reports and through close looking; the role of ground plane and background in depiction, especially in its relation to the figure as well as to narrative; and finally, the manifestation or occlusion of ground and background in period art theoretical commentary. This body of writing is analyzed especially in regard to its potential to make a complex argument about ground's role in art historical teleology and sequencing from gold ground painting to tenebrism.

In moving between these areas, this book takes an approach to image and text that could be called—or indicted as—"formalist." This word carries connotations of nefariousness. Scholarship in the humanities tends to impute to a method that places greatest emphasis on artefacts themselves a politics of containment and exclusion that is reactionary.[24] However, in the North American context, the association of formalism with a conservative political stance can be argued to have had more to do more with the political climate during the Cold War, when formalist readings became prevalent, than with the actual political agendas of contemporary critics interested in form. Meanwhile, humanist scholarship tends to associate with progressive liberal politics a method that treats artefacts as enmeshed in social contexts and dependent on historical circumstances, and for that reason grants as much attention to these contexts and circumstances as to the artefacts themselves. And yet, an academic obsession with dismantling formal containers—the nation-state, the relegated domestic sphere, or the penal system—has done little to disrupt the operation of such forms in social life.[25] In some quarters of the academy, this interest in "socially" progressive art history has even given rise to the expectation that scholars ought directly to reflect aspects of a marginal identity in their scholarship and professional person. Art historians of color, for example, are somehow expected to address their race and ethnicity in ways that are immediately recognizable, categorizable, and consumable. It remains an open question whether such assumptions contribute as much toward ensuring that the said scholars "stay in their lanes" as toward showcasing a (possibly rather superficial) level of "diversity," "equity," and "inclusion."[26] Let us ponder for a moment the formalism of the "lanes" or "fields" which structure the research and teaching in art historical departments: while professing to be antiformalists, some scholars have erected new restrictive forms that have the effect of sealing subdisciplines within given identities. White Euro-American scholars themselves, it should be said, rarely come up against these pernicious underlying assumptions.

In her book *Forms: Whole, Rhythm, Hierarchy, Network* (2015), Caroline Levine convincingly argues that while overtly social and political approaches postulate a cause-and-effect relationship between milieu and work, the artwork is always already present and is not an immediately direct effect of the social.[27] In lieu of using the work of art primarily as a point of departure to excavate the social conditions related to its patronage, creative inception, and production, I place emphasis first on paintings' formal qualities and prefatory processes of making, not in search of ideal wholes or integral forms, but rather on the trail of tensions and complexities in figural contour and arrangement, texture and tonal value of brushwork, and the conjunctions and (especially) disjunctions in a composition that hold the viewer in suspense. The internalizing of groundwork's possibility does make the social dimensions of the artwork significant, though only through the initial step of attentive looking. That is to say, when the viewer once stops to grasp groundwork's interpretive possibilities, the social dimensions of form (here understood as including ground) then become necessary for an enriched experience of the painting. The artwork may not be a direct effect of context. Even so, it presents its significance as inextricable from the residue of the "social"—the entire lived and material world, now partly inaccessible, which surrounded the circumstances of its making.

Consequently, to render into prose the dissonant complexities of figure and ground in the Renaissance picture, this book engages with Renaissance art criticism to anchor theoretically its thesis about how the pictorial ground formulates certain models of sense-making within a historically specific social realm. Attentiveness to the dynamic use of figures of speech, imagery, and narrative devices in biographies and treatises contributes to a shift in art historical method, from a data- or concept-driven analysis based on the single lexical or semantic unit to a more process-oriented mode of close reading. Equally revealing is when these texts pass over and write around the ground, leaving gaping ellipses or blanks in the texture of their prose. The bringing of these texts more holistically into dialogue with the paintings enables a greater permeability between text and image, with the effect of an intermedial transfer of analytic devices. Language can certainly be "a conspiracy against experience," as Michael Baxandall famously claimed in *Giotto and the Orators* (1971). Yet as Baxandall's own preoccupation with language as analytical scaffolding demonstrates, careful description of an artwork deepens and refines that experience, while also providing an occasion to interrogate and historicize the very linguistic medium of art historical inquiry.[28]

Hence, my use of visual and verbal formalisms does not aspire to impose wholeness and unity, or aim to inhibit interference or rupture. Meanwhile, interrupting the encroachment of social context onto an artwork's form can paradoxically open up a larger network of referents. The groundwork of the Renaissance picture addresses, models, or comprises an experimental field wherein an awareness of historically specific compositional processes resolves into comprehension of the social domain. Much Renaissance scholarship on the social function of the image speaks to the constructed or fashioned nature of representation. Yet while intending to address the image overall, analyses that point out the constructed nature of representation privilege the figure, and thereby understand the construct of the image through analogy with the figure. An approach to the image from the viewpoint of ground replaces constructedness with contingency. The "look" onto the image is enriched with the awareness that painting does not necessarily posit the figure as autonomous—in fact, the very attempt at self-constitution necessarily always fails when we acknowledge the image's seams and ruptures. Instead, groundwork as a method conceives the figure and figuration through their interdependency with the ground. In turn, the groundedness of the figure provides a theoretical frame to direct our attention to the "peripheral" and the transitive properties of bodies and their locations; to include not only the *who*, but also the *where*.

This book, then, aims to tell the "deep story" of the picture, one that is often occluded but that is fundamental to the picture's very existence and necessary for its comprehensive understanding. Ever since Vasari's germinal work, the ground has, in varying degrees, emerged into, disappeared from, and then reappeared in art historical descriptions. As Christopher Wood observes in his account of the history of art history, Alois Riegl would identify the interchangeability between figure and ground, and therefore the interruption of the distinctions between the two, as constituting "the template of the modern Western artwork." In this new artefact, figure and ground exist in a fluid exchange, permitting the artefact "as a whole to cohere and detach itself from the rest of the world, as if the work itself were now a figure set off against the ground of life."[29] However, it is not the aim of this study to see ground in the Renaissance picture in teleological terms, as a preliminary, if foundational, step toward modernist arguments concerning flatness or the perception of depth in painting, painting as a layered structure and foldable surface, or the dissolution of figure/ground oppositions.[30] While the figure/ground distinctions can be undone, ground endures as a constant variable in the conditions of what defines painting as a medium.[31] As Toni Morrison reminds us, paraphrasing A. S. Byatt, the ground was always there, "[we] knew it was always there, and have always known it was as it was, though we have now for the first time recognized, become fully cognizant of, our knowledge." Morrison applies Byatt's observation in her study on the invisibility of Black presence in criticism. As she states, "it requires hard work not to see."[32] Aside from recuperating the ground as a category that merits critical examination, I am also intent on grasping the dilemma of its exception in our current models of art theoretical interpretation. What does it mean to exist as something so present as to escape notice but also so peripheral as to escape attention?

The figure/ground distinction can be undone and yet endures over time. In identifying groundwork as a blind spot in art historical analysis, this book also represents a divergent approach to certain assumptions concerning chronology and progression that are prevalent in the discipline referred to as "art history." On one hand, the narrative of these chapters seems to follow, even underscore, a progression of the compositional operations undergirding the Italian Renaissance picture, from gold ground in the Trecento to the darkness in tenebrist painting circa 1600 and beyond. Yet in tracking these shifts, I am less interested in imputing these visible changes in the picture to external causes and forces. It is not my view that the "rise of science" accounts wholly for the emergence of landscape, or that "skepticism" explains dark grounds.[33] I argue that the apparent modalities of ground actually inform and absorb or subsume, rather than replace, one another. Gold ground, while seemingly discarded in the Renaissance due to the increased valuing of mimetic skill over material application, continued to inform groundwork. Chiaroscuro and tenebrist paintings depend, as does gold ground, on the tension between nearness and distance to engineer their aesthetic and narrative effects. Impasto brushwork, which activates the materiality of the canvas support, has much to do with the convention of tessellated surfaces in mosaics. The historical orientation of this book, in other words, seeks not only to present a history of ground as ever present, but also to give value to the temporally dissonant juxtapositions that ground evokes.

History is thus pursued through excavation, through an attempted return to the origins of picture making deep within the physical picture itself, through the stratified layers of paint that sit above the prepared support.[34] Strangely enough, the deeper we penetrate and the closer we come to the "ground zero" of painting, the stranger the view on and into the artwork becomes. There is nothing more afigural or anticipatory than a joined panel or blank canvas awaiting the application of the material ground. The power of ground lies in its material, mimetic, and interpretive potential: to find history inside the picture, within its depths.

1

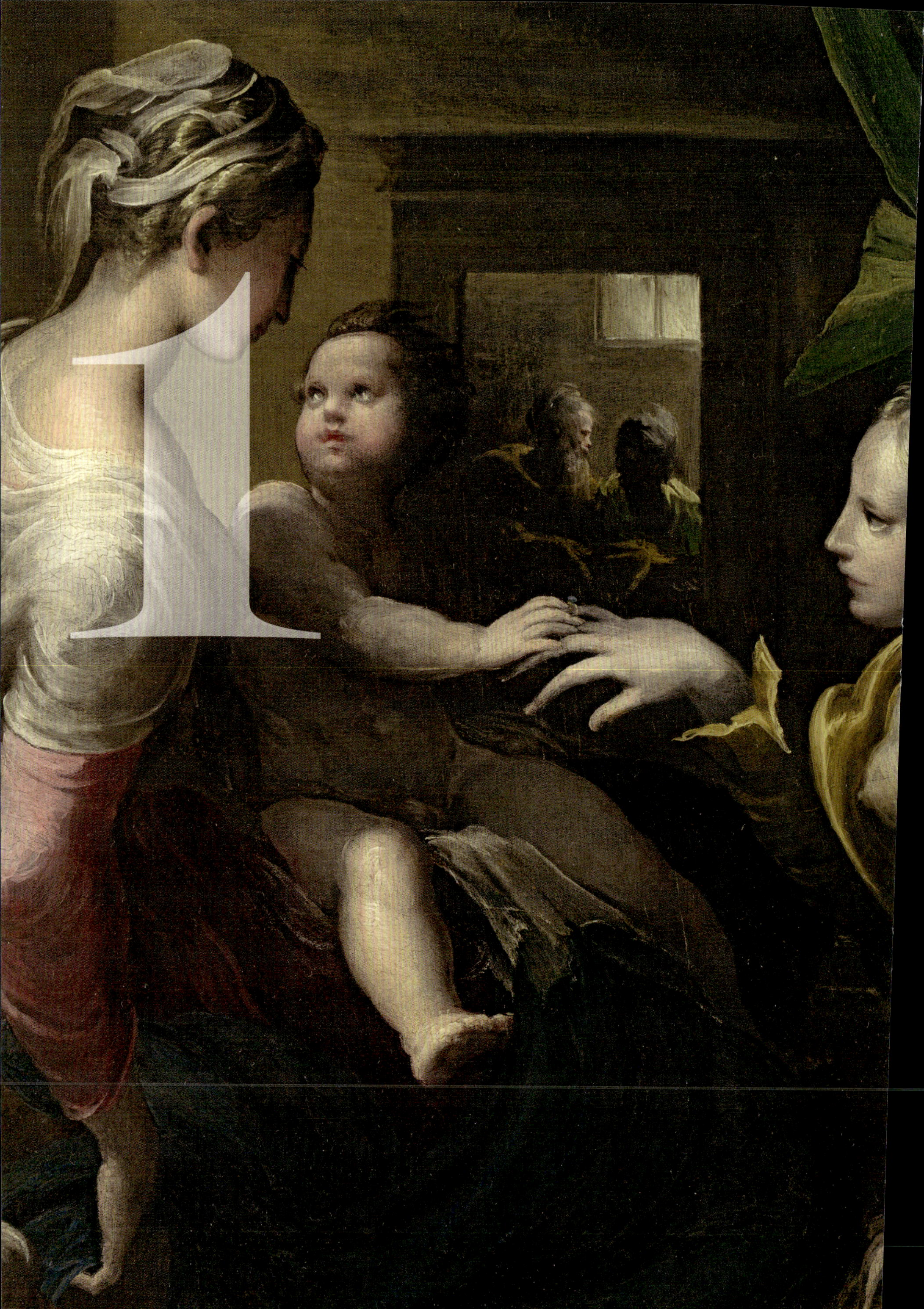

Words for Grounds

Of the many vignettes about the visual arts recounted in Pliny the Elder's *Natural History*, two regarding the origins of painting remained indelible in the imagination of Renaissance artists and writers on art. The first of these attributes the discovery of painting to the act of tracing a line around the shadow of a beloved. In one variation of the tale, the daughter of Butades, a potter from the Greek city-state of Sicyon near Corinth, falls in love with a young man about to depart for a journey. "And when he was going abroad," Pliny recounts, "she drew in outline on the wall the shadow of his face thrown by the lamp." Elsewhere in the *Natural History*, Pliny affirms that "all agree that [painting] began with tracing an outline around a man's shadow," and consequently, he adds, "pictures were originally done in this way." In the second origin story, Pyrrhus, a king who waged war against Rome, had in his possession an agate gemstone. As Pliny phrases it, "nature unaided," through patterns and markings, made the stone appear to portray the Nine Muses, along with Apollo holding his lyre. To these two origin stories about painting, we can add a third that was equally important for Renaissance thinking about the arts. Ovid's *Metamorphoses* tells of Narcissus, the beautiful youth who did not love until he encountered his own reflection. Writing centuries later, the humanist and architect Leon Battista Alberti wrote in his treatise *On Painting* that "the tale of Narcissus fits our purpose perfectly. What is painting but the act of embracing by means of art the surface of the pool?"[1]

These origin stories ally the inauguration of painting with shadow, pattern, and reflection.[2] They are examples of "metaphorology," a term the philosopher Hans Blumenberg coined to describe how discursive thinking about foundational principles preempts itself in myths, fables, or figures of speech. Resisting ready definition or summary, parables and metaphors narrate the beginnings of things, foreshadow their demise, and orient pathways to larger theoretical claims. More than ornamental rhetoric, metaphor points in Blumenberg's view to the mode of thought that occurs before concepts have been settled and have coalesced into hard-edged semantic

Detail, Figure 1.4

units or differentiated terms. In his introductory essay to *Paradigms for a Metaphorology*, Blumenberg likened the domain of the imagination to "a catalytic sphere from which the universe of concepts continually renews itself, without thereby converting and exhausting this founding reserve."[3] Myth and metaphor, the long and short forms of imaginative thought, function similarly, by providing a means to grasp connections and provide explanation without sharp delimitation. Metaphorology "seeks to burrow down to the substructure of thought, the underground, the nutrient solution of systematic crystallizations." In addition, an approach based in metaphorology "aims to show with what 'courage' the mind preempts itself in its images and how its history is projected in the courage of its conjectures."[4]

The primordial myths and metaphors of painting bear what Blumenberg called "a roving anticipatory quality" that offers a way to revisit and reorient our understanding of the Renaissance picture.[5] A rich body of scholarship has pondered the implications of these origin myths for our understanding of mimesis, from the shadow understood as the image of the other, to the reflection as the image of the self, to the pattern as an image made by chance and nature. Let us add one more component: in its primordial stage, painting as a medium comes into being in and through certain physical and pictorial conditions: namely, a ground. In these myths, the ground takes various guises: it is a wall, a slab, and a pool of water. The Corinthian maiden draws around her beloved's shadow "on a wall" (in pariete). Ground as vertical enclosure stands on the edge between domestic interior and distant destination, between the shared physical presence of the couple and their eventual dissolution into observer (the daughter) and absent sitter (the beloved). In the second story, the agate stone ground, with its pitted grain, acts as both carrier of fantastical patterning and physical substrate. The image that comes out of it encodes the passion of the earth's own processes of change and posits an essential connection between nature, divinity, and artifice. Finally, in the last of these classical accounts, Narcissus, "having lain on the earth" (humi positus), gazes at his own reflection and offers his lips to "the deceptive pool" (fallaci fonti). As Hubert Damisch suggests, this myth conceives painting as a projection on a planar surface in two dimensions. Yet the aqueous surface is only the uppermost layer. Alberti describes Narcissus as embracing the "superficie del fonte"—the pool's surface, underneath which water collects in the bedrock. In his rendering of the Ovidian tale, Plotinus notably mutates the pool into a river into which Narcissus plunges to find his avatar. Each of these grounds—wall, rock, and pool—relates in varying ways to the multiple grounds in the Renaissance picture: ground as material, ground as depicted platform or terrain, and ground as background. These grounds shape the material, and ultimately the affective, dimensions of the image as a physical vestige of togetherness and separation, as an impermanent fluctuation, and as a site of fantasy.[6]

In the Renaissance, these classical myths about painting's origins were translated, glossed, and sometimes rendered as paintings themselves. For his Florentine residence, Giorgio Vasari painted a variation of the myth of the Corinthian maiden in which the act of tracing the shadow becomes the beginning of self-portraiture (fig. 1.1). Painters such as Titian, Sebastiano del Piombo, and Daniele da Volterra engaged heavy lithic supports as representational vehicles, discovering figuration in the "pre-existing" material, a practice that will be discussed in chapter 3. The myth of Narcissus, too, received pictorial realization by such artists as Filarete and the followers of Boltraffio, though most powerfully by Caravaggio, as will be addressed in chapter 5: his rendering dedicates almost half of the canvas to the evanescent aqueous ground that shows the reflection of the doomed youth.

Simultaneously, in this era when the theory of art began to develop as an autonomous genre, discussion about the fashioning and function of grounds in painting grew and coalesced around critical key terms. The language of Renaissance art theory began to identify ground not only as a

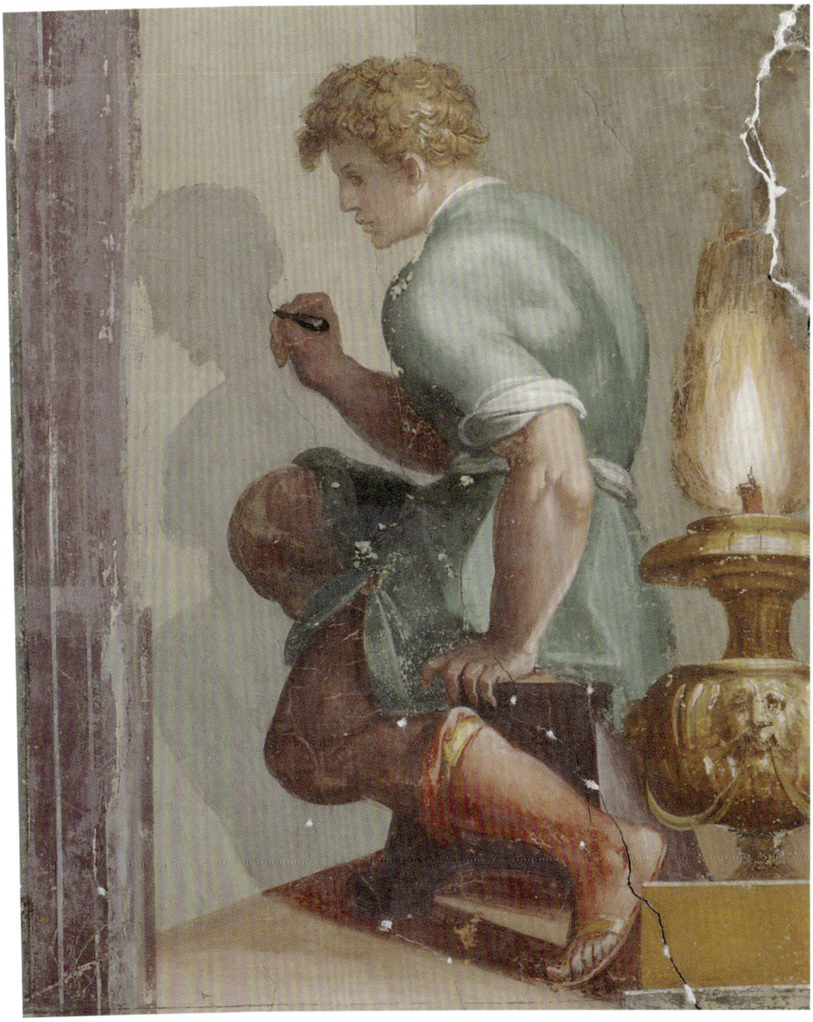

Fig. 1.1. Giorgio Vasari, *Gyges the Lydian Tracing His Shadow*, 1572. Fresco. Casa Vasari, Florence.

material element, but also as an agent in the pictorial field. Ground was not just there; it exerted effects on the material, composition, and interpretation of the Renaissance picture. In other words, these theorists began to identify *groundwork*, the exploration of ground for its possibilities with respect to facture, composition, and meaning.[7]

The complexity of the discourse surrounding grounds in the Renaissance is suggested by the presence of several words for what we now take as ground, whose denotations and connotations bled into one another. This lexical spectrum not only speaks to the multilayered nature of the painting process; it also points to how writers on art were attempting to make sense of, in order to locate and prescribe, ground's place in painting. The following sections elaborate on the three semantic areas of ground that make up our interpretive framework.

GROUND AS MATERIAL PREPARATION

The first semantic area of ground in painting pertains to the material preparation of the support. In her examination of period documentary sources on grounds, Jilleen Nadolyn points out that *gesso*, the combination of gypsum (calcium sulphate) and a binder (frequently a type of animal glue) is the term that most often refers to this preparatory layer. Variations on this substantive include *ingessatura* and even the more specific *preparazione a gesso e colla*, a preparation of gypsum and glue size. The word *gesso*, as in English today, also has a verb form: "gessare dictam tabulam" was a standard phrase in contracts stipulating that painters were required to provide their supports with a preparatory layer. Treatises on painting deploy the verbs *ingiessare* or *ingessare* in their prescriptions and explanations of the painting process. As paintings shift from wooden panels to other supports, predominantly canvas, other terms appear or take on an expanded set of meanings. Jill Dunkerton, Marika Spring, and more recently Angela Cerasuolo have excavated the usage and semantic range of this technical vocabulary. The word *imprimatura*, roughly though not exactly synonymous with our English "priming," is a case in point. Imprimatura might designate a supplementary layer of size or drying oil that serves to reduce the absorbency of the ground. When pigmentation is added, imprimatura also describes a painting's initial base color. A nearly equivalent though more flexible term was *mestica*. In his *Vocabolario Toscano dell'Arte del Disegno* (1681), an invaluable period lexicon of techniques and materials, Filippo Baldinucci defined mestica as a "mixture of different earths and pigments ground in walnut or linseed oil: it is applied on panel and canvases which are to be painted: artists also call it imprimatura." Mestica, like imprimatura, could refer to a mixture of base colors from which the painter could work up a composition. Yet mestica could also refer to the specific order in which gradations of color are to be laid down on the painting surface.[8]

What did this material ground do? A couplet from *Der Teufels Netz* (c. 1441), a German satirical didactic, speaks to its necessity: "The ground they did not prepare as they ought / Thus is the work for naught." (So hand sie den grund nit wol berait. / Darumb ist es verlorn arbait.) Just as society needs a stable foundation free from vice, the poem declares, so too does a painting require a ground in order for it to endure. The ground functioned to protect the support while also preventing it from absorbing liquid paint, which, like the pool of water in the Narcissus myth, lingers on top as a visual surface. Grounds also smooth and diminish irregularities in the support material. On panel, they furnish an appropriate surface on which to execute gilding, and in certain cases, can be modeled and shaped to achieve effects in low relief, as in pastiglia work. On canvas, the ground applied with a grounding knife fills in the open weave of the textile support, or if the painter elects, can be withheld to enhance textural effects. The ground thus provides base of color as well as texture that the painter can exploit in subsequent layers of paint.[9]

Ground, therefore, was crucial for a picture's appearance and durability. Application of the ground was a laborious part of the painting process, which required time, expertise, and appropriate studio space. Documents therefore occasionally mention artists' legal obligation to carefully prepare their panels: a contract dated 1442 between Priamo di Piero della Quercia and the Opera of San Michele of Volterra stipulates that the artist will apply a gesso ground with size on the entirety of the painting surface. The proper application of ground also received commentary in period treatises on art. The painter Cennino Cennini devotes some two dozen chapters to the topic in the early Renaissance text *Libro dell'arte* (c. 1390). As though to suggest the complicated and crucial nature of executing a ground, he even recommends that the artist pray before confronting the panel: he should invoke "the name of the most holy Trinity" and the "glorious Virgin Mary." Technical examination has revealed variations to the instructions set down in Cennino's text. Even so, the procedures he lays out were generally standard for panel painting in the Trecento and Quattrocento. Therefore, it is worthwhile to summarize his instructions for how grounds should be applied—on what surfaces and with what material parameters and consequences.[10]

Cennino's chapters on grounds call attention to the tremendous labor that the manufacture of the Renaissance picture entailed, even before a composition was realized. The elaborate procedure would first begin with removing any flaws on the front side of the panel. For a complex work, such as a polyptypch or large altarpiece, dowels or dovetail inserts would join multiple panels together. Battens, or long strips of wood, would then be fastened on the back to secure the construction against the natural movement of the wood due to any fluctuations in temperature and humidity. The front surface of the panel would then receive a coat of size, a glue made from the skin of an animal such as rabbit, kid, or sheep. The addition of canvas, parchment, or other fibrous materials further stabilized the panel against inevitable variations in the atmosphere. At this point, gesso ground would be applied to the panel. The gesso itself could take two forms: *gesso grosso* contains coarser particles of gypsum; *gesso sottile* contains gypsum that has been allowed to soak in water for about a month until, in Cennino's words, it becomes as "soft as silk." *Gesso grosso* and *gesso sottile* would be applied in sequence. Extant paintings from the period generally feature one coat of *gesso grosso*, while the layers of *gesso sottile* could approach as many as ten. The application of the ground would create a brilliant white, hard surface; this in turn would be sanded down until, as Cennino describes, it "becomes like ivory." The panel would then be ready for preparatory drawing, the application of red bole, and the laying down of gold leaf to realize a gold ground. The gesso ground could extend to the picture's edges. For paintings well through the fifteenth century, the frame was a structural component of the panel's construction. In certain cases, the front face of the panel would be carved from a piece of wood, leaving the beveled edges to assume the role of framing device. In these instances, both panel and frame received preparatory coats and gilding, so that ground is implicated in every corner of the picture.[11]

Chapter 2 will offer a more extensive treatment of gesso ground in relation to gold ground, the intriguing instance where the ground emerges on the picture's surface. For now, it is worthwhile to consider instances when the gesso ground, seemingly submerged beneath layers of paint, has a direct bearing on the final appearance, and ultimately the effect and objective, of a work. Paintings of certain artists, particularly those from northern Italy, feature an additional layer, the imprimatura, which reduced the absorbency of the gesso ground while enhancing its luminosity. The Venetian artist Palma Vecchio, a contemporary of both Giorgione and Titian, was among several artists who chose to exploit this layer's chromatic potential. The inventory of his studio taken after his death in 1528 is interspersed with descriptions of paintings, which indicate their subject matter (mostly Madonnas, saints, and landscapes) as well as their varying states of completion ("meza facta" is a recurrent phrase). In cases where panels or canvases were unfinished, the notary indicated whether they had been prepared with "zesso bianco" (white gesso) or "zesso beretin" (*beretin* here being a Venetian word for ash or gray). Technical analysis has suggested that in Palma's *Blonde Woman* (c. 1520), a portrayal of ideal female beauty (fig. 1.2), white gesso ground contributes to the luminosity of the figure's pale and radiant skin, which is rendered in layers of translucent oil paint. Meanwhile, the dark areas surrounding the figure have been prepared with a darkened ground, in a technique called "local priming." In Palma's groundwork, the brilliant ground is allowed to shine through the paint, and this radiance becomes the hallmark of feminine beauty in the Petrarchan tradition. The ground's effect is paradoxical: Palma "gets closer" to the ground by allowing the brilliant white gesso to shine through; yet the figure's brightness mobilizes the trope of remoteness and unattainable beauty in courtly poetry. Ground works from below but then is kept at a distance.[12]

→

Fig. 1.2. Palma Vecchio, *A Blonde Woman*, c. 1520. Oil on panel (77.5 × 64.1 cm). National Gallery, London. Mond Bequest, 1924.

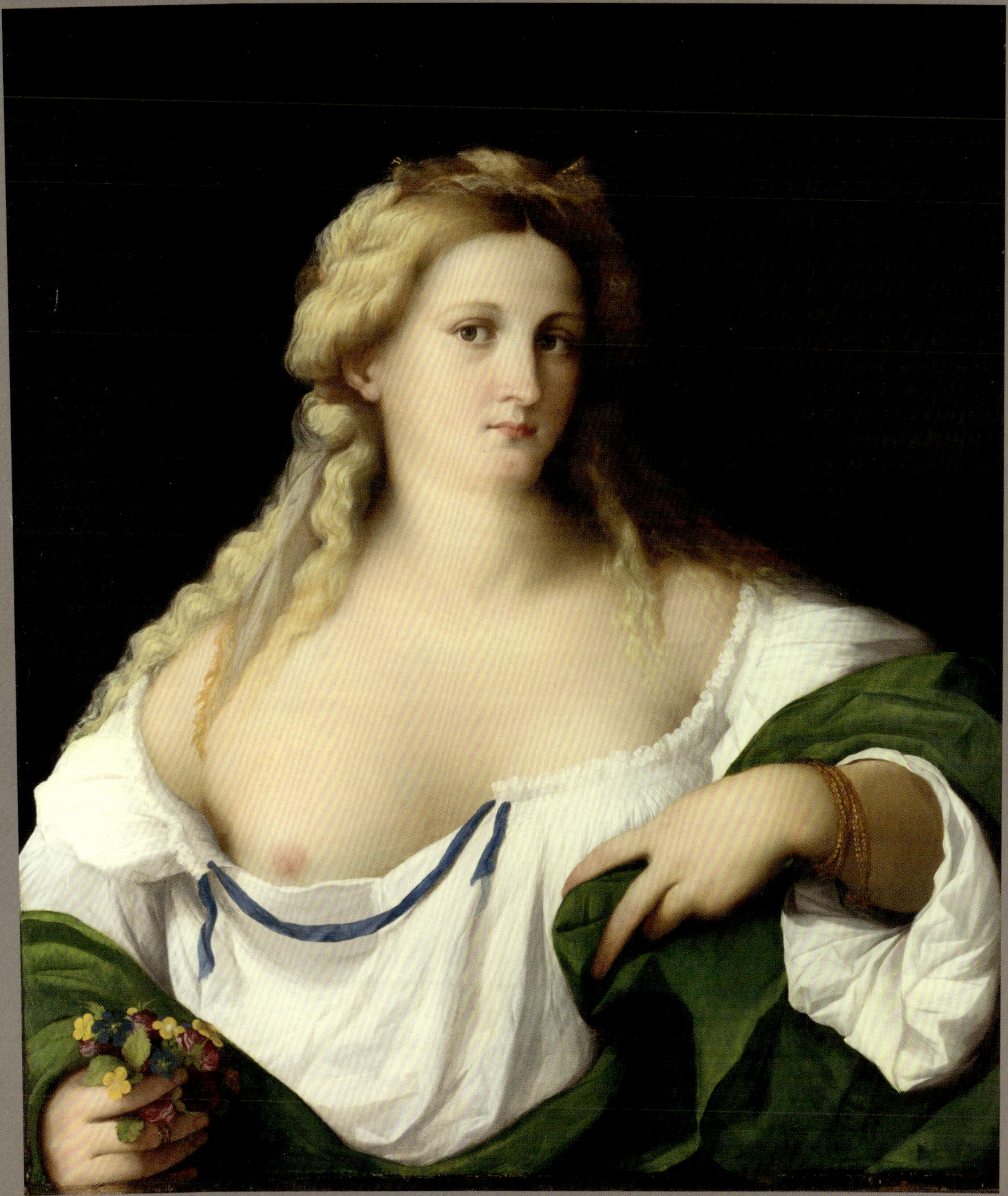

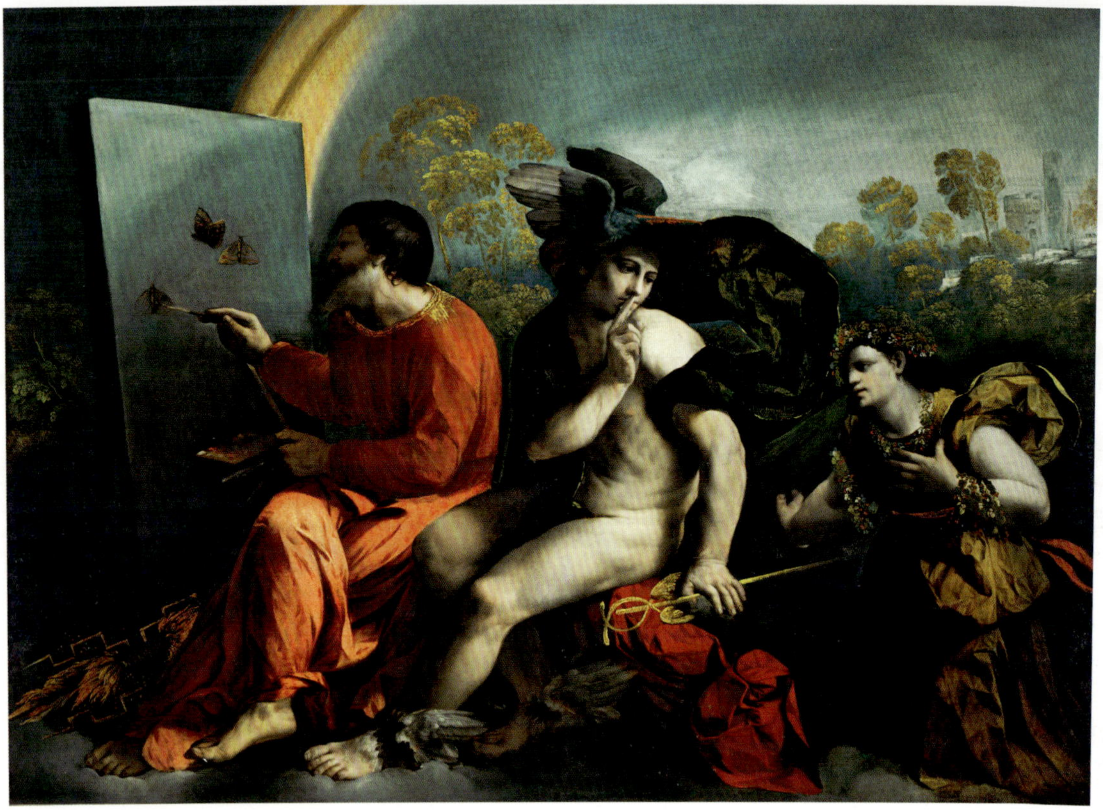

The increasing use in the fifteenth century of canvas instead of panel as the main physical support for a painting is a subject of frequent commentary in art historical accounts of technique.[13] But just as gesso grounds on panel were fundamental to a picture's durability, and in some cases also drove its meaning and stylistic ambitions, grounds on canvas were just as integral. For these textile supports, the interstices of the weave are smoothed over by grounds, which are flicked onto the canvas by a knife to partially fill in the depressions and graze the tops of the threads. At times, support and ground worked together to convey certain effects: fine weaves with evenly spread grounds could approximate the smooth surface of panel, whereas coarser weaves such as those used by Tintoretto could achieve the impression of relief when paint was roughly applied.[14] In Tintoretto's work, the linear seams in the canvas could even at times direct where the artist decided to place lateral horizontal lines or vertical breaks between figures in his compositions.[15]

Fig. 1.3. Dosso Dossi, *Jupiter, Mercury, and Virtue* (*Jupiter Painting Butterflies*), c. 1524. Oil on canvas (112 × 150 cm). Wawel Royal Castle, Kraków.

In tandem with these changes in supports and their preparation was the emerging practice of artists' working with colored grounds. The imprimatura applied to the gesso ground could contain pigments displaying a range of tonalities. In the sample of paintings from the National Gallery, London analyzed by Jill Dunkerton and Marika Spring, darker grounds incorporated "lead-white, various forms of black, umber, yellow and red earths, lead-tin yellow and less commonly, red lead, vermilion, and assorted pigments described as 'palette scrapings.'"[16] Ground absorbs the studio's "trash." Darkened imprimatura demanded delicate artistic judgment and skill. The sixteenth-century painter and writer on art Giovanni Battista Armenini warned that "oil, as experience proves, naturally darkens all colors and at the same time it makes them fainter, so that the darker the underlying imprimatura, the dirtier they get."[17] Painting registers the passing of time from the bottom up.

Dosso Dossi was among the many sixteenth-century northern Italian painters who deftly deployed colored grounds to achieve varying levels of luminosity. Dosso's imprimatura frequently consisted of a mixture of clay, lead white, charcoal, and brown earths. In his *Jupiter, Mercury, and Virtue*, the muted tones of this ground are visible toward the bottom and partly on top of the canvas on which Jupiter has begun to paint (fig. 1.3). This ground has a temporal valence insofar as its discernibility indicates that Jupiter has not completed but rather is still in the process of painting butterflies hovering on the canvas's surface. In the painting's upper zone, the chromatic complexity of this ground facilitates the impression of fluctuating atmospheric and lighting effects, further enhancing the impression of action and transience. Ground works metaphorically: sky is compared to an almost blank grounded canvas awaiting the painter's brush.[18]

Chromatic shift in grounds entailed new approaches in paint application. Whereas a light ground invites the rendering of linear shape in dark, a colored preparation encourages a description of form in light. Consequently, with an increasing tendency toward colored grounds, painters came to practice what Dunkerton and Spring have called a "broader style of painting," deploying light and thick paint to model form. Parmigianino was one of many sixteenth-century painters who explored the possibility for bravura sweeping brushwork afforded by a darkened ground.[19] A number of paintings from the 1520s feature a noticeable shift from light gray grounds seen in his earlier work to considerably darker grounds. In his *Mystic Marriage of Saint Catherine*, he left the dark brown priming layer exposed, allowing it to stand out in between the breaks of rapid brushwork (fig. 1.4). In other passages, shadows and layers of dark paint are built on top of the colored ground, enhancing tonal contrast. Parmigianino's groundwork partakes in the bravura handling of the brush, which in turn enhances the physical immediacy of the somber setting and tactility of swirling curtains and drapery.[20]

Darkened grounds laid in with bold brushwork engaged with art critical discourse in a period that prized such qualities as *prestezza* (quickness) and the *non finito* (artful unfinishedness) in painting. Such colored grounds were critical for the development of what Michel Hochmann has called "tonal painting," an approach to chromaticism pursued by Titian, Caravaggio, Domenico Fetti, Rubens, and Rembrandt. In this view, ground as material

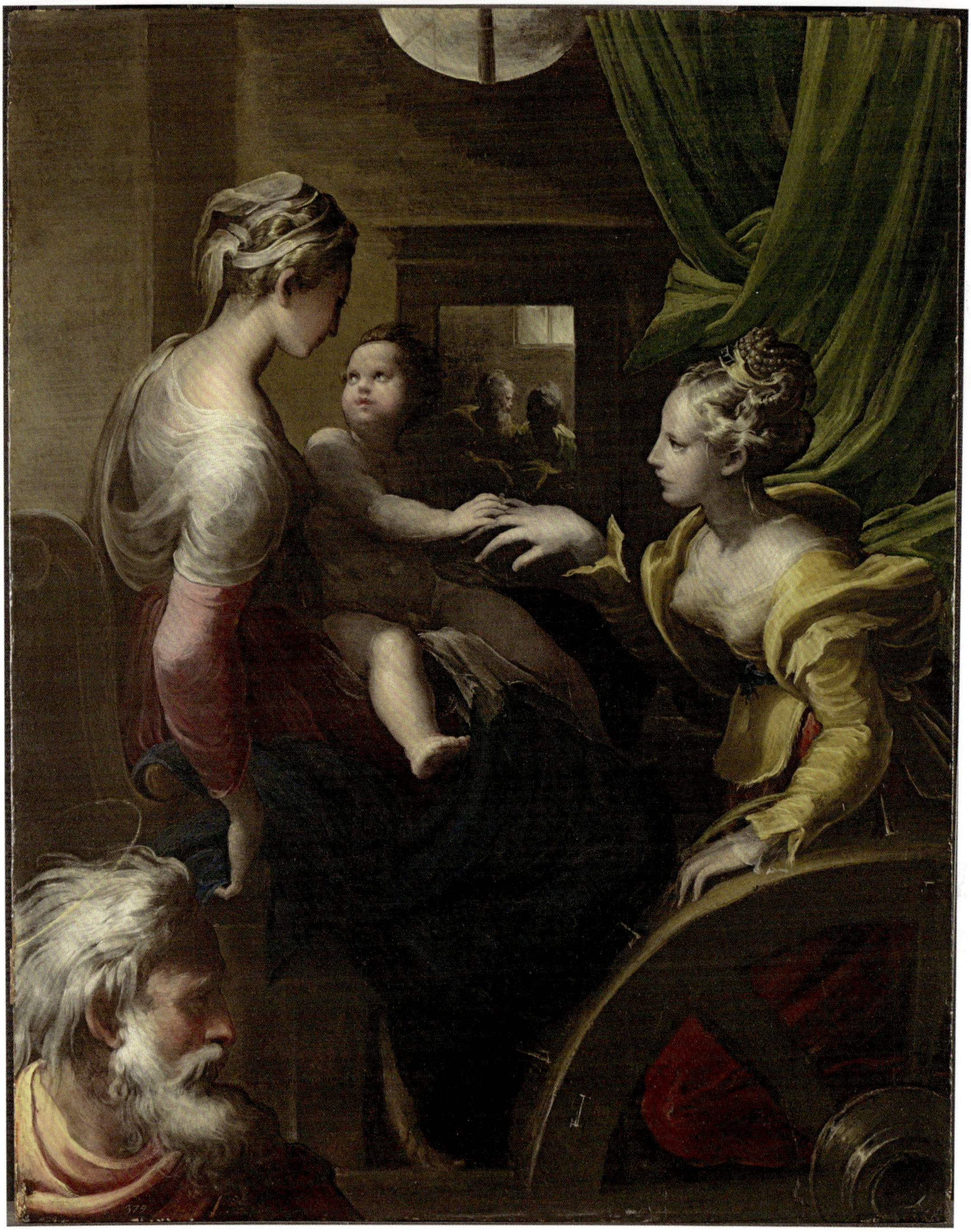

Fig. 1.4. Parmigianino, *The Mystic Marriage of Saint Catherine*, c. 1527–31. Oil on panel (74.2 × 57.2 cm). National Gallery, London. Bought, 1974 (NG6427).

preparation is not merely preliminary in the sense of making the picture ready for future use. Ground is already painting.

GROUND AS PLANE AND TERRAIN

When the picture is no longer looked at as a material expanse, but instead is looked into as a fictive world, the word "ground" comes to refer to the represented surface on which bodies stand. Stumpel considers this notion of ground as a natural or architectural base critical to the development of pictorial composition: "There is always, apart from the saint himself and the background, something like the ground on which he stands." He clarifies that "by ground, I now mean the platform his feet are resting upon."[21] The period term to designate this particular zone in the picture is *piano*, defined in a mathematical context as "that which has, in its surface, equality in all its parts."[22] This ground is fundamental, since it functions as the vehicle "whereby the consistency of the painted world can be established—and consequently tested by the beholder." *Piano* and related expressions such as *linea del piano*, referring to a base or horizon line, were standard terms in Renaissance treatises on mathematics, surveying, and perspective.[23]

While it certainly also serves as a geometric concept, piano can shed its regularity and evenness in accordance with a picture's subject matter. A synonym for piano in this sense might be "terrain," a word that calls attention to the geological features of land. In fourteenth-century painting, the piano frequently appears as a cliff or ragged ridge, as it does in Duccio's *Noli*

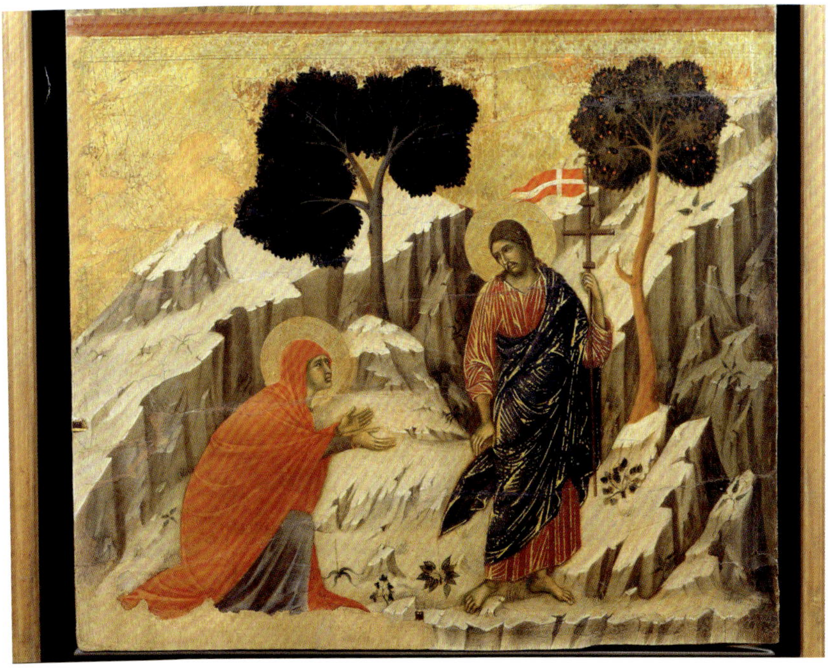

Fig. 1.5. Duccio, *Noli me tangere* from the *Maestà* altarpiece, 1308–11. Gold and tempera on panel (51 × 57 cm). Museo dell'Opera Metropolitana, Siena.

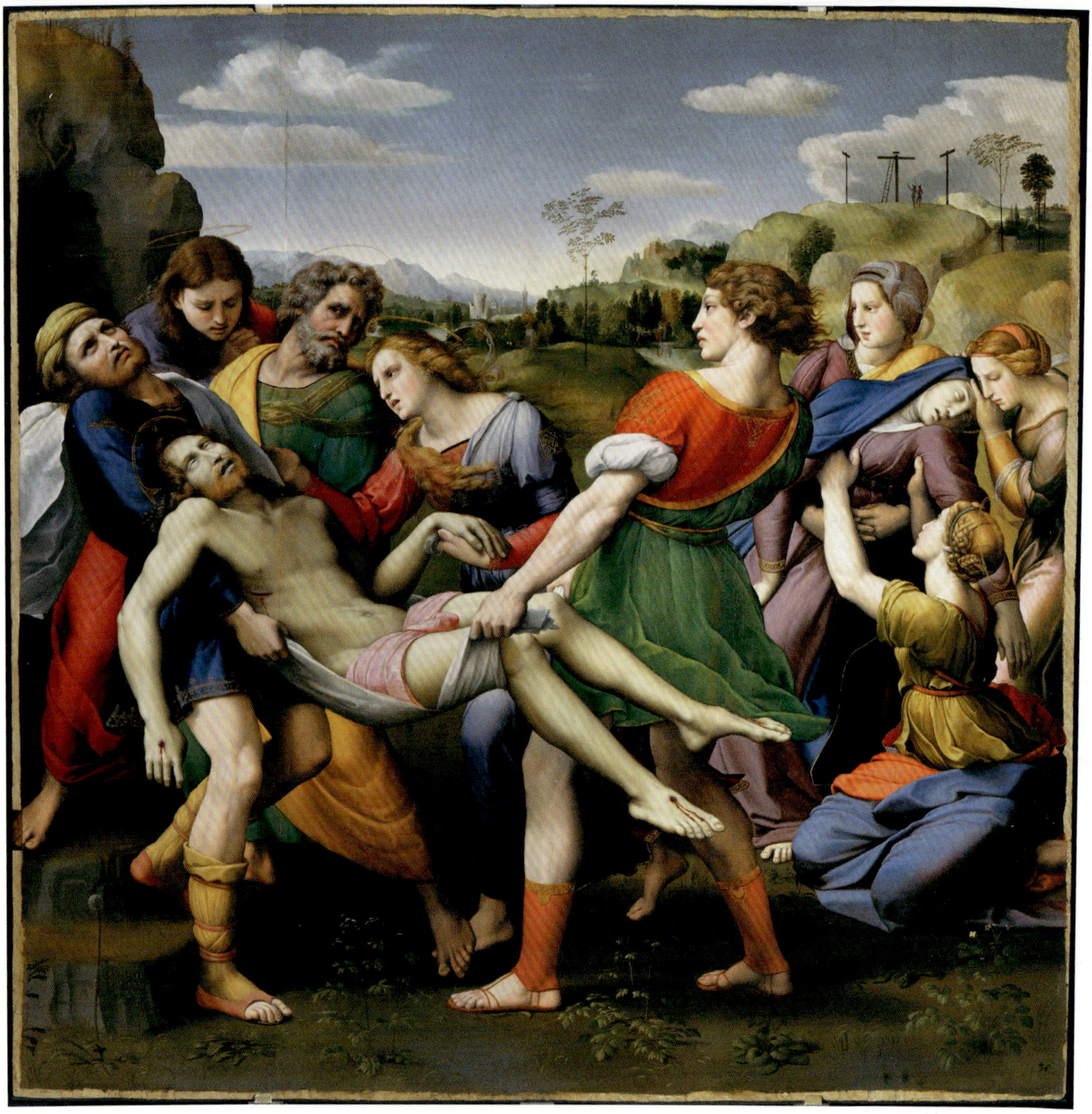

Fig. 1.6. Raphael, *Deposition*, 1507. Oil on panel (184 × 176 cm). Galleria Borghese, Rome.

me tangere (fig. 1.5). Here Christ stands and Mary Magdalene kneels on the jagged ground. This terrain bridges and separates: clefts establish continuity between the folds in the Magdalene's drapery and the chrysographic lines in Christ's robes. Yet the piano also registers the distance, both spatial and affective, between the two figures. The cliffs, emphatically oriented upwards and to the right, amplify Christ's shift away from the Magdalene. Ground as terrain enacts groundwork, by intensifying bodily gesture and underscoring the miraculous event of Christ's appearance in the early morning light, which is reflected on the surface of the jagged rock face. Additionally, there is a metaphoric element of arduous ascent that is represented by the rockscape. From the Magdalene's position of kneeling in reverence, she can eventually ascend to Christ. Duccio translates the logic of Jacob's Ladder to the earth itself.[24]

Groundwork in relation to terrain resonates with, and yet in critical ways departs from, a concept that T. J. Clark described in a series of lectures as "ground-level painting." For most painters, Clark suggests, ground-level painting is of little importance, given that the ground as such is often taken for granted. For example, in Raphael's *Deposition*, the earth merely serves as "pure support for the action above—the falling and holding and balancing, with its intricate criss cross of movement sideways, close to the picture plane" (fig. 1.6). The earth, according to Clark, has not "the least resistance or material character of its own."[25] But this is too categorical: close looking reveals that Raphael deftly used the ground plane to place and display his own signature (RAPHAEL. / VRBINAS. / M.D.VII). The incised name appears on the stone block that acts like a step leading to Christ's tomb, so that the viewer must read it before identifying the location of the sacred grave. And as Rona Goffen has claimed, the signature on the ground sits just

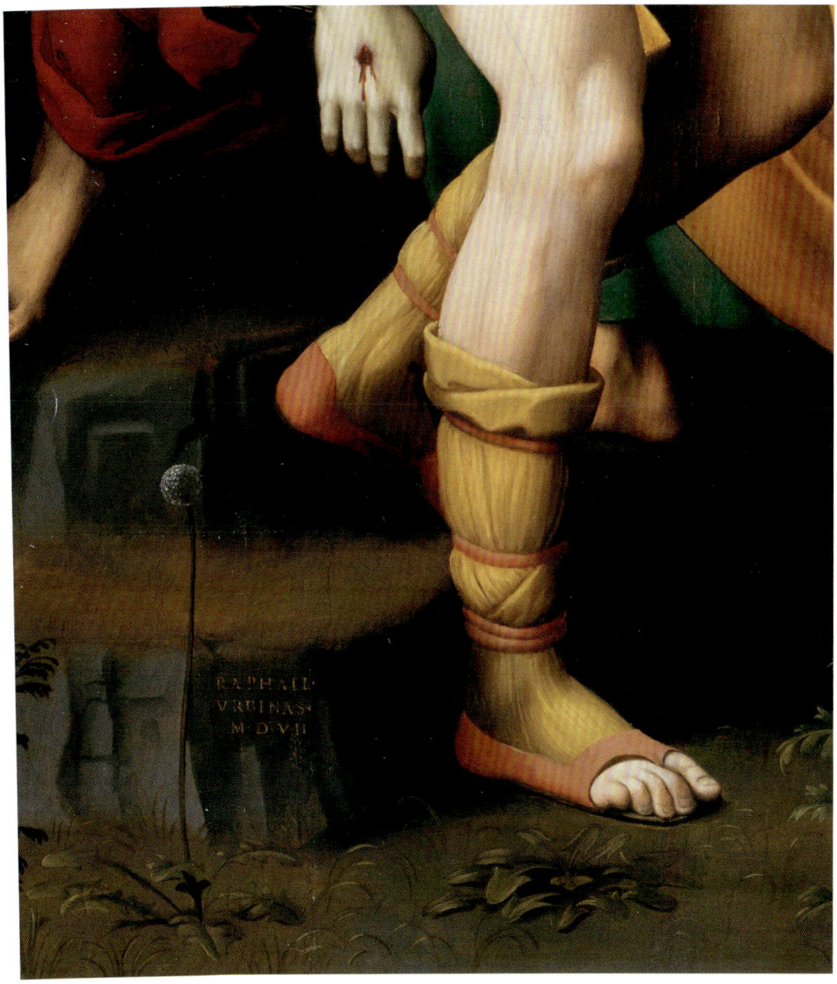

Fig. 1.7. Detail from Raphael, *Deposition*, 1507. Oil on panel (184 × 176 cm). Galleria Borghese, Rome.

beneath Christ's hanging left arm as a synecdoche for the artist's hand itself (fig. 1.7).[26] Clark then discusses those painters who do engage in ground-level painting. For them, the ground "becomes something other than a notional 'plane' established in a system of equal spatial coordinates or dimensions; it becomes a level, a grounding, a limit condition of the human; and further it becomes a world in itself, level and yet not level, firm and yet locally unreliable, fissured, fractured, intricate—a world of levels as opposed to an image of levelness." Ground-level painting is interested in the ground's "weight-bearing or body-balancing qualities" and depicts the moment of contact between upright man and the ground plane. Poussin and Bruegel, two representatives of ground-level painting, deploy the ground level to point to the affective, gustatory, and even erotic dimensions of personhood.[27]

It is important to draw a distinction between ground-level painting and groundwork, although they seem to overlap. Ground-level painting is primarily engaged in the matter of how ground as terrain registers one of the chief characteristics of the human species, namely bipedalism. As Clark puts it, "standing on one's hind legs is a great fact of human existence whether or not it is thought of within an evolutionary frame. For whatever reason—within whatever ideological matrix—some artists come to see it as the key to our being in the world."[28] David Summers has presented similar arguments regarding how the "uprightness" of the human body relates to the orientation of the image hanging on the wall.[29] Groundwork, by contrast, is not only interested in the human form as it ascends from and descends to the ground plane. Ground-workers, if we may so call them, are those painters who deploy ground to create a series of reverberating effects that bear directly on narrative action and meaning in the picture. Visual incident distributes itself between figure and ground, with emphasis placed on their conjunctions and disjunctions.

What is more, ground unfolds metaphor. To return to the example of Raphael's *Deposition*, the little sprouts signaling the Resurrection are arguably in an eschatological sense the most important part of the picture. Groundwork thereby marshals the plane to become a *Bedeutungsträger*, a carrier of meaning that shapes pictorial composition and its reception. In its extreme form, groundwork can compete with and sometimes supersede figure, drawing attention away from the body and toward itself.

How else might groundwork operate through the plane? How artists mobilize the grid pavement, one of the most conventional ground planes in fifteenth-century painting, provides an important test case. Whereas the grid, or *vellum*, is most often associated with organizing and controlling the overall picture plane, the geometrically ordered "checkerboard" floor also elicited commentary. "The method of dividing up the pavement," Alberti declared, "pertains especially to that part of painting which, when we come to it, we shall call composition." He includes it among those aspects of painting that were "totally unknown to our elders because it was obscure and most difficult." Even contracts from the period attest to the importance of the

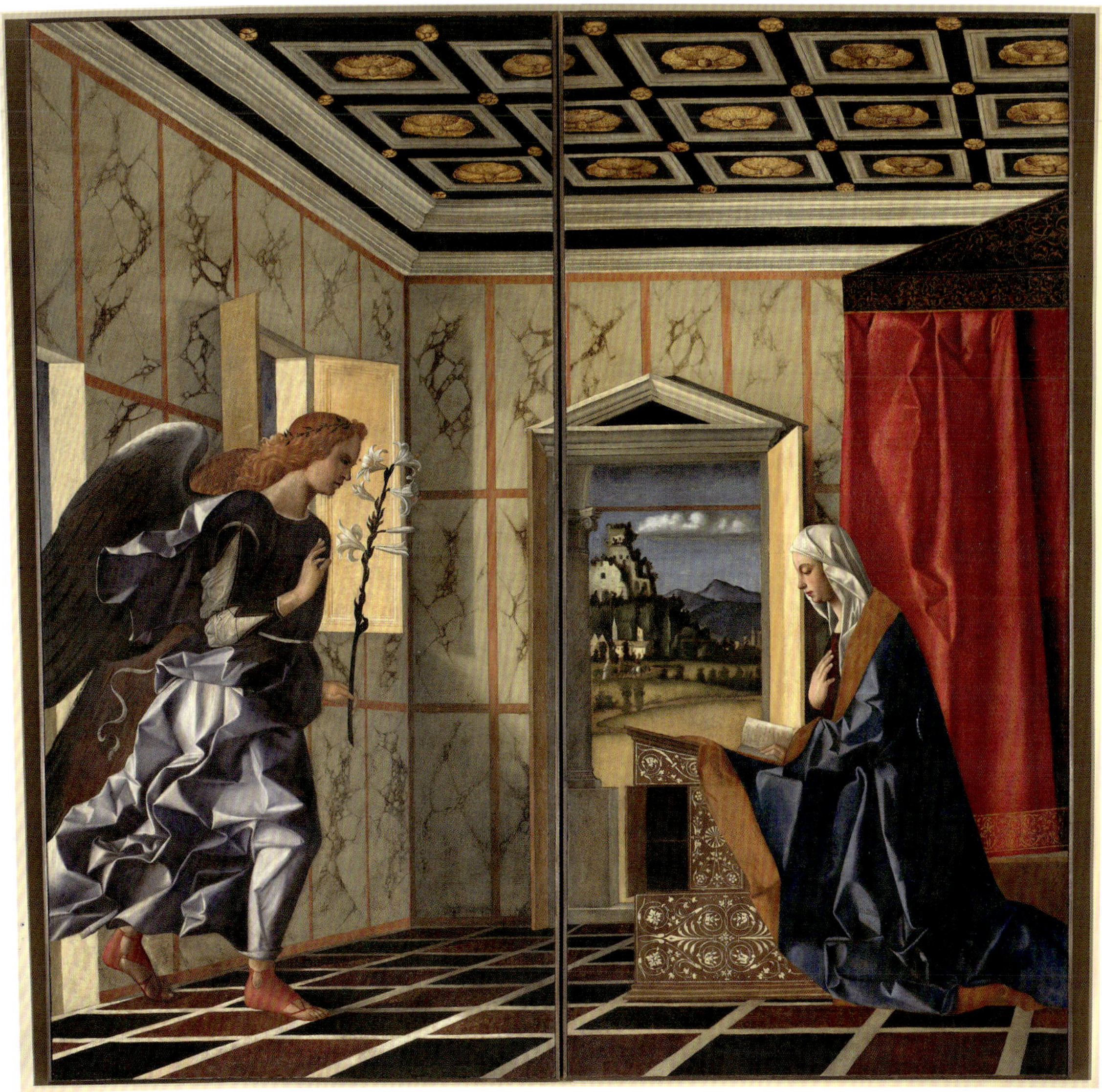

grid as a pictorial task. One such agreement was drawn up between a painter who wanted his son to learn the art of painting and Squarcione, the Paduan painter best known as Mantegna's master. According to the contract, Squarcione agreed to teach his charge "the principle of a plane with lines drawn according to my method, and to put figures on the said plane, one here and one there, in various places on the said plane, and place objects, namely a chair, bench, or house, and get him to understand these things." The grid, then, was fundamental to locating objects, and by extension, understanding organization in a composition itself.[30]

The checkerboard pavement could also act as a more complex compositional device affecting the visibility and intelligibility of a narrative. This is

Fig. 1.8. Giovanni Bellini, *Annunciation*, c. 1500. Oil on canvas (224 × 210 cm). Gallerie dell'Accademia, Venice (formerly in Santa Maria dei Miracoli, Venice).

the case for a painted pair of organ shutters, once located in the church of Santa Maria dei Miracoli in Venice (fig. 1.8). Attributed to Giovanni Bellini and dated to the beginning of the sixteenth century, the panels portray the Annunciation unfolding in a domestic setting that resembles the church's opulent interior, clad with marble revetment. The checkerboard ground is part of the grid schema that dictates the chamber's overall spatial disposition: all of the side walls and even the coffered ceilings feature a network of intersecting lines. The purpose of the grid goes beyond conveying the impression of geometric rigor. The grid also imparts the strangeness of Gabriel's stance, which moves between stepping and floating: while the angel's right foot is flexed on a sienna-colored tile, the other hovers between ground and mid-air. The shutters' display above the ground intensified this sense of suspension, for the organ was installed in a loft above the raised presbytery's left-hand side.[31]

The checkerboard ground becomes an instrument of what Wolfgang Kemp has termed the "chronotopos," the dynamic use of setting to segment, and in this case, impart the "when" of, pictorial narrative.[32] The square tiles allow the viewer to ascertain the number of steps between the Archangel Gabriel and the Virgin, a distance traversed by miraculous light streaming in from the *fenestra* (and here, the window's open shutters are meta-pictorial references to the deployable organ shutters themselves). The viewer is encouraged to measure in steps the time remaining between this scene and the delivery of the ultimate message. Bellini's checkered ground seems to say, "It will be soon," just as Duccio's rocky cliffscape says, "It will take time."[33]

While Bellini's *Annunciation* intimated these compositional possibilities, later painters would explore in a more pronounced fashion how a ground organized as a grid might implicate the upper and lower registers of pictorial space in the service of dramatic storytelling. Tintoretto laid out the pivotal event of the *Finding of the Body of Saint Mark* (1562–66) on a checkerboard pavement (fig. 1.9), in this case, the floor of the church in Alexandria, where the saint is buried before his *furta sacra* to Venice recedes far into the distance. The pavement serves not only as a measuring device to ascertain the height of the wall tombs from which corpses emerge. Once again associated with speed, the floor tiles rush back toward the brilliantly lit stone slab, opening to the catacombs, into which two figures descend to search for the saint's holy body. As in Pliny's myth of the Corinthian maiden, we confront human and shadow, though this time the figure moves not laterally across the earth, but downward into it.

Although the grid typically reveals the order on the surface, here it also suggests what lies beneath that surface, or a vertical series of surfaces. Tintoretto extends the grid to occupy three dimensions. As we saw with Bellini, the grid allows viewers to measure narrative progress through the actors' physical movement from left to right or foreground to background (or vice versa). In the *Finding*, Tintoretto also overturns this narrative convention.

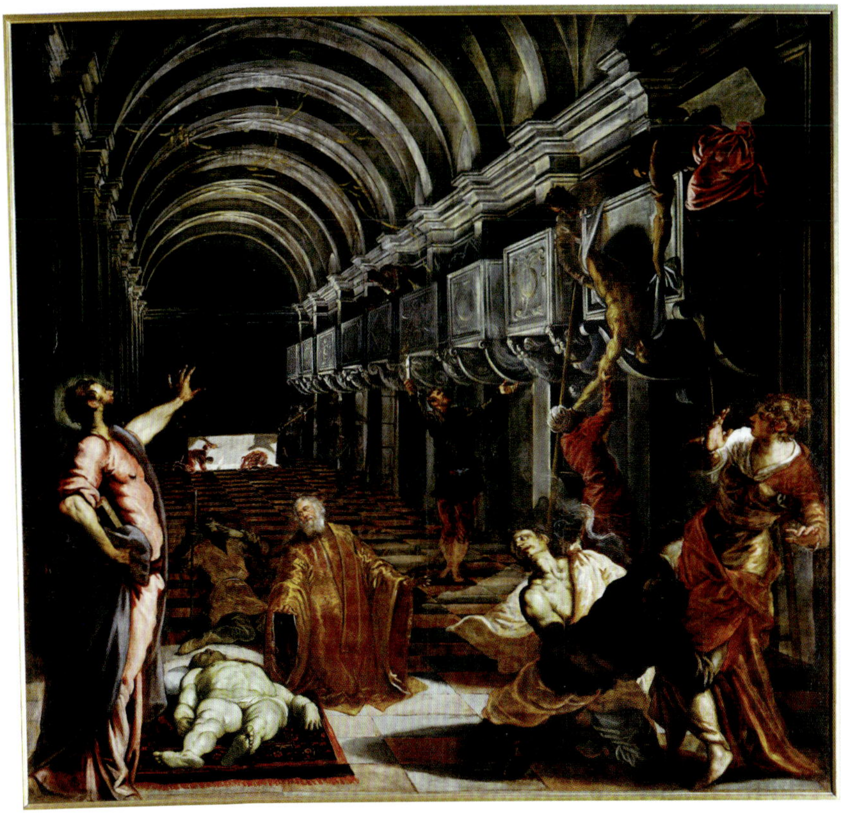

Saint Mark, his arm seemingly stretched along the picture's cunicular expanse, halts the search for his own body, which has already been exhumed and placed in the foreground. The pavement signals not where action has happened or will happen, but instead where it must be suspended. The subject of the *Finding* thereby acquires a force of urgency that surpasses a rote recital of hagiographic events. Tintoretto's groundwork loosens the geometric rigidity of the zone of the ground: just as the grid of the floor is tunneled under and layered over (with the carpet beneath Saint Mark's body), the narrative also takes on multiple topographic levels. The grid becomes a space of unpredictable action, holding the viewer in suspense, at the same as it references actions in the past that are visible and known.[34]

FROM FOREGROUND TO BACKGROUND

In generating a series of effects on, and emerging from, the ground as plane and terrain, groundwork acts through the picture, moving along the entire passage from foreground to background. Sometimes this movement is abrupt, as in Tintoretto's painting, where the floor slab raises and rotates the ground plane to become background. Later writers on art sought to classify the relation between near and far. In his *Analysis of Beauty* (1753), the British

Fig. 1.9. Jacopo Tintoretto, *The Finding of the Body of Saint Mark*, 1526–66. Oil on canvas (396 × 400 cm). Pinacoteca di Brera, Milan (formerly in the Scuola di San Marco, Venice).

painter William Hogarth observed that to achieve the quality of simplicity, "painters [. . .] divide their [compositions] into fore-ground, middle-ground, and distance or back-ground." While it is uncertain whether painters consistently thought of their compositions in these terms—dividing them up, as Hogarth prescribed, "into three or five parts or parcels"—the various spatial zones in the picture often exist in continuity and immediate connection with one another.[35]

The background's antipode, the foreground, that part of the view nearest the viewer, is integral to understanding how the picture engages in space-making and meaning-making. We might therefore ask, "What is the route to the background? What work does the viewer have to undertake to culminate the journey through the "half-opened door" to "another world"

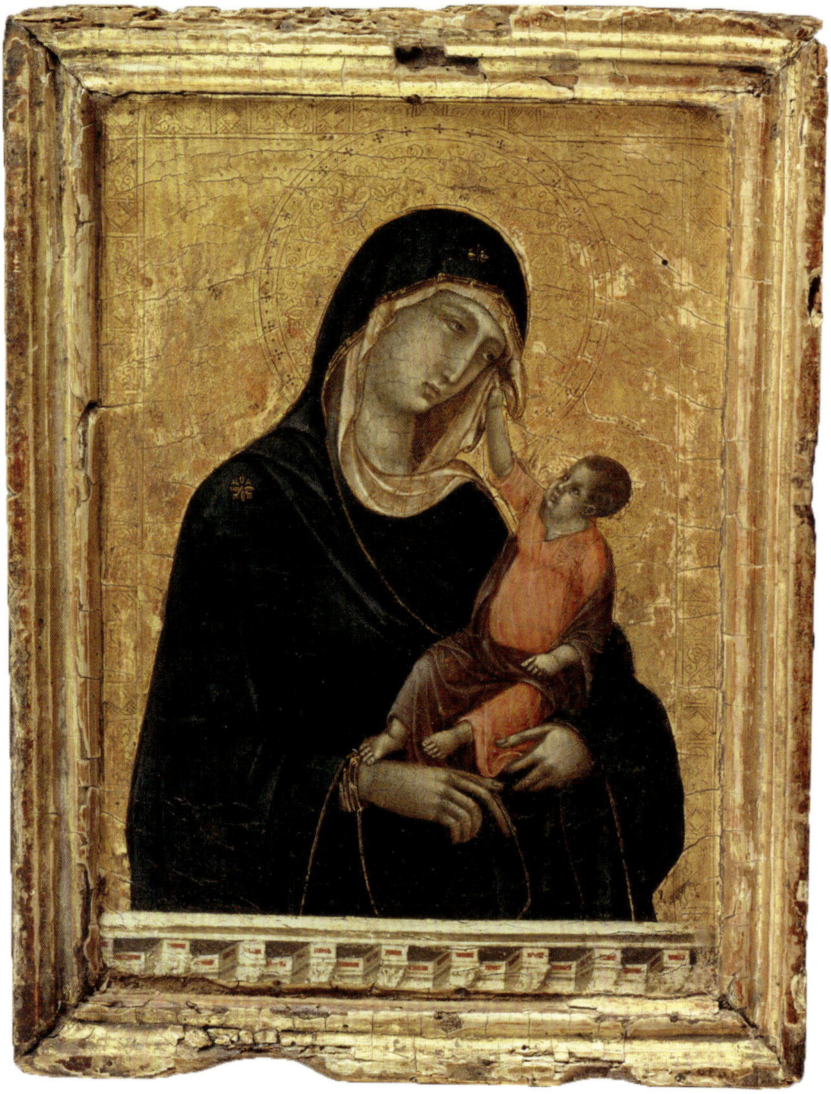

Fig. 1.10. Duccio, *Madonna and Child*, c. 1300. Tempera and gold on panel (overall, with engaged frame, 27.9 × 21 cm; image surface 23.8 × 16.5 cm). Metropolitan Museum of Art, New York. Purchase, Rogers Fund, Walter and Leonore Annenberg and The Annenberg Foundation Gift, Lila Acheson Wallace Gift, Annette de la Renta Gift, Harris Brisbane Dick, Fletcher, Louis V. Bell, and Dodge Funds, Joseph Pulitzer Bequest, several members of The Chairman's Council Gifts, Elaine L. Rosenberg and Stephenson Family Foundation Gifts, 2003 Benefit Fund, and other gifts and funds from various donors, 2004 (2004.442).

(as André Malraux and Maurice Merleau-Ponty described the encounter with the medium of painting)?[36] Painters' consideration of this question can be seen in a trio of examples, briefly considered here, that problematize the foreground, occasionally referred to as the *primo piano* in period texts, as a way into the pictorial field.

Similar to an operatic recitative, the musical declamation preceding an aria, the foreground acts as a prelude: it brings the beholder into relation with the picture and establishes the conditions for viewing. At times, the foreground registers authorship (through the insertion of signatures) and reflects on the aims of representation itself. To invoke Duccio once again: the Sienese master's *Madonna and Child*, dated to the last decade of the fourteenth century, conceives its foreground in novel terms as an illusionistic parapet (fig. 1.10). This ledge can be considered as the picture's double edge, its second frame. For Louis Marin, such encasing devices display "a remarkable polysemy between supplement and complement, gratuitous ornament and necessary mechanism." Here the parapet as frame foreshadows the action of Christ, who seems to push away his mother's veil to better fix his gaze on the Virgin. The veil might be likened to a dissolved or elastic parapet, framing the face of the Virgin, underscoring her status as the *fenestra coeli*, window to heaven. The mechanism of the foreground as frame also dictates the terms of the picture's viewership. Aside from mediating the space of the beholder and the gilt realm the Virgin inhabits, the parapet with its foreshortened corbels compels the viewer to kneel. While the checkerboard encouraged viewers to imagine traversing horizontal space, the parapet implies height. The picture rises up, the viewer crouches. Christ reaches up to Mary, and thus while the viewer is encouraged to kneel on one hand, he or she also reaches, ascends. The foreground underscores the beholder's position as subject, here understood in a physical and devotional sense as a body with legs and arms, who both kneels before and reaches toward in order to contact the divine.[37] The parapet, in truncating the Virgin, does away with the problem of how to show her footing and thus enables her to seem fully situated in a celestial space.

In our second example, the foreground invites reflection on representation itself, the forms it can take, and its capacity not only to imitate and surpass nature but to outlast it as well. Titian expanded the semantic potential of the foreground in his treatment of the parapet in *Portrait of a Lady* (1510–12), also known as *La Schiavona* (fig. 1.11). In her sensitive reading of the work, Maria Loh calls attention to the complex relationship between foreground and figure, how the woman stands "on the threshold between different realities," engaged in and engaging the viewer in "a simultaneous game of hide and seek and of show and tell."[38] One participant in this ludic enterprise is the lady's left hand, foreshortened and emerging from the depths of her voluminous sleeve to rest on the foreground's edge. Her fingers graze the proverbial "fourth wall" separating actor and spectator. When the hand emerges from the sleeve, figure touches ground. As in the Duccio example

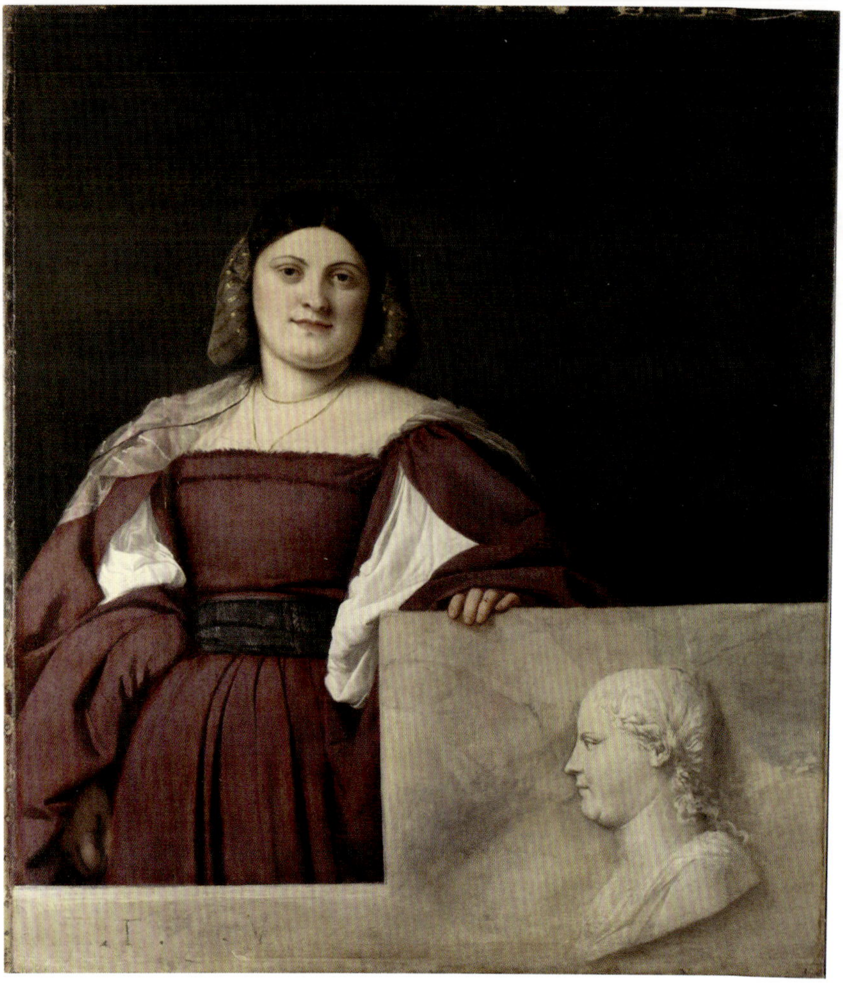

Fig. 1.11. Titian, *Portrait of a Lady* (*La Schiavona*), c. 1510–12. Oil on canvas (119.4 × 96.5 cm). National Gallery, London. Presented through the Art Fund by Sir Francis Cook, Bt., in memory of his father, Sir Herbert Cook, Bt., 1942 (NG5385).

discussed above, the half-length format suppresses the sitter's moment of figural contact with the ground as floor. Both painters seem to be drawing a relationship between the standing ground of the viewer and the pictorial foreground behind which the sitter is shown. In other words, the painting relocates the boundary between viewer and sitter inside the picture itself.

The parapet also elicits and places pressure on analogies between the different media involved in representation. Just as the woman projects from the dark gray ground behind her, so too does her sculpted avatar emerge in relief from the veined marble ground. Here, the relief portrait is rendered by more painterly means than is her "painted" portrait behind the ledge: quivering brushstrokes describe the relief portrait's braids and falling curls, as well as the garment's edges and neckline. The relief's throbbing blue vein embedded within stone is a meaningful detail: the blood vessel invokes the many myths in which humans are created from stones, images appear in stone, sculptures come to life, or even in which people are petrified. The

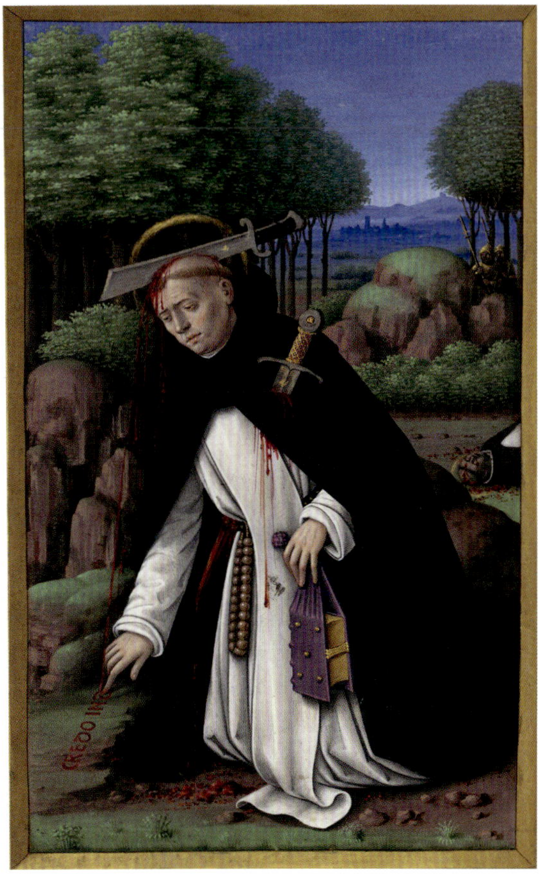

foreground here provides the structure where Titian can argue for *ars potior natura*—art more powerful than nature[39].

In *La Schiavona* as in Raphael's *Deposition* discussed previously, the ground serves as a matrix for script. In Titian's painting, the ledge was inscribed with the double majuscule "V.V.," later modified into "T.V.": these initials could have referred to some such humanist motto as "virtus et veritas" (virtue and truth), or "vivens vivo" (the living subject), or even the artist's name (Tiziano Vecellio). Inscriptions can be made in any number of grounds: foregrounds often feature artists' signatures and *cartellini*—illusionistically rendered pieces of paper showing a name and date.[40]

The inscription can appear in and on the ground, as it does routinely in visualizations of the death of Saint Peter Martyr, who, as recounted in the Golden Legend, having been bludgeoned with an ax, wrote "CREDO IN DEUM" (I believe in God) on the ground with his own blood (fig. 1.12). The presence of script in paintings, in conceiving the picture plane as a writing surface, draws attention to how the medium of painting migrates from and through the various media that feature graphic marks (on supports such as vellum, the printed page, panel, canvas, and fresco).[41]

Fig. 1.12. Jean Bourdichon, "Death of Saint Peter Martyr at Verona." Parchment. From *Horae ad usum romanum* (*Grandes Heures d'Anne de Bretagne*), c. 1500–1508. BnF Ms. Latin 9474, fol. 179v. Départment des manuscrits, Bibliothèque nationale de France, Paris.

Script on the ground plane, in demanding that the viewer focus enough to be able to read—or at the very least, to recognize the presence and authority of letters—transforms the field surrounding or behind the script into background. This effect at times also paradoxically turns figure *into* ground. In the *Allegorical Portrait of Dante*, attributed to an artist in the circle of Agnolo Bronzino, the book coexists, even competes, with the body of the Florentine poet, which is transformed into a background for the display of verse (fig. 1.13).[42] The forty-eight lines from *Paradiso*, Canto 25 beginning with the words "Se mai continga," inscribed as they are on the verso and recto of the book, call for a diagonal mode of viewing, not from foreground to background of the picture, as is conventional, but instead from lower left to upper right, which is also the direction of Dante's spiritual ascent from the flames of the Inferno to the Mount of Purgatory. Dante's gesture is self-effacing: instead of frontally presenting his verse, he twists his head away, beholding the scene in the background that emerges from the text in the foreground.

In the progression from foreground to background, the figure usually occupies the middle ground, which is the primary focus of the viewer's attention. But that focus can wander and drift. Incidents of meaningful distraction upon the ground as terrain challenge and supersede the semantic centrality of the figure. In both *La Schiavona* and the *Allegorical Portrait of Dante*, the foreground underscores the themes of transience and remembrance. Titian's sitter places her hand on the slab that bears her effigy in relief. Dante too places his hand on the book, asserting the immortality of his writing as opposed to his body, which is twisted as if to show its impending recession from view, its ultimate death and internment, through which it will become a part of the ground.

Writing motifs pass back and forth from ground as the earth, the place where feet touch to support the body, to foreground, the part of the picture that seems closest to the viewer. It seems as though painters are confronting the question, "How can I most effectively make contact with the viewer, by extending this space inward, or by requiring the viewer to focus or pause here?" Returning to Wharton's observation that the ground is "the real picture [. . .] which had its birth in the artist's brain," the ground seems to be the place where the space of the painting becomes the locus of painterly thought.

GROUND AS BACKGROUND

While artists sometimes drew sharp distinctions between ground as platform and ground as background, these two pictorial elements often blended into each other, facilitating a convincing representation of spatial recession. Correspondingly, the semantic boundaries of certain terms for grounds and backgrounds became open and pliable.

For example, the word *piano* is defined in period dictionaries as a surface

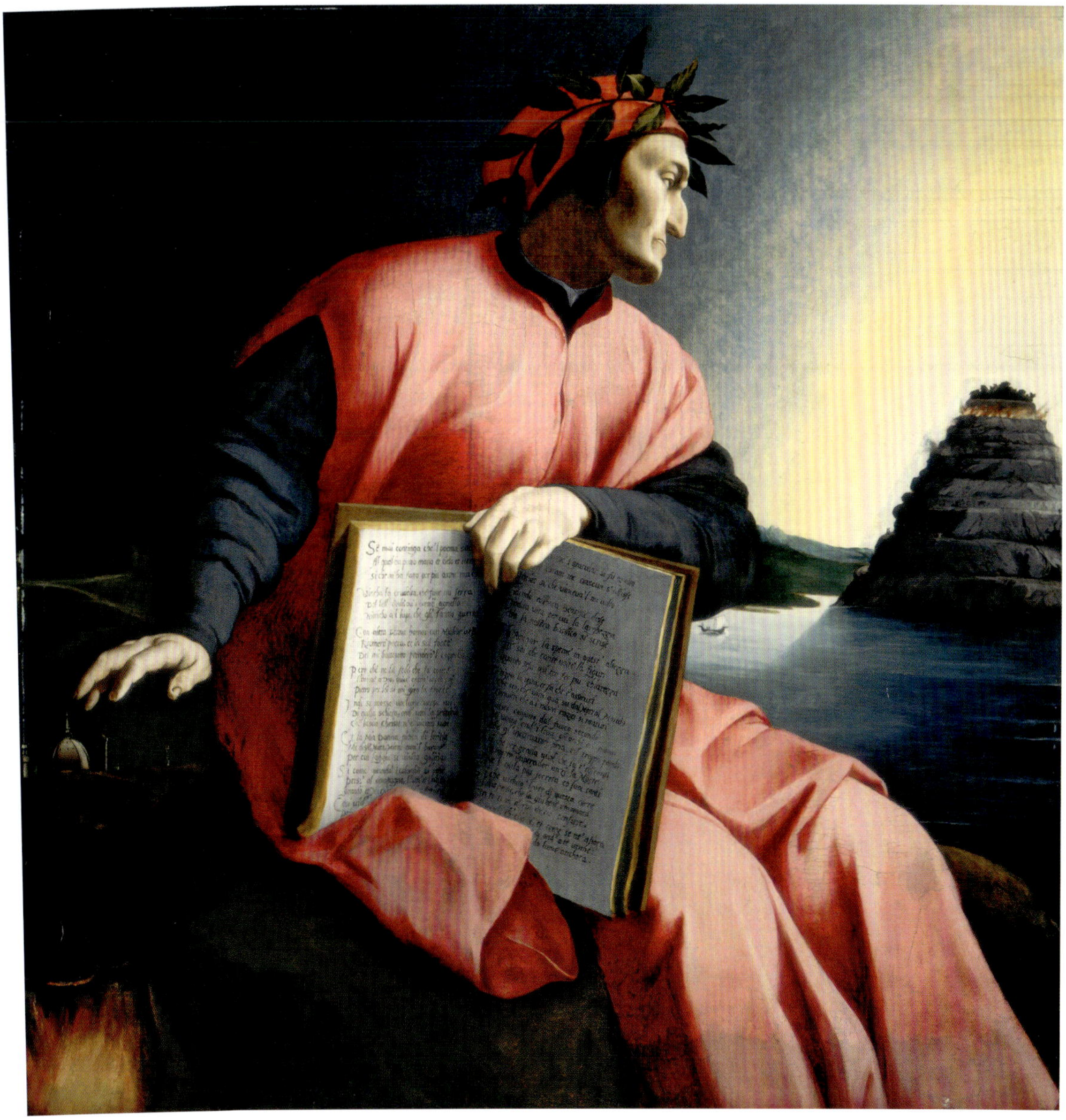

Fig. 1.13. Circle of Bronzino, *Allegorical Portrait of Dante*, late sixteenth century. Oil on panel (126.9 × 120 cm). National Gallery of Art, Washington, DC. Samuel H. Kress Collection, 1961 (1961.9.57).

with "equality in all its parts" (cognate with the English "plane"). Piano as platform is also closely allied with the concept of ground as setting. The terms *sfondo* and *sfondro* refer to scenery assembled for ephemeral decorations or stage sets. In landscape painting, *sfondato* also refers to a distant view or the effect of breaking through the confines of a containing wall or plane.[43] An etymological relative of *sfondo* is *fondo*, meaning depth or recession (from the Latin *fundus*: base or bottom) often in opposition to a figure *a rilievo*, a body projecting from the pictorial field into the viewer's space. Another lexical set includes the words *lontano* and *lontananze* (from the Latin *longe*: far), signifying the illusion of spatial depth, and more specifically, landscape views that recede far into the background. Paolo Pino, in his treatise on painting *Dialogo di pittura* (1548), grants lontani a secondary status by asserting that while his own compatriots excel at imitating the figure, northern *oltramontagni*—in other words, artists who live far away, "over the mountains"—are expert in lontani. Other words in the lexicon delineate specific subject matter: *aeri* for skies, *paesaggi* for landscape views, and *casamenti* and *prospettiva* for representations of architecture.[44]

One word in particular, however, has prominence in the lexical map we have been charting: *campo*. In his philological analysis of the term in art literary sources, Jeroen Stumpel demonstrated that *campo* acts as a powerful equivalent period term for what we now refer to as ground. Derived from the Latin *campus*, *campo* primarily refers to an even, open plane or field, but it can also refer to a place of action, battle, or debate. Here one thinks of the lines in Dante's *Purgatory* about artistic rivalry: "Once Cimabue thought to hold the field [campo] / as painter; Giotto now is all the rage, / dimming the luster of the other's fame." In art literature, the term *campo* emerges as a flexible verbal instrument, addressing all three areas of ground. For example, Cennini deploys the word to refer to the act of laying in the ground of a panel. "Bear in mind," he recommends, "that a panel needs to be laid in more times [più volte campeggiata] than a wall."

Campo could occasionally designate the area where figures stand and appear. Raffaello Borghini remarks in *Il riposo* (1584) that the painter "must avoid placing tall and standing figures in the front row, for they block those in the second row from view, and take up a large part of the campo." He continues, "The judicious painter will seek to make his figures in front either in a sitting or kneeling position, or some other low attitude, in order to leave space for other figures, houses or landscapes [casamenti e paesi]." *Campo*, however, more often referred to what we now call background, specifically the space between, behind, and even above the figures. So Giovanni Battista Armenini explained in his precepts on painting that in Perugino's rendition of a Crucifixion, "all kinds of things were created in the field of the sky [in campo celeste], with the finest blues, as this was of the greatest pleasure to people in those simple days."[45]

My intention is not to assert a one-to-one correspondence between each of the three semantic areas of ground and any of these terms. For every instance when *campo* refers to ground as material preparation, documents reveal that *gesso* is also operative. Some writers refer to the background not with *campo*, but with *piano*, as does Alberti in *On Painting* (1435): he understands space more through an interest in its underlying geometric principles, and hence favors the more Euclidian concepts of "plane" and "surface." Instead of insisting on a strict separation between these concepts, I want to lay emphasis on the very impulse to formulate words for grounds. This drive suggests that writers on art in the Renaissance were engaged in diagnosing the conditions of the painting medium—its fundamental

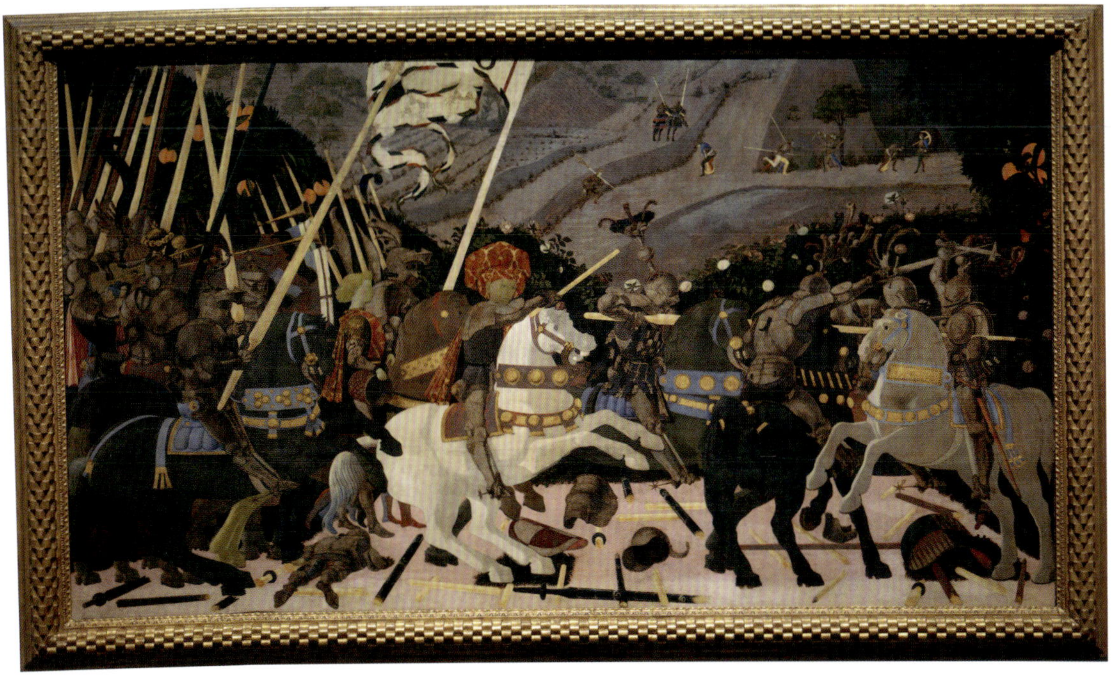

elements and potential for pictorial representation—through the ground, and the multiplicity of available terms suggests a chorus of voices. As the different painters developed their own solutions to the challenges of groundwork, the different art writers used their own words to identify the locus of these actions.

A germinal source is Vasari's *Lives*, not in the artist biographies but in the introduction to the *Three Arts of Design*, the often overlooked but fascinating appendix to the *Lives*, which treats the materials and technique of architecture, sculpture, and painting. Here Vasari defines painting as a medium in terms of ground: "Painting, then, is a plane covered by fields of colors, on a surface of panel or wall or canvas, around different outlines which, through the skill of good design of encompassing lines, surround the figure." The basic unit of painting is a "plane [piano] covered with *campi di colori*, on a surface of panel or wall or canvas." Not only does the definition describe the conventional process of painting—beginning with the outer edges and leaving figures in reserve; the statement articulates what painting is, in respect to the other arts, with spatial and material terms that implicate support, plane, and pictorial field—the multilayered and complex strata we now name "ground."[46]

This philological and compositional resonances of the term *campo* converge in Paulo Uccello's famed battle paintings (fig. 1.14). Here, according to Stumpel, the detritus of war has "been distributed in such a way as to form the inescapable pattern of a geometric piano." Burioni goes on to note how the lances function not only as instruments of war deployed

Fig. 1.14. Paulo Uccello, *Niccolò Mauruzi da Tolentino at the Battle of San Romano*, c. 1438–40. Egg tempera with walnut and linseed oil on poplar (182 × 320 cm). National Gallery, London. Bought, 1857 (NG583).

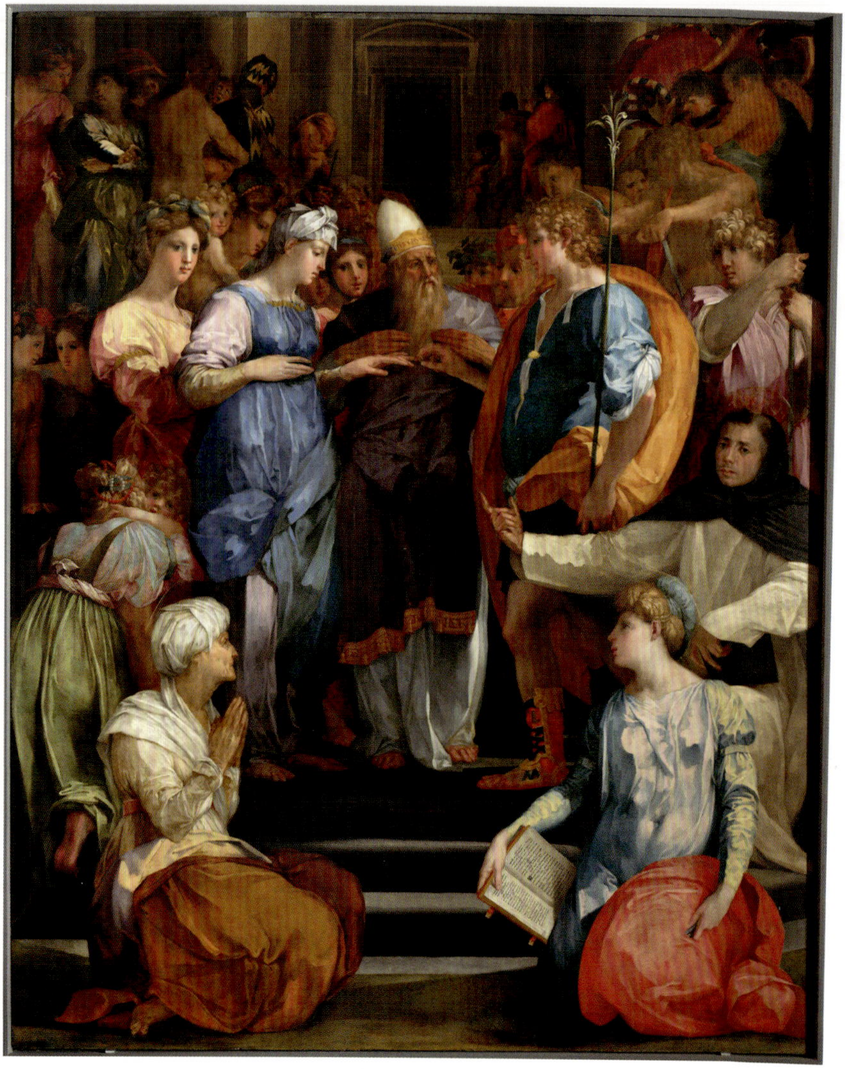

Fig. 1.15. Rosso Fiorentino. *Marriage of the Virgin*, 1523. Oil on panel (325 × 250 cm). San Lorenzo, Florence.

by the figures jostling for space but also as measuring sticks that extend foreground into background. By means of his skills in foreshortening and composition, Uccello creates a scene of disordered order. Battleground merges into another type of campo: the semicultivated fields and pathways in the distance, where the battle dwindles to one-to-one combat and another pair of figures retreats. Their relative isolation heightens the drama of war. In building up different levels of space in these battle scenes, Uccello makes fruitful use of the semantic potential of *campo* as evoking both a visual zone and a field of military engagement.[47]

Background—the part of the picture farthest from the principle object of contemplation—is not always seen by art writers of the period as significant. Vasari, for instance, states that Rosso Fiorentino produced such rich figural invention, as in his *Marriage of the Virgin* (1523), that he never needed

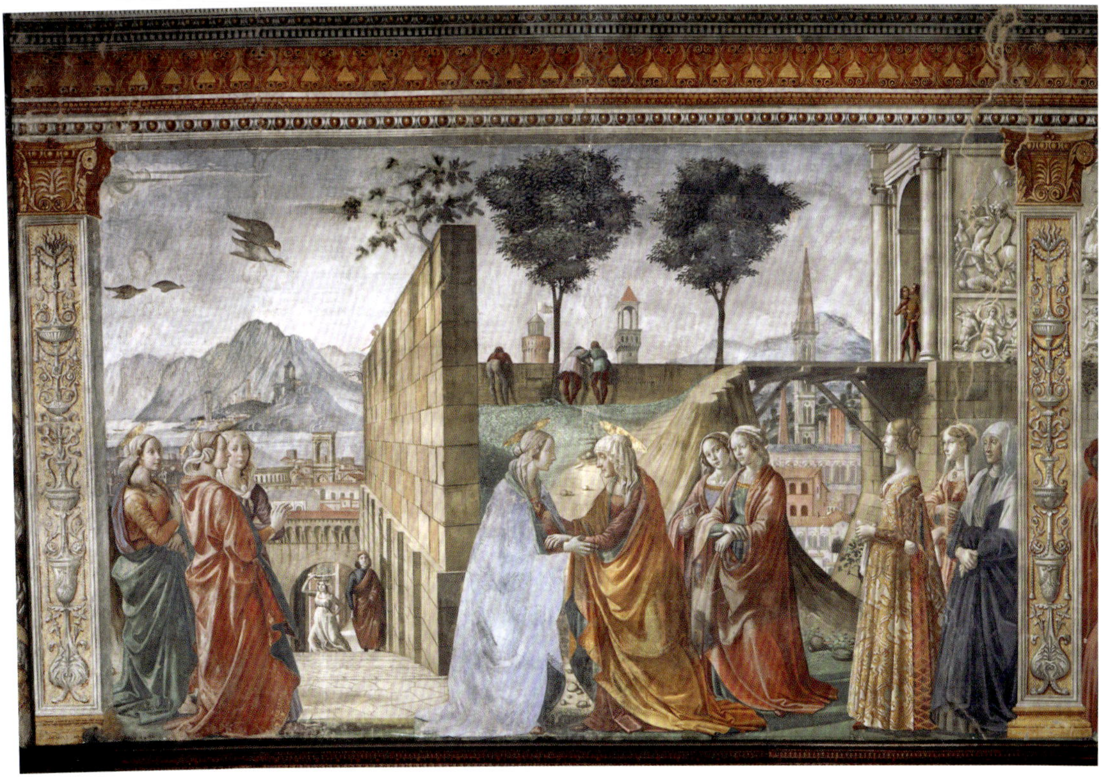

to create any background whatsoever ("niente di campo") (fig. 1.15). As other writers have frequently pointed out, Rosso devised a compositional scheme where figures crowd out the ground. Conversely, the painting might also be said to create a mutant ground from figure itself. Rosso creates a bodily structure that brings the architectural orders normally present in a background to life: the tall and elongated figures function as living, breathing columns that both organize and participate directly in the narrative scene. Yet Vasari's comments raise an important question: under what conditions can background stop functioning as a mere backdrop; that is to say, a subordinate compositional entity? When does background begin to accomplish groundwork by departing from norms to achieve a series of semantic and critical consequences?[48]

Complex thinker that he is, Vasari does acknowledge a number of possibilities. He praises an artist of no less a stature than Raphael for recognizing that "painting does not consist of representing nude figures alone." Rather, painting possesses what Vasari calls "a large field" (un largo campo). He provides a list of forty-seven pictorial elements as candidates for placement in that field, among them buildings, landscapes, draperies, costumes, and meteorological effects. Vasari cites period contracts that require artists to fill in the grounds behind figures with "landscapes and skies," "buildings, castles, cities, mountains, hills, plains, rocks, costumes, animals, birds, and beasts of

Fig. 1.16. Domenico Ghirlandaio, *The Visitation*, c. 1485–90. Fresco, pre-restoration. Tornabuoni Chapel, Santa Maria Novella, Florence.

every kind" (fig. 1.16). This prescription to "fill in" had its roots in the classical notion of *parergon*—literally "that which surrounds [para] the main work [ergon]". The humanist Paolo Giovio, for example, praised Dosso Dossi for his *parerga*, defined as "the pleasant diversions of painting," which comprised rocks, groves, rivers, and the "far distant prospects of land and sea." As both Ernst Gombrich and Thomas Puttfarken have pointed out, Giovio's statement contains the germs of classifying painting in terms of distinct subject matter, or genre—and in fact Giovio summarizes his characterization of *parerga* as "cuncta id genus spectatu oculis iucunda" (all that kind of thing that is pleasing to the eye). Vasari weaves together these two strands—one contractual, the other critical—not only to define the components of pictorial variety; for his deployment of the term *campo* also raises the question of *where* these elements ought to be placed, and how they should be distributed throughout the pictorial field. Background can pass into groundwork through conceiving itself as an aperture; there, the picture opens itself up to the representation of the world's variety, demonstrating in the process the artist's repertory of subject matter and skill.[49]

This automimesis, the disclosure of artistic selfhood that emerges through the very act of representation, need not always look out into the external world, toward the adjunct of landscape. The background can also be a place where the picture announces whence it has come, declaring the very material and mimetic conditions that make representation possible. One work that approaches its background in this manner is the *Madonna dell'Impannata* (1512–13), given to Raphael and his workshop (fig. 1.17). Vasari mentions that the banker Bindo Altoviti first commissioned it for his palazzo in Florence, though it now serves as the altarpiece for the chapel of Duke Cosimo I's new apartments—which, Vasari does not fail to add, were "built and decorated by me." Demonstrating a close up and firsthand knowledge of the work, his description characteristically praises the artist's rendering of the figures with respect to their affect, stance, and placement. Christ's smile brings joy to the spectator, while the Virgin's facial features—her eyes, forehead, nose, and lips—demonstrate modesty, grace, honor, and virtue. Christ's twisting posture animates his nude body, its calibrated placement linking the left and right sides of the figural grouping. Vasari's evaluation of the painting terminates with the following phrase, "and for background there is a casement, in which he devised a linen covered window [*inpannata*] that gives light to the room wherein are the figures."[50]

It is striking that Vasari singled out the background for description—the linen-covered window that centuries later gave the picture its title. The passage as a whole departs in significant ways from his definition of painting discussed above: there he states that painting is in essence a field of colors surrounding lines that in turn encompass the figure. His description of the *Madonna dell'Impannata* marks a provocative reversal: it ends, rather than begins, with the campo. While he darkens a majority of the ground to enhance figures projecting out of the picture plane in relief, Raphael

→

Fig. 1.17. Raphael, *Madonna of the Cloth Window Covering* (*Madonna dell'Impannata*), c. 1514. Oil on panel (160 × 126 cm). Galleria Palatina, Palazzo Pitti, Florence.

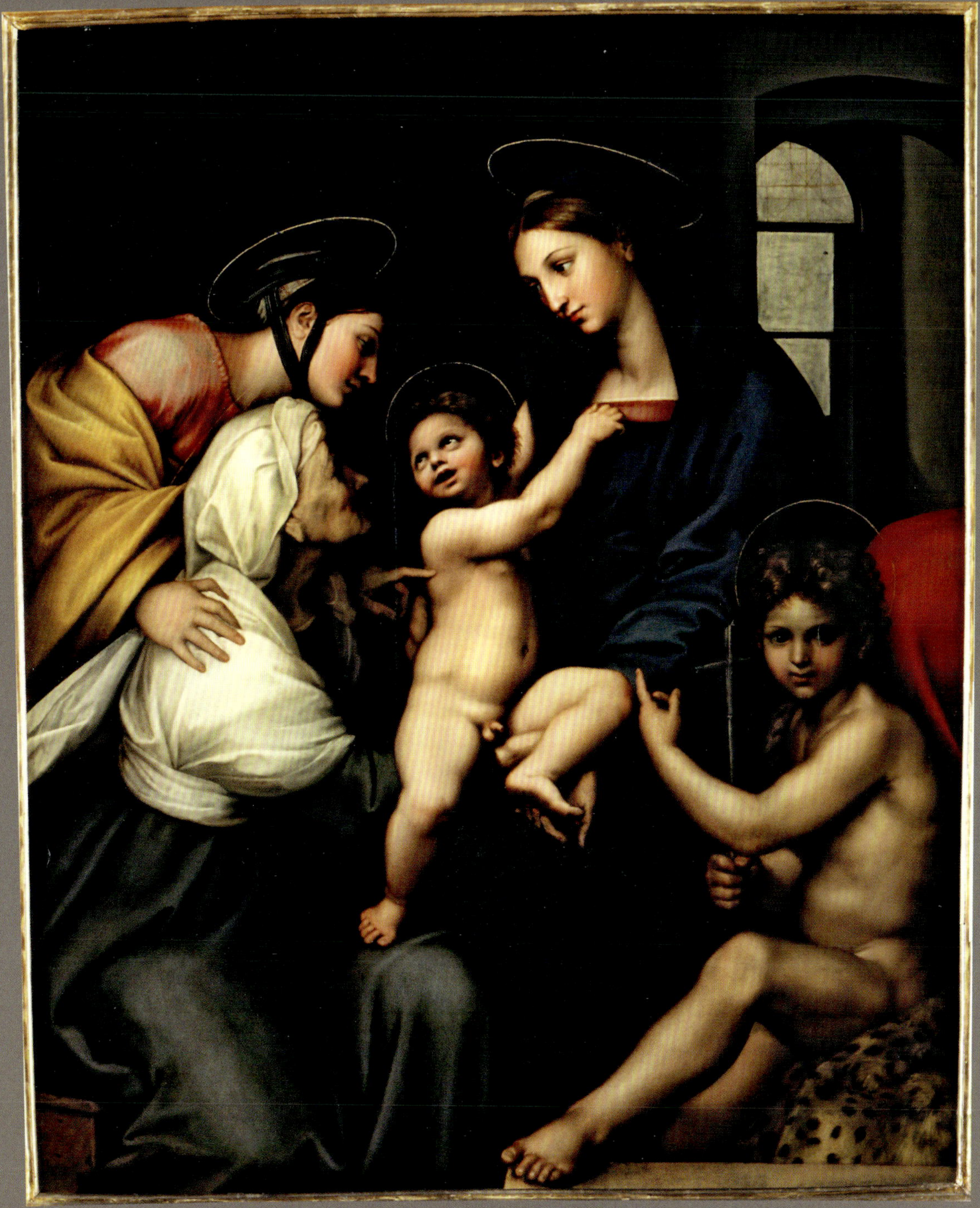

transforms the last third of the background to the right into a source of light, a window. Period dictionaries define "impannata" as a window furnishing "composed of several wooden frames over which paper or textile is stretched." The textile—usually linen—was steeped in turpentine to make its surface translucent. While impeding the entry of water and wind, *finestre impannate* introduced light into the domestic interior. Inventories of grand households, such as those of the Este, Tornabuoni, and Medici, mention the presence of these; they also appear in inventories of artists' homes such as that of Santi di Tito's residence drawn up shortly after his death. On a material level, the impannata was similar to the canvas on which a painter would lay down paint. These "window canvases" could be decorated with an insignia or device, as seen in the windows painted with religious emblems in Sodoma's rendering of a Benedictine cell (fig. 1.18).

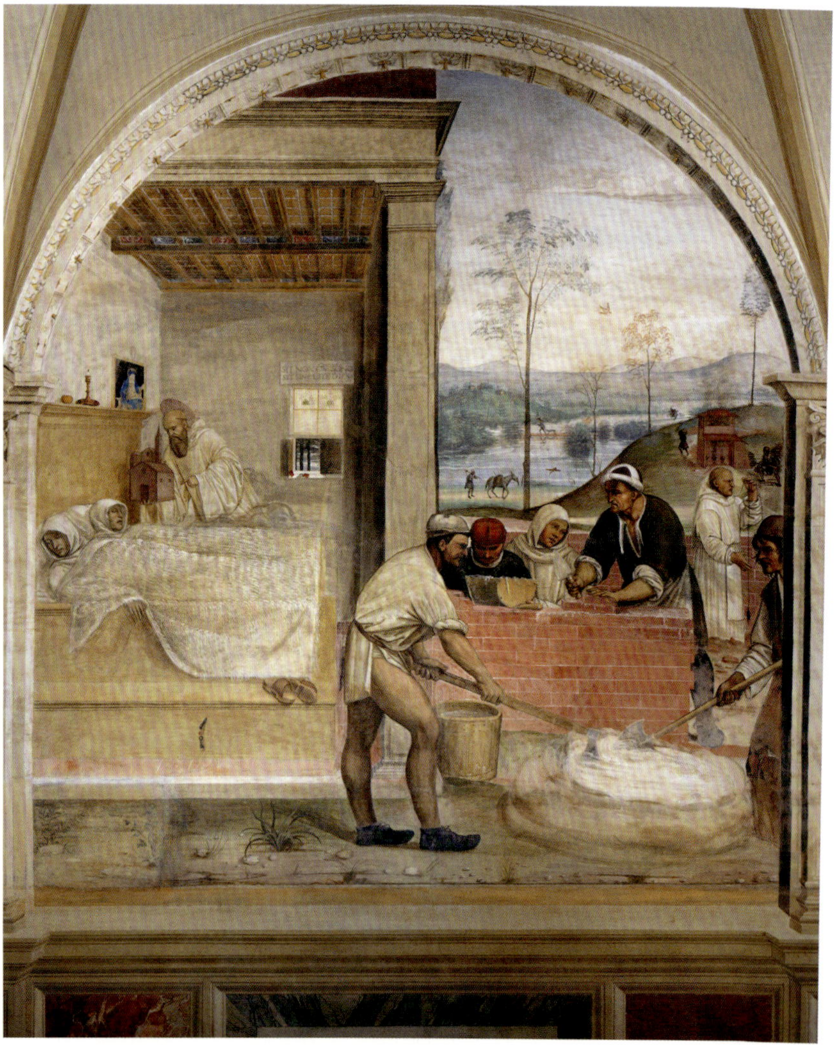

Fig. 1.18. Giovanni Antonio Bazzi, called Il Sodoma, *Saint Benedict Appears to Two Monks* (*The Life of Saint Benedict*, scene 32), 1505–8. Fresco. Abbey of Monte Oliveto Maggiore.

Raphael's background aims to describe domestic ambience. Assessing the deeper import of the campo is a matter of delicate judgment, especially given that the two extant preparatory drawings for the painting do not show the background. Technical analysis conducted during the two campaigns of cleaning, most recently in 2016, has pointed toward a highly sensitive handling of paint in this specific area of the picture, which attests to a degree of deliberation by Raphael and his workshop. Meanwhile, the bulk of scholarship has been devoted to identifying the role of hands in the painting.

Yet the background and its groundwork—the series of effects the ground creates in the picture, both compositionally and semantically—has elicited little commentary. Surprisingly, one of the longest and most insightful meditations on the painting and its spatial interior comes from the twentieth-century architectural theorist Robin Evans. In a now famous essay entitled "Figures, Doors and Corridors" (1978), Evans characterized fifteenth-century altarpieces portraying the Holy Family as elevated, figuratively, above the viewer and staring out into nothing, thus demonstrating a "holy and untouchable tranquility." In contrast to this hieratic sensibility, Raphael's figures have "descended from their pedestal to be engulfed by animated groups . . . not so much composed in space as joined together despite it. They look closely on one another, stare myopically into eyes and at flesh." These protagonists communicate with one another as much by touch as by sight. Evans then correlated what he called the figures' gregariousness with the snug interior space depicted in the painting and with Raphael's architecture, as in his plan for the Villa Madama with its accumulation of spaces and "matrix of interconnected rooms." The *Madonna dell'Impannata* displays a carnality that shines through "the various signaling of gestures."[51] Evans' argument is more evocative than historically grounded. A more likely reading, one oriented toward the painting's theological resonance, would understand the passage of light through the cloth and its monochromatic representation in terms of the Incarnation. The connection between radiance, textility, and tactility emphasizes the physical presence of Christ as redeemer in the physical world.[52]

In the following chapter, I will argue that Gentile da Fabriano contrasts the monochromatic effects of gold ground with the polychromatic figure in order to dramatize Christ's incarnation. In Raphael's painting, too, a gleaming monochromatic field seems to contain in a state of potentiality what then becomes actual in the figural group. In the description of these refined and glowing figures, brushwork is barely visible, as though they appear miraculously, not by human hand. By contrast, the window demonstrates a rough, virtuosic brushwork. In representing the coarse fibers of linen and the stitched-together pieces of cloth, Raphael and his workshop permit the priming of the panel, the visible layers of campi, to erupt. As opposed to the luxuriant cloth of honor hung on the left, the window's covering is patchwork, a field of stitched-together linen fragments, a campo composed of campi. The patchwork's patterning, squares traversed by diagonals,

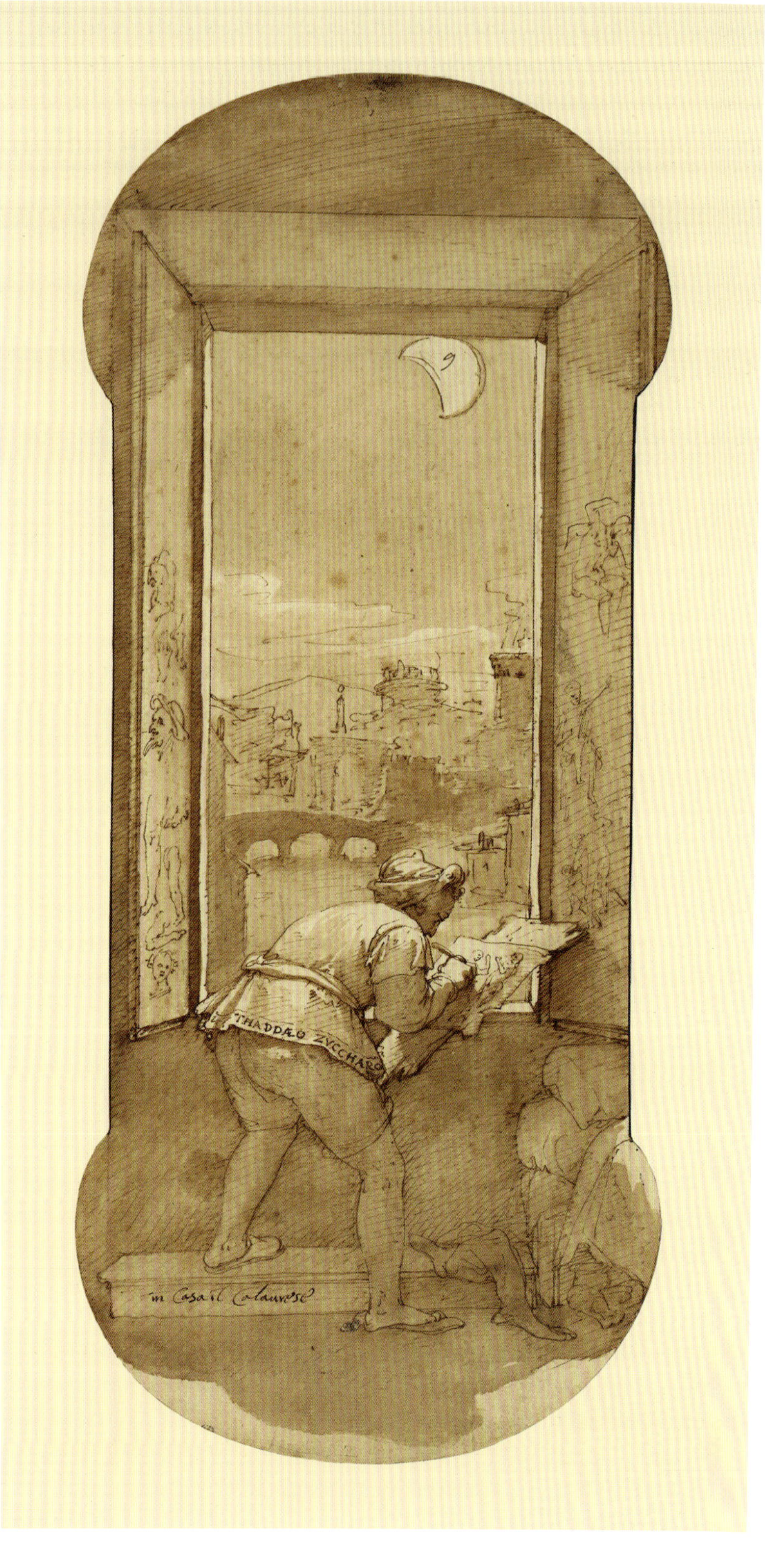

Fig. 1.19. Federico Zuccaro, *Taddeo Drawing by Moonlight in Calabrese's House*, c. 1595. Pen, brown ink, and brush with brown wash over black chalk on paper (42.1 × 17.7 cm). J. Paul Getty Museum, Los Angeles.

demonstrates the organizing principles of the intertwined figural composition.[53] In the "gregarious" figures, who are connected by shared glances and touching, this geometry becomes flesh: St. Anne's hand weaves itself under Christ's leg to support him; the Virgin's hand supports his foot; Elizabeth's horizontally pointing finger and John's upward pointing figure form a kind of warp-and-weft.

This background also invites reflection on the relation of craft to painting. In Federico Zuccaro's series narrating the life of his elder brother Taddeo, window coverings also become the site of artistic process. One scene shows Taddeo crouching, sketching away by moonlight (fig. 1.19). Covered with drawings of figures after the antique in various states of motion, the open window casements function as an improvisatory sketchbook where Taddeo replicates in miniature the monumental wall paintings he is studying in Rome, the frescoes of Polidoro da Caravaggio on palace facades or Michelangelo's *Last Judgment* in the Sistine Chapel. The foldable panels make up a modest triptych dedicated to the study of art, with diligent Taddeo as the protagonist who, as the inscription reads, "sends sleep away from his eyes, and sloth from himself." Similarly, the carefully stitched impannata in Raphael's painting introduces into the scene of the opulently clad Holy Family an element of simplicity and humility, qualities that Vasari stressed in his description of the Virgin's expression. Instead of making a distinction between craft and art, Raphael through this background shows the significance of the former in the miraculous transformation that is the latter.

GROUNDWORK AND THE POSSIBLE

In summary, the three areas of ground—material preparation, plane, and background—act as more than just auxiliary physical or spatial components in the Renaissance picture. They participate in what we have called "groundwork." This is ground's capacity to move from simply occupying an area of a given composition to producing a series of *effects*. Ground can govern how the picture comes into being as a physical object, how it manifests itself visually and configures meaning. Groundwork is thereby distinct from two operative categories in art history. The first of these is constraint. Scholarship that thinks from the aspect of constraint tends to understand the work of art as an unmediated precipitate of physical conditions and social norms, and therefore would understand ground as determined by its material and by contractual obligations. The second is freedom, or the idea that the artist's creation is self-willed. Groundwork introduces a middle way between these two poles, conceiving the campo as the terrain of the possible. If the ground harbors the mythical origins of the picture, it is also where thinking about painting—about the role of its practitioners and the site of its history—can begin.

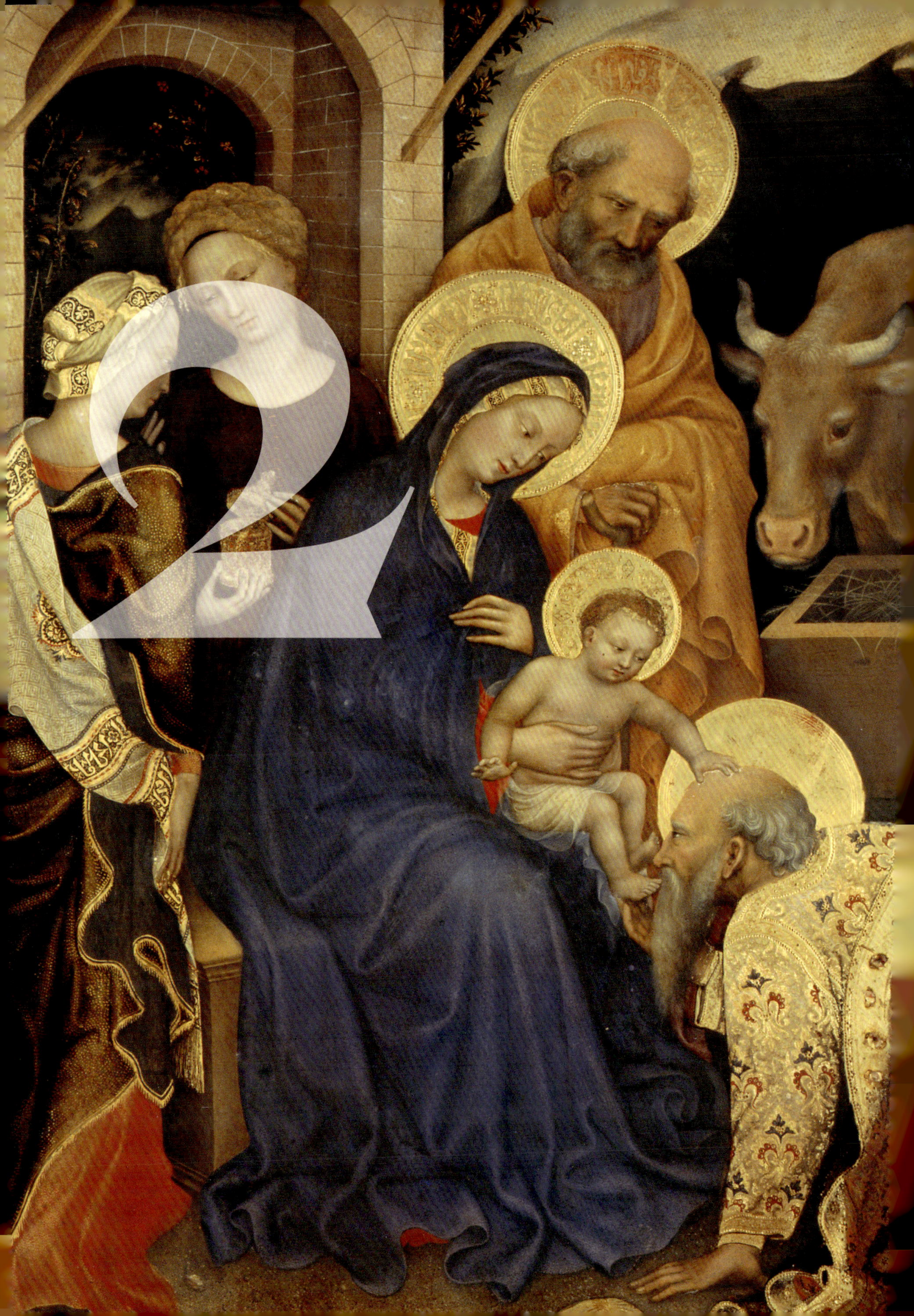
2

Possibility: Angels in the Ground

> Si vous aviez vécu autant que moi vous sauriez qu'il n'est qu'une seule chose matérielle dont la valeur soit assez certaine pour qu'un homme s'en occupe. Cette chose . . . c'est L'OR. L'or représente toutes les forces humaines. [. . .] Eh ! bien, l'or contient tout en germe, et donne tout en réalité.
>
> (If you had lived as much as I have, you would know that there is only one sole material thing whose value is sufficiently certain for a man to bother with it. This thing . . . is GOLD. Gold represents all human forces. [. . .] Gold contains the germ of everything, and, in reality, it gives everything.)
>
> **Honoré de Balzac, *Gobseck* (1830/42)**

The world opens itself up to the individual willing to seek it. So declares the Swiss historian Jacob Burckhardt in his foundational account *Die Kultur der Renaissance in Italien* (1860). Part IV of the book, entitled "The Discovery of the World and of Man," opens with a sentence that is long, ponderous, and triumphant in tone: "Freed from the countless bonds which elsewhere in Europe checked progress, having reached a high degree of individual development and been schooled by the teachings of antiquity, the Italian mind now turned to the discovery of the outward universe, and to the representation of it in speech and form."[1] In other writings, Burckhardt demonstrates how works of art exemplify the dichotomy between medieval imprisonment on the one hand and Renaissance freedom on the other. His extended essay "Das Altarbild" (The altarpiece), composed toward the end of his life and published posthumously in 1898, sets painting on gold ground—panels covered and decorated with gold leaf—against the Renaissance picture's openness and spatial unity. "The altarpiece," he states, "now completely released from gold ground, has been the birthplace of *true* air, and *true* clouds in painting; indeed, only here did landscape as well achieve such a beautiful

Detail, Figure 2.6

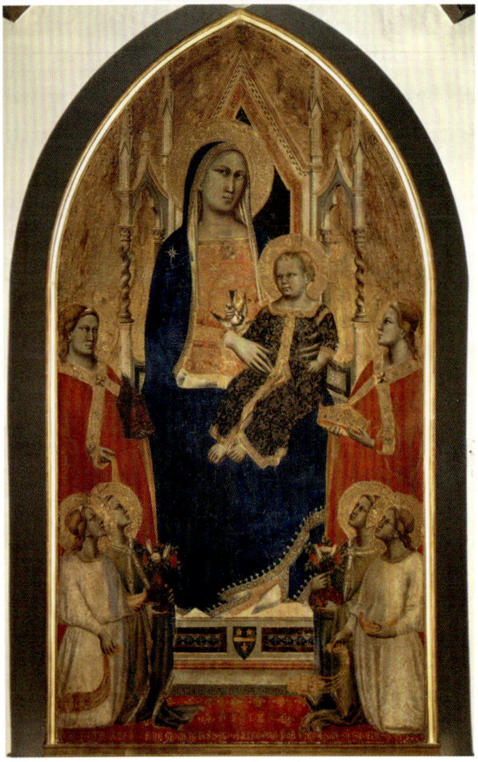

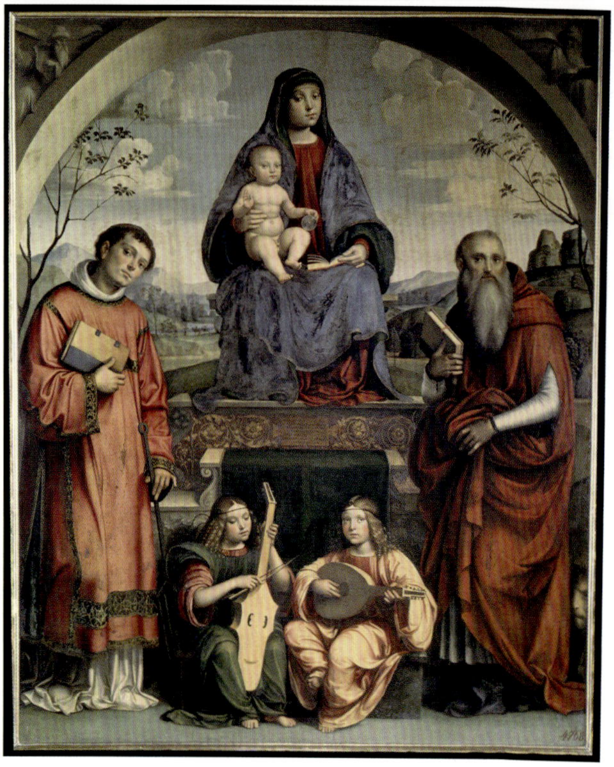

(LEFT)
Fig. 2.1. Taddeo Gaddi, *Madonna with Child and Angels*, c. 1330–35. Tempera and gold leaf on panel (91 × 48.5 cm). Gallerie degli Uffizi, Florence.

(RIGHT)
Fig. 2.2. Francesco Francia, *Madonna and Child Enthroned with Saints Lawrence and Jerome*, 1490. Oil and tempera on canvas (193 × 151 cm). State Hermitage Museum, St. Petersburg.

and festive existence."[2] In the landscapes of such artists as Francesco Francia, views of nature open up the altarpiece to the world. Burckhardt terms these depictions "festive" because, in his view, the flatness and closure of gold ground represent an ideological preoccupation with the other world at the expense of this one (figs. 2.1, 2.2).[3] This opposition between gold ground and nature, otherworldliness and worldliness, resonates in "Auf Goldgrund" (1860/82), a poem written by Burckhardt's admirer and compatriot Conrad Ferdinand Meyer. The first stanza recounts a journey from gallery to countryside: "I went late today to the museum, where the saints, the supplicants stand out against the gold grounds. Then I strode through the fields, towards the hot glow of the evening."[4]

Whether or not they agreed with Burckhardt that gold ground represented a limited preoccupation with the present world, cultural historians writing in the early decades of the twentieth century would reinforce the notion of gold ground as otherworldly, representing divine light and transcendent space.[5] Alois Riegl in *Die Spätrömische Kunstindustrie* (1901) described Byzantine gold mosaic as an "ideal spatial ground."[6] The Danish art historian Julius Lange claimed (*Ausgewählte Schriften*, 1912) that gold ground in certain instances presented "a picture of God's kingdom, the fire of heavenly love."[7] Writing in the wake of the October Revolution, the Russian Orthodox priest and polymath Pavel Aleksandrovič Florenskij described gold ground in Byzantine icons as intimating a vision of an invisible world through molten metal.[8] In his popular book of world history *The Decline of the West* (1918), Otto Spengler interpreted gold ground as "an express assertion of the existence and activity of the divine spirit. [. . .] For a thousand years this treatment of the background was held to be the only one metaphysically—and even ethically—possible and seemly in representations of the Christian legend."[9] Ensuing scholarship would reiterate this notion of gold ground as an "echo of Paradise," "timeless space," or a "field of divine immanence."[10]

The understanding of gold ground as "a sign for transcendence or pious narrow-mindedness," in Cornelius Claussen's words, corresponds more with Romantic notions of the Middle Ages than with the historical medieval period.[11] Ernst Gombrich already disputed the conventional understanding of gold ground in his review of Josef Bodonyi's *Entstehung und Bedeutung des Goldgrundes in der spätantiken Bildkomposition* (1932/33). Rather than understanding gold ground as a sign of divine space, Gombrich raised the possibility that these grounds were essentially "materials, metal, that is to say, in fact: Gold."[12] Gombrich suggested that, as opposed to the otherworldliness of gold proposed by scholars such as Bodonyi, one ought to emphasize the *Dinghaftigkeit* (thingness) of gold: its weight, prestige, and costliness.[13]

More recently, in an article unassumingly entitled "Marginalien zum Thema Goldgrund" (1983), Ellen Beer urged scholars to ask, not what gold necessarily *meant,* but what it *was*. In particular, Beer called for understanding gold as a material—a precious material to be sure—but a physical substance all the same. Gold's "material character," as Beer phrased it, lent itself to artistic handling as seen in the punch work, incisions, and relief-like effects that appear in manuscript illumination, metalwork, and painting.[14] Recent scholarship has indeed flipped the coin to explore gold's worldliness. Anne Dunlop proposes that gold ground painting has the capacity to present "a microcosm of God's created universe." When contained in the field of painting, gold and other precious materials, such as lapis lazuli, are "materials of an ambiguous and complicated status, neither fully animate nor inanimate, present and yet tied to a world elsewhere."[15] Gold ground, for instance, might allude to the early modern networks of trade and travel. We can consider the example of King Mansa Musa of Mali: part of the lore about this ruler surrounded his pilgrimage to Mecca in 1324–25, when his abundant distribution and expenditure of gold caused a significant deflation of its value.[16] In his description of Musa's travels, the historian al-ʿUmarī wrote that the Malian king "left his country with 100 loads of gold"—by some estimates, approximately seventeen tons.[17] The account of the West African king functions as an allegory of the source and sovereignty of gold as a faraway and valuable commodity. As a devout king, Musa practices charity to such an extent that gold is devalued: otherworldliness impinges upon worldliness.[18]

GOLD GROUND AS A SITE OF POSSIBILITY

When it comes to inhabit the picture, gold ground interweaves gold's range of associations: purity, rarity, and incorruptibility; monetary value; along with chromatic and reflective material properties. It is, as Victor Michael Schwarz has described, "a powerful lever which the painter can apply in a whole variety of ways in order to intensify and structure the perception of the picture."[19] We might extend this insight by proposing that gold ground pivots between worlds, material and immaterial, worldly and otherworldly. More specifically, the elasticity and dynamism of gold ground is a function of gold's material behavior, its malleability and ductility. These terms refer to gold's capacity to be hammered into thin sheets, stretched in multiple directions, and shaped and indented to create forms, both thick and thin, with gradations of brightness and darkness.

Malleability and ductility, I propose, constitute gold ground as a site of the possible—a term that I employ in its classical sense. In his *Metaphysics*, Aristotle explored two interrelated senses of the possible (*dynamis*). The first of these is associated with *potestas* (power or force). This refers primarily to the power of physical and moral force but can also describe the power of a word, a number that is squared, and military strength.[20] In Renaissance art literature, *potestas* and its vernacular equivalent, *potere*, describe the power of artist and creation. Gold ground becomes an arena where the artist demonstrates his power in handling and mastering materials. The second sense of the possible relates to *potentia* (in the vernacular *potenziale*), that is to say, the state of "not yet" being or happening. Aristotle described "the potential Hermes that the sculptor perceives in the wood" (*Metaphysics*, 6.1048a32–33). Notably, Aristotle designates artists such as the architect, the musician, and the sculptor as figures who can effect a passage from potentiality to actuality (*energeia*). Potentiality, in his definition, is the possibility for the occupation to remain unfulfilled. Hence, an interpreter of Aristotle claims, the architect is powerful in that he is also capable of *not* building: "potentiality is the suspension of the act."[21] I would like to extend this designation in using the term "mimetic potential" to describe the capacity of gold ground to achieve a middle way between always latent potentiality and full actuality. Gold ground anticipates and achieves tenuous representation on the painting's material surface.

Two well-known sources elaborate gold ground as a site of the possible with respect to both power and potential. The first is the so-called *Libro dell'arte*, composed toward the end of the fourteenth century by the artist and writer on art Cennino Cennini. The second is a gold ground panel, *Madonna and Child with Angels* (c. 1405), by Gentile da Fabriano, whose engagement with gold ground is often read in connection with Cennino's text. In both of these sources, gold ground becomes a terrain where the artist can explore the conditions of the possible, can dramatize not what painting is, or should be, but rather what it can be and become. Whereas one-point perspective posits a measurable and contiguous spatial relationship with the viewer, gold ground introduces a space and a viewing experience that is much more indeterminate. At the same time, it presents viewers with perceptual and semantic possibilities to grapple with, and ultimately make sense of, the represented world before their eyes.

In forming generalizations from gold ground to the groundwork of painting writ large, the ground becomes the place where actions might possibly have taken place or could still possibly take place, while the human body is the supposed vehicle of action. Groundwork recalls and anticipates, reflects and suggests. Groundwork lays down conditions of possibility that interweave art making and sense making. As the open field of painting, ground is the place in the picture where things can happen. To pay attention to groundwork is to bring into view possibilities that have remained latent and invisible. The beholder, in a state of captivation, looks, scrutinizes, and imagines conceivable outcomes, both anterior and posterior.

GOLD GROUND AND ARTISTIC POWER

While Cennino's *Libro* is often described as a mere "recipe book," art historical scholarship has also acknowledged the intellectual ambitions behind this germinal text. Cennino may even have envisioned the work as an art literary showcase, designed to win the attention of *literati* and courtiers at the da Carrara court in Padua, where the artist is documented to have been in 1398 and 1401.[22] Wolf-Dietrich Löhr sees the *Libro* and other Trecento art literary evidence as part of the "growing attention for the painter's practice, his mastery and transformation of raw materials which serve as material and means." In this view, Cennino represents a movement toward understanding artistic power (*potere*) as the agency that enables the artist's hand to manipulate and effect what Löhr calls the "metamorphosis of materials."[23]

In the *Libro*, phrases such as "how you can," "it can be," or "as you will" recur, also with respect to the making of gold ground. Here are a number of examples:

> How you can gild with green earth on panel.
> You can also do it as they used to in the olden days.
> Pat the gold as lightly as you possibly can.
> Watch [. . .] so that you always go about saving as much gold as you can.
> In the winter, you can gild as much as you want.[24]

Recipe books generally say, "Do this," not "You can do this." The *Libro* therefore differs from a straightforward instruction manual by connecting artistic power with the ability to judge and decide how to act in many different possible situations. Through his use of the modal verb *potere* (to be able), Cennino's voice urges the artist to exercise his judgment, ability—in other words, his power over gold in the process of creating an auriferous field.

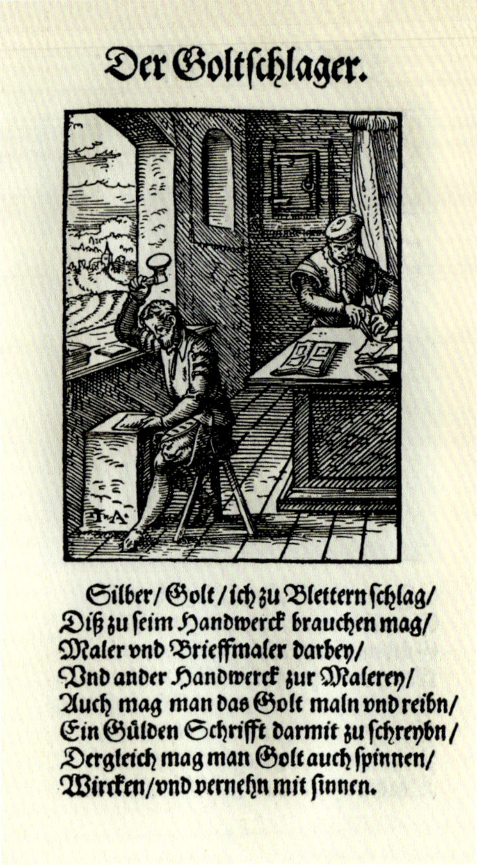
Der Goltſchlager.

Silber/Golt/ich zu Blettern ſchlag/
Diß zu ſeim Handwerck brauchen mag/
Maler vnd Brieffmaler darbey/
Vnd ander Handwerck zur Malerey/
Auch mag man das Golt maln vnd reibn/
Ein Gülden Schrifft darmit zu ſchreybn/
Dergleich mag man Golt auch ſpinnen/
Wircken/vnd vernehn mit ſinnen.

Fig. 2.3. Jost Amman, "Der Goltschlager" (The goldbeater). Woodcut. From *Das Ständebuch*, 1568.

The prerequisite to handling gold leaf was its discerning procurement. "When you want to know about gold," Cennino advises, "have a look when you buy it." He further specifies, "Take it from a good goldbeater and have a look at the gold."[25] Goldbeaters were specialized artisans with independent workshops, who also provided gold and silver leaf for a variety of purposes. *Battiloro* in Florence, for instance, were incorporated into the Arte di Por Santa Maria, the city's silk weaving guild. Gold and silver thread, formed by attaching metallic strips to an adhesive substrate and wrapping them around a core yarn, was integral for the production of luxurious silk fabrics such as brocade and raised velvets.[26] In Venice, the complete guild register, or *mariégola*, of goldbeaters is unfortunately not extant, but transcriptions of some of its contents found in other documents indicate that *battiloro* or *batiorii* worked with *tiraoro* (literally "gold pullers") to provide gold leaf to textile weavers, miniature illuminators, book binders, and leatherworkers.[27] Aside from their professional ties with painters, some goldbeaters were related to artists by family: Sandro Botticelli, who himself trained as a goldsmith, had an older brother Antonio who for some years owned his own *battiloro* shop.[28]

As Cennino suggests, goldbeaters possessed varying degrees of skill. A woodcut from Jost Amman's *Book of Trades* (1568), albeit a sixteenth-century source from north of the Alps, offers a representation of a goldbeater's workshop (fig. 2.3)[29]. Gold was often supplied in the form of minted coins, such as the Venetian ducat or the Florentine florin, which were melted and flattened by rollers, to emerge as long strips ready to be cut into squares. The goldbeater then inserted these sections between parchment leaves and beat them repeatedly and forcefully until the gold achieved microscopic thinness.[30]

The verses beneath the woodcut describe how the "Goltschlager" beats silver and gold for the handwork of illuminators and painters and also spins gold into twisted strands for textiles.[31] Cennino himself addresses how the malleability of gold enables transformation from coin to artistic material. A Venetian ducat, he observes, can yield up to one hundred forty-five leaves of gold, although more than one hundred leaves should not be derived from a single coin, for the sake of quality.[32] Gold leaves were sold wholesale in bundles of one hundred, and extant contracts demonstrate that in certain cases painters purchased thousands of gold leaves to fulfill their commissions. The gilt framing components (now lost) for Leonardo's *Virgin of the Rocks* altarpiece, to mention a particularly notable example, would have required approximately twenty thousand gold leaves.[33]

If gold ground testifies to an artist's capacity to leverage his professional contacts outside the studio, it also demonstrates how artists managed gold's material behavior. Laying down gold leaf swiftly on the moistened bole demanded expert timing and keen awareness of the studio's thermal conditions. Cennino recommends that the artist gild in the winter, when the weather is mild and damp, because humidity prevents the moistened bole from drying too quickly. Care should also be taken that drafts do not blow the gold leaves away. The stone used to burnish the gold ground should be held to the artist's chest in order to warm it and remove dampness. Burnishing, too, should occur in the winter; in the summer, he says, the artist should move quickly and "gild one hour, burnish the next." "What if," Cennino asks, "[the weather] is too cool and something comes up that means gold ground needs to be burnished?" The panel should be kept "in a place which experiences some warm currents." And if the weather is too dry? "Keep it in a damp place." Laying gold ground, like fresco painting, is a seasonal endeavor, subject to climatic conditions to which the artist must be sensitive.[34] Artists' "pictorial intelligence," their knowledge of how pictures are made, look, and work, also entails some degree of environmental adaptation.[35]

The malleability of gold, its capacity to be hammered, pressed, and shaped, invites the artist's *potere* by opening up possibilities of mark making. To mutate a term from Alfred Gell, gold ground is "sticky": it attracts techniques, patterns, and effects from the adjacent arts of metalworking and textiles, notably in basins and silks from North Africa and the Levant.[36] Medieval Islamic vessels, such as the basin made for Sultan al-Nasir Muhammad ibn Qalawun (d. 1341), produced in either Cairo or Damascus between 1330 and 1340, were made of base metal and inlaid with silver and sometimes gold; their gleaming and glittering surfaces seem to have been fashioned to convey the overall impression of gold (fig. 2.4).[37]

Cennino's language itself invokes intramedial exchange: to instruct in the working of gold ground, he deploys a battery of verbs that might refer to both painting and metalwork. The artist must "gild, burnish, scratch, stipple, and pick out details." To render figures in gold grounds, the painter ought to "get a needle attached to a stick and start scratching." To mark out haloes, one begins by "picking out the figures against the ground, following the little marks that you will see, which you incised with the needle." As in metalwork, fashioning gold ground entails marking out, cutting, polishing, and engaging with the material at close range.[38]

Cennino draws particular attention to what he calls "granare a rilievo," granulation or stippling, which he describes as "one of the loveliest branches" of painting.[39] Granulation involves pricking the soft gold ground with a needle-like instrument to form clusters of minuscule punch marks; the point clusters catch and scatter light, or as Cennino puts it, "sparkle like millet grains." By contrast, the surrounding burnished gold ground is perceived as dark. Gold paradoxically becomes shadow. Cennino himself pursued this technique, as seen in the painting of a *Beatified Bishop*, now in

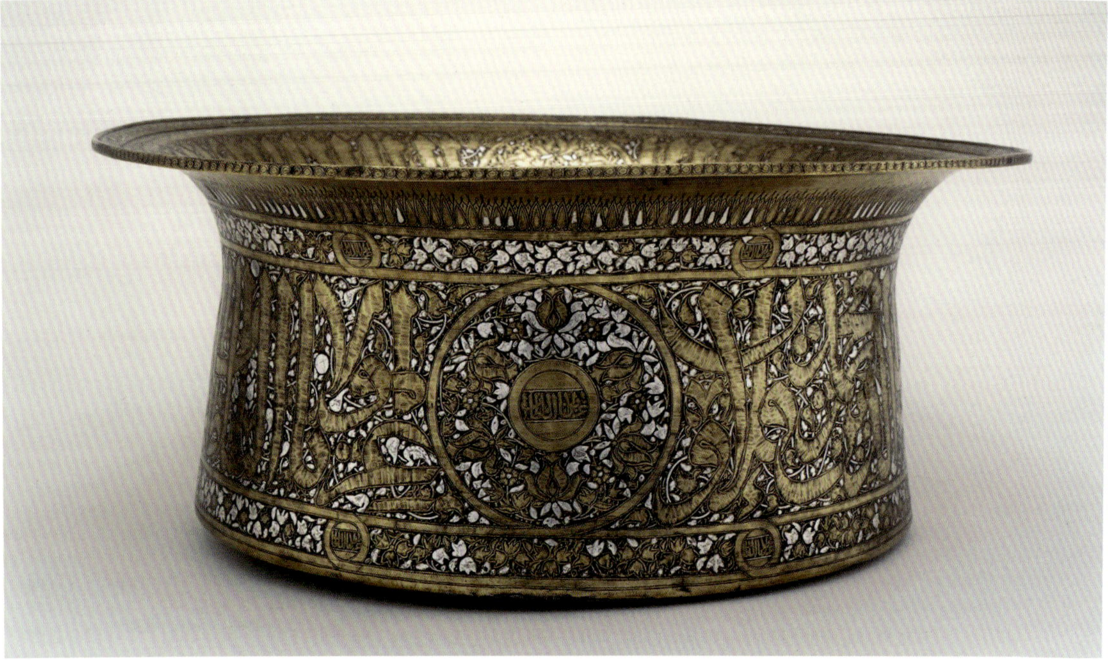

Fig. 2.4. Basin decorated with the name, titles, and blazon of the Mamluk sultan al-Nasir Muhammad, c. 1320–41. Raised brass with gold, silver, and black inlays (diameter 54 cm). British Museum, London.

Berlin (fig. 2.5).[40] In the bishop's crook, point clusters articulate the lion's limbs, fur, and mane. Stippling in relief not only brings gold ground into the third dimension; it allows this supposedly monotonous gleaming surface to generate subtle pictorial effects through interplay between light and shadow.

Cennino points to the chromatic range in gold ground when discussing the art of burnishing: "When will you see that the ground is completely burnished? When the gold comes out almost dark, it is so shiny."[41] I will return below to the interpretive issues at play in granulation, but for now, the following point merits emphasis: to consider how gold ground pivots between the "unworldly" or "worldly," we must first account for its basic conditions and what sorts of artistic intervention it enables—in other words, how it functions as the ground of the possible. With respect to artistic *potere*, or power, the artist's realm of possibility depends, among other things, upon professional contacts, climatic conditions, and malleability. Invention is not restricted to the painted parts of the panel. In gold ground, Cennino declares, the artist works "con sentimento di fantasia, e di mano leggiera" (with a sense of imagination, and a light hand).[42]

GOLD GROUND AND MIMETIC POTENTIAL

Gold ground is also a site of the possible in relation to *potentia*, or mimetic potential. Gold ground intimates visual form, generates analogies across media, and dynamically opens up possible worlds, both microscopically and macroscopically, for the acute viewer. Material malleability generates semantic

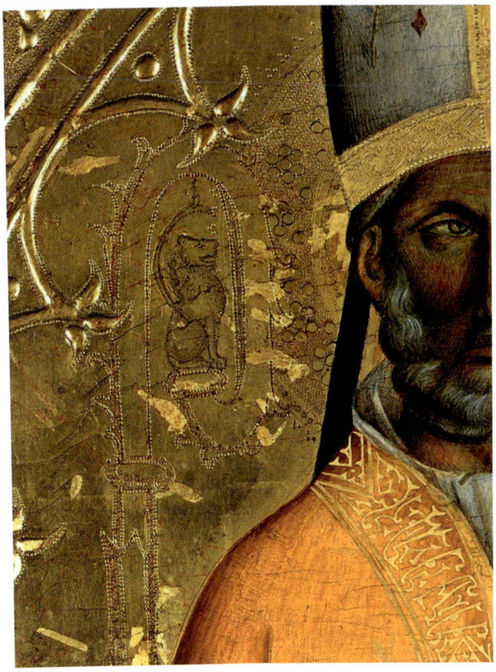

malleability. As becomes evident in the next chapter, as painting moves toward representational ground later in the fifteenth century, the capacity of ground to invoke other media, shift states, evoke action beyond the represented event will continue as a fundamental property.

The work of Gentile da Fabriano (c. 1370–1427) provides a model for thinking about the mimetic potential of gold ground. In the most abridged description, Gentile is conventionally heralded as a key art historical protagonist who marks the transition from the ornamental and crafted qualities of the "International Gothic" to the newfound naturalism of the Renaissance. A prime example is his famed *Adoration of the Magi* (1423), executed for the Strozzi family chapel in the church of Santa Trinita, Florence (fig. 2.6).[43] Hovering above the figures, many of whom are adorned with sumptuous fabrics and crowned with haloes, is the Star of Bethlehem. To convey the luminosity of this heavenly sign, through a series of diminutive brushstrokes, Gentile describes light touching the tips of leaves, the barren hills, and the dark interior of Christ's manger. Notably, this naturalism is not wholly illusionistic, executed through paint alone. It is fundamentally metallic, though the effect extends beyond the materiality of metal.

Gentile's strategy moves between using gold's reflective properties to produce light and depicting light through a graduated application of bright paint. The Star is composed of a gold ground base upon which layers of tempera are applied, and lines are then scratched to convey the impression of shooting rays. Gentile scratched away the upper paint layer of the Magi's elaborate costumes to describe lustrous damask silk fabrics by means of the

Fig. 2.5. Detail from Cennino Cennini, *Beatified Bishop*, c. 1400. Gold leaf and tempera on panel (overall 121 × 105.5 cm; image surface 99.8 × 44.6 cm). Gemäldegalerie der Staatliche Museen zu Berlin.

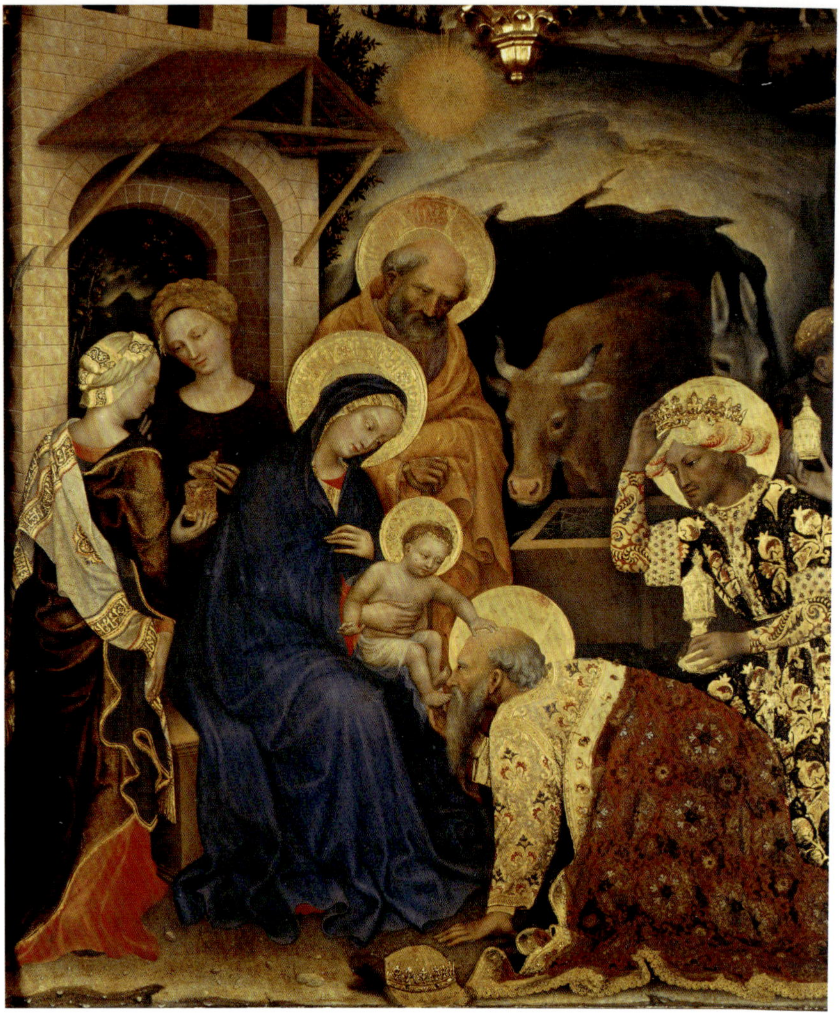

Fig. 2.6. Detail from Gentile da Fabriano, *Adoration of the Magi*, 1423. Gold leaf and tempera on panel (300 × 282 cm). Gallerie degli Uffizi, Florence.

underlying gold leaf. The artist also applied gold leaf beneath the paint that describes the triangular awning above the Holy Family to suggest light falling over the manger.[44] In an earlier *Nativity* (c. 1420–22) (fig. 2.7), Gentile uses the same method to characterize how celestial illumination irradiates the pasture where the shepherds watch over their flock—"An angel of the Lord appeared to them and bathed them in light" (Luke 2:9). The gold ground in the upper register reads as the source of light that falls on the gleaming hills and fields in the landscape.[45] Metallic leaf is thus wielded by the artist to enable the mimetic description of light. In these paintings, gold ground as a site of mimetic potential is a field where making and representing, material and illusion, flatness and depth, light and shade emerge, coincide, and collaborate.

In both of these Nativity scenes, the gold ground that would conventionally occupy the upper half or most of a panel's surface area now

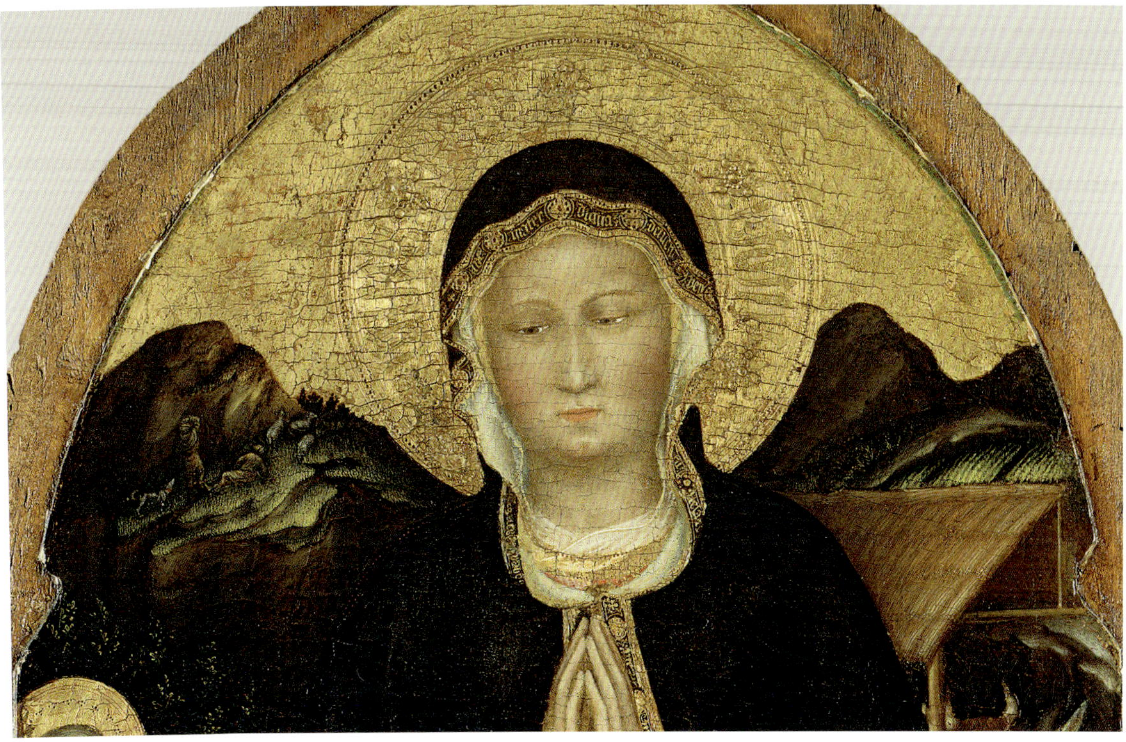

retreats to the highest part of the picture. Instead of being used for the sake of its own luminosity, gold is placed in service to the representation of luminous bodies. Gentile's work thus offers an opportunity to take stock of gold ground's shifting functions in the medieval and early modern periods. Whether it intimates divine space or refers to the preciousness of metal and its reflective properties, gold in the medieval icon often works "pre-mimetically": the gold leaf that covers the panel's surface, with notable exceptions, does not primarily depict illusionistic effects. Gold behaves like gold. In Gentile's paintings, however, this indexical use of the material (whereby gold signifies goldenness) is adapted to the service of mimesis: gold leaf is covered with paint, which is then scratched to allow the metal surface to shine through and render a portrayal of heavenly bodies. Gold ground's material properties (such as its tendency to form a thin layer) takes on a "stratigraphic potentiality," in that it lends itself to be covered with other layers which can then be scratched off.

METALLIC PAINTING

In one of Gentile's earliest extant works, his *Madonna and Child with Angels* (c. 1405), gold ground empowers the semantic charge that runs throughout the picture (fig. 2.8).[46] Almost half of the panel's surface area is covered with gold leaf, which thus undoubtedly enhances its visibility from far away, possibly

Fig. 2.7. Detail from Gentile da Fabriano, *Nativity*, c. 1420–22. Gold leaf and tempera on panel (72.1 × 42.6 cm). J. Paul Getty Museum, Los Angeles.

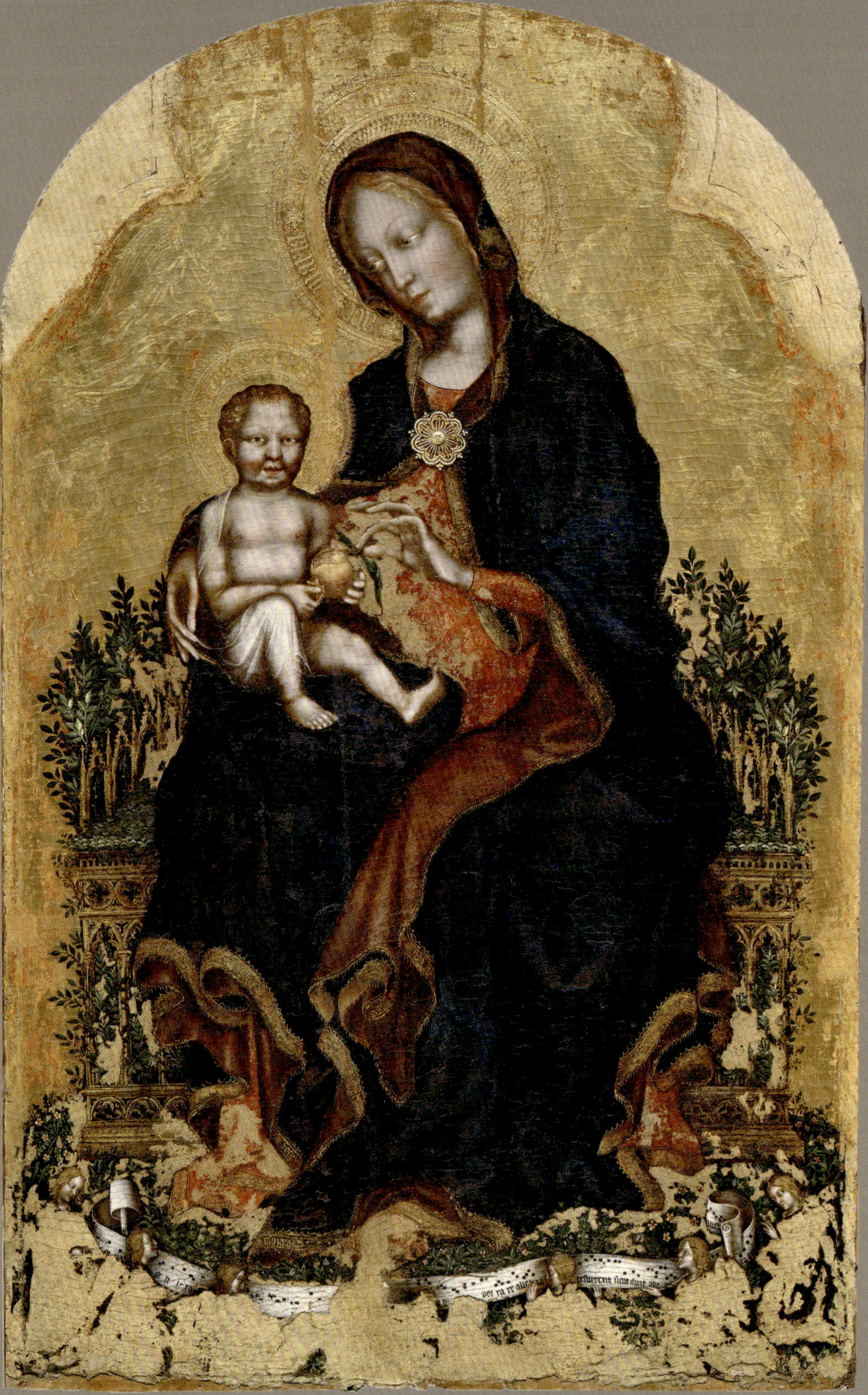

in a dark and cavernous space. At the same time, details in the gold ground reward a different kind of viewing at close range. In this work, Gentile begins with a more "pre-mimetic" and iconic use of gold (which he then experiments with by scratching into it for the sake of mimesis) and then develops a more mimetic use of gold by exploiting its ability to depict a volume through light and shade.

Frustratingly, knowledge about the work's execution, patronage, and original display—which would enable a fine-grained reading of its contemporary reception—remains elusive. Scholarship on the panel, however, has established, if not the facts, then the probable conditions behind its making and exhibition. Based on its style, the panel was most likely painted during Gentile's sojourn in Venice, or else in Lombardy. Its intended destination was further afield, in the Basilica of San Domenico in Perugia, a city where the artist had long-standing family ties. The patron, though still unidentified, could have been a member of one of Perugia's prominent families, perhaps the Graziani, who resided in the Porta San Pietro district close to San Domenico and regularly left legacies, commissioned works of art, and endowed chapels for the basilica. Bartolommeo degli Acerbi, the prior of San Domenico from 1386, and a patron for other works of art for the basilica, has also been proposed as a possible client. The panel's original location in San Domenico remains unknown, though it has been suggested that it was installed in the chapel of San Giacomo, in an area that is now the basilica's sacristy. Hence, it was originally located in a publicly accessible chapel, which also would have permitted close-up viewing. Documented as being located in the basilica's novitiate in 1861, the panel remained in San Domenico until 1863, at which point it entered the collection of the Galleria Nazionale dell'Umbria in Perugia, where it is currently exhibited.

The meticulous detail accorded to virtually every element in the picture would have called for scrupulous visual attention. This remains the case in spite of its slightly damaged condition. Losses are apparent in Christ, the Virgin's robe, and most visibly in the lower zone in the figures of angels. The elongated and curved panel was cut on top, and unpainted portions in these upper areas indicate that it was originally set in a trefoil framework as the central panel of a triptych. Despite the losses, we can discern the figural components that interweave iconographic themes of glorification, humility, and resurrection. The Virgin as Queen of Heaven sits enthroned and embraces Christ, holding a pomegranate as a proleptic sign of the Passion and eventual Resurrection. Alluding to the Virgin's humility and purity, rose bushes with unopened buds surround and weave in and out of gilt open tracery, ogee arches, and other microarchitectural features. This throne stands in a *hortus conclusus*, or enclosed garden, an iconographic amalgamation of the Madonna Enthroned with the Madonna of Humility. In the panel's lower zones, seven angels hold a banderole that displays verse from the *Regina coeli*, a "call and response" sung during the Easter Vigil mass. Other inscriptions on the Virgin's halo and the hem of her mantle reinforce the themes of

←

Fig. 2.8. Gentile da Fabriano, *Madonna and Child with Angels*, c. 1405. Gold leaf and tempera on panel (115 × 64 cm). Galleria Nazionale dell'Umbria, Perugia.

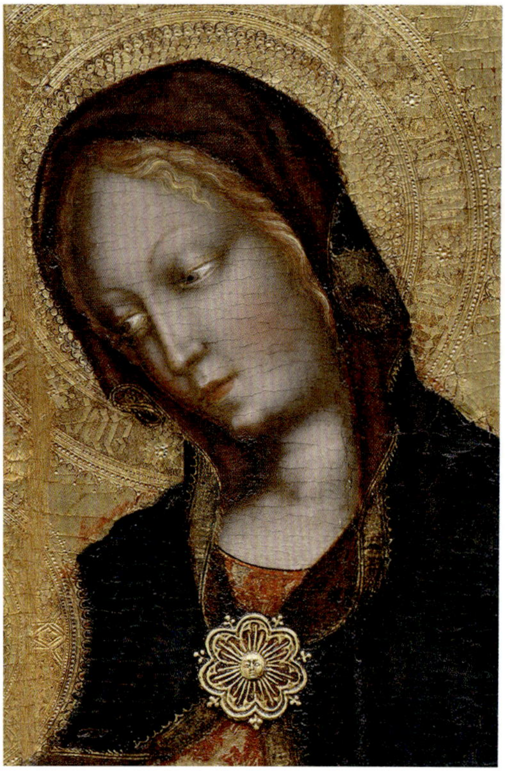

Marian exaltation and resurrection. These last two elements in particular—the halo and the hem—demonstrate Gentile's familiarity with Venetian and northern European metalwork and his power to translate its effects on panel. Andrea De Marchi, in fact, has employed the lexical compound *orafo-pittore*, or "goldsmith-painter," to describe Gentile's ambition to paint with metal.[47]

In the Perugia panel, instances of this "metallic painting" abound. The Virgin's blue mantle, now faded, is painted on a sheet of silver leaf; passages throughout this area were delicately scraped away to create floral patterns and script. This silvery ornamentation would complement the strangely gray hue of the Virgin's flesh, while contrasting with the gilt elements in the rest of the picture. The Virgin's stucco clasp, which is gilt, figures the sun and its rays, and thereby evokes the verse "a woman clothed with the sun" (Revelation 12:1), which is often applied to the Virgin.

Gentile used various techniques, including mordant gilding, to suggest light glinting off the leaves of the rose bushes, the throne's microarchitectural ornament, the Virgin's blond tresses, and the scale pattern covering her red robe (fig. 2.9).[48] Here he applied fine lines of mordant, an adhesive substance, to create patterns across specific areas on the painted surface. Small pieces of gold leaf were then placed over these passages and would adhere, while the excess gold was brushed away. Of mordant gilding, Cennino states that the gold used "should be the most beaten out and the most delicate

Fig. 2.9. Detail from Gentile da Fabriano, *Madonna and Child with Angels*, c. 1405. Gold leaf and tempera on panel (115 × 64 cm). Galleria Nazionale dell'Umbria, Perugia.

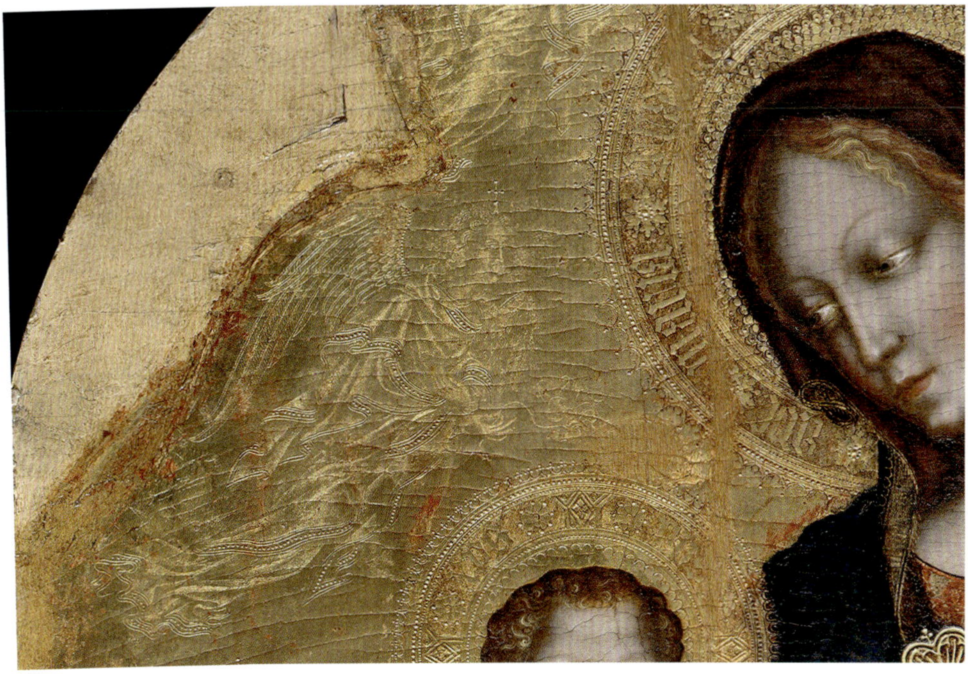

[. . .] that you can find." When this technique is expertly done, "your handiwork will come out like fine hairs, which is the most beautiful work."[49] Mordant gilding hence simulates gold's ductility, its capacity to be stretched into the thinnest of threads. This visual analogy also refers to the artist's use of his materials. For Gentile paints *with* metal. The artist in his potency manipulates the inert substance of gold to produce figural naturalism, as in the case of the Virgin's hair.

OPUS PUNCTORIUM

The most remarkable example of Gentile's deployment of metallic painting occurs in the gold ground itself (fig. 2.10). Here, the artist harnesses the mimetic potential of gold ground, its capacity to dramatize the process by which representation comes into view. The viewer discerns, though with some difficulty, diaphanous angelic forms inhabiting the area surrounding the Virgin and Christ. Only apparent when photographed in raking light or seen in person, the two uppermost angels hold a crown above the Virgin enthroned. The four below hold lilies, whose connotations of purity complement the unopened rose buds in the garden.

To render these diaphanous forms, Gentile incised slender lines in the gold ground to articulate the angels' figural contours. A circular punch was used to ornament the hem of their robes with a series of dots. Between and spilling out of these schematic outlines, clusters of points, created by the *granare* technique, read as faces, hair, wings, and drapery. These pin-sized

Fig. 2.10. Detail from Gentile da Fabriano, *Madonna and Child with Angels*, c. 1405. Gold leaf and tempera on panel (115 × 64 cm). Galleria Nazionale dell'Umbria, Perugia.

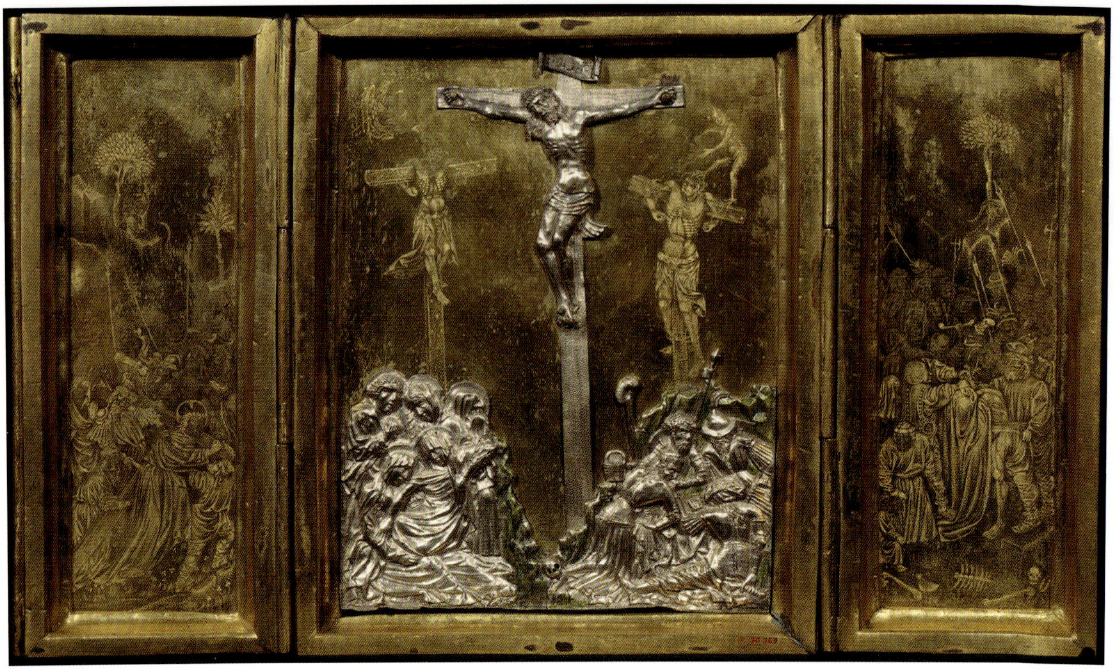

Fig. 2.11. Unknown Netherlandish or French, *Triptych with the Way to Calvary, the Crucifixion, and the Disrobing of Jesus*, c. 1420. Gilded copper, silver, and paint on panel open 24.8 × 41.9 × 1.9 cm; closed 24.8 × 21.2 × 3.9 cm). Metropolitan Museum of Art, New York. Gift of J. Pierpont Morgan, 1917 (17.190.369).

concave depressions catch and scatter light, while the surrounding gold ground, burnished smooth, paradoxically provides shading by contrast. When employed in service to description of the figure, stippling loosens the distinction between figure and ground by nestling the figure within the ground itself. The constellation of points describes volume while the untouched surrounding forms a defining contour.

As a site of potential, pounced (minutely perforated) ground becomes something beyond itself by forging analogies with period metalwork. Frequently cited as a comparandum is a copper-gilt triptych showing the *Crucifixion* between the *Carrying of the Cross* and *Christ Disrobed*, now in the Metropolitan Museum of Art, New York (fig. 2.11).[50] Attributed to a Franco-Flemish goldsmith, the triptych is dated to the early fifteenth century and thus is roughly contemporaneous with the Perugia panel. Appearing in embossed silver relief in the foreground are the figures of Christ, the Marys, and Roman soldiers. The two thieves as well as the narrative scenes on the side panels feature what fifteenth-century inventories described as "travail pointillé," "greneté," and "poincoinné," in French, or as "opus punctorium" or "punctile" in Latin.[51] Just as in Gentile's Perugia panel, delicate depressions in the Franco-Flemish triptych articulate volume by scattering light, creating areas of brightness that stand out against the darker gold ground (fig. 2.12). Gentile may have seen comparable pieces of this refined metalwork, in the form of reliquaries, processional crosses, and jewelry, during his residence in the early fifteenth century at northern Italian courts and in the Republic of Venice.[52]

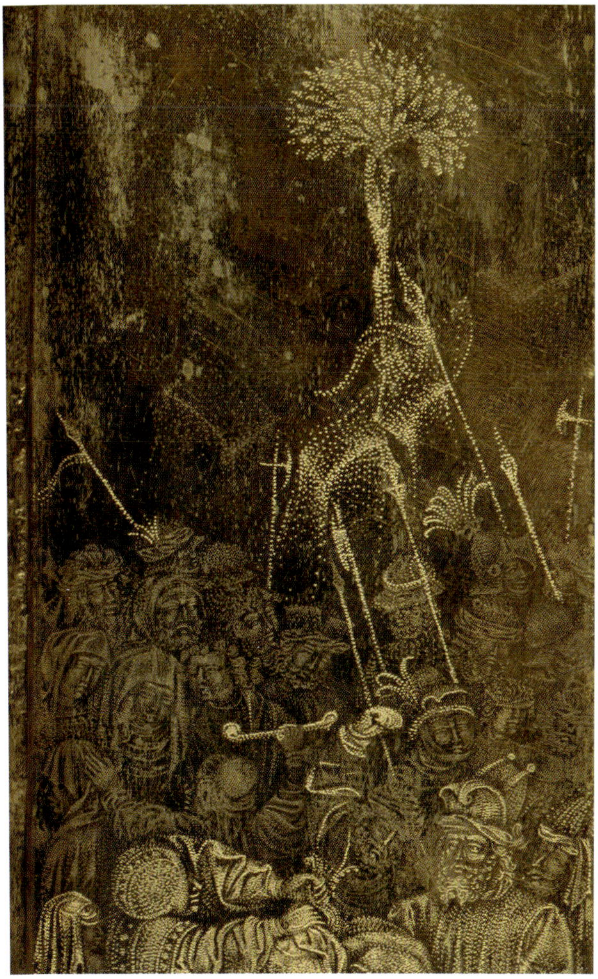

Fig. 2.12. Detail from Unknown Netherlandish or French, *Triptych with the Way to Calvary, the Crucifixion, and the Disrobing of Jesus*, c. 1420. Gilded copper, silver, and paint on panel (open 24.8 × 41.9 × 1.9 cm; closed 24.8 × 21.2 × 3.9 cm). Metropolitan Museum of Art, New York. Gift of J. Pierpont Morgan, 1917 (17.190.369).

The presence of opus punctorium in gold ground across media invites us to deepen the analogies between painting and metalwork. Gold was a medium that Renaissance painting supposedly disavowed, so the art historical narrative goes, in its progression toward illusionism.[53] Yet through opus punctorium, goldwork can achieve the effect of brushwork, suggesting volume by modulating light and shade. This subtle chiaroscuro even verges on *sfumato*, appearing to hover though in fact it is anchored in stippled ground. Picture and metalwork also approach relief: the points in the field generate oscillating forms that appear to protrude into the foreground and recede into the background.[54] What we see is a type of relief in reverse: the forms that seem to project outward are due to cavities in the ground. The points in the field indicating volume read as brilliant white or gray; opus punctorium thereby also evokes monochrome grisaille painting, a technique sometimes deployed to imitate bronze relief.[55] Pounced ground is a fertile ground, propagating shoots of transmedial reference.

A WORKSHOP OF LOOKING

The common denominator to these transmedial analogies is the demand for close, attentive viewing that punch work demands. The so-called period eye must squint to draw visual incident from the ground. Observers, in fact, commented on the necessity of close looking when taking in Gentile's stippled grounds. The Sienese humanist Sigismondo Tizio in 1526 described this granulation in his history of Siena, a manuscript of which is now in the Vatican Library.[56] His remarks pertain to angels in the background in Gentile's fresco of the Madonna of the Notary.[57] The painting, once in the Campo in Siena, has been destroyed.[58] However, the artist's extant fresco in Orvieto allows us to imagine the appearance and effect of the lost Sienese mural (fig. 2.13).[59] As Tizio describes,

> Gentiles Fabrianensis pictor eximius Virginis imaginem ceterorumque sancotorum non hoc anno, ut fertur, pro foro publico apud tabelliones depinxit, sed sequenti perfecit. In imis vero sub Virgine circulus est, in quo Iesu Christi in sepulcro mortui consistentis, quam pietatem Christiani vocant, a dextris ac sinixtris angeli duo sunt, aereo colore tam tenue picti, tamque exili lineatura in tufeo lapide ut, nisi quis etiam ostensis acutissimum figat intuitum, conspicere non valeat.
>
> (The distinguished painter Gentile of Fabriano painted an image of the Virgin and other saints for the notaries in Campo not in this year, as is said, but completed it in the following year. In the lower portions, under the Virgin, is a circle, in which to the right and left of Jesus Christ lying dead in the tomb, which the Christians call the Pietà, there are two angels painted in a bronze color so finely and with so thin an outline in the plaster that, unless someone fastens an extremely keen gaze on them when they have already been pointed out, it is not possible to see them.)[60]

In Tizio's Latin, the gaze required to see the two angels must be "acutissimum," literally "most sharp," derived from *acus*, (needle), a word befitting the stippling technique. Without a gaze as sharp as the stippler's needle, it is not possible to see his work. The hypothetical fulfillment of this possible act of looking is further qualified by the necessary presence of an expert, someone who can point out the stippled ground to the observer. What is implied is what we might call a "workshop of looking," a practice of observation that is collaborative and pedagogical. Someone points out and someone else sees. Opus punctorium asks for a community of viewers to make out and make sense of its formal subtlety. The ground's mimetic potential demands an audience in the plural, with physical and visual access to a work that must be close at hand.[61]

→

Fig. 2.13. Detail from Gentile da Fabriano, *Madonna and Child*, 1425. Fresco. Duomo, Orvieto.

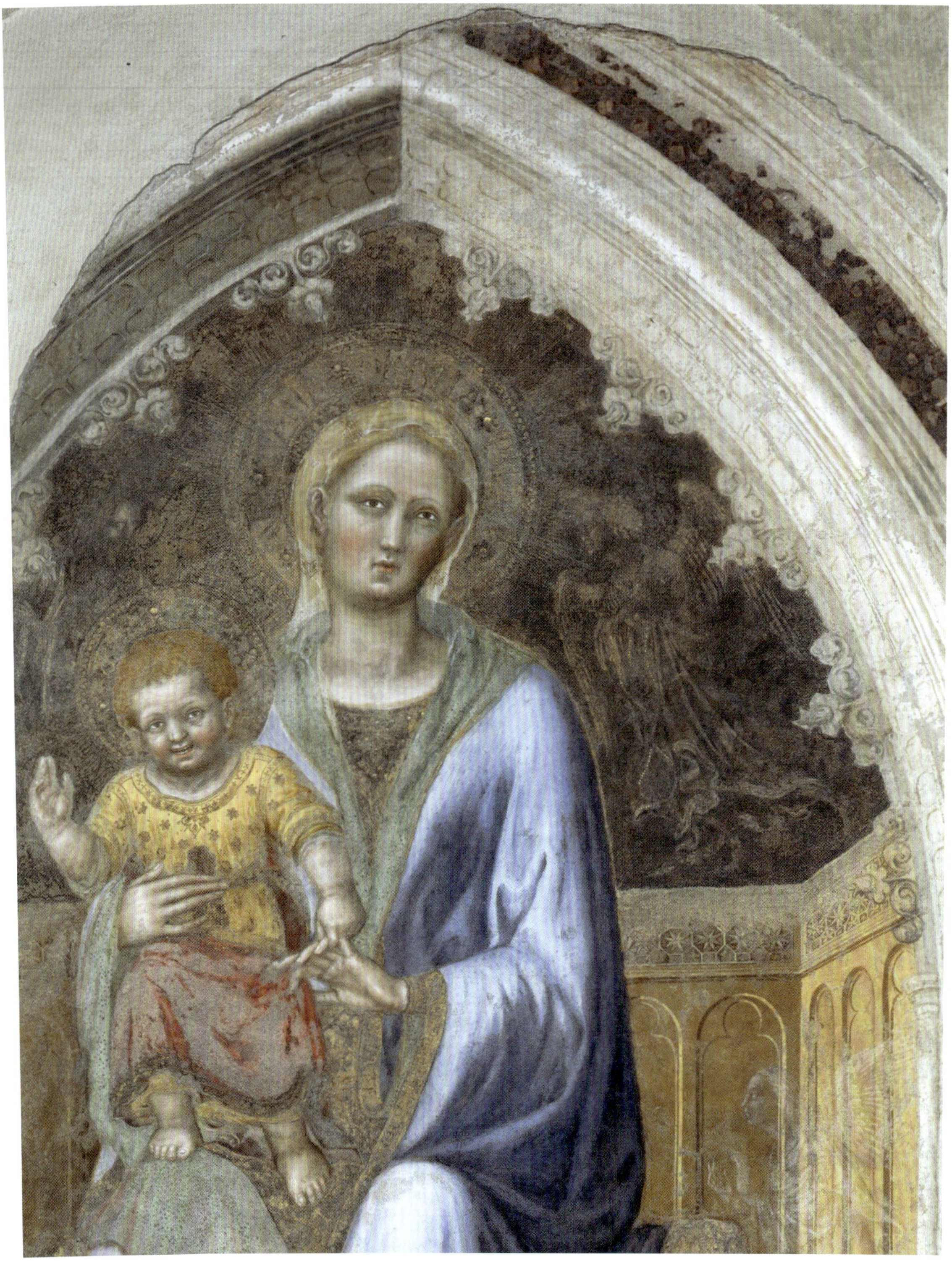

In the subsequent history of painting, following Burckhardt's account, mimetic potential in the picture's background will come to be actualized. Meanwhile, as I will argue in the next chapters, potentiality—that which can happen or can come into view—remains an important dimension of ground. Groundwork in the Renaissance picture will begin to make visible, or actualize, different modalities of ground, ranging from the hardest and most durable of stone bases to fluid and molten substances that yield beneath one's feet. Stable foundations can become unsolidified and dissolve. The painter mimetically depicts the stages of ground that progress from potentiality to actuality, and back again. The painting of ground, and the beholding of ground, themselves become pictorial events that indicate and actualize ground's possible states. The question becomes not what painting is, but what painting can be.

ANGELS IN ANGLES

Returning to the Perugia panel, we might ask what as a devout viewer one might have gained by fastening one's gaze on Gentile's gold ground. On a basic level, the pounced ground reinforces the panel's subject matter, given that the angels bearing crown and lilies further exalt the enthroned and humble Virgin. But something more is at play. The gold ground, undulating as it does between radiance and darkness, flatness and diaphanous figuration, stages its potential by injecting temporal and spatial dynamism into the panel. Here we might recall Alberti's well-known remarks on gold in painting. In addition to criticizing painters' disproportionate use of gold in their panels, Alberti disapproved of the material's dynamic qualities. Gold endangered pictorial illusion, since it appears differently according to lighting and viewing angle: "one can observe that, after you have placed gold on a flat panel, the major parts of those surfaces that one needed to represent as bright and brilliant appear dark to observers; and other surfaces, perhaps, which should be darker, appear more luminous."[62]

Elaborating on Alberti's remarks, Schwarz aptly notes that gold ground introduces "an uncontrollable piece of reality in the artful simulation of the picture."[63] In the Perugia panel and other paintings, however, the difficulty that gold ground poses for the act of seeing proves to make it suitable for the depiction of otherworldly beings whose presence is not consistently visible. Gentile's dramatization of gold ground's potential recalls a pun made by Saint Bernard alluding to the notion that angels are God's eyes and ears. Urging followers of the Rule to be steadfast, Bernard stated, "In every public place, in every *angulus* [corner], respect thy *angelus* [angel]."[64]

Diaphanous angels such as Gentile's appear in other panels as well as in frescoes in other settings. But in light of the intended destination of the *Madonna and Child* in the Basilica of San Domenico, it is worth bearing in mind that the Dominican friar Thomas Aquinas devoted a substantial portion of his *Summa theologica* to angels. Among the many topics he confronted regarding the nature, appearance, and actions of angels, Aquinas speculated on their place, motion, and time (1:QQ.52–53). His points of inquiry covered such questions as "Whether in passing from place to place the angel passes through intervening space?" and "Whether the angel's movement is in time or instantaneous?" Aquinas did not restrict angels to a specific place and instead argued that they move swiftly through infinite space from indeterminate locations, which he called the "wherefrom" and "whereto."[65] "Since the points in every magnitude are [. . .] infinite in potentiality," he reasons, "it follows that between every two places there are infinite intermediate places." These swift-moving immaterial beings exist in many different nows, "since time is nothing else than the reckoning of before and after in movement."[66] While I do not wish to draw too direct a parallel between Aquinas's angelology and Gentile's work, the angels that emerge and disappear from view in the Perugia panel find a ready analogy in Aquinas's description of angelic behavior. As messengers moving between "wherefrom" and "whereto," now and another now, in a field of infinite points, angels appearing and disappearing via the malleability of gold and its reflective qualities dramatize the potential of gold ground to bring a celestial world into and out of vision, both temporally and spatially. Whereas one-point perspective offers a rationalized, fixed, and measurable depiction of the world, Gentile's points on a field speak to the possibility of a world whose appearance fluctuates according to the viewer's own viewpoint. The line of vision from the viewer to the cluster of points in gold ground is not straight but beguilingly oblique.

THE GROUND OF INCARNATION

Does the potential of this gold ground ever become actualized? In the specific example of the Perugia panel, potentiality culminates in the appearance of the miraculous, the representation of Christ incarnate.[67] Gentile's opus punctorium underscores the artist's power to dramatize gold ground's potential through the holographic angels that appear and disappear from view. Christ, however, is "there," clear and present. By divine incarnation, the otherworldly erupts into the worldly. Gentile's panel explicitly contrasts the indeterminate state of the numinous with the appearance of Christ in the flesh. Two different pictorial modes represent these ontological states of potentiality and actuality. While opus punctorium achieves tonality by paradoxically turning gold ground into shadows and concave depressions into light, the tonal modulation of paint renders the volumetric and polychrome substance of flesh. Gentile seems to be essaying an argument about how painting can depict the divine incarnation through *chromatic* incarnation.

A long exegetical tradition, in fact, drew comparisons between a painter's coloring of a figure and the prophesied fulfillment of God's law through the birth of Christ. In his gloss on Hebrews 10:1, the early Church Father John Chrysostom remarked that "for as in painting, so long as one [only] draws the outlines, it is a sort of 'shadow.'" The application of colors,

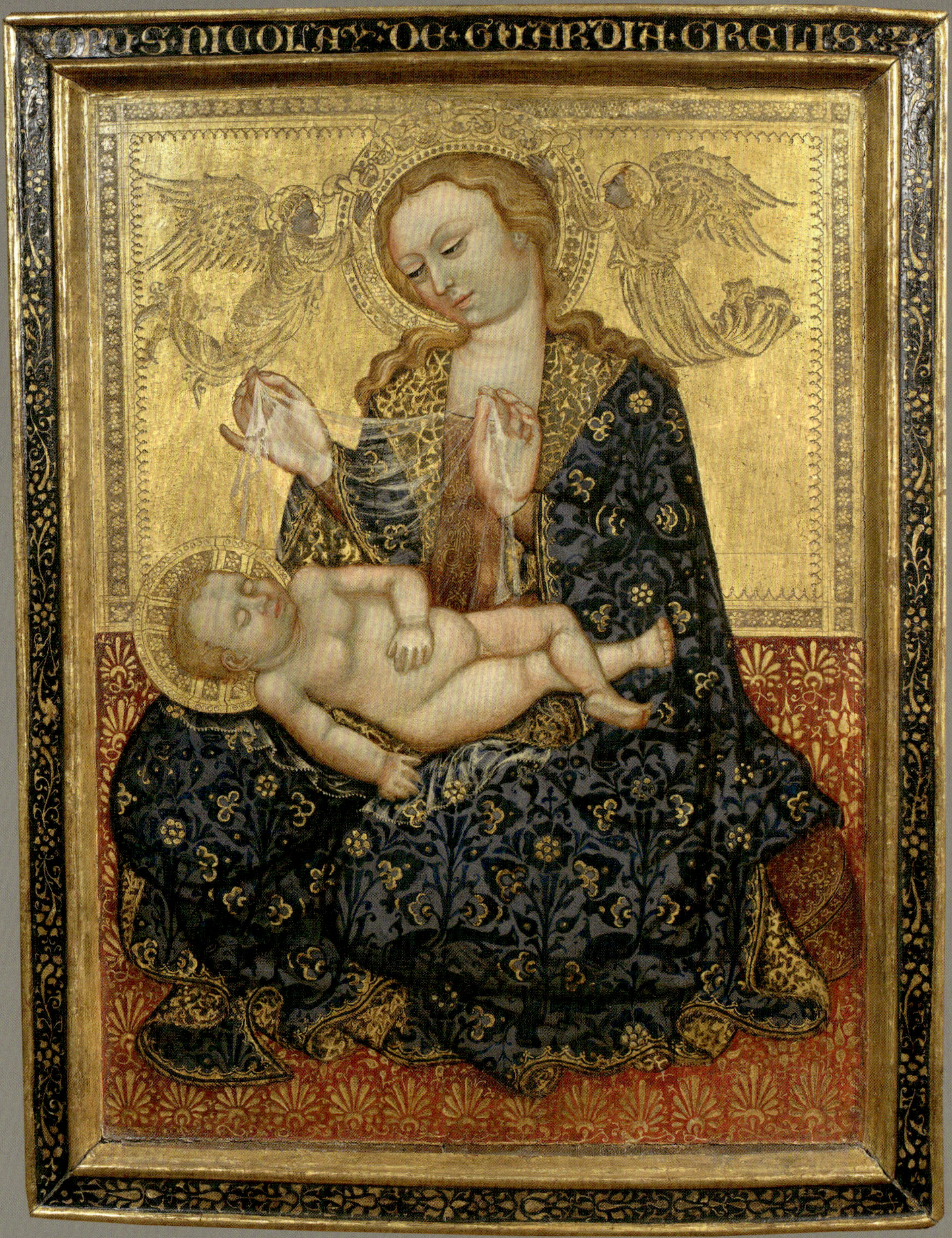
OPUS·NICOLAY·DE·GUARDIA·GRELIS

however, realizes what outlines in a picture merely suggest: "but when one has added the bright paints and laid in the colors, then it becomes 'an image.'" In a similar way, Chrysostom declares, "something of this kind also was the Law." The divine Incarnation realizes that which "was a shadow of good things to come."[68]

It is therefore significant to note that along with the many chapters devoted to gilding, Cennino's *Libro* refers no less than forty-five times to what he terms "incarnatione," the task of applying colors to render skin tones and bodily substance.[69] In period sources, however, *incarnatione* more commonly referred to divine incarnation.[70] In the Perugia panel, Christ's divine enfleshment is made doubly apparent through its juxtaposition with gold ground and the phantom forms floating there. We might even say that Christ's translucent robe, a nexus of hatched and cross-hatched lines, is a veil that is drawn aside, revealing his body. Several works, such as a panel by Nicola da Guardiagrele, closely follow Gentile's model of stippled gold ground against figures.[71] It is highly suggestive that these panels feature what Leo Steinberg memorably called the "sexuality of Christ," whereby the Son of God's genitalia is either exposed or prominently displayed (fig. 2.14).[72] Gold ground provides, both in the literal and figurative sense, the "background" to the depiction of Christ's humanity. Ground anticipates the coming of the figure.

GOLD GROUND AND BEYOND

The lines from Balzac's *Gobseck* cited in the epigraph could be summarized as follows: "Gold, not God, makes all things possible." Whereas the villainous usurer in the *Comédie humaine* speaks of possibility in the sense of possession and speculation, groundwork in the Renaissance picture gives another slant to the meaning of gold's possibility.[73] In Cennino's text and Gentile's panel, gold's inherent malleability enables ground to become a site of the possible, a field where artistic power exploits mimetic potential. Ground unfolds a spectrum of material, medial, perceptual, and devotional possibilities, which facilitates continuous passage between worlds, artisanal and climatic, pictorial and metallurgical, physical and ethereal. The shimmering auriferous field seems reluctant to settle in any one domain.

Yet Gosbeck is adamant about another property of gold that renders it a vehicle of possibility: its monetary function. Not its softness but its status as hard cash. Of course, when *battiloro* transformed coins into leaves, gold ceased to function as money, becoming instead an artistic material. In his *Contribution to the Critique of Political Economy*, Karl Marx inserted the following observation: "Gold is fixed capital; floating only in so far as it is consumed for gilding."[74] Gold's value as a universally accepted form of currency "floats," that is, diverges and dissipates, when it is hammered into leaf and awaits a second life as a gilt surface bearing artistic worth. Gold ground

←

Fig. 2.14. Nicola da Guardiagrele, *Madonna and Child*, c. 1423–25. Gold leaf and tempera on panel (67 × 51 cm). Gallerie degli Uffizi, Florence.

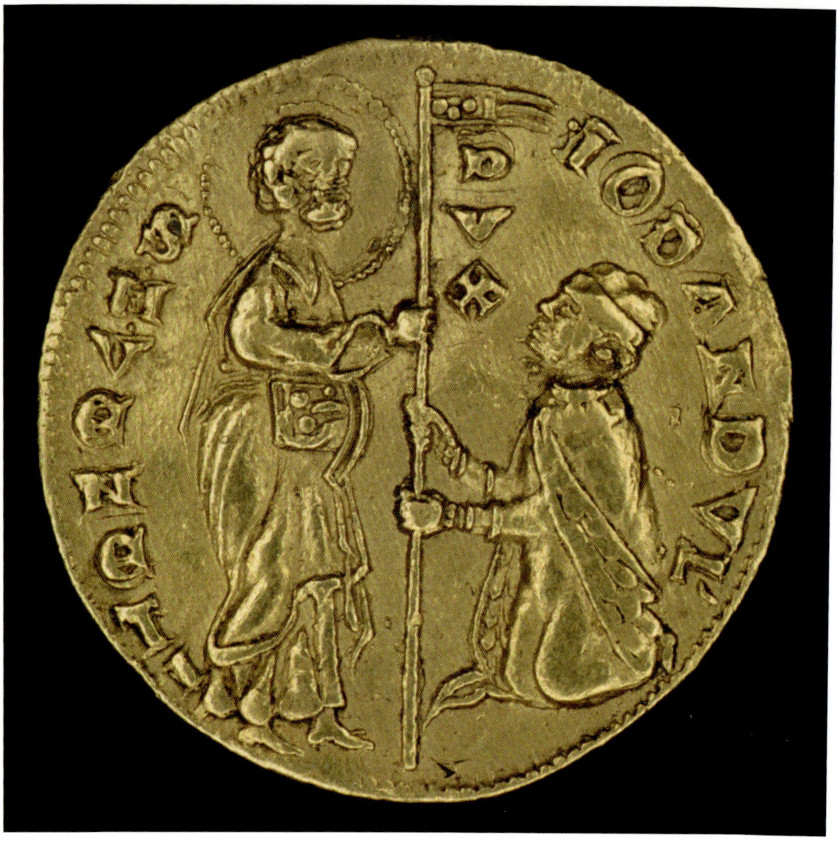

dramatizes the transformation of exchange value into use value. Could it be, however, that gold ground retains an imprint of its former life as currency?

The Venetian ducat, along with the Florentine florin, was the commonly accepted currency throughout the Mediterranean: in 1532, the French pilgrim Denis Possot remarked that "from Venice to Jerusalem no one takes money of gold unless it be of Venetian coin."[75] The 3.5 grams of gold in the Venetian ducat traveled throughout the early modern world, bearing the figures of Christ, Saint Mark, and the Doge standing proud in relief (fig. 2.15). In a strange sort of reverse engineering, the gold ground in Gentile's altarpiece is the opposite of relief, given that the bodily forms are indented with the prick of a needle. While small gold coins in their multiplicity, with their tiny and often unscrutinized images, move through and across all areas of the mercantile world, Gentile's groundwork turns the logic inside out—the viewer experiences a single, expansive, and stationary image on a microscopic scale, such as when considering the individual threads of the Virgin's hair. The artist's representation of the infinitesimal, however, points to the infinite height, depth, and breadth of the numinous.

Fig. 2.15. Ducat of Venetian Doge Giovanni Dandolo, 1280–89. Gold, 3.51 grams. British Museum, London.

Gold ground offered itself to artists and viewers as a site where forms —or worlds—come into and pass out of appearance. For its later art historical interpreters, gold ground became something else, a contested site in a cultural clash between advocates of positivism and rationality and those of beauty and transcendence—and it was claimed and reclaimed to suit their ideological objectives. In the fifteenth century, the objectives of the naturalistic ground establish themselves as "naturalized" and inevitable: gold ground is subsumed by the distant view; or, through linear perspective, by the measurable interconnection between the figure in the picture and the viewer facing and standing before it. The victor would appear to be the mathematical construction of illusionistic space. And yet, latency and possibility—the power of artistic skill and mimetic potential—as a condition of ground will continue to drive the power of images.

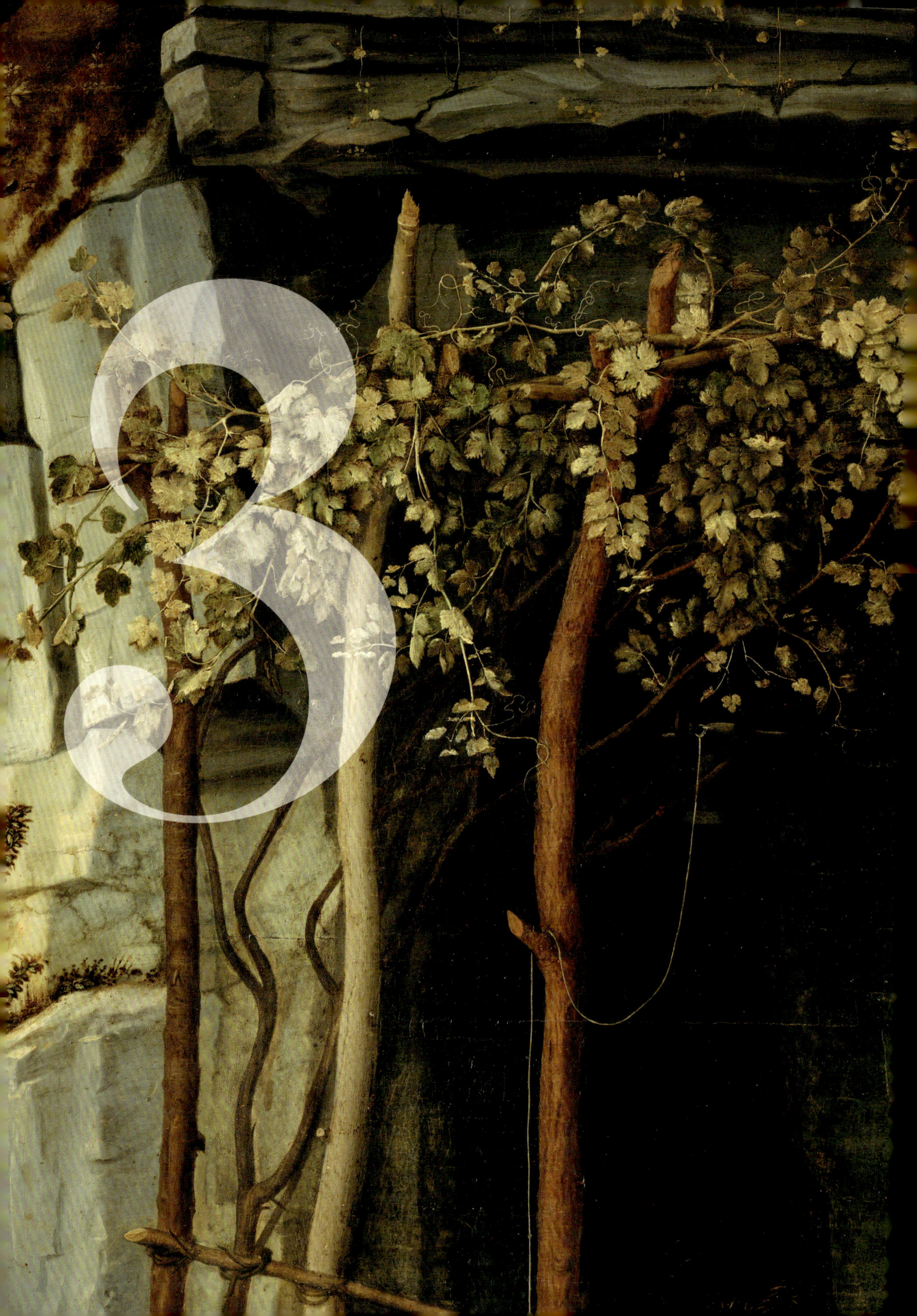
3

Metamorphosis: Rockland, Fissure, Marshland, Cave

FROM THE DUST OF THE GROUND

In a well-known episode in Vasari's *Lives,* Cimabue comes across the young Giotto drawing while tending sheep in the countryside near Florence. Vasari recounts that the shepherd boy was seen making portraits of his sheep on "*flat and clean slabs of stone* with a slightly pointed rock."[1] The anecdote marks a decisive step in Vasari's narrative of the visual arts' progression toward naturalism. Vasari not only portrays Giotto drawing from life; in casting the budding artist as a shepherd boy in bucolic surroundings, he connects the natural setting with the advent of the *maniera moderna*—the modern approach to art making. Aside from abandoning the awkward and misshapen bodies in Italo-Byzantine painting, which Vasari condemned as "monstrous figures," the artistic descendants of Giotto will relinquish gold ground and the mosaic medium, among other characteristics of Trecento art, as Vasari's biographies progress.

In the place of these grounds, the viewer beholds a natural expanse, including landscapes and the effects of weather and time of day, "skies turbid or serene [. . .] the splendor of the sun."[2] Never mind that gold ground would have a long life beyond its supposed demise, such as in the works of Gentile da Fabriano discussed in the previous chapter. Even Jacob Burckhardt, who celebrated the yielding to landscape of the backgrounds of altarpieces, acknowledged that well into the sixteenth century, artists such as Mariotto Albertinelli would continue to use gold ground.[3] But for Vasari, such instances were momentary glitches in his narrative: after being confined for centuries by gold ground, the Renaissance picture, most especially through the art of Raphael, will at long last open itself to a "campo largo"—a wide field—that will encompass representation not only of the human figure but also of the surrounding world.[4]

However much the scene of Giotto drawing in the countryside anticipates the renewal of art, the fable is also significant with regard to another aspect of art making that has often escaped critical attention. Vasari names and describes, albeit in the briefest terms, the instruments enabling the

Detail, Figure 3.1

advent of naturalism. The flat slabs of stone that constitute the support and stylus are taken directly from the ground beneath the artist's feet; in other words, from the geological landscape. Vasari's anecdote of Giotto thus resonates with earlier vignettes about artistic discovery and creation in which earth and rock play a pivotal role. Origin stories narrate that the first humans are shaped from earth: "Then the Lord God formed a man from the dust of the ground" (Genesis 2:7). In Leon Battista Alberti's Latin comedy *Momus*, from the 1450s, the character Charon, the ferryman to the underworld, recounts a creation story that he has heard from a painter: humans were made from clay mixed with honey or warm wax.[5] Charon's viscous material, like the biblical ground in its malleability, both "concentrates and radiates," in the words of the French philosopher Gaston Bachelard; it gives form "the expansion of infinite things."[6] Scattered throughout ancient and early modern art literature are also instances where the refined viewer discerns form within and among the naturally occurring swirls and spots in precious marbles.[7]

In Vasari's account, rock comes forth as the twofold means by which the artist Giotto generates his transcription of nature: the artist imparts his line with stone on stone, one sharp, the other smooth. The delineation of naturalistic form emerges from friction; stone—sharp and jagged or flat and smooth—allows for the figure to take its place in the physical ground of the image. Giotto makes graceful, animate marks with the most unpromising material, the obdurate matter of stone. As divine power molds earth into human beings, artistic power transforms hard, gray, lifeless rock into an almost living, almost tangible scene.

DURABILITY AND FRAGILITY

In fact, slate, marble, and alabaster became popular materials for pictorial supports in the decades before Vasari was writing. Their use allowed figuration to emerge directly from and upon a ground of stone. The material properties of these stone grounds resonated with art theoretical debates and theological exegeses of the period.[8] A painting on stone collapses sculpture and painting into a single object and thereby resolves the *paragone*—the early modern debate in which Vasari and others attempted to define artistic media through comparison.[9] Meanwhile, when employed as a ground, stone can refer to its other uses. For example, slate can serve as a touchstone for assayers, who test precious metals by rubbing them against the rock to leave a trace; therefore, the slate ground employed in Titian's *Ecce Homo* compels devout viewers to measure themselves and their spiritual progress against the exemplar of Christ.[10] References to the technique and effect of these "pitture su pietre" stress their durability. A letter written in 1530 to the humanist Pietro Bembo reports that the Venetian artist Sebastiano del Piombo "has found the secret to using the most beautiful oil pigments to paint on marble, which will make painting nothing less than eternal. As soon as the colors are dried they are united to the marble in such a way that they are almost petrified."[11] Figuration, having emerged from the ground, then also fuses with the ground and assumes its durability. In attempting to endure eternally, to extend indefinitely forward in time, paintings on stone also register the desire to arch backward and return to a primordial moment of art making.

Ironically, Vasari's text would prove to be more resistant to the teeth of time than many of these pictures painted on slabs on stone. Layers of paint can flake and break off, disintegrating skillfully executed brushwork.[12] Due to their weight and heft, paintings on slate are liable to crack, or, when assembled for large-scale altarpieces, can be in danger of collapsing. In these situations, painting no longer has the advantage over sculpture of greater transportability and durability.[13] In his *Considerazioni della pittura* (1619–24), the Sienese physician and art critic Giulio Mancini criticized paintings on stone under the classical rubric *pretium fragilitas*—price comes from fragility. To employ stone as a ground for paintings, Mancini charges, is to "transform gems into glass" and to "rob them of their perpetuity." A miniature on slate painted by Jacopo Ligozzi, he admonishes, "in being dropped was broken into pieces."[14] Thus stone as a supporting medium for paintings, while it has the potential to endure when left untouched, also runs an increased risk of destruction through rough handling.

Visual artefacts often compromise the ideals of aesthetics. The desire for the picture to offer an unmediated view onto nature—or to emerge directly from the elements of nature—is frustrated by any number of contingencies. While Giotto's sheep appear to bring stone to life, a painting on stone that proclaims eternal durability can crack when dropped. The impulse to mimesis not only casts the shadow of deception on the walls of Plato's cave. The *interruption* of form is latent in the walls' very (geological) makeup, through cracks, fissures, and other irregularities on the surface. A breach of continuity or potential stoppage is built into the ground almost as if to prepare for the moment when the veil of artifice is lifted and the inevitable limitations of a given material are revealed. Ironically, in its breakage, the fragile ground lays bare the virtuosity that is needed to transform constitutive materials into art.

Hence, when an artist makes a depiction of fissured rocks, this image does not exclusively encode its own disintegration. While a rockscape depicts the raw materials of creation, its features are placed in service to the composition so that intentionally represented cracks can function as connecting lines that distribute narrative and figural allusion throughout a picture.[15] In fifteenth-century paintings of rocky terrain, a crack in the ground becomes a route along which metaphors that involve the figure in solitude, overlaps in temporalities, and elisions between landscape and waterscape can develop. Moreover, when faced with such fissures as indicate dramatic tectonic action, the viewer is compelled to ask not just, "What happened to this figure?" but also, "What happened in this place?" and, "What will happen next?" When penetrating more deeply into the pictorial narrative, the question becomes, "From where and to where will this action go?"

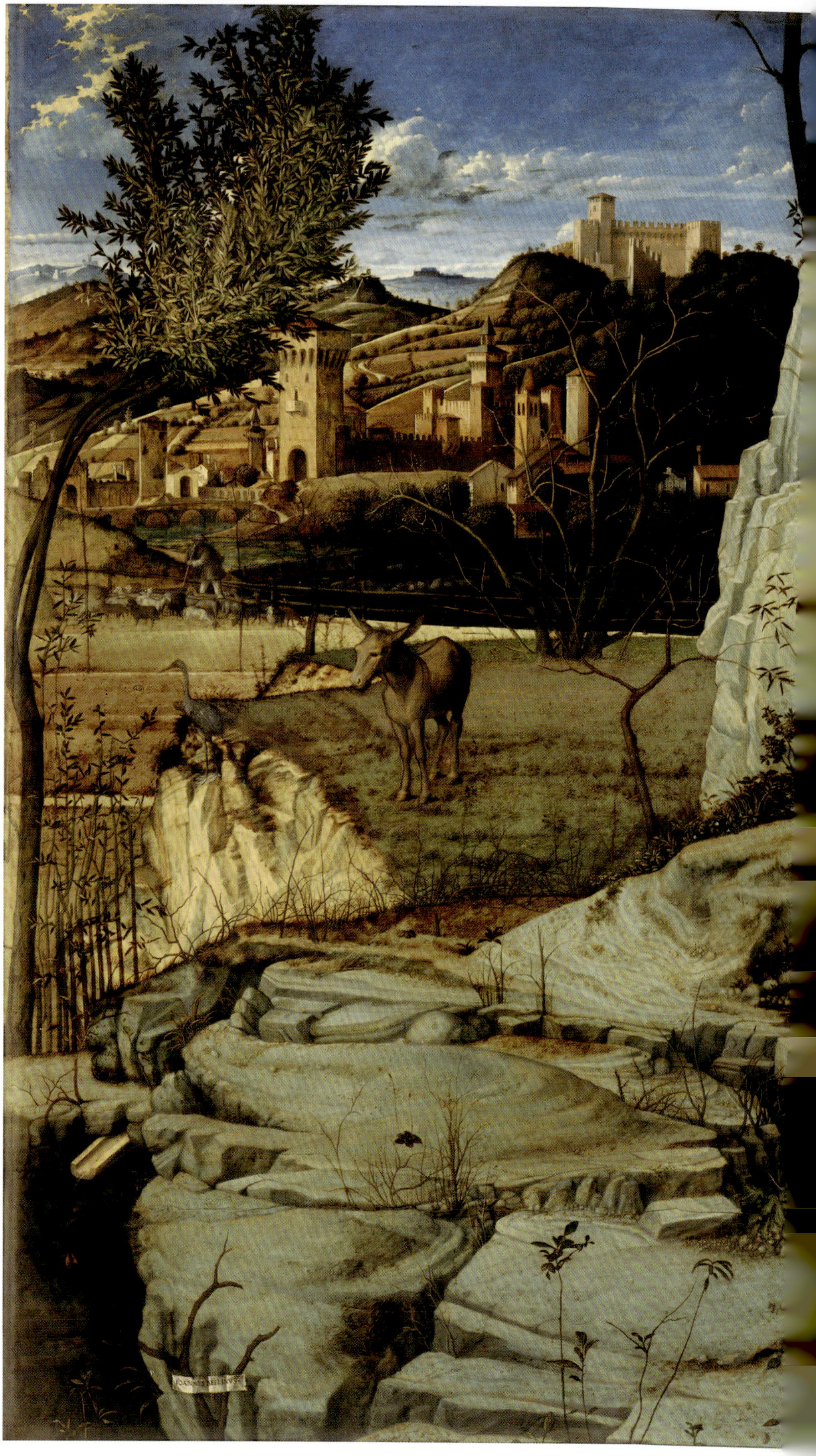

Fig. 3.1. Giovanni Bellini, *Saint Francis in the Desert*, c. 1476–78. Oil on panel (panel 124.6 × 142 cm; image surface 124.1 × 140.5 cm). Frick Collection, New York. Henry Clay Frick Bequest, 1915 (1915.1.03).

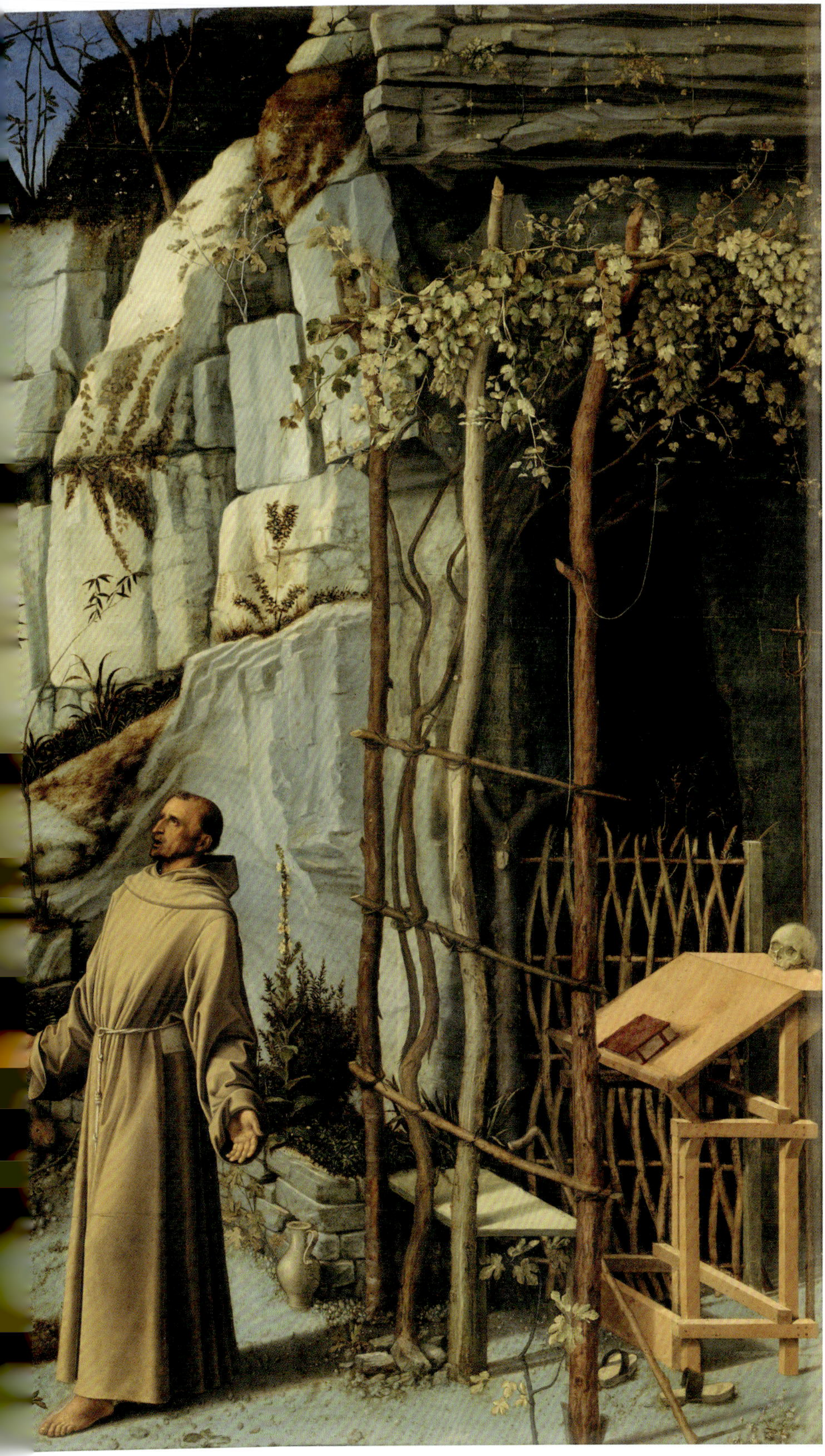

SAINT FRANCIS IN THE DESERT

Giovanni Bellini's *Saint Francis in the Desert*, dated c. 1475–78 (in the Frick Collection, New York), stands in this book as a paradigmatic image (fig. 3.1). Scholarly interventions have stressed such aspects as the panel's enigmatic subject matter, the circumstances of its patronage, and its relation to modes of Franciscan devotion in Renaissance Venice.[16] An invaluable contribution and a key point of reference for the present discussion is the volume *In a New Light: Giovanni Bellini's* St. Francis in the Desert (2015), published in connection with the Frick's monographic exhibition of the painting. Authored and edited by Susannah Rutherglen and Charlotte Hale, *In a New Light* combines technical analysis with fine-grained readings of the composition and relevant sources to confront long-standing iconographic questions. Does this painting depict the stigmatization, the moment when a seraph imprints the signs of Christ's wounds on Francis's body?[17] If so, why does the painting exclude the seraph and other key components of that miraculous event? Previous depictions portray Francis's lifted arms, easily discernible wounds on his hands, feet, and side, and rays that bind the saint with the angel and cross (fig. 3.2). Perhaps Bellini's panel portrays an altogether separate event from the saint's biography: his open mouth might signal vocal celebration of the creatures of the world and God's creation. Alternatively, the panel's elements and iconography might allude simultaneously to several disparate episodes of the Francis narrative.

Given that the prevailing models of art historical analysis are for the most part driven by the figure, Bellini's inversion in this painting of the conventional hierarchy that places figure over ground further adds to the difficulty of clarifying the work's subject matter. Instead of the body assuming the most prominent position, it is the background—the area that surrounds Francis and against which he stands—that dominates the picture plane. As Otto Pächt observed in his formalist reading of Bellini, in this painting "landscape is no longer an accoutrement or simply a background tapestry." It has instead become "the central feature of the composition."[18]

What mediates the disparity between Francis's diminutive figure and the expansive ground is the painting's middle ground. The piled-up mass of rocks upon and against which Francis is standing alludes to La Verna, the mountain where Francis, having left behind the noise of the city in order to pray and undergo penance, received the stigmata. Though it seems to depict an unruly wilderness, a mountain crag with haphazardly distributed details, this middle ground is the result of carefully planned panel construction and the laying in of color together with more improvisatory and gestural moments of brushwork.

The support and its preparation—the material ground—are instrumental in conveying the welling up of luminous shelves of stone. Almost architectonic in its construction and finish, the wooden support is formed from three horizontal poplar panels. As was customary in fifteenth-century painting practice, Bellini applied over this support several layers of gesso

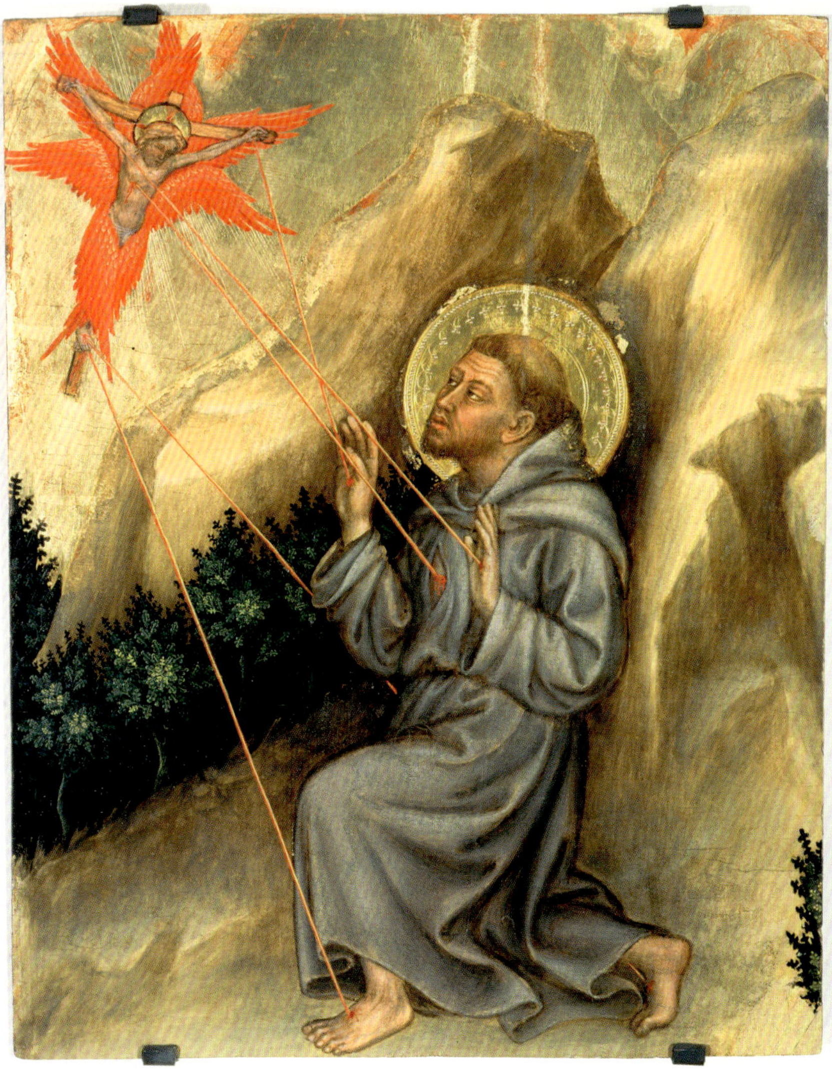

ground. This provided a smooth, even, and brilliant surface on which to apply the underdrawing, which he executed with a fine brush using a fluid carbon-based paint.[19] Reflectography indicates that unlike other elements in the background, such as the well delineated architecture of the townscape, the rock face was underdrawn in a loose, suggestive manner. Bellini indicated crevices and shadows with hatched lines, while other elements of the rock face were suggested with elaborate cursive forms. Serving more as a guide than a directive, the underdrawing of La Verna was then covered with imprimatura, composed of white lead pigment and oil, which was smeared over the entire surface of the panel by hand. This priming layer not only sealed the underdrawing, guarding it from alteration during the painting process; the reflective white preparation also imparted a limpid brightness to

Fig. 3.2. Gentile da Fabriano, *Saint Francis Receiving the Stigmata* from the *Valle Romita Polyptych*, c. 1408. Gold and tempera on panel (48.9 × 37.8 cm). Pinacoteca di Brera, Milan.

the overlying layers of paint, effectively lighting the panel from the ground up.[20] In the represented scene, the blue sky in the background is one source for the light that strikes the laurel tree (with such apparent force that it twists and bends) and the prominent rock face behind the saint. Hence, although writers such as Vasari and, later, Burckhardt may have celebrated paintings of this period for having overcome gold ground, the employment of the open background as a medium for the distribution of light demonstrates an affinity with gold ground, or rather, a continuation of its function.

RADIANT ROCK

As previously discussed, art historians through the nineteenth century promulgated the still widely held narrative that illusionistic experiments in spatial depth and distance replaced "archaic" gold grounds. In performing this replacement, the work of art transformed itself from object to image, from a material thing in the world to a representation of the world. The faraway horizon in Renaissance painting heralded, as Spengler put it, "the appearance of something profane and worthy."[21] However, Bellini's landscape backgrounds, in spite of their lyrical and meditative nature, complicate the association between Renaissance painting and secular naturalism. "Depth becomes a threshold to divinity": Birgit Blass-Simmen offers this observation in relation to the artist's portrayal of the Resurrection, where Christ is pictured ascending above and through horizon and sky (fig. 3.3). Bellini's backgrounds, she concludes, "assume their place between gold ground painting with inherent transcendental meaning and the landscape backgrounds of the following generation."[22] To substantiate this claim, she marshals the literary scholar Albrecht Koschorke's assertions on the "opening of the horizon" in early modern painting: empirical spatial depth does not force itself into the former ground of painting (i.e., gold ground) without assimilating this ground to itself. That which seems to be evacuated is instead subsumed. The vestigial traces of an obsolete medium become apparent if they are sought.[23]

Hence, Bellini's painting retains aspects of gold ground even as it develops a new approach. To portray the sky pierced with clouds and rays of light, Bellini experimented with varying proportions of precious ultramarine and whites. One valuable substance, gold, is replaced by another, lapis lazuli, the semiprecious stone that was crushed and laboriously processed to make ultramarine, which Cennino described as "a glorious, lovely, and absolutely perfect pigment beyond all the pigments."[24]

As was demonstrated in the previous chapter, gold ground features varying levels of relief. Bellini's sky also features relief: the edges of clouds, for instance, were raised with impasto, or thick layers of paint (fig. 3.4). To render the diagonal rays of light streaming from the clouds, a brush loaded with a pale red and yellow paint was dragged directly over the ultramarine sky: the streaks of rough, bright paint over the blue expanse grant a physical texture to the light. Gentle ridges and curlicues delineating wisps of cloud

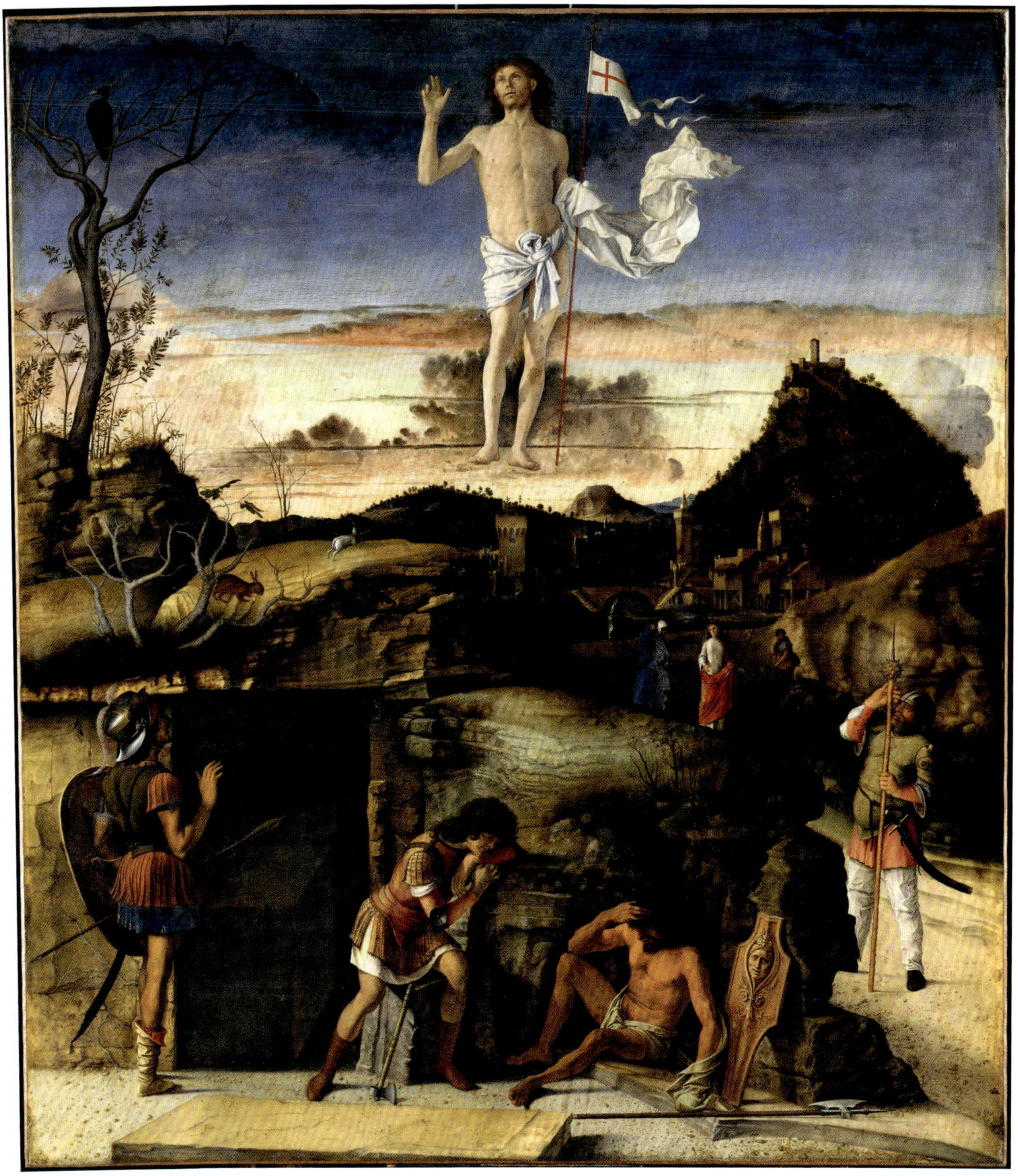

Fig. 3.3. Giovanni Bellini, *Resurrection of Christ*, c. 1475–79. Oil on poplar wood, laid down on canvas (148 × 128 cm). Gemäldegalerie der Staatliche Museen zu Berlin.

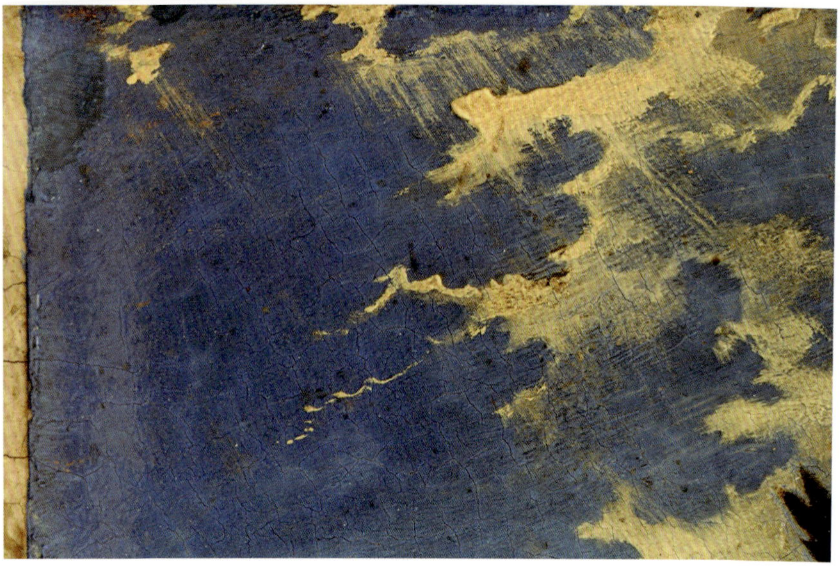

Fig. 3.4. Detail from Giovanni Bellini, *Saint Francis in the Desert*, c. 1476–78. Oil on panel (overall 124.6 × 142 cm; image surface 124.1 × 140.5 cm). Frick Collection, New York. Henry Clay Frick Bequest, 1915 (1915.1.03).

stand out from the cerulean sky.[25] It could be said that Bellini drew on the effects, although he did not employ the material, of gold ground.

In the painting's middle ground, Bellini enriches the rock face by alluding to and adapting mosaic, which was the Venetian form of gold ground par excellence. In a later work, the *San Giobbe Altarpiece* (1487), Bellini simulated the glittering field of an apse mosaic by laying down gold leaf over an orange-red layer consisting of bole and lead white (fig. 3.5). The patches of gold leaf on the left-hand side of the apse overlap and merge to create a unified area of radiance. On the right-hand side, however, the sections of gold leaf are placed at intervals, allowing the darker bole to show through. The irregular pattern of darker areas between patches of gold suggests the uneven scattering of light and shadow on a roughly tessellated surface.[26] In such illusionistic depictions of mosaic, the medium of oil painting effects a comparison between itself and its pictorial antecedent.[27]

In the painting of Saint Francis, Bellini went beyond this and *transmuted* the medium of gold ground mosaic in the shelves of glowing rock that make up Francis's backdrop, the sacred mountain of La Verna. The matrix of radiant stone blocks approaches the logic of mosaic through its fragmentation, verging on tessellation, of the surface (fig. 3. 6). To make the rock face appear radiant, Bellini laid in underlayers of warm yellow paint beneath passages of pale blue on the reflective white ground: this intricate layering of color imparts what has aptly been termed a "celadon hue" to La Verna.[28] Complementing the makeshift chapel with its bell and crucifix, the mosaic-like rock face thus brings the interior of a metropolitan church to the desert. Underscoring the translation of gold ground outdoors, plant life bursts forth between the enlarged tesserae.

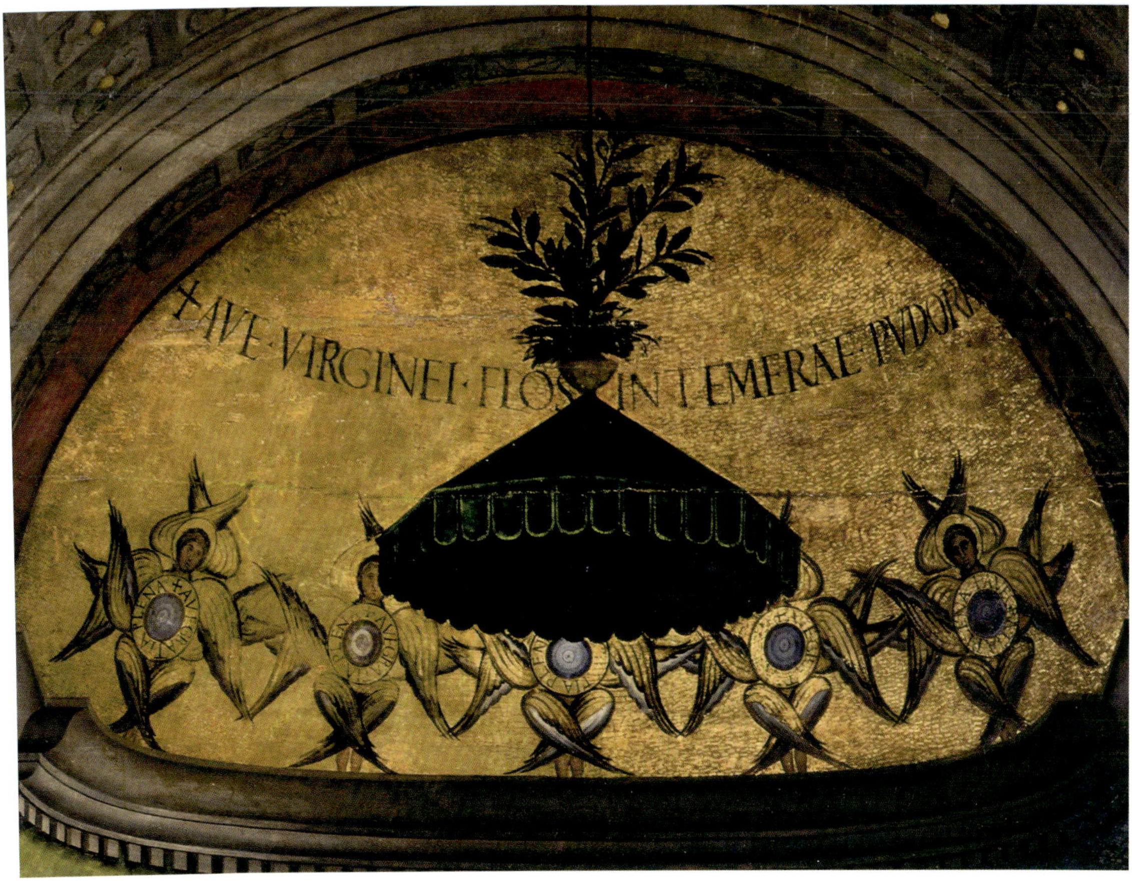

The *Little Flowers of Saint Francis*, a fourteenth-century collection of episodes from the saint's life, describes the miraculous events depicted in the painting. According to this text, "all of Mount Alverna [that is, La Verna] seemed to be on fire with very bright flames, which shone in the night and illumed the various surrounding mountains and valleys more clearly than if the sun were shining over the earth."[29] As Johannes Tripps has discussed, in paintings of scenes from biblical narrative, rocks often convey the manifestation of supernatural light,[30] by reflecting it toward the viewer. In works such as the *Annunciation to the Shepherds* (Cappella Baroncelli, Santa Croce, Florence) executed by Taddeo Gaddi in the 1330s, folds in the rock floor modulate a miraculous illumination that blazons the birth of Christ (fig. 3.7). In the Frick panel, the reflective surface of the rock face allows Francis to appear illuminated, as though on stage. The steps on the bottom left transform the rocky ground into a proscenium where the drama of the sacred event takes place. The rising piano of this stage leads the eye toward the makeshift altar and darkened apse of this chapel, an interior space of worship that has been broken apart into constitutive elements—a slab, a crucifix, a bell.

Fig. 3.5. Detail from Giovanni Bellini, *San Giobbe Altarpiece*, c. 1478. Oil on panel (471 × 258 cm). Gallerie dell'Accademia, Venice.

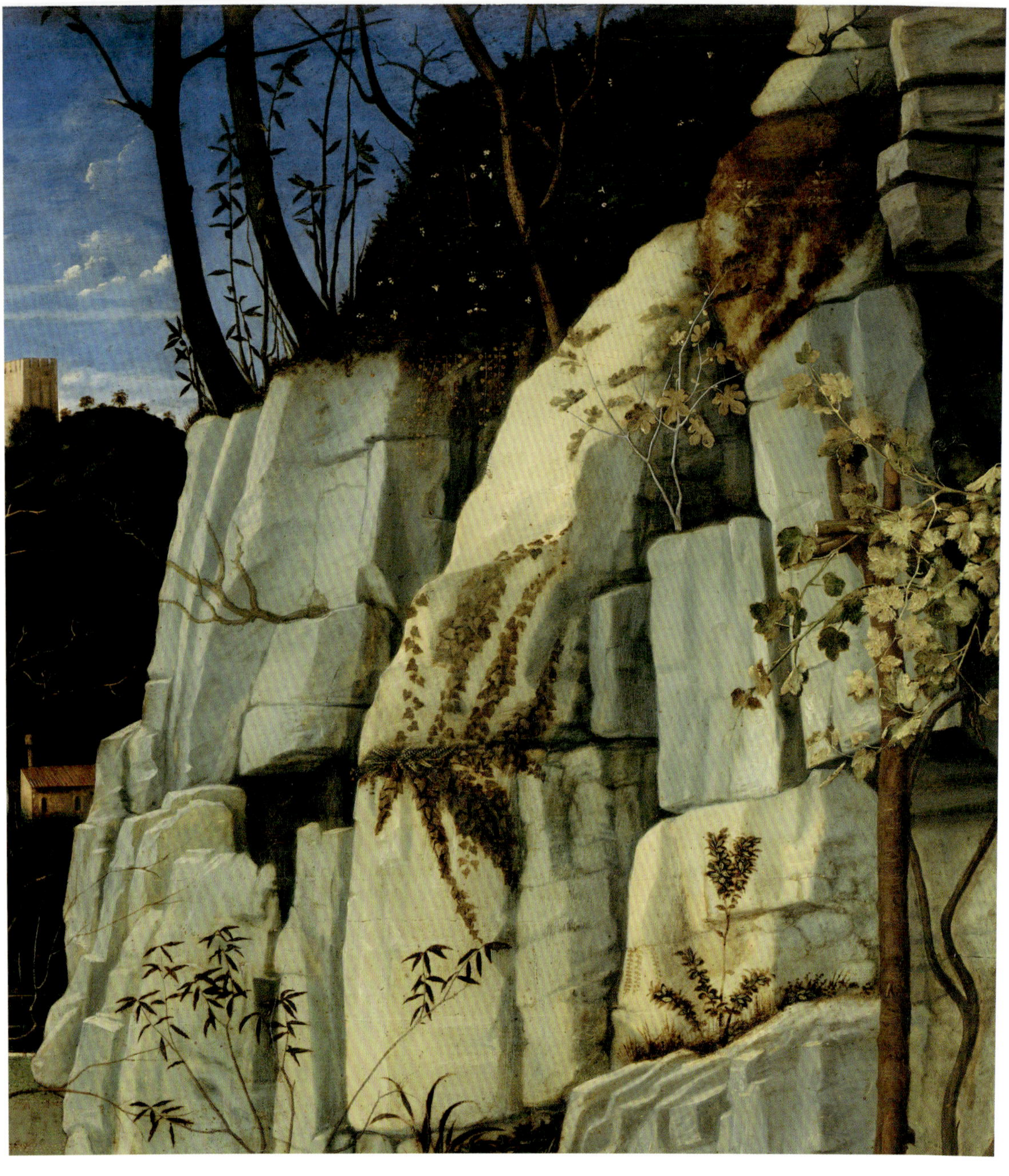

Fig. 3.6. Detail from Giovanni Bellini, *Saint Francis in the Desert*, c. 1476–78. Oil on panel (overall 124.6 × 142 cm; image surface 124.1 × 140.5 cm). Frick Collection, New York. Henry Clay Frick Bequest, 1915 (1915.1.03).

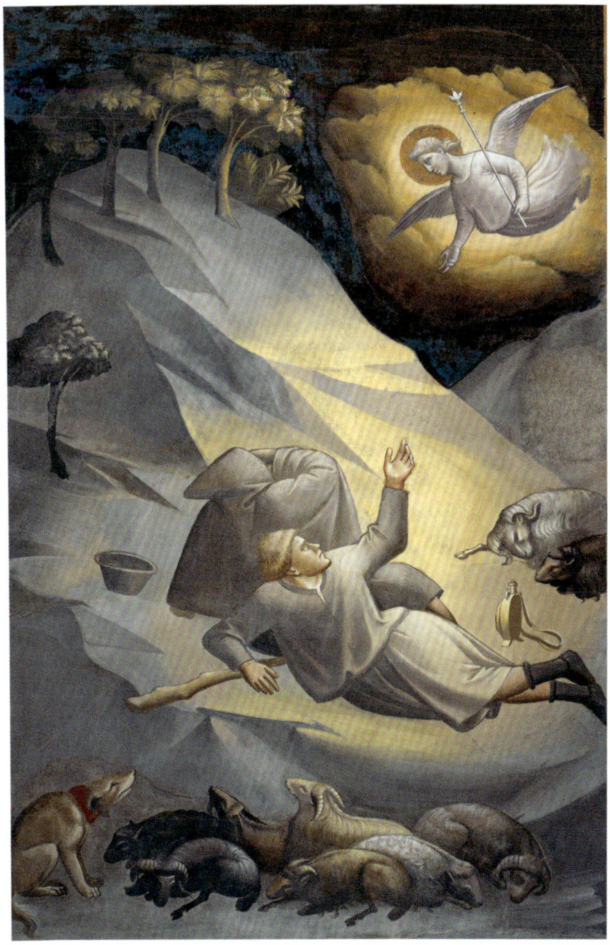

CRACKS

In painting the rock face, Bellini worked in an open and fluid manner, frequently departing from the underdrawing to describe the rough blocks of stones and their jagged edges. Working wet-in-wet, he rendered shadows in the crevices by dragging a brush filled with dark paint through the light blue layer before it was fully dry. On the craggy edges, swiftly applied strokes of thick white paint describe light directly striking the cliff. While Bellini certainly followed the outlines provided by the underdrawing of the rocky mass and aqueous foreground, he deployed gestural and spontaneous brushstrokes, in correspondence with the sudden tectonic forces that break apart rock.[31] The local application of multiple layers of color and wet-in-wet technique further enhance the multiple levels of relief on a mountain textured with crags that rise above smoother, exposed bedrock below.[32] Bellini's brushwork is paradoxical: the speed, fluidity, and improvisation of painting breaks apart the rock face in the very process of its creation.

Fig. 3.7. Taddeo Gaddi, *Annunciation to the Shepherds*, c. 1328–33. Fresco. Baroncelli Chapel, Santa Croce, Florence.

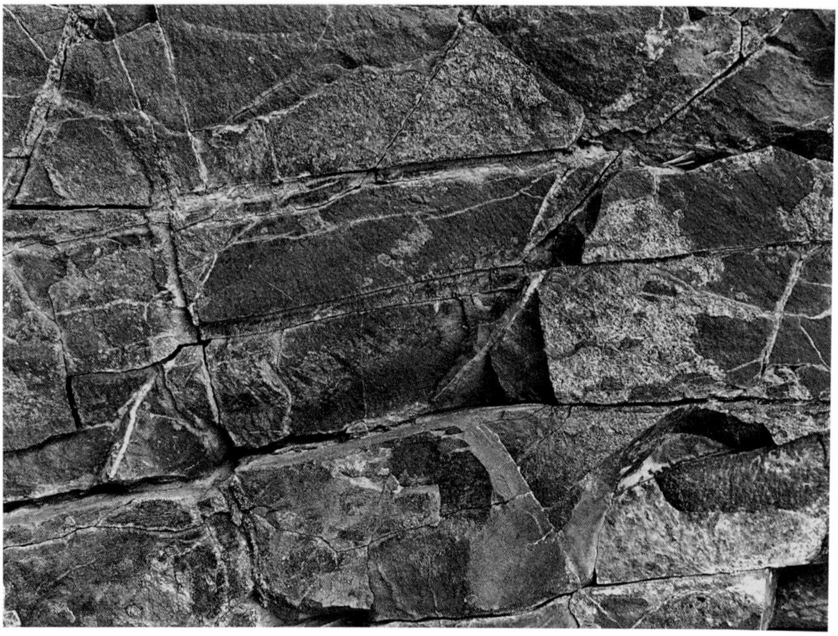

Fig. 3.8. Stone wall showing cleavage and fracture.

Two terms deployed in geology and the material sciences describe mechanical behaviors of stone when it breaks. "Cleavage" refers to breaking along regular lines, while "fracture" refers to irregular breaking. The variable sensitivity of rock materials and the structure of their grain produce differing tendencies to breakage. Hence, fissures can have an identifying function. Certain types of rock (such as feldspar) can cleave into horizontal and vertical planes (fig. 3.8) while other types cleave obliquely or in two dimensions. Meanwhile, wispy lines that diverge from the grid indicate fracture. Cracks allude visually to tectonic events, whereby at some point in the past, tension, compression, and stress caused rupture. Humans' early ancestors searched for stones that had broken to form sharp edges, which were useful for cutting nutritious meat and marrow from bone. Eventually, *Homo habilis*, an early hominid species, discovered that smashing rocks against one another would create sharp edges. The prototypes of flints, spears, and knives were born. As materials scientist Mark E. Eberhart observes, the phenomenon of fracture constituted the first human technology: "the way a material fails can define its use."[33] In our narrative, the sharp edge becomes significant as an artist's tool—as stylus and palette knife. The earth's raw materials offer up the tools for nature's mastery at the same time as natural forces reduce the products of artifice to nature once again.

In the Frick painting, Bellini employs fracture and cleavage, both natural and human-induced, to organize his composition. At the center of the picture, the vertical edge of the rock face separates the mountain wilderness from the pastures beyond it and frames the view of the town still farther beyond. The rock face, meanwhile, is cleaved into megaliths and, to the right, opens to reveal a cave. Directly behind Francis, striations define a rock garden, where carved blocks have been built into a human-made wall or shelf. From here toward the left of the painting, the artful blocks and fissures seem to dissolve into a cascade of visibly once-molten rock that flows toward the foreground. At the picture's lower edge, rock hardens again, as is signaled by the carved steps, which allow a gradual descent before the rock face drops off into a crevice. A gutter spout reveals that a spring is feeding a stream along the painting's central, diagonal fissure, which is replete with vegetation in different stages of growth and decay.

The cracks in Bellini's rock face signify more than just the rugged wilderness where Francis undertakes his devotional practice in solitude. Just as a host of varieties of flora burst from between the picture's cracks and crevices, a compositional strategy of fragmentation allows the complexity and fertility of ground to emerge. Through the ground, Bellini unfolds Francis's experience of solitude, the overlap between the biblical past and eschatological history, and the particular fifteenth-century interest in renewing centers of spiritual retreat in the Venetian lagoon. Through their multiplicity, the grounds in this painting—the distant view, the stratified backdrop, and the unstable foundation—energize the apparently stationary figure of Francis into an active vehicle whose multiple stages of transformation can be traced along the route that is the painting's diagonal line in the composition, which depicts a crack.

PAST VIEWS AND FUTURE PROSPECTS

As previously described, the ridge's jagged profile in the middle ground cuts diagonally across the painting, opening up a view of the town nearby and separating Francis from civilization (fig. 3.9). Bellini thus effectively creates two paintings in one. André Chastel termed this pictorial device "un tableau dans un tableau" (a painting within a painting).[34] This pictorial doubling accentuates the distance between the desert and civilization. While separate, both elements exist within view of one another, a visual relationship that underscores the definition of one (solitude in the wilderness) as dependent on its antithesis (community in the city).

In other paintings of hermit saints from around this time, Bellini likewise employed stone's cleavage to convey the isolation of the figure and distance from habitation. In his panel of *Saint Jerome in the Desert*, dated to the same period as the Frick painting, the jagged rock face overhangs and protrudes toward the saint: his blocklike forehead and angular and tanned body work as a visual extension of the crags (fig. 3.10). The viewpoint from below confirms the saint's spiritual loftiness.[35] Meanwhile, the shelves and roof of rock frame the prospect of the nearby city. Bellini positions the town so that, while not far away, it is at some remove.[36] Desert saints never lived in what the historian Peter Brown termed "splendid isolation" from towns and villages. While imbued with an aura of strangeness that lent them spiritual

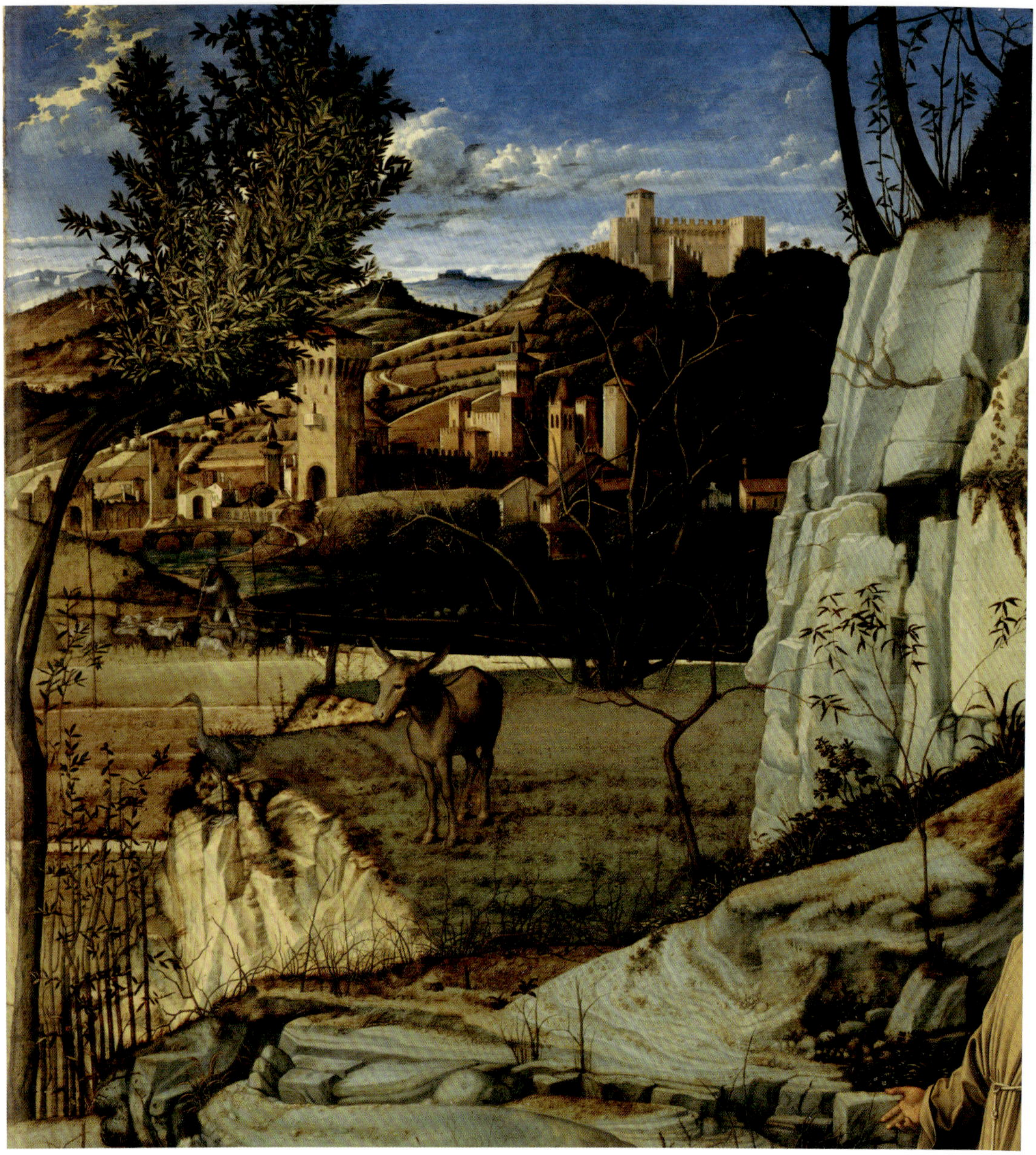

Fig. 3.9. Detail from Giovanni Bellini, *Saint Francis in the Desert*, c. 1476–78. Oil on panel (overall 124.6 × 142 cm; image surface 124.1 × 140.5 cm). Frick Collection, New York. Henry Clay Frick Bequest, 1915 (1915.1.03).

authority, these holy figures mediated the seemingly unbridgeable worlds of countryside and town, peasantry and patriciate. Desert saints dwelled close enough to intervene in the political affairs of a city and to capture the imagination of its inhabitants, and yet far enough away to rise above quotidian life.[37] This sense of near distance or removed proximity gives the realms of city and country a certain amount of fluidity.

Distance quells the noise of human life while allowing desert saints to take in a visual panorama of the civilization they have left behind. The

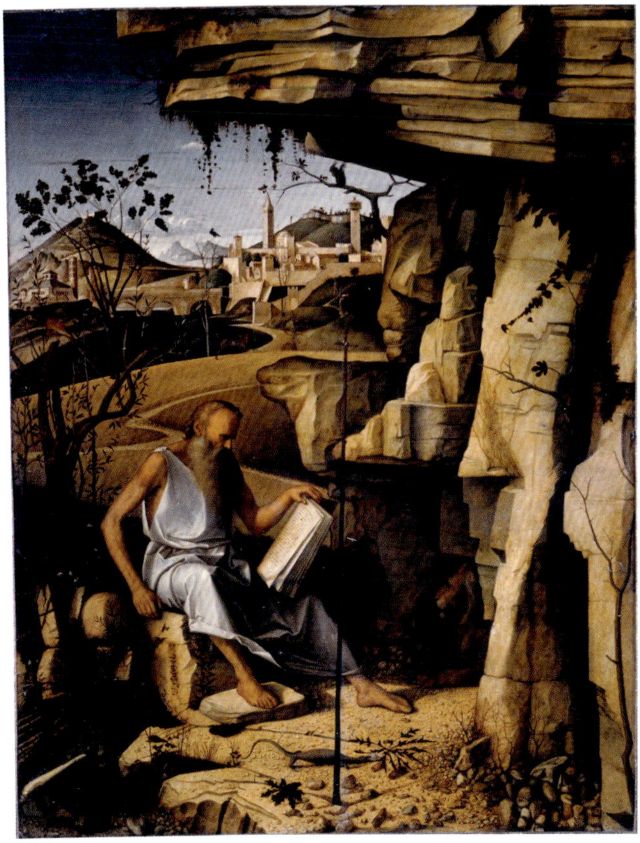

Legenda maior (1263), an early biography of Francis composed by Saint Bonaventure, narrates that the saint, "relinquishing the restlessness of the crowds, sought out the secrets of solitude and a place of quiet desire." Divine providence leads Francis "to a high place called Mount La Verna" which is described as apart (seosorum), literally "turned towards itself" (se-vorsum), a word that implies the introspection the saint will undertake on the sacred mountain.[38] In the painting, a visual analogy between Francis's body and the buildings of the town undergirds this distinction between crowd and self. Francis's upright posture, echoing the towers in the townscape, calls to mind his status as a pillar of the Church or the architect of its repair.[39] But whereas in the town the towers stand in multitude, Francis stands in solitude. As in his panel of *Saint Jerome*, Bellini ultimately replaces the analogy between the saint and the towers with that between himself and the mountain, so that the height and isolation of La Verna dramatize Francis's separateness and spiritual stature.

The effect of quiet in the painting is a product of Francis's perspective from his solitary place of meditation. This silence allows us to reflect that pictorial backgrounds not only record the topography in the distance but can also be positioned in retrospect. Jerome, in reflecting on his withdrawal

Fig. 3.10. Giovanni Bellini, *Saint Jerome in the Desert*, c. 1480. Oil on panel (151.7 × 113.7 cm). Gallerie degli Uffizi, Florence.

into monastic life, evokes his former life in the city in what hasbeen described as a "split time frame": "Oh how often when I was living in the desert, and in that vast solitude, scorched by the burning sun, which provides monks with a savage dwelling-place, did I imagine myself surrounded by the pleasures of Rome" (*Epistulae* 22.7).[40] For Francis, too, it can be assumed that the town nearby offers the backward glance of memory.

ELSEWHERES

As previously stated, the positioning of the hermit at a certain remove from town enables him to live apart while retaining the town as a point of reference. Perhaps because of this dual relationship, some viewers of the Francis picture perceive the town as "nearby" (propinquo) while others see it as far away. Interestingly, in period sources the word *lontani*, meaning "distances" or "distant areas," was used to refer to parts of a painting that were perceived as far from the viewer. In her essay exploring this overlooked art critical term, Blass-Simmen points to the word's appearance in correspondence dated November 1502 between Giovanni Bellini and agents acting on behalf of the famed patron of the arts and collector Isabella d'Este, Marchesa of Mantua.[41] Through an intermediary, Bellini stated that the painting he could offer to make, in addition to portraying the Madonna and Child with Saint John the Baptist, would include "qualche lontani et altra fantaxia" (some distant views and other fantasies). At this moment in the development of the art lexicon, the designation "lontani" stood alongside better-known terms for landscape, such as *paese* (land or town) or *paesaggio* (landscape). The word would continue to have currency well into mid-sixteenth-century Venetian sources.[42] It encodes a sense of otherness ascribed to ground, an abstract "out there." *Paesaggio* appears more concrete and would emerge as the standard term to point out scenes in the distance in the Renaissance picture.

In another often-cited letter to Isabella d'Este, dated January 11, 1506, Bembo described Bellini's habit of "always wandering [vagare] according to his desire in the pictures, such that they might satisfy whoever looks at them."[43] To wander, of course, is to roam without purpose or intended destination. Yet to traverse a visual field demands a mental foothold: if not a path, then notches and ledges where the mind can step, push itself forward, even backtrack as it explores.[44] In the case of the painting of Saint Francis, as the eye traverses the background, into the lontani, it continues to seek out and stop at several figures. There is the shepherd tending to his flock, the heron perched on the rock, and the donkey standing to its side. On the one hand, these figures bear symbolic meaning: the donkey may refer to Christ's entry into Jerusalem on Palm Sunday, which is referenced in the darkened entrance of the city gate, and which served as a precedent for Francis's journey to La Verna by means of the same animal.[45] In addition to this narrative reference, these figures mediate the connection between Francis and the town in the distance as the ground is traversed visually.

In his insightful essay entitled "Elsewhere," Al Acres examines fifteenth-century painters' use of such "staffage figures," so-called accessory elements that are strategically positioned to offer a sense of scale and enliven landscape. Such "concentrated lures of attention," Acres writes, "manage not merely to draw the eye beyond the foreground." They work "to slow its [the eye's] itinerary there in a way that resists perception of the background as mere surplus."[46] The figures in the middle distance allow the eye to linger in that space and thereby enable the viewer to gauge Francis's remove from civilization.

While lontani might lie beyond, Bellini positions figures in the distant area approaching this "elsewhere" to signal the route by which this visual destination might be reached. While the overhang frames the view of the town, placing desert and civilization side by side in a dialectic relationship, Bellini opens up the middle ground to introduce a third variable in this relationship, which raises the idea of ground as a site of recurring motion. The central crack and the staffage figures present the ground as traversable space, or a space that needs to be traversed. Continuous motion is a necessary part of the relationship between these two endpoints.

The deferred arrival in the lontani also bears temporal connotations. Dante notably uses the phrase "mondo lontana" to refer to future time: the fame of the Virgin endures and will endure, he emphasizes, in a world that is not immediately, but eventually, to come (*Inferno* 2.58–60: "la dama ancor nel mondo dura, / e durerà quanto 'l mondo lontana.") As has often been noted, the idealized urban architecture in Bellini's town, as well as its elevated position, prompts association with Mount Zion, "the city of the living God, heavenly Jerusalem" (Hebrews 12:22).[47] The painting's lontani thus turn toward the prophetic future, the place that Francis hopes some day to reach.

The serrated edge of the rock face cuts into and reveals the distant view as occurring not in the present but in an anticipated future. What seems to be a timeless panorama, in which the town is a fortress against change and the fields are acted upon by the repeating seasonal cycle, simultaneously subsumes both Francis's personal history, since he has left the town for a secluded life, and world prophecy, since the town can also represent the New Jerusalem. The seemingly static background view thus encompasses "what was" and "what will be." More generally, this painting demonstrates how backgrounds can compress into a single vision knowledge of local topography, memory, and a hoped-for future. Porous to time, backgrounds are a matrix through which memory and prophecy flow.

Groundwork achieves the synchronized presentation of temporally distinct scenes. A compelling parallel to Bellini's geological temporality can be found in the *Madonna delle Cave* (c. 1488–90), a work close in date to the Frick picture, executed by the artist's brother-in-law Andrea Mantegna (fig. 3.11). The open mouth of the Christ Child, prone on Mary's lap, corresponds to the opening in the quarry in the background, where stonemasons hammer and carve on different levels in the bedrock. While the portrayal of artistic

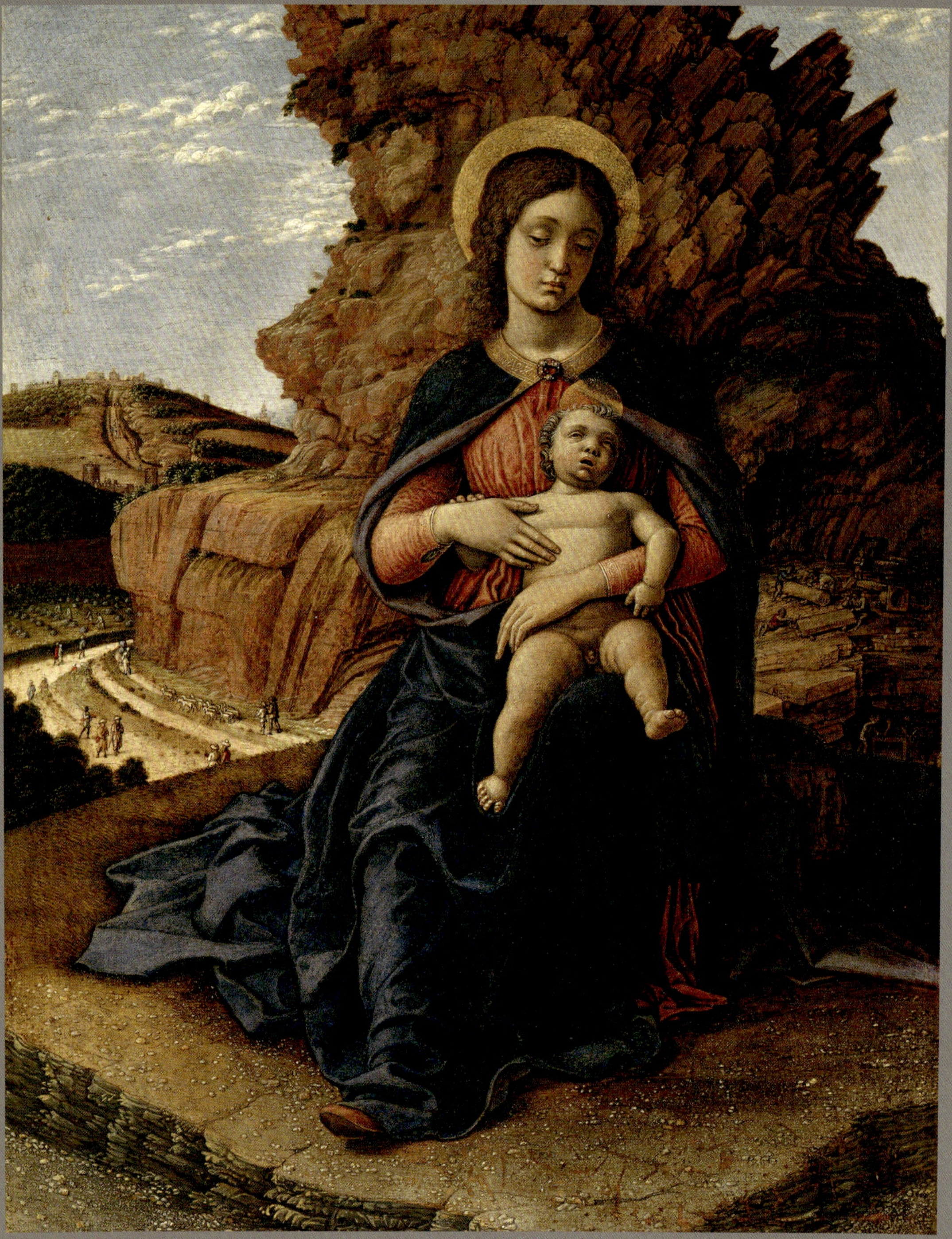

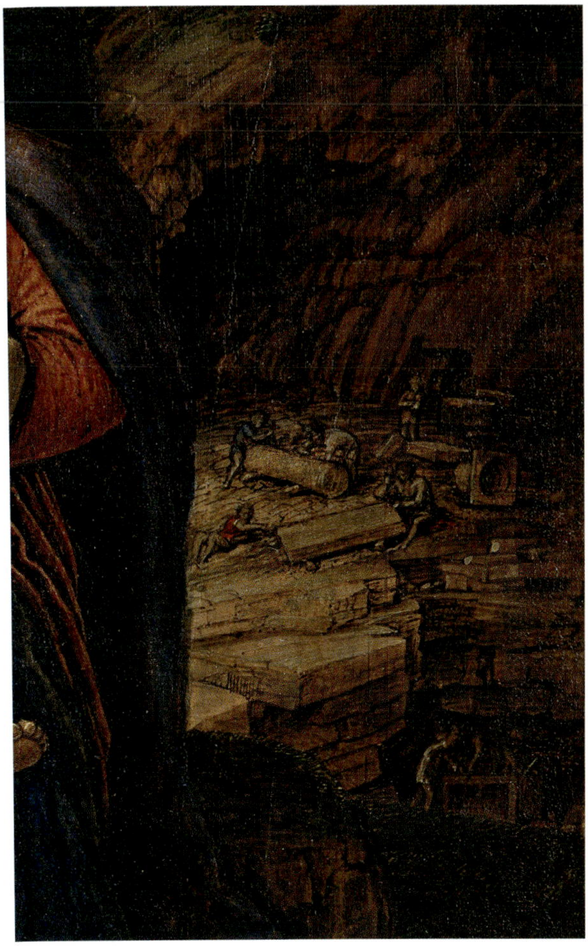

creation can refer to the genesis of the world, and by extension, the incorporation of humans in sacred history, in this instance Mantegna deploys stonemasonry to signal a complex temporal scheme, in which the future overlaps with both the past and continuous present: artisans in the background shape the Arma Christi, the column on which Christ will be bound and whipped, and the sarcophagus in which his body will be placed (fig. 3.12). The activity of quarrying and sculpting in the depths of the earth alludes to how future time promises to enact the historical drama of the Crucifixion.[48]

←

Fig. 3.11. Andrea Mantegna, *Madonna of the Caves* (*Madonna delle Cave*), c. 1466. Tempera on panel (29 × 21.5 cm). Gallerie degli Uffizi, Florence.

(ABOVE)

Fig. 3.12. Detail from Andrea Mantegna, *Madonna of the Caves* (*Madonna delle Cave*), c. 1466. Tempera on panel (29 × 21.5 cm). Gallerie degli Uffizi, Florence.

BRUSH AND CHISEL

Within the rocky outcrop itself, Bellini mobilizes the fracture of stone not only to simulate and allude to the mountain setting of La Verna. The jagged lines embed Francis's hermitage in the surrounding wilderness while breaking apart and articulating the ground. These cracks introduce Francis into the desert, inserting him into a continuum that extends to primordial history.

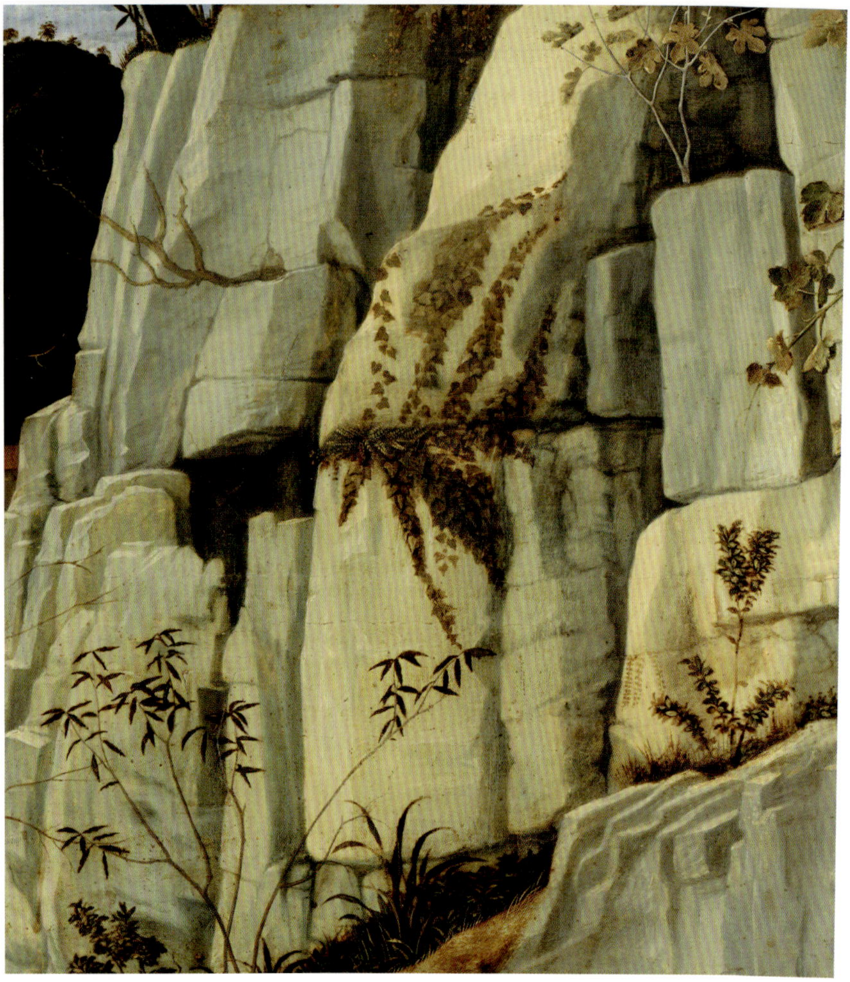

Fig. 3.13. Detail from Giovanni Bellini, *Saint Francis in the Desert*, c. 1476–78. Oil on panel (overall 124.6 × 142 cm; image surface 124.1 × 140.5 cm). Frick Collection, New York. Henry Clay Frick Bequest, 1915 (1915.1.03).

A figure standing on a stable and even plane in a picture often signals the present tense, announcing to the viewer, "Here I am." Bellini destabilizes the ground's planarity and conventional reference to the *hic et nunc*, the here and now. In doing so, he moves his depicted desert away from the art of painting and closer to stonework. In works of monumental construction, as in geology itself, passage into anteriority can be signaled through descent through successive layers, as well as through weathering, whereby layers are worn away. Bellini's painting of stonework prizes the strata that are revealed when stone is broken apart, as well as the smooth polish that results from weathering. Bellini thus underscores the "work" that is entailed by the artwork: "l'artista, / Ch' ha l' abito dell' arte e man che trema" (*Paradiso* 13.77–78; the artist who has the habit of art has a hand that trembles). In these verses, Dante encapsulates the push and pull between artistic volition and the awful resistance of the material.[49] Bellini's painting thus also speaks of the sublime difficulty of managing his material.

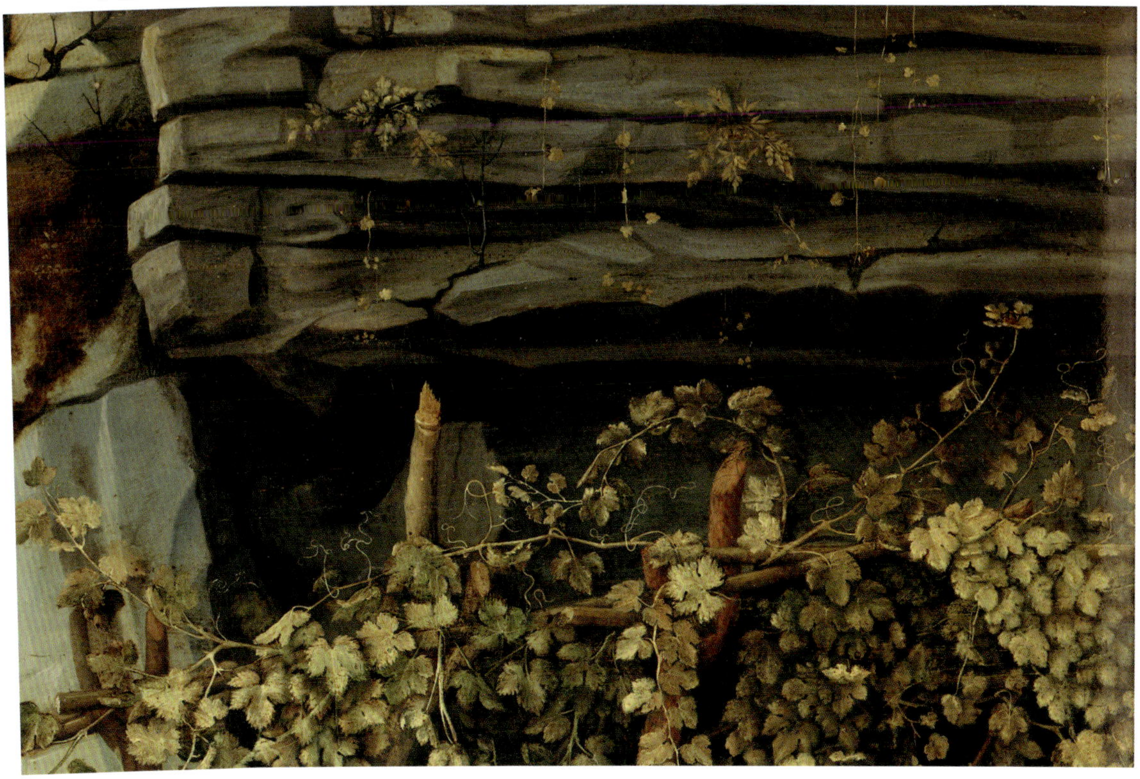

The rock face, which conveys steep vertical depth, shows the rough rectilinear forms that are the product of cleavage. These forms also resemble roughly dressed blocks of stone (fig. 3.13). Some of their surfaces appear polished and some have sharpened edges or patterns that appear to have been carved out with stonemasons' tools—chisels, claws, rasps, or trowels.[50] Bellini arrives at painterly contour by handling the brush to jab and pick at stone forms, so that painting models itself upon stone carving.[51] Additionally, the monochrome of the middle ground, its gray-blue tonality, allies this part of the painting with stonework. Meanwhile, the depicted rock face itself approaches architecture. The compressed planes above the hermitage read as either a lintel or cornice projecting lines of molding. Five dark gray lithic strata, fractured and sprouting weeds, bridge and surmount the vertical sides of the cave's entrance (fig. 3.14).

Francis's shelter and study, with its grape vines and framework of broken branches, is depicted in a pastoral mode. Despite its location in "the desert," his abode appears idyllic and verdant, with little evidence of the hardship of rural life, such as to appeal to the city dweller.[52] Fittingly, the geo-architectural formations of the textured blocks in the middle ground suggest parallels with the architectural feature known as rusticated ornament (*opus rusticum*). Connoting naturalness and solidity, this type of course and rough stonework is visible on fifteenth-century Renaissance Venetian buildings,

Fig. 3.14. Detail from Giovanni Bellini, *Saint Francis in the Desert*, c. 1476–78. Oil on panel (overall 124.6 × 142 cm; image surface 124.1 × 140.5 cm). Frick Collection, New York. Henry Clay Frick Bequest, 1915 (1915.1.03).

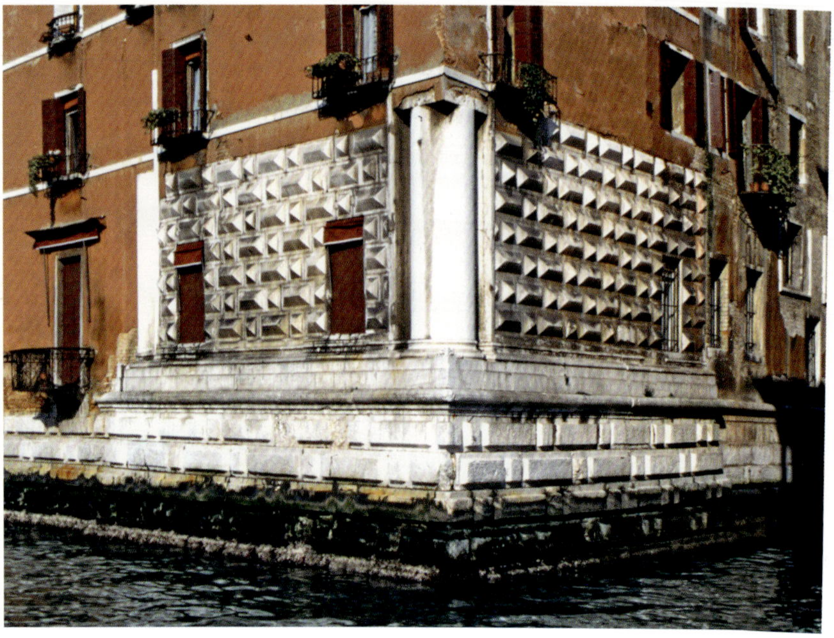

most enigmatically on the so-called Cà' del Duca, which was begun in 1457 and left unfinished.[53] Attributed to Bartolommeo Bon, this fragment of a palace floating on the Grand Canal presents a highly refined and stylized version of the naturally occurring blocks in Bellini's painting (fig. 3.15). At the foundation level, near the water emerge rows of rough-faced blocks. Above this are superimposed stacks of course stonework and diamond motifs sculpted in high relief. The panels in the foundation read as shining bright white; in the story above, the diamond patterned blocks cast shadows: the stones become a middle gray and fully dark hue when observed from the side. Such rustication transfers chiaroscuro effects, often thought to be the domain of painting, to the medium of architecture. Doorways and portals displaying variations of rusticated motifs would later feature in such architectural treatises as Sebastiano Serlio's *Extraordinary Book of Doors* (1551).[54] Bellini explores rustication's fluid relationship between architecture cut into living rock and dressed masonry.

STRATIFIED TIME

Of the cornice, Leon Battista Alberti writes in *De re aedificatoria* (3:9) that this type of molding requires care from the architect: its position on a facade's upper reaches gives it visual prominence; its structural role is to bind different parts of a construction at the point where it is most likely to give way.[55] Hence, a cornice should express the stable tectonics of a construction. But Bellini's molding is fissured. There are weeds growing out of the cornice (see fig. 3.14). Below that, grapevines hang from the wood structure. This vegetation leads

Fig. 3.15. Bartolomeo Bon and others, detail of stone base from the *Cà' del Duca*, begun 1457. Rio del Duca, Venice.

the eye downwards toward the darkness of the portal in the rock face—as it were, a massive opening in the ground. The cracks effected by cleavage break up the rock face into layer on layer. They insert the desert scene deep into vertical space, and simultaneously through stratified time to the distant past.

To be sure, not until the seventeenth century were theories conceived according to which the passage of time could be fathomed by studying a sequence of superimposed layers of sediment, such that the deeper one progressed into the earth, the further back in time one went.[56] Even so, a passage from Alberti's fifteenth-century treatise on architecture, written a generation before the Bellini painting, intimates this temporal understanding of stratification well before its scientific codification. Describing the work of "perscrutatores" (prospectors) who locate hydraulic sources in the earth, Alberti writes that these water seekers "have observed that the whole crust of the earth, and mountains in particular, consists of page-like strata, some denser, some more rarefied, some thicker, some thinner." Aware of geological depth, the prospectors note that "in mountains these skins are heaped and piled up one above the other [. . .] the layers run in continuous steps from either side of the mountain to the very center" (*De re aedificatoria*, 10:4).[57] The successive layers of stone not only formed mountains over the course of time; these strata also indicate the passage of time.

Alberti's conception of geologic layers as "pages" or "skins" is highly suggestive if we intend to read Bellini's depicted geology as itself metaphoric for visualizing layers of a superimposed temporal sequence. Located at some remove from the city—at a temporal remove from the futurity of the New Jerusalem—Francis's living conditions are likened to an Edenic primordial habitation. Yes, this is the wilderness, but it is a wilderness that provides necessary and ample materials for human dwelling (fig. 3.16). Vitruvius, who was widely read in the Venetian ambient in the late fifteenth century, described the early humans who built the first dwellings: "they began, some to make shelters of leaves, some to dig caves under the hills, some to make of mud and wattles places for shelter, imitating the nests of swallows and their methods of building" (*De architectura*, 2.1.2).[58] A woodcut in Cesare Cesariano's translation of Vitruvius, published in Como in 1521, shows early humans weaving together branches and gathering rocks in order to build the earliest abode (fig. 3.17).[59] In Bellini's painting, the structure of woven branches around the cave portal hence recalls the organic origins of architectural form.

Bonaventure, the Franciscan theologian and philosopher who wrote Saint Francis's biography, believed that in his communion with animals, the saint achieved integration with an Edenic paradise that preceded the Fall.[60] Other hermit saints living in the wilderness, such as Jerome, were also considered "new Adams."[61] Bellini's painting, by embedding the figure of Francis within the stony landscape—along with a donkey, a heron, and a rabbit—likewise conjures a time before humans were alienated from nature. The hospitable wilderness presents itself as a return to the Garden of Eden.

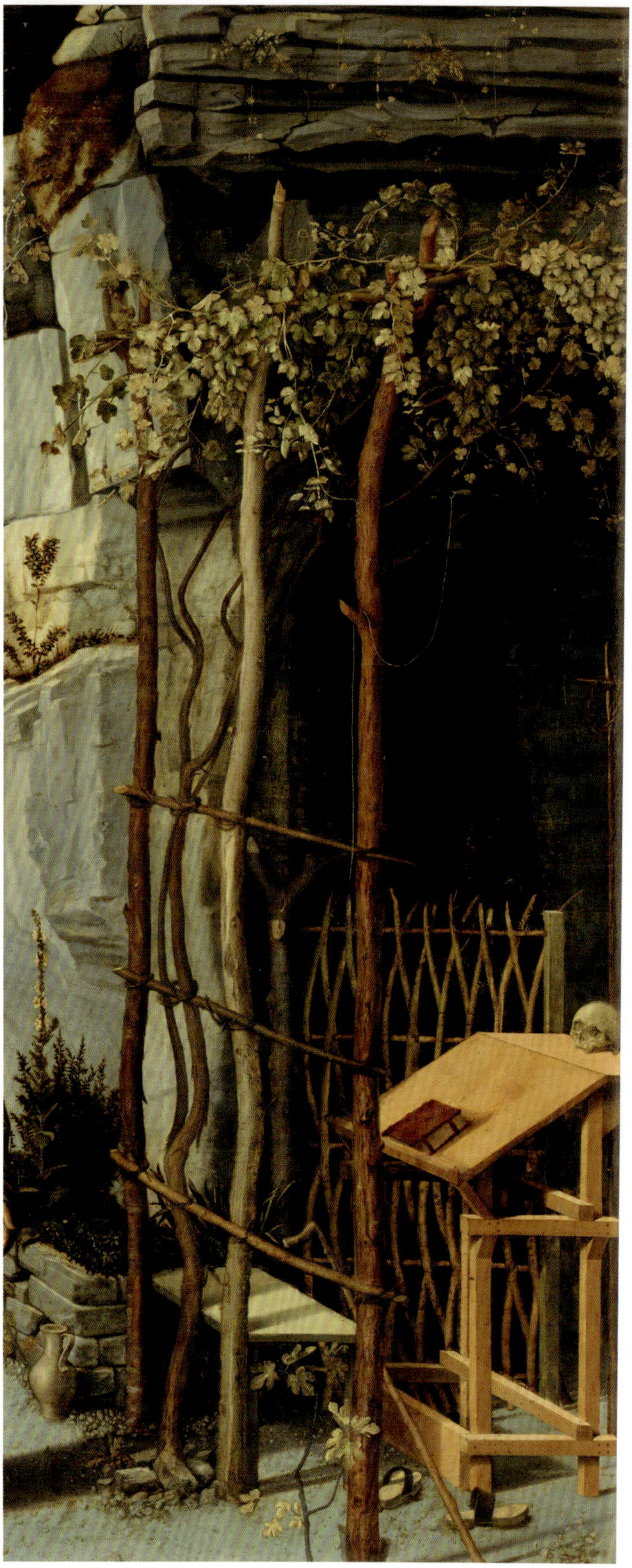

Fig. 3.16. Detail from Giovanni Bellini, *Saint Francis in the Desert*, c. 1476–78. Oil on panel (overall 124.6 × 142 cm; image surface 124.1 × 140.5 cm). Frick Collection, New York. Henry Clay Frick Bequest, 1915 (1915.1.03).

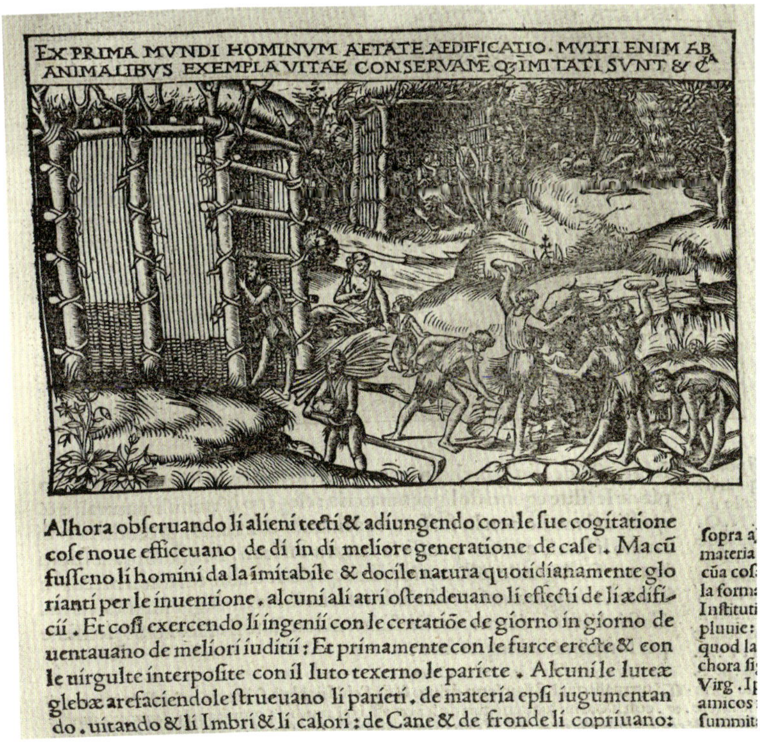

EX PRIMA MVNDI HOMINVM AETATE AEDIFICATIO. MVLTI ENIM AB ANIMALIBVS EXEMPLA VITAE CONSERVAM̃E Q; IMITATI SVNT & C^A

Alhora obſeruando li alieni tecti & adiungendo con le ſue cogitatione coſe noue efficeuano de di in di meliore generatione de caſe. Ma cũ fuſſeno li homini da la imitabile & docile natura quotidianamente glorianti per le inuentione. alcuni ali atri oſtendeuano li effecti de li ædificii. Et coſi exercendo li ingenii con le certatiõe de giorno in giorno deuentauano de meliori iuditii: Et primamente con le furce erecte & con le uirgulte interpoſite con il luto texerno le pariete. Alcuni le luteæ glebæ arefaciendole ſtrueuano li parieti. de materia epſi iugumentando. uitando & li Imbri & li calori: de Cane & de fronde li copriuano:

Meanwhile, the grapevine, whose spry tendrils demonstrate Bellini's mastery of curvilinear form, bear Eucharistic associations and implicitly shift the viewer's attention forward in time: Christ's blood redeems the fall of humankind and its banishment from Eden.[62]

THE ROCK OF GOLGOTHA

In the middle ground, Bellini attends to the visual manifestation of a sudden event. Indicating abrupt motion, the fissures that break the tower of stone into an irregular grid of rough-hewn blocks evoke the climax of biblical narrative: Christ's Crucifixion and powerful natural and supernatural events that followed. The Gospel of Matthew recounts that after Christ died, "the curtain of the temple was torn in two from the top to the bottom. And the earth quaked, and the rocks were rent. And the graves were opened: and many bodies of the saints that had slept arose" (Matthew 27:51–52). In this succession of short clauses, the jarring rhythmic pattern and passive voice that leaves the agent unnamed evoke Old Testament theophanies—the breaking through of God's presence into the physical world.[63] In 1 Kings 19:11, the Lord appears to the prophet Elijah through billowing gusts and the rending of the ground: "And behold the Lord passeth, and a great and strong wind before the Lord over throwing the mountains, and breaking the rocks in pieces."[64] The earthquake on Golgotha also has typological parallels with the prophecy of Isaiah

Fig. 3.17. Cesare Cesariano, "The First Human Dwellings." Woodcut. From *Di Lucio Vitruvio Pollione De architectura libri dece*, 1521.

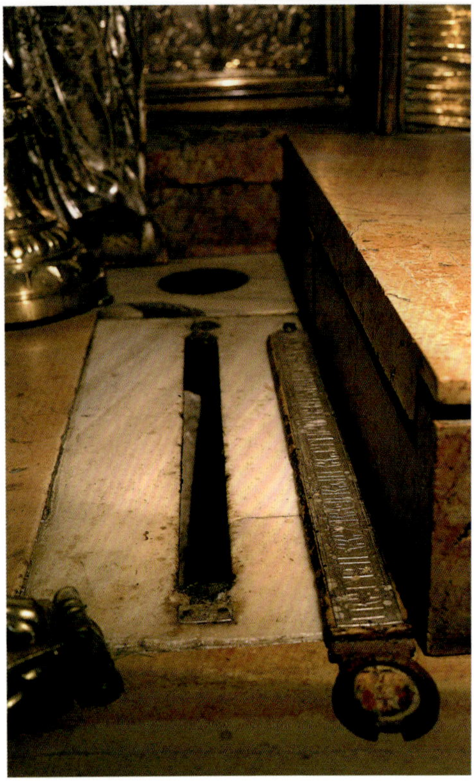

24:19–20: "with breaking shall the earth be broken, with crushing shall the earth be crushed, with trembling shall the earth be moved." In the Vulgate, the repetition of the hard sounds of Cs and Ts evoke the cracking of the earth: "Confractione confringetur terra, contritione conteretur terra; commotione commovebitur terra." In the Hebrew, the guttural repetition of H sounds produces more of the sense of upheaval, as though the earth were turning over on itself: "ro'ah hit'roaah haaretz por hit'Por'rah eretz mot hit'mottah aretz / no tanu eretz kashikor v'hit'nod'dah kam'lunah v'khavad aleyha posh'ah v'naf lah v'lo tosiyuf qum."[65]

In the Church of the Holy Sepulchre in Jerusalem, the Rock of Golgotha, also known as the Mount of Calvary, is incorporated in the Chapel of the Crucifixion. Fissures in the rock, believed to have been rent in the wake of Christ's death, are currently visible under glass. A marble plaque and Greek inscription citing the verses from Matthew, presumably installed in the nineteenth century and removed during the course of archaeological restorations from around 1960 to 1980, once covered these fissures (fig. 3.18).[66] Yet before these interventions concealed the rock from view, the clefts, fissures, and apertures in stone were readily available to pilgrims' sight and touch. As Yamit Rachman-Schrire has demonstrated, late antique and medieval travelers consistently described and meditated on the form, narrative reference, and allegorical meaning of these cracks. As presented in these travel accounts, cracks opened up physical and metaphorical apertures through which the body and mind of the pilgrim could enter into and testify to a sensorial encounter with sacred history.[67]

Rachman-Schrire's observations merit summary here. The anonymous author of the *Itinerarium* (c. 570), identified as a pilgrim from the northern Italian town of Piacenza, writes that on reaching the Holy City he prostrated himself and kissed the ground. Inside the Lord's Tomb, as he describes it, "you can see the place where he was crucified, and on the actual rock there is a bloodstain. Beside this is the altar of Abraham [. . . and] next to the altar is a crack, and if you put your ear to it you hear streams of water."[68] The crack becomes a resonant cavity, rich with acoustic sensation. The pilgrim from Piacenza not only sees, but listens to the Holy Sepulcher. The crack deepens his immersion in the tomb's history and its connection to an aquiferous underground.

Fig. 3.18. Fissure said to have been caused by the earthquake at the moment of Christ's death, near the Greek Orthodox altar, Calvary. Church of the Holy Sepulchre, Jerusalem.

Correspondingly, in the Bellini picture, a spout juts out at the point where the central fissure that cuts across the picture terminates. An underground channel or stream is thus implied that irrigates the rock and enables it to sprout lush vegetation. Like the other signs of cultivation in the picture, the spout indicates that the "desert" is in fact a tamed wilderness. In the overwhelming sense of quiet that this picture constructs, water trickling from a spout offers an acoustic impression of liquid spilling into the abyss.[69]

Other pilgrimage accounts of Jerusalem emphasize that pilgrims to the Rock of Golgotha treated its depressions and cracks as points of entry where they might physically introduce themselves to the event of Christ's crucifixion and bring themselves closer to his former corporeal presence. In his travel narrative, the twelfth-century German pilgrim Theoderich describes how "pilgrims plunge their head and face" into the hole in the Rock where the cross was once inserted "out of the love and respect that they bear to him who was crucified." In a type of baptism—a descent into emptiness instead of water—the traveler temporarily exchanges Adam's skull for his own, and puts himself into a grave in order to emerge again. To the right, Theoderich continues, Mount Calvary "displays a long, wide, and very deep rift in the pavement, where the rock was rent asunder when Christ died. Yawning above and in front with a frightful cleft, it proves that the blood which flowed from Christ's side as He hung upon the cross found its way quite down to the earth."[70]

The crack receives and directs the flow of Christ's blood away from his body and channels it deep into the earth. Like the stream that irrigates the rock in Bellini's painting, Christ's blood will change the nature of the earth itself from hard and hostile to pliant and nourishing. The image of Christ's blood trickling down into the cracks "quite down to the earth" can also be brought into connection with the viewer's "entry into the picture" along the cracks. Through these channels, the viewer's sensorial reception of imagery becomes the fructifying juice, as it were, that allows the picture to spout forth in the imagination of reader and viewer.

Pilgrimage accounts written in the years contemporary with the Frick Bellini reiterated this fascination with the clefts and apertures in the Rock of Golgotha. Felix Fabri, another Dominican friar, composed an account of "wandering"—his *Evagatorium*—after his two journeys to the Holy Land in 1480 and again in 1483–84.[71] Fabri writes that, on entering the chapel of Mount Calvary, "now before our eyes was displayed that wondrous stone, that desirable rock." Beholding the socle-hole in which the cross was inserted, the pilgrim exclaims, "no one was there who could withhold himself from tears and cries." Calling for the breaking of the heart in sight of the rending of the most obdurate matter, he rhetorically asks, "Who could have so hard a heart that it would not be rent in that place, where he beheld before his eyes the hardest rock to have been rent?" (quis enim tam durum cor habere posset, quod non scinderetur in loco, ubi oculis suis videt scissam petram durissimam?). Fabri then describes the crack that is believed to have formed after Christ's death. He sees it, touches it, and attempts to enter it: "We went up to this rent one after another, and kissed it, putting our heads into it and as much of our bodies as we could." In these accounts in which pilgrims placed their bodies inside the breach in stone, there is an ecstatic

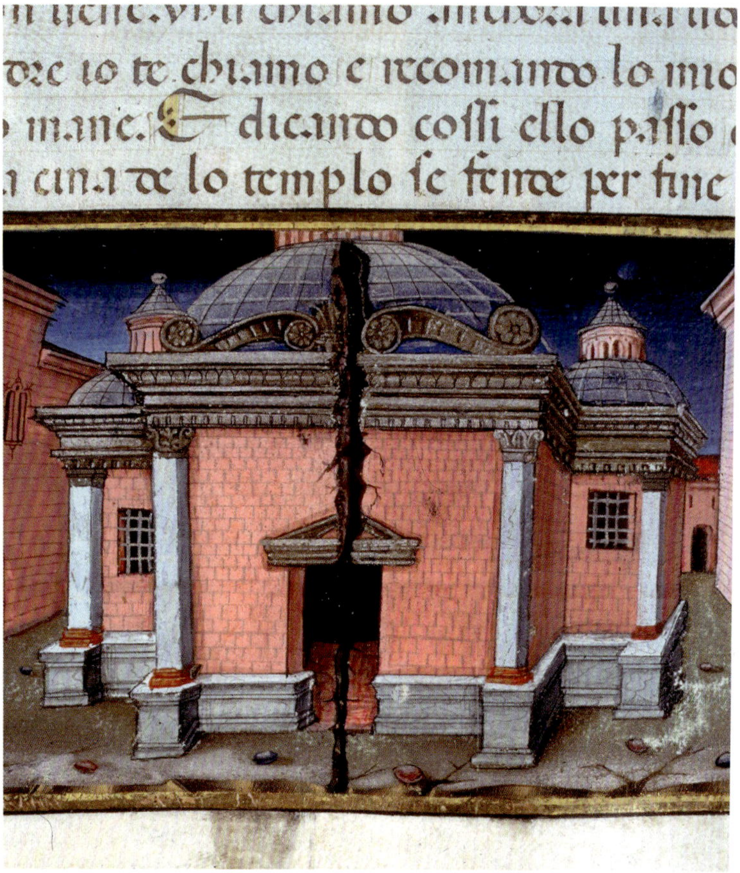

Fig. 3.19. Cristoforo de' Predis, *The Temple Destroyed after the Death of Christ*, 1476. Miniature on vellum (6.98 × 12.7 cm). Il Codice Varia 124, c. 119v. Biblioteca Reale, Turin.

interpenetration of body and ground, just as Christ's blood was understood as having used this entry to penetrate and revitalize the earth.[72] This circulation takes new form as streams of pilgrims come to the holy site in order to return home and bear witness.

Key examples in fifteenth-century northern Italian imagery related to the Holy Sepulcher combine modes of visualizing space to figure the crack as a vehicle for devotional viewership. Folio 199v of the famous *Varia 124* (Biblioteca Reale, Turin), an illuminated manuscript of the New Testament executed by the Milanese artist Cristoforo de' Predis for his patron Galeazzo Maria Sforza, the duke of Milan, depicts the Temple destroyed after Christ's death (fig. 3.19). The perspectival scheme directs the eye onto the stage of the Temple's urban setting. Superimposed on the central orthogonal line is a vertical fissure. It runs down the entire length of the miniature, from the torn temple veil to the rocks opening up the graves of saints. Breaking the temple in two, the crack enlarges the portal, as if to invite the eye to enter into the depths of the Holy Sepulcher.[73] The minuscule scale of the de' Predis miniature with its severed groundwork does not draw in the physical body of its viewers. Something equally profound is called for—imaginative entry.

LIQUID WAX

In the legend upon which Bellini's painting is based, the rock of La Verna draws Francis's body inside itself. The painting depicts Francis standing against a tower of stone, alone on the mountain (fig. 3.20). Among the mountain's crags, in its openings and recesses, the saint found salvation in addition to solitude. The *Little Flowers* recounts the following miracle. During the Feast of the Assumption—the miraculous event when Mary is taken bodily into heaven—Francis undertook a holy fast on the mountain "with great abstinence and severity, mortifying his body." One day, moved by the spirit, he emerged from his cell and decided to pray inside a cavity hollowed out from a rock. Below, "a horrible and fearful precipice" plunged "at a great drop to the ground." The Devil suddenly appeared. Having nowhere to flee, the saint "immediately turned around, with his hands and face and his whole body against the rock." God never lets his servants suffer more than they can endure, the narrator recounts. And so, by a miracle, the rock to which Francis clung "yielded itself to the form of his body," taking hold of him. "As if he had put his hands and face into some liquid wax," the narrator continues, "the shape of his face and hands was imprinted onto that rock." The saint thus escaped the Devil.[74]

In this miracle of "liquid wax," Francis's body passes through different states. He mortifies his flesh and crouches inside a cavity. Later visual interpreters of the episode, such as the seventeenth-century artist Jacopo Ligozzi, chose to emphasize the saint teetering at the brink of an abyss (fig. 3.21).[75] Yet the most significant transformation in this episode congeals his body into rock. As if to provide evidence of the miracle to future observers, Francis's face and hands are impressed into the liquefied stone as a seal is pressed into wax. This imprinting was the chief means of authentication in early modern Europe. Writing in 1390, the Franciscan friar Bartolomeo of Pisa declared that the imprint of Francis's hands in the rock "appears to the discerning today."[76] The image of melting wax itself recurs in period writings about Francis. Ubertino da Casale's mystical work *The Tree of the Crucified Life of Jesus*, itself written on La Verna in 1305, recounts that when Jesus appeared to Francis, the saint's heart "turned to wax, melting inside him." Ubertino further explains that "divine love has the power to melt [. . .] and the power to shape, as wax flows onto the mold of a seal."[77] Instead of describing the metamorphosis of an inner affective state, the story of the miracle on La Verna involves a physical transformation that merges figure with ground. The cliff "hollowed itself out" (si cavò), a reflexive verb that expresses how the ground manages to undo itself around the form of the saint's body. Ironically, Francis gets out of trouble (a situation that can be expressed in Italian as *cavarsene*—to extract oneself) by merging with the rock face (cave). In turning away in fear and imprinting his face and palms into the wall, Francis enacts a union between fore- and background. The miracle creates a form of sculptural relief, the negative impression of the figure, as in a die or stamp. The position of Francis's body is transient, but its imprint is not.

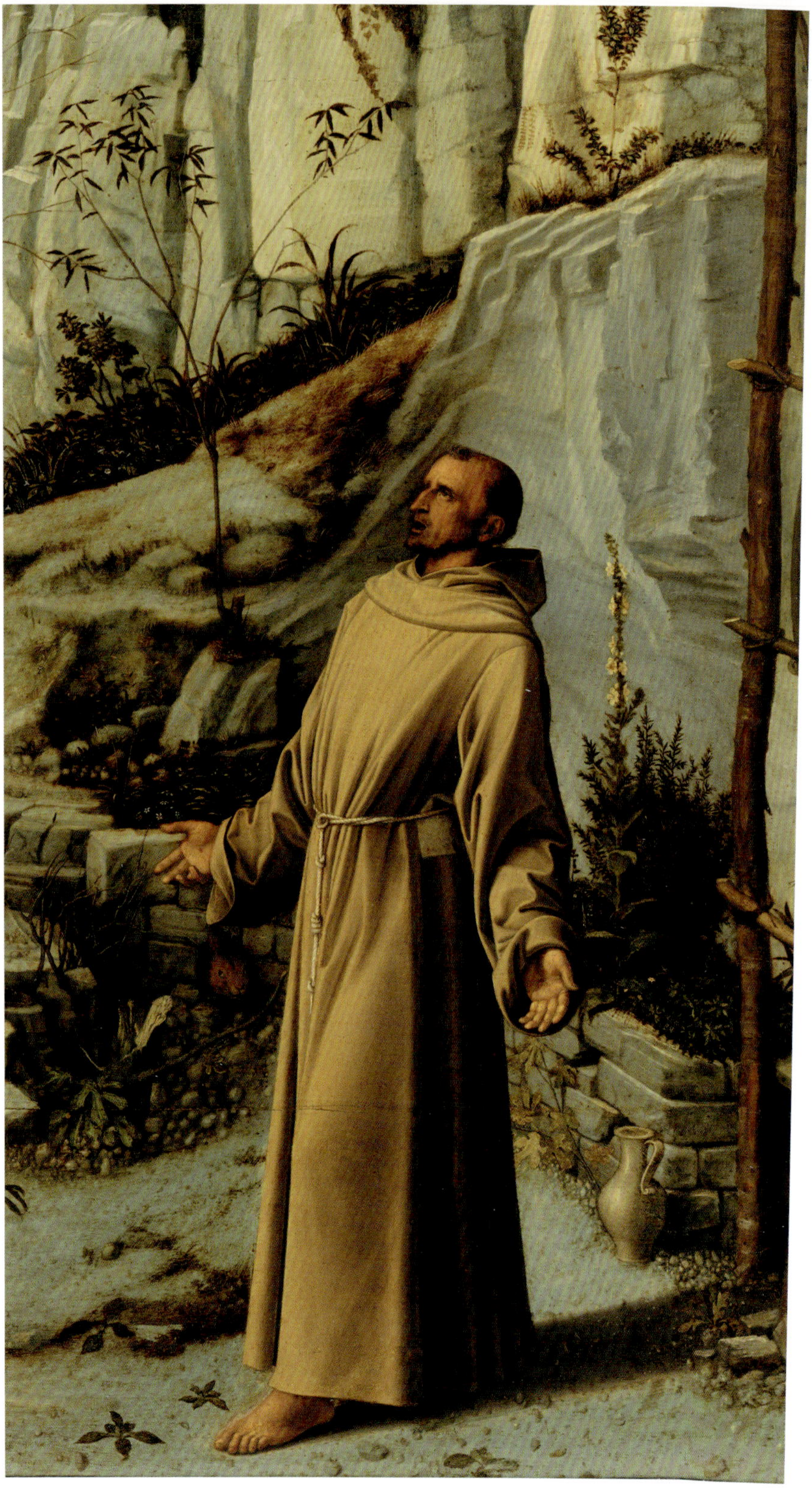

Fig. 3.20. Detail from Giovanni Bellini, *Saint Francis in the Desert*, . 1476–78. Oil on panel (overall 124.6 × 142 cm; image surface 124.1 × 140.5 cm). Frick Collection, New York. Henry Clay Frick Bequest, 1915 (1915.1.03).

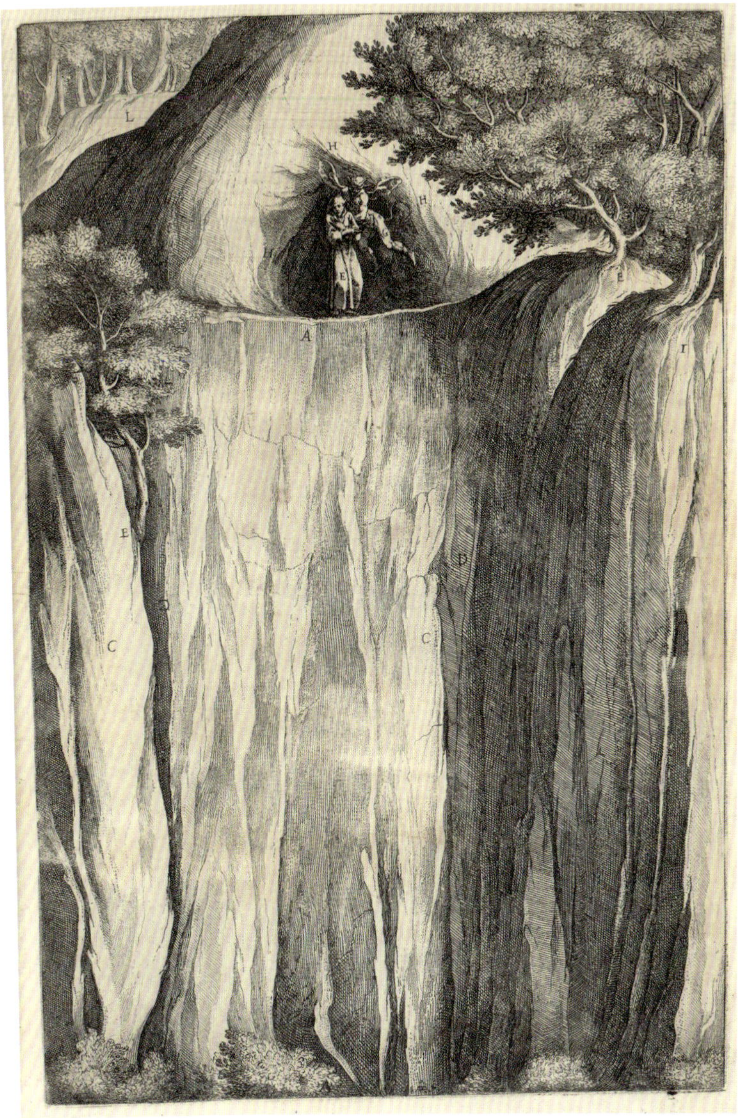

Fig. 3.21. Jacopo Ligozzi, print made by Raffaello Schiaminossi, "The Temptation of Saint Francis." Etching (book 43.3 × 30 × 1.8 cm). From Fra Lino Moroni, *Descrizione del Sacro Monte della Vernia*, 1612. National Gallery of Art, Washington, DC. Acquisition funded by a grant from The B. H. Breslauer Foundation, 2013 (2013.67.9.15).

Drawing upon precedent, Bellini molded the rock face behind Francis to allude to the miracle. The series of tunneling ridges behind the saint in Marco Zoppo's rendition of the Stigmatization, a work Bellini himself had occasion to study, has been interpreted as the rock face "caving in" to save the saint from the devil (fig. 3.22). In the Frick panel, Francis's brown robes glow against what Rutherglen and Hale have aptly termed the "glacial blue cast" of the escarpment.[78] At the same time, the triangular niche closely follows his contours, enclosing and containing the saint. In *The Passionate Triangle*, Rebecca Zorach has eloquently described how the geometric form of the triangle had deep theological resonance for certain early modern thinkers. According to them, the triangle, rising as it does from horizontal

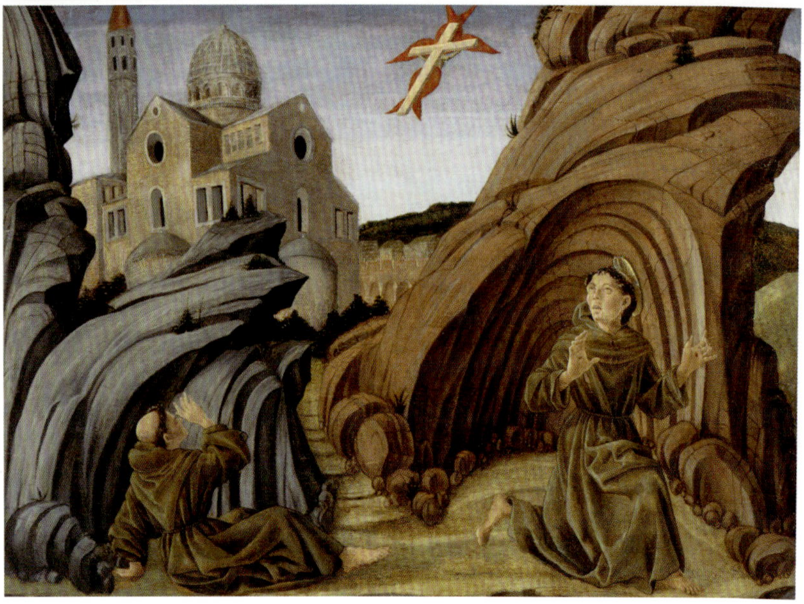

base to single point above, symbolizes the ascent from the terrestrial to the celestial, the material to the spiritual.[79]

While Francis embodies this notion of spiritual ascent, Bellini inflects the potentially symmetrical form of the triangle with jagged edges and stepwise bevels that embed the figure in the ground. The saint seems to sink into the rock face, which coalesces around his body. To describe the shadows in the depression adjacent to Francis's face, Bellini painted wet-in-wet: he dragged a brush loaded with brown paint through a light blue underlayer, still moist. For the cliff's jagged edges, he alternated strokes of dark paint and white highlights to convey strata of rock interleaved with shadows. As Rutherglen and Hale observe, "the molten, fluid quality of oil paint evokes with poetic immediacy the legendary melding of the rock to the saint's form."[80] The fractured yet malleable ground behind Francis's body becomes capable of inward recession as well as outward projection.

The ostensibly obdurate medium of stone thereby offers a model of flexible mediality. It could be said that through Bellini's use of the Francis legend, painting goes beyond a mimetic process, whose objective is to portray the ground, and becomes a metamorphic process, which acts to transform what it portrays. The artist begins from rock and turns the rock into fluid paint.

Fig. 3.22. Marco di Ruggero, called Marco Zoppo, *Saint Francis Receiving the Stigmata*, c. 1471. Tempera on panel (35.1 × 46.7 cm). Walters Art Museum, Baltimore. Acquired by Henry Walter with the Massarenti Collection, 1902 (37.544).

THE EMPTY CAVE

The crack provides a mode of entry into the picture that is more unfettered and flexible than the dictates of linear perspective can allow. Bellini deploys the crack in the Frick picture not only to direct the power of sight but also to ramify it. A network of fissures inscribes the irregular rock face, which terminates toward the panel's right in Francis's cell. With the skull, hanging cross, and crown of thorns at far right—a combination that was unusual in Franciscan iconography at this time—the cave acts to represent Christ's tomb.[81] The history of Franciscan ties with the Holy Sepulcher supports this iconological correlation: in 1342 Pope Clement VI issued *Gratiam agimus* and *Nuper carissimae*, bulls that officially appointed the Franciscans to act as custodians of the Holy Land, a privilege that continues to the present day.[82] The *Little Flowers* reiterates the link between Calvary and the rugged Apennine landscape that is so intimately connected with Francis. The text recounts how Francis, while in meditation at his hermitage, was "gazing at the form of the mountains and marveling at the great chasms and openings in the massive rocks. And he began to pray and then it was revealed to him by God that those striking chasms had been made in a miraculous way at the hour of Christ's passion when, as the Gospel says, 'the rocks split.'"[83] In the text itself, Francis in the act of beholding seems physically overwhelmed by the massive stones and their irregular lines. The echoing superlatives ("grandissimi fissure [. . .] sassi grandissimi") accentuate the magnitude of the clefts and rocks while diminishing Francis's relative size, which is further reduced as we imagine the saint kneeling in prayer.[84] In Renaissance antiquarianism, broken rocks and fissures are most often associated as topoi with weathering and the mournful passage of time.[85] Yet in the *Little Flowers*, chasms contain a prophecy of renewal. As the author states, it was foretold at the time of the earthquake in Jerusalem that the Passion of Christ would be renewed on La Verna ("perché quivi si dovea rinnovare la passione del nostro Signore Gesù Cristo"). The prophecy's fulfillment is testified through the imprinting of the stigmata on Francis's body. To justify and reinforce this connection, the author draws on the authoritative words of Mark ("secondo che dice il Vangelista"). Beyond referring to destructive collapse or rupture, La Verna's cracks disclose and reveal religious truth.

FULL EMPTINESS

In Bellini's painting of Saint Francis, the fissures and clefts in the rock face constitute a *Bedeutungsträger*, a visual instrument that actively carries meaning by its presence in the pictorial field. The crack, a symptom of stone's material behavior in the physical world, figures the background as a compositional framing device, an architecture that emerges from a natural substrate, and the venerated site of death and resurrection. What is more, this fracture in stone opens up the painting's middle ground to negative space, which bears further Christological resonance. The bell string hanging against the cavity on the panel's far right-hand side allows the viewer to discern the cave's depth when it might otherwise appear as an opaque flat plane (fig. 3.23).

Bellini inserts such black zones in the pictorial field in other paintings as well, notably in the *Resurrection of Christ*, painted in the same period as the Frick painting, and now held in the Berlin Staatliche Museen.[86] The soldier's

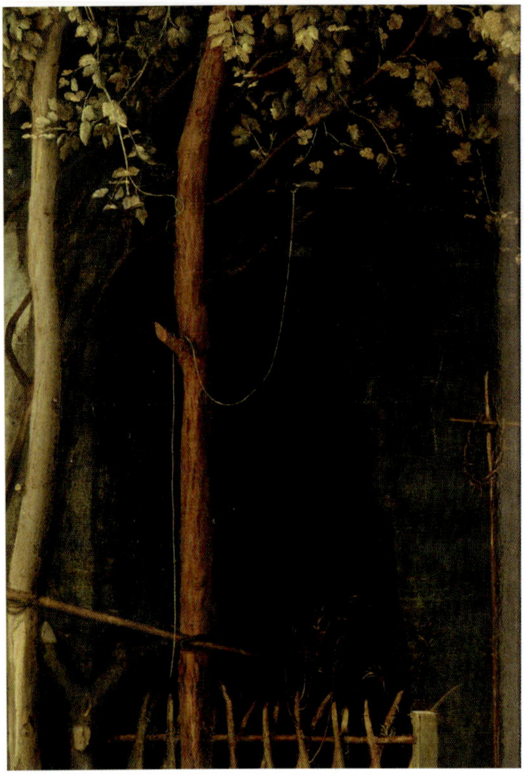

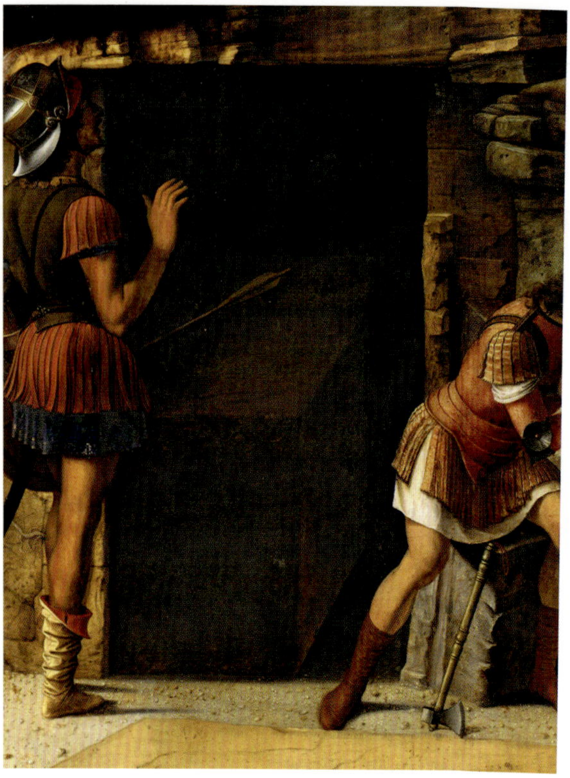

(LEFT)
Fig. 3.23. Detail from Giovanni Bellini, *Saint Francis in the Desert*, c. 1476–78. Oil on panel (overall 124.6 × 142 cm; image surface 124.1 × 140.5 cm). Frick Collection, New York. Henry Clay Frick Bequest, 1915 (1915.1.03).

(RIGHT)
Fig. 3.24. Detail from Giovanni Bellini, *Resurrection of Christ*, c. 1475–79. Oil on poplar wood, laid down on canvas (148 × 128 cm). Gemäldegalerie der Staatliche Museen zu Berlin.

hand, lifted in surprise at Christ's ascent, points to the tomb's empty depth. The stone slab recedes in the distance (fig. 3.24). While ostensibly indicating the Redeemer's elevation, the soldier's hand also touches the ungraspable dimensions of darkness. Commenting on the spatial qualities of color, Leonardo da Vinci observed that "black, like a broken vessel, is not able to hold anything."[87] In both the New York and Berlin panels, Bellini interposes black zones, which are mediated through cracks splintering the rock face, to convey the miraculous emptiness of the tomb.

This darkness alludes to what is not granted to view inside the cave: the absent and resurrected body. Heightened chiaroscuro conventionally represents relief and can thereby simulate tactility, as in the projecting pieces of broken rock above the cave opening, which seem to thrust toward the viewer. Yet irregular chiaroscuro—the uneven distribution of light and shade such as becomes evident farther to the right where the stone cornice flattens into a shadowed middle tone—can also dramatize the deferral of tactility as the surface texture becomes less tangible. Darkness and depth postpone, yet can promise, too, the encounter with the figural.

In the *Resurrection*, the empty cave entrance is the primary actor. In the painting of Saint Francis, the cave entrance, now to one side of the painting, is echoed by a second gaping hole or aperture: Francis's open mouth (fig. 3.25). Already in the painting's underdrawing, Bellini took pains to

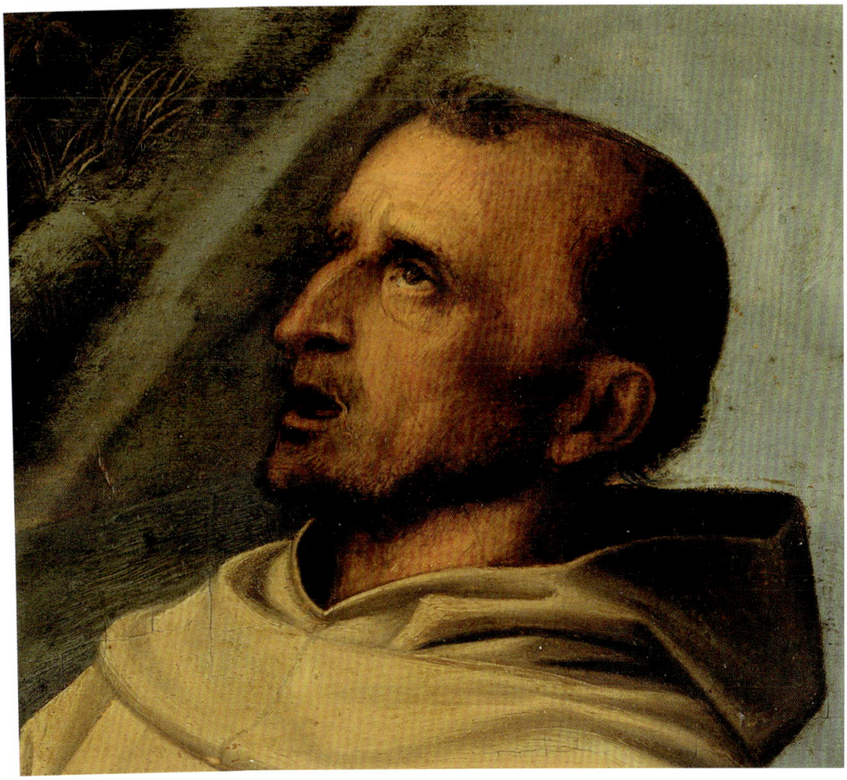

delineate the saint's face and mouth with a series of finely hatched lines.[88] He then laid in the shadows surrounding Francis's lower jaw and inside his mouth before describing the saint's reddish lips and tongue with thin layers of color. Francis's mouth is miniscule when compared to the scale of the painting; yet the dark area inside his hood duplicates the mouth's space, as though to amplify it. In constructing the other void—the cave's entrance—Bellini applied gradations of increasingly darker paint—moving from green-gray to black—to indicate recession into depth. The contours of the rock shelter echo the silhouette of Francis's hooded figure such that his body might snugly fit within. Whereas the outer rock face turned to liquid wax to contain Francis and thus save him from the devil, the cavern seems to promise to absorb him completely. It could be said that just as his body merges with the rock, Francis's soft mouth, about to speak or sing, at the same time becomes the cave.

The archaeologist Doug Bailey observes that holes are not simply voids or pockets of empty space. Introducing discontinuity or detour on a given surface, holes are visual events that "disrupt and alter perspectives." Concavities, in particular, "define boundaries between perceived parts," since they necessitate the presence of an edge, which draws attention to the passage between two distinct entities: surface and depth.[89] In the Bellini, the apertures of mouth and cave underscore by force of contrast the exterior of the

Fig. 3.25. Detail from Giovanni Bellini, *Saint Francis in the Desert*, c. 1476–78. Oil on panel (overall 124.6 × 142 cm; image surface 124.1 × 140.5 cm). Frick Collection, New York. Henry Clay Frick Bequest, 1915 (1915.1.03).

saint's face and the rock face. And yet, under the condition of their visual analogy and mediation by the dark folds in Francis's robe, these concave holes—one small, the other monumental—dissolves boundaries between figure and ground. Enmeshed in the harmonious chromatic range of the foreground's earth tones, the correspondence between open mouth and cave encourages the viewer to perceive the dissolution of Francis's body in the masses and caverns of La Verna. The mutual dissolution of figure into ground posits an eventual return to an elemental unity.

THROUGH THE MARSHES

In the earliest known written source on the painting, the author's sensitivity to format, orientation, and depth of field loosens the centrality of the figure that tends overwhelmingly to govern art writing, and introduces a degree of complexity in sixteenth-century conceptions of pictorial composition. In 1525, the Venetian connoisseur Marcantonio Michiel described the painting while making notes on works of art located in Venice and throughout Lombardy and the Veneto. More than a series of dry inventories, Michiel's handwritten observations on loose sheets of paper, which he compiled and revised in the course of two decades, have been properly characterized as blending reflections on style, provenance, historical categorization, materials, techniques, and artistic collaboration.[90] While Michiel's notes remained unpublished until 1800, they have been considered by scholars to constitute the beginnings in the Venetian ambient of an art critical lexicon whose terms had not yet been consolidated and codified.[91] In the physical manuscript, the frequent crossing out of words, insertions, revisions, and use of different inks are graphic testaments to the process whereby Michiel jogged his memory, reconsidered, and worked out his responses to artworks on the folio page.[92]

The rich, compressed, and often enigmatic nature of these notes is apparent in the entry on Bellini's *Saint Francis*, which Michiel saw in the private collection of the Venetian patrician Taddeo Contarini. Jotted down in bold script in dark brown ink, the entry appears toward the top of the folio with a blank space beneath, a mise-en-page that gives Michiel's words prominence. The description reads, "La Tavola de l' S.[an] Franc[esco] ꝺ nel deserto, a oglio, Fo opera d[e] Zuā[n] Bellino, cominciata da lui a M[esser] Zuān Michiel / e ha ū[n] paese propinquo finito et ricercato mirabilmente." (The panel of Saint Francis in the wilderness, in oil, was the work of Zuan Bellini, initiated by him for Messer Zuan Michiel, and [it] has a town nearby, marvelously finished and refined."

The painting's title as furnished by Michiel gives equal weight to person and place, to Francis and the setting, "deserto," an uninhabited place in contrast to the city. The preposition "nel" (in [the]) underscores the figure's insertion within its rugged surroundings, after Francis has removed himself from the city and withdrawn into the wilderness. Michiel also divides the entry into two parts, which themselves roughly correspond to the painting's main compositional parts of foreground and background. The first is the information concerning support, title, medium, and patron (coincidentally also named Michiel, though whether a close family connection existed between the two has not been confirmed).[93] The second is signaled with the clause beginning "ha" ([it] has), which identifies the feature of the nearby village, given that "paese" most likely refers in this particular instance to a piece of land that is cultivated and inhabited.[94] In imagining the choreography of Michiel's eye and hand, it seems plausible that the principal fissure in the rock face that separates the wilderness from the city prompted him to introduce a syntactic break in the entry, which is followed by a new clause referring to the background setting. He underscores the visual qualities of immersive depth (the title of the painting is given as *San Francesco* ***nel*** *deserto*) and recession into the near distance ("un paese propinquo").

Rosella Lauber has recently also called attention to another aspect of Michiel's ductus, which may lend insight into the painting's connection with an actual "desert" in the Venetian lagoon. Examining the manuscript's paleography, Lauber noticed that the writer first wrote "San Francesco d[. . .]", before crossing the "d" out and replacing it with the conjunction "nel." This lapsus indicates that Michiel, when observing the painting, may have initially been thinking of the Franciscan convent island of San Francesco *del* Deserto, located two to three hours away by gondola from the metropolitan center of Venice.[95] In 1220, on his return from a journey to the Levant, Francis was reported to have stayed on the island. In his biography of the saint, the *Legenda maior*, Bonaventure relates that during his sojourn there, Francis, walking "per paludes Venetiarum" (through the marshes of Venice) miraculously quieted the singing birds.[96] In the decades preceding and in the very years during which Bellini is believed to have executed his painting, the Observant branch of the Friars Minor sought dogal and papal sanction to restore worship and engage in continuous prayer on the island, a process that required repairing and enlarging the church dedicated to the stigmata.[97]

For the patron Zuan Michiel, Bellini's painting may have invoked the island's vigorous campaign of Observant devotional practice. In concert with the papal and dogal decrees, Bellini's groundwork can be said to support an implicit visual connection between the painting's rocky *deserto* and the Venetian lagoon. As Marilyn Lavin astutely observed, the rock ridge that flows like lava behind and past Francis echoes the shape of the saint's bare foot. Observant Franciscans rigorously adhered to the regulation against friars wearing shoes: "the rule of the discalced friars thus is likewise the rule of the rocks."[98] Francis here appears in fact to possess a pair of sandals, discarded beneath his lectern. Nevertheless, the correspondence between foot and liquid-like ground dramatizes the unstable and sensory qualities of the saint's barefoot perambulation "through the marshes of Venice." The island of Saint Francis del Deserto itself was described in a fifteenth-century papal bull as standing "in certain marshes and in the marine and watery parts of the diocese of Torcello."[99]

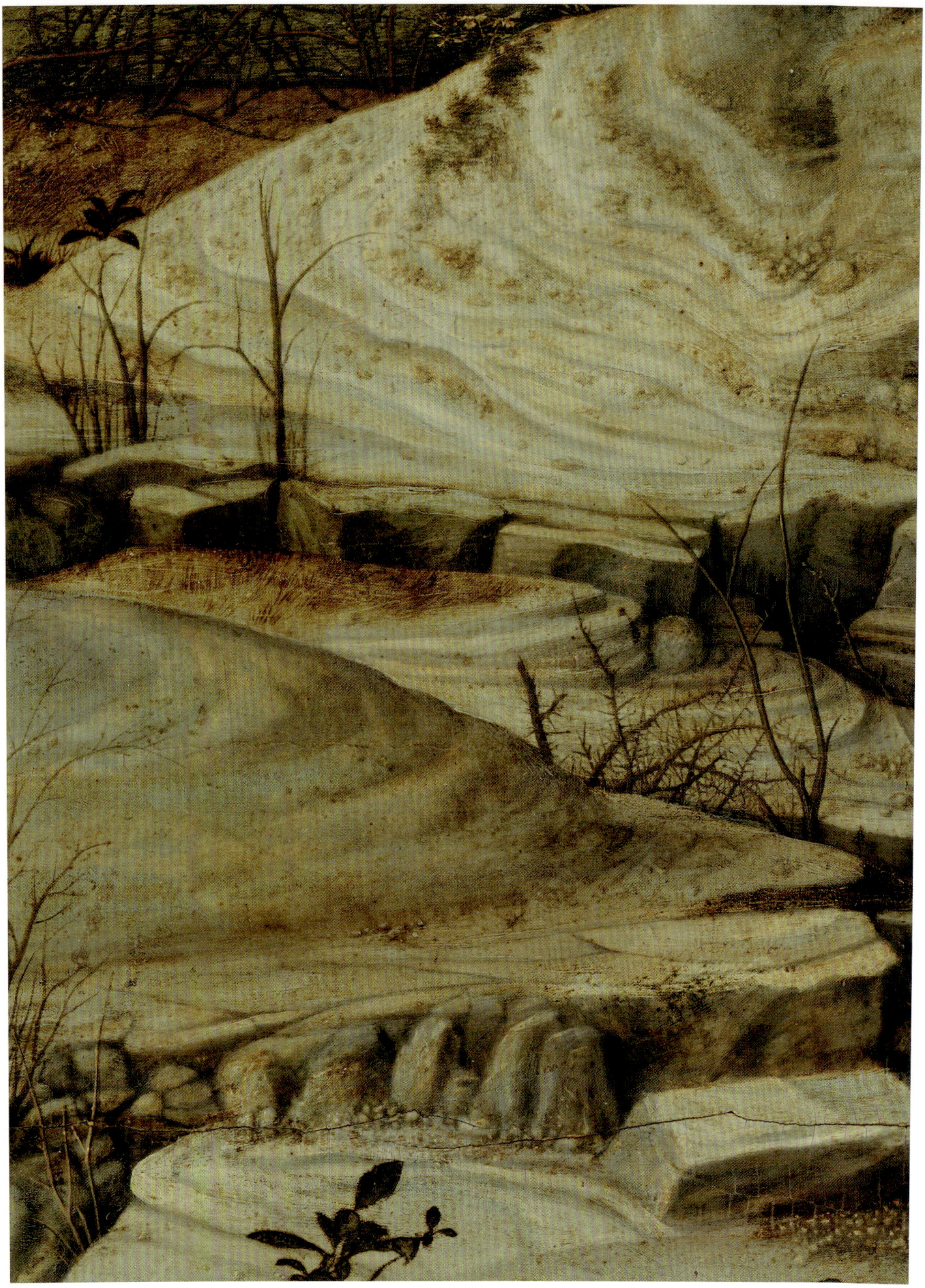

The inextricable intertwining of water and land in the painting's foreground gives further support to the shift in our discussion of Bellini's groundwork from crack to liquefaction, and from stonework as a model back to the liquid medium of paint. Hence, while the painting describes the mountainous desert of La Verna, we also see traces of an aqueous desert (fig. 3.26). The stone formations behind and next to Francis resemble a succession of pools that accumulate and overflow. Their syncopated formal rhythms recall how the tides alternately inundate and expose the mud flats, shallows, and marshes in Venice's unique estuarine environment.

Period representations of the lagoon used thinly applied layers of oil paint and subtle modulations of color to indicate the gradations of depth distinguishing sea, shallower water channels, and mud banks (fig. 3.27).[100] In stretching the geological topography of La Verna toward the marine environs of San Francesco del Deserto, Bellini likewise deployed successive underlayers to interleave stone with sea. The strategy of superimposition—which is seen in the painting's subject matter in the piling up of rocks in the cliff face and corresponds, in the painting's facture, to the accumulation of medial references (mosaic, relief sculpture, and architecture) and in its composition, to the synchronous presentation of narrative moments (the Crucifixion of Christ, and Francis's departure from civilization)—also extends to an enfolding of topographic allusions. Over the gray-greenish bed of rock to Francis's right, Bellini painted blurry splotches of brown pebbles. Their irregular grouping replicates the drift and flow of sediment beneath a current. In the same passage, faint gray contours alternate with expressive strokes of white impasto paint to evoke a cascade washing the surface of stone. The superimposed layers of translucent colors convey the impression of looking through, not at, an aqueous rock formation.

Farther toward the painting's bottom edge, reeds choke the splits and cracks articulated with jagged strokes of dark paint. On the lower bed of rock, curvilinear lines of dark paint on the gray blue stone suggest a smooth, liquid swirl. Amidst the stone's cool tones, Bellini also intermingled highlights of honey-colored paint as though to suggest the glint of warm light off water. Francis's habit is painted with the same rich brown, thereby implying close kinship between saint and stone. All kinds of ontological distinctions are being bridged here: near and far, past and future, solid and liquid, body and rock. Further below, toward the panel's extreme lower edge, Bellini's color combinations create other unexpected spatial congruences. The dark leaf hanging on the twig could mistakenly be seen as floating on the surface of a blueish-gray pool of water. Then immediately to the left, Bellini drags a broad swath of dark paint downward, which splinters off to indicate a sequence of stair-like clefts in the rock.

The material world appears unsettled and fluid, at least for a moment, before it solidifies again.[101] The obdurate material of stone moves between and passes through quasi-geological cycles of fragmentation, liquefication, and solidification.[102]

←

Fig. 3.26. Detail from Giovanni Bellini, *Saint Francis in the Desert*, c. 1476–78. Oil on panel (overall 124.6 × 142 cm; image surface 124.1 × 140.5 cm). Frick Collection, New York. Henry Clay Frick Bequest, 1915 (1915.1.03).

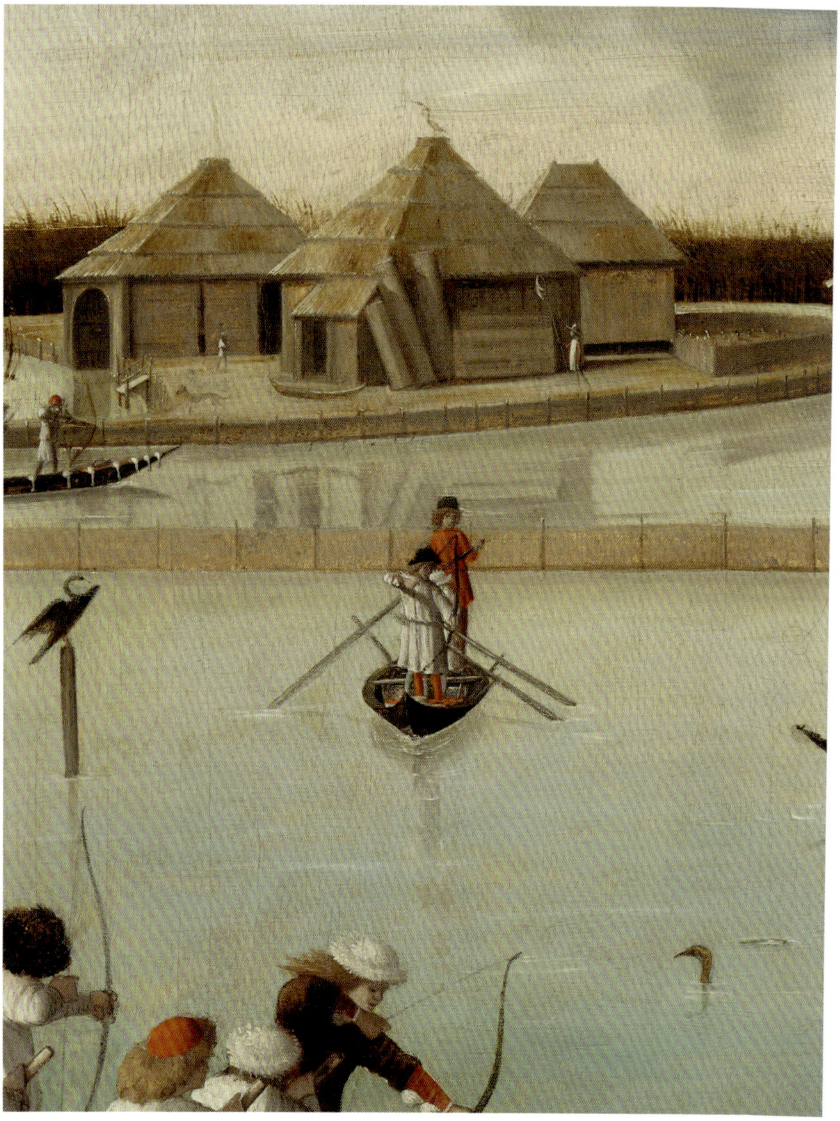

Fig. 3.27. Detail from Vittore Carpaccio, *Hunting on the Lagoon*, c. 1490–95. Oil on panel (75.6 × 63.8 cm). J. Paul Getty Museum, Los Angeles.

By ancient tenet, stone was considered a form of liquid, petrified. Alluding to the natural-historical ideas of Aristotle and Theophrastos, Seneca observes in his *Naturales quaestiones* (3.15.2–3) that "in the earth also there are several kinds of moisture," which "change from liquid to stone" (in lapide ex liquore vertuntur). Stone held on to a quantity of water in order for its elements to amalgamate.[103] In the painting, therefore, the lava-like creep might be seen in relation to the other hydrological sources in the landscape. Far in the distance, a river flows beneath the broken bridge (a symbol of Francis's role as builder of the Church). Meanwhile, at the panel's lower left, the drain spout implies the presence of a subterranean stream that drains into the crevasse below.[104] River and stream are coaxed or traversed by the products of human ingenuity. However, Bellini's groundwork in the foreground seems to describe a type of flow that passes through several distinct states.

One evocative description of lava flow specifically can be found in *De Aetna* (1496), a Latin dialogue concerning volcanic phenomena written by one of Bellini's patrons, Pietro Bembo.[105] Asked to describe the descent of lava in a volcanic eruption, one speaker in *De Aetna* remarks, "[S]treams of fire come swirling down in a thick flood as the flames drive them on, and spread all over the surrounding country [. . . ;] the flood then stands hardened like a glacier, until a second lot of streams come down [. . . and] as that one hardens, another inundation supervenes and does the same, and this happens again and again."[106] Moving between images of fire, stone, ice, and water, Bembo's verbs of action—"despumare" (swirl), "flui" (flow), "indurescere" (harden), "conglaciare" (freeze)—might well characterize the viscous flow of rock in the painting, which follows a successive cadence of "going ahead" and "pulling back."

More than merely alluding to the lagoon topographically, the foreground imagines Francis, while depicting him as stationary and erect, in the act of walking "per paludes Venetiarum," with emphasis on the preposition that signals motion in relation to place. The foreground condenses and enfolds the actions of continuous narrative into itself. Like Bachelard's honey, groundwork "concentrates and radiates."

NATURE'S *PATHOSFORMEL*

The legendary Giotto in Vasari's *Lives* generates his line with stone on stone. Bellini imagines stone as itself producing line. Preceding human interventions or even animal life, the crack is the original line, occurring spontaneously as a result of natural processes. Given its formal and semantic import in Bellini's painting, the crack might even be considered the earth's *Pathosformel*—an expression of the ground's animated and dynamic movement—which bears on the panel's representation of place and characterization of the saint.[107] As a further sign of the fissure's significance, Bellini applies his signature to the crack in the foreground (fig. 3.28). The *cartellino*, or small piece of parchment, that displays his name in humanist script is crinkled, echoing the rugged stone surface.[108] The twig that catches the cartellino grows up from below the picture, from out of the crevasse, pointing to the depths beneath the foreground. More than simply declaring authorship, the cartellino through its proximity to a significant site of geological cleavage and fracture indicates these phenomena as central principles informing the compositional logic, and therefore the meaning, of the picture.

Bellini thus might be said to locate his authorial presence in the ground of the image. Rather than reinforcing foundational notions of art making, this move puts pressure on them, opening up the picture to explore the transformation and transmutation of materials, media, and notions of line. The textured impasto of clouds in an ultramarine sky draws on relief effects

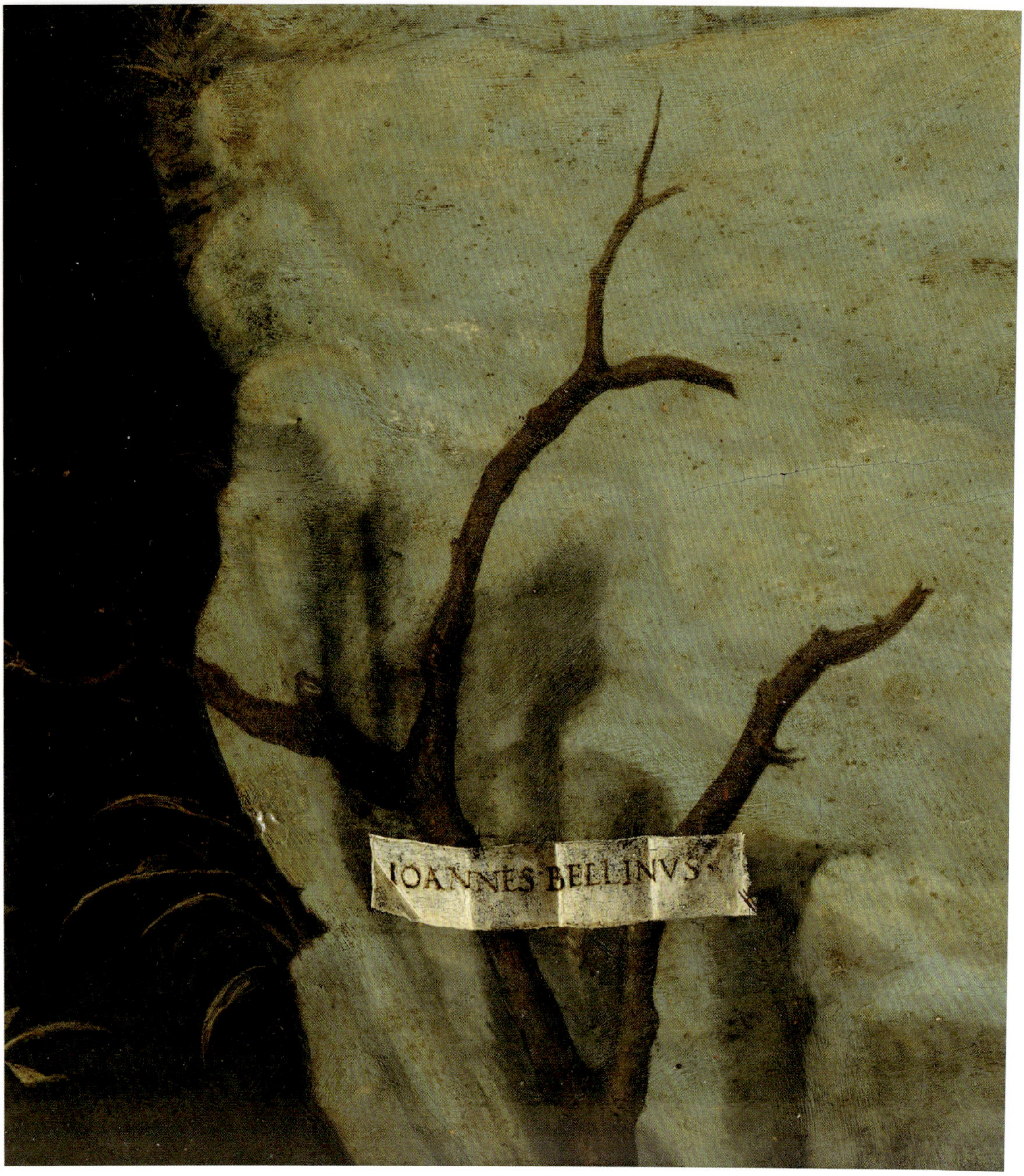

Fig. 3.28. Detail from Giovanni Bellini, *Saint Francis in the Desert*, c. 1476–78. Oil on panel (overall 124.6 × 142 cm; image surface 124.1 × 140.5 cm). Frick Collection, New York. Henry Clay Frick Bequest, 1915 (1915.1.03).

of gold ground, albeit through white lead and lapis lazuli, other mineral ores excavated from the earth. Radiant stone blocks approach the tessellation of mosaics and architecture nestled in living stone. The side of a cliff liquefies into wax, preserving the imprint of the figure. Rock erupts a viscous flow of paint that brings the mountain path to marshland. Stone splits to reveal an expanse of darkness that disrupts the beholder's calibration of surface and depth. Francis leaves the obscurity of his cave study to face a glittering gold ground transmuted into paint. In his meditation on mimetic stone and its fissures, Bellini locates a picture making that begins from below, in the ground and background.[109]

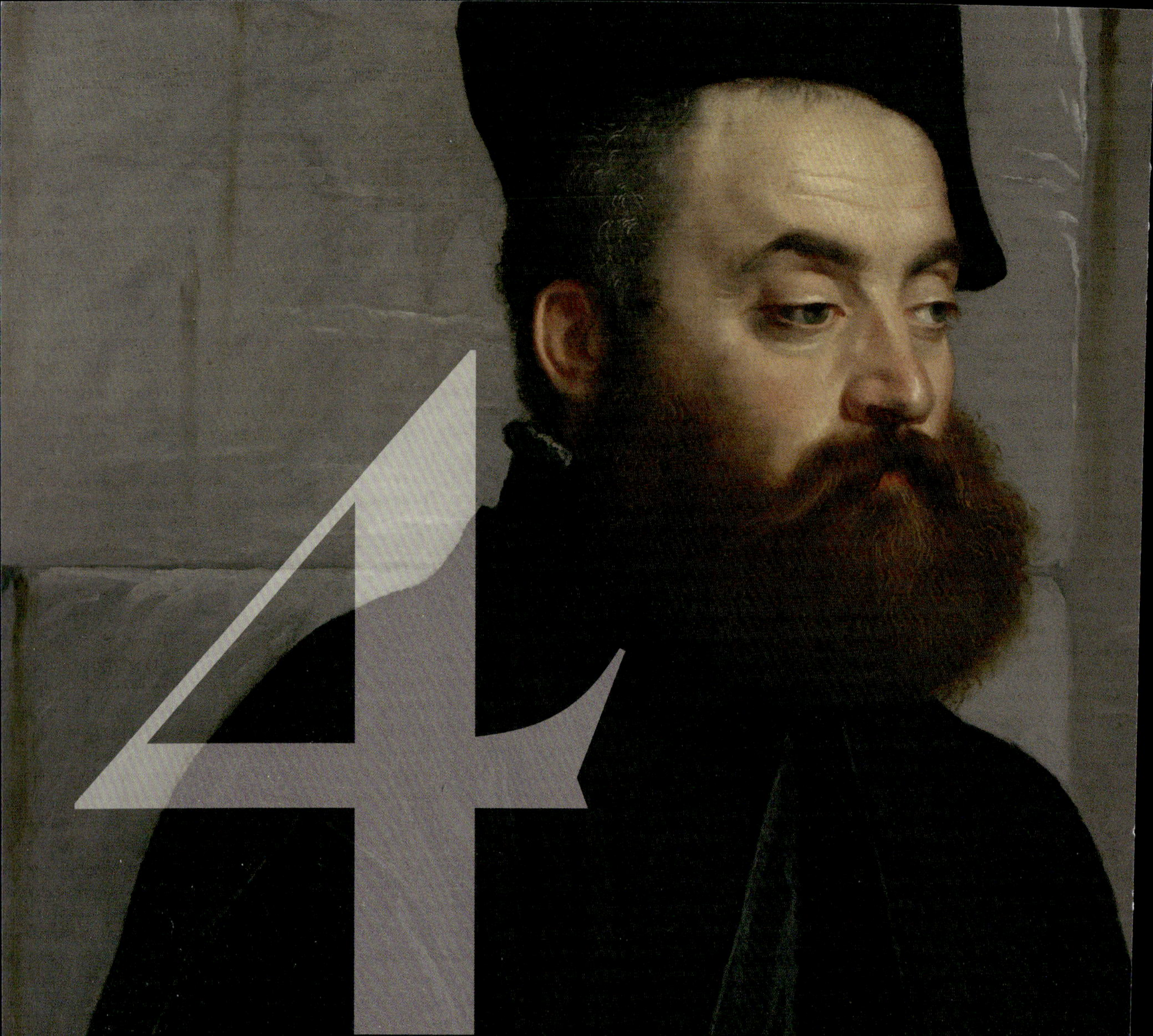
4

Articulation: Walled Figures, Figured Walls

Within this wall of flesh
There is a soul[.]

William Shakespeare, *The Life and Death of King John*, act 3, scene 3

In the Frick Bellini, Francis stands barefoot, supported by the radiant gray piano, or floor. While demonstrating moments of pliability, the stone platform nevertheless anchors the saint, holding him instead of allowing him to fall into the dark abyss. Francis's bodily stance is contingent upon his "circum"-stance—the area that surrounds his pose and motivates his posture. The steep cliff provides the context for the rock wall immediately behind him, the vertical structure that encloses and locates his figure. Alluding to Francis's salvation, the hollowed-out rock face is the berth from which his transfiguration will occur as *alter Christus*, another Christ.

As the setting for the mythical origin of painting and sculpture, the wall marks a boundary for figural presence and the discernment of form. As Pliny the Elder recounted (and as was discussed in chapter 1), the Corinthian maiden draws an outline around her lover's shadow on a wall. The tale refigures the wall from a structure of domestic enclosure to a liminal space of presence and absence. There the lover will pause for his portrait before setting off on his journey. The wall is therefore also a place of loss, since the lover is grasped only vicariously through the outlines of his profile. The wall first contains, then commemorates, the beloved.

In the Francis miracle, the divinely inspired wall is able to sustain the saint bodily and save him from a fatal descent—as it were, when the floor falls out from under him. In Pliny's tale, although the lover is released into the world and to his death, the vertical elevation retains his imprint. As monochromatic field, the wall becomes the site where painting thinks about what it is by thinking about what it can hold, and what is relinquished.

Detail, Figure 4.5

In other episodes from art literature, the wall in its bare state itself is found to contain meaningful forms. In his notebooks, Leonardo declares that if "you look at a wall splattered with stains or [inlaid] with a variety of stones" a resemblance to landscapes, battles, or "strange faces and costumes, and an endless variety of objects [infinite cose]" can be discerned.[1] Leonardo's amorphous marks on the wall or in the grain of stone itself offer themselves to the viewer's interpretive faculty. The wall can be thought of as a projection screen, first for the Corinthian maiden's desire—and loss—and then in the case of Leonardo, for the whole expanded field of unconscious activity.[2] For Bellini's Saint Francis, while the rock wall shows a remarkable formal elasticity, it becomes imprinted with one specifically meaningful image—the body of the saint in a state of miraculous deliverance. In all of these cases, the natural or built wall represents a world of matter that stands ready to reflect human experiences of erotic reminiscence, artistic fantasy, or spiritual transport. The wall contains the potential to evoke figuration beyond its plain planeness.

It is against these art theoretical and hagiographic contexts that we can interpret the pictorial positioning of figure against wall. The painting's ground, in the figure or trope of the depicted wall, becomes an unacknowledged actor that exposes and enfolds the body within its depths. In a type of feedback loop or cycle, the wall offers to view and then engulfs the subject. In portraits by the northern Italian artist Giovanni Battista Moroni (1520/4–79), this chapter's protagonist, the wall seems to represent a hermetic seal or denial of access. Even so, ground as wall is simultaneously shown to receive attributes of memory, affect, interiority, and motion that the figure itself declines to express. In these paintings, which were made almost a century after *Saint Francis in the Desert*, human characters and walls in the Renaissance picture can still be seen as entering into a fluid exchange of attributes. Hence, along a trajectory that starts from gold ground's mimetic potential, whereby figuration comes into and passes out of view, ground increasingly takes on the charge of narrative potential. In other words, the ground becomes the place of impending action, which is alluded to, even promised, and yet momentarily deferred.

AN INCONGRUOUS PAIR

There couldn't be a figure more incongruous with Bellini's Saint Francis than Moroni's so-called *Il cavaliere in rosa* (*The Man in Pink*) (fig. 4.1). Dated 1560, the portrait's sitter has been identified as the patrician Gian Gerolamo Grumelli, the scion of an aristocratic Bergamasco family.[3] In contrast to Francis's rough robes of brown sackcloth, Grumelli wears a magnificent costume of pink silk and silver thread. Though he was born more than three centuries after the historical Francis, the nobleman in his material status embodies what the saint himself had once been—before he forsook wealth, stripped himself bare, and pursued the ideal of Lady Poverty in "the streets and piazzas of the city," as

→

Fig. 4.1. Giovanni Battista Moroni, *Portrait of Giovanni Gerolamo Grumelli* (*The Man in Pink*), 1560. Oil on canvas (216 × 123 cm). Fondazione Museo di Palazzo Moroni, Bergamo. Lucretia Moroni Collection.

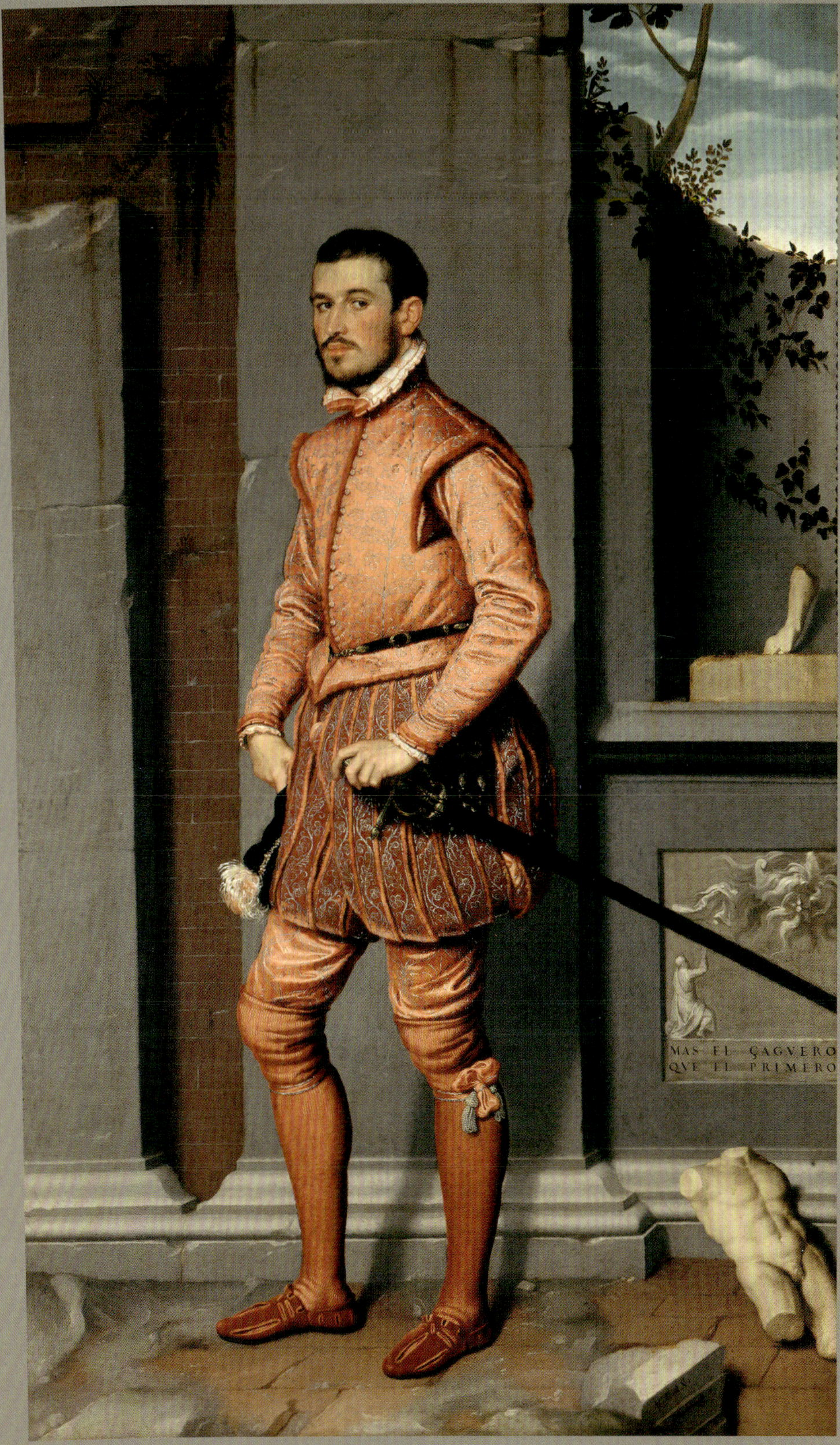
MAS EL ÇAGVERO
QVE EL PRIMERO

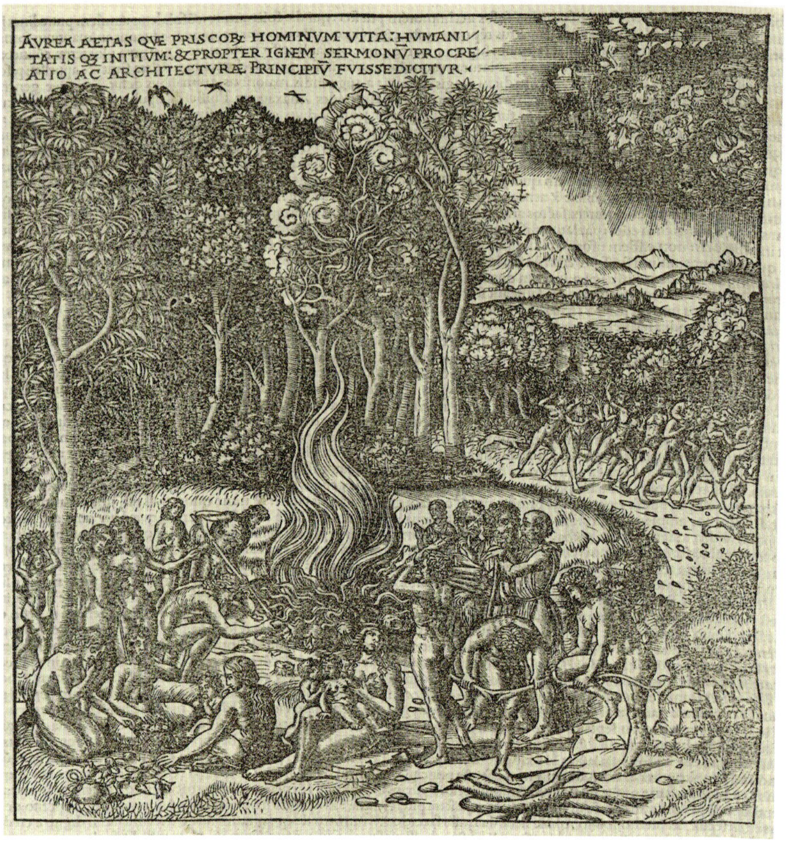

Fig. 4.2. Cesare Cesariano, "Discovery of Fire in the Golden Age." Woodcut (20.9 × 18.3 cm). From *Di Lucio Vitruvio Pollione De architectura libri dece*, 1521.

one thirteenth-century allegory narrates.[4] Beyond costume, there are additional disjunctions between the two images in respect to posture (rigid astonishment versus casual ease), contact with the viewer (oblique versus direct), and attributes (humble knotted rope versus leather belt and fine rapier).

Francis and Grumelli, however, both interact with a gray background wall. The walls in Bellini and Moroni move between the categories of natural formation, built form, and crumbling ruin; at times they are even and expansive, at times minutely fissured. In the works of both artists, bodies project from the vertical plane and yet are embedded in it. This spatial ambiguity mirrors how these walls convey temporal suspension: what happened before the moment depicted in the image and what will occur after it are held at bay. In the case of Grumelli, the architectural enclosure presents decay and puts forward the flush of the amorous victor. Walls register the charge of temporality or are imprinted with it. Comparing this seemingly incongruous pair of paintings enables us to get at a fundamental condition of the Renaissance picture: namely, the artist's calibration of a body's stance in and against a neutrally colored plane. For if the portrayed figure declares, "This is me," then the wall adds the adverb of place to this statement: "Here I am," or "Here I stand."

Moroni's portraiture offers a case in point. Sitters ranging from members of the northern Italian elite to craftsmen such as the subject of *The Tailor* inhabit his canvases, while many of these portraits feature gray grounds. Some of them present a generalized gray chromatic field behind the sitter, while others depict the sitter in a gray architectural enclosure including floor or pavement and especially walls—dappled and shadowy planes—that stand behind the figures. Gray grounds envelop and frame the body. They rise, crumble, and, when inscribed with words, even speak to us. Gray grounds precipitate views onto the outside world or the world beyond. In them, Moroni stitches in pockets of shadows so that even his discernably representational grounds become areas of obscure emptiness.

In spite of their visual interest and variety, Moroni's gray grounds are often dismissed as mere "foils," planes of color that set off and contrast with the figure.[5] What I want to propose instead is that Moroni's characters exist in a state of interplay with their supporting structures. His sitters seem stoic and distant, but they are not entirely inscrutable. It is to the gray ground that Moroni displaces access to their inner life. There in the ground, emotion is hinted at though not shown, suggested though not fully revealed. The figure takes on properties of the wall and the wall takes on properties of the figure. What results from this transfer are what we might call "walled figures" or "figured walls."

LIFE IN COMMON

Of course, beyond its role as a screen or matrix for images, the wall serves to provide shelter as well as functioning to contain and divide members of social groups. The ancient Roman architect Vitruvius recounts in his treatise *De architectura* (2.1–3) that "once upon a time, in a certain place, trees, thickly crowded, tossed by storms and winds and rubbing their branches together, kindled a fire." Ignited by chance, this first of fires terrified the primordial humans, who lived like animals "in forests and caves and woods." When the fire subsided, these bipeds approached the remaining flames and found comfort from the warmth. Fire generated "concourse among men, deliberation and a life in common" (fig. 4.2).[6] The first humans went on "to make shelters of leaves, some to dig caves under the hills, some to make of mud and wattles places for shelter."[7] Thus emerged a nascent form of the polis—the territory of the state, the body politic, and a discourse on the exercise of power and governance.

In the prologue to his own treatise on matters pertaining to architecture, *De re aedificatoria* (1485), Leon Battista Alberti disputes this ancient vignette and instead locates the beginnings of society in the constitutive elements of building.[8] Although, in Alberti's words, "some have said that it was fire and water which were initially responsible for bringing men together in communities," in his view it was without a doubt the structures of the wall and roof that "drew and kept men together." Two terms drawn from the Vitruvian lexicon characterize the role of these walls in this first human settlement:

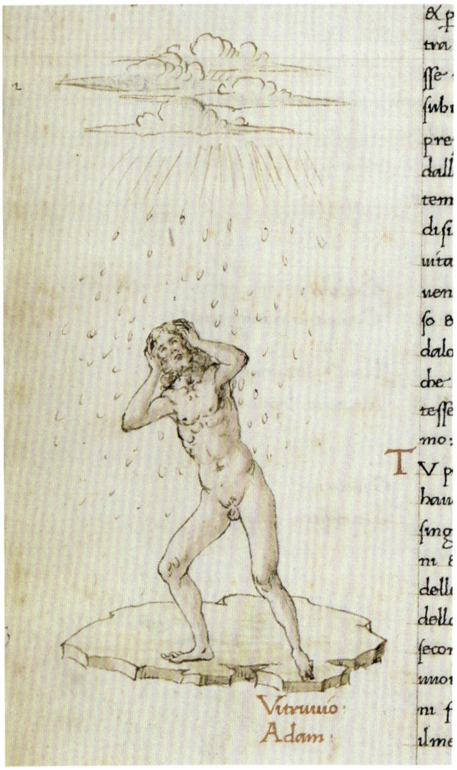

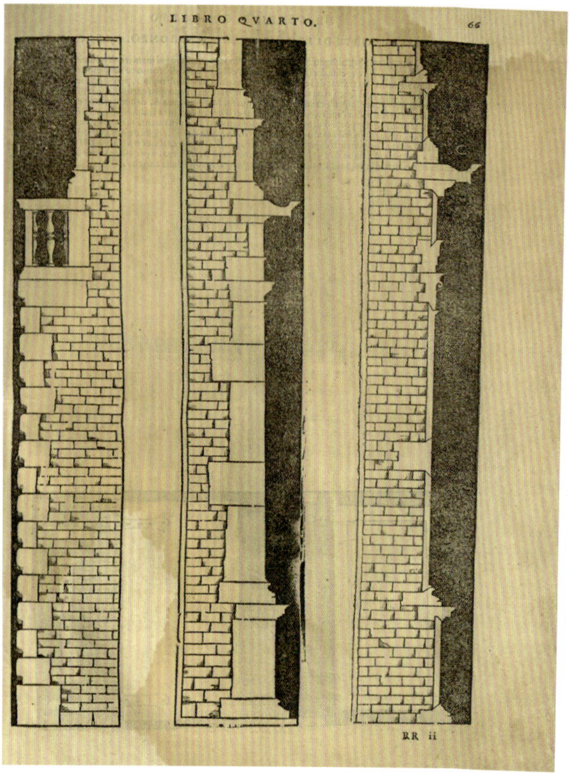

(LEFT)
Fig. 4.3. Antonio Averlino, called Filarete, "Adam Protecting Himself from the Rain." Pen and ink on paper (manuscript 29 × 40 cm). From the *Codex Magliabechianus*, c. 1465. BCNF Ms. II.I. 140, fol. 4v. Biblioteca Nazionale Centrale, Florence.

(RIGHT)
Fig. 4.4. Unknown Italian after Sebastiano Serlio, "Three Sections Showing Examples of Setting Live Stone with Brick." Engraving. From Sebastiano Serlio, *Quarto libro d'architettura di Sebastiano Serlio*, first published 1537.

contenere (literally "hold together," that is to say, surround and contain) and *conciliare* (call together).[9]

Later in his treatise, Alberti elaborates on the purpose of walls. "In the beginning," he writes, "man looked out for settlements in some secure country." To protect themselves from "piercing cold and stormy winds," early humans built walls out of the ground on which a covering could be laid. But these walls did not wholly contain. Primeval man "opened windows and doors in the walls, from floor to roof, so as to allow entry and social gathering within." In addition to facilitating the formation of social bonds, these walls "let in the sunlight and the breezes at the right time, as well as [. . .] let out any moisture and vapor that may have formed inside the house." Walls not only contain and call the first humans together. Permitting the entry of elements conducive to health and discharging noxious ones, the vertical plane between floor and roof both provides shelter and secures physiological well-being.[10]

Widely circulated in the vernacular in the sixteenth century, Alberti's work stood alongside architectural treatises on the Renaissance bookshelf. It was, in fact, listed in the inventory of books belonging to one of Moroni's close artistic collaborators.[11] Alberti takes an approach to the wall that differs from the historical and technical treatments by Serlio and Palladio. He provides a critical point of departure for us to formulate a conceptual understanding of the wall in Moroni's portraiture, and the Renaissance picture at large: namely, that the wall as ground holds together ideas surrounding figural stance, the expression of affect, and imminent action.

Alberti's words about *contenere* and *conciliare* can be used to identify the function of the supposedly nondescript wall in the Renaissance picture. The wall acts as what we might call "contingent containment." The architect and theorist Filarete in his *Trattato di architettura* (1461–64) depicts another human figure from the distant past, the biblical Adam, attempting to shelter himself from the first rain. The triangular placement of his hands, Filarete argues, was the origin of the pitched roof; the sides of his body were the first walls of civilization (fig. 4.3).[12] While this image presents architecture as seeking to provide Adam with an ever more durable shelter in which he may contain his body, architecture can only ever promise to do so temporarily.

In this scheme, flesh becomes building. Later architects active in northern Italy and contemporaneous with Moroni discussed more technical aspects pertaining to the construction of the wall—its structural integrity and material makeup. In 1537, the initial installment of Sebastiano Serlio's treatise *General Rules of Architecture* appeared in Venice. In an excursus on architectural ornaments in stone, Serlio illustrated three types of brick walls bonded with stone facing, each of which exemplifies a different degree of durability and requires a different amount of time to build (fig. 4.4).[13] Glossing both Vitruvius and Pliny the Elder, Andrea Palladio in his *Four Books on Architecture* (Venice, 1570) analyzes six types of ancient wall construction. One variety of wall, observed in Turin, consists of river pebbles sliced in half. A wall made of irregular stones in Palestrina resembles patterns of ancient pavement.[14]

The wall indeed becomes a marker of culture, a place of display. It is where a society announces to itself and others, "We live here." It encloses the figure defensively, limiting view beyond its confines. At the same time, this containment is contingent. The figure can be ejected beyond the wall; or else the wall can crumble away, alluding to a future oblivion or an elemental past. Less than representing fixity, then, the gray walls in Moroni's paintings are temporary, even tenuous. However "civilized" Moroni's figures appear to be, alienated by time and custom from the first humans in these accounts, the primordial function of the wall as an instrument of congregation and containment constitutes the ground of the artist's portraits.

HOW TO PAINT A GRAY BACKGROUND

While giving the appearance of stout masonry, the gray walls that constitute Moroni's architectonic backgrounds are material artifice. They are the uppermost strata that sit above layers of paint applied on cloth; specifically, canvas, his preferred material support.[15] Throughout his career, Moroni worked with a variety of canvas weaves: tabby and herringbone, and later, heavier twill weaves.[16] On these supports, the artist first applied a layer of gesso, a mixture

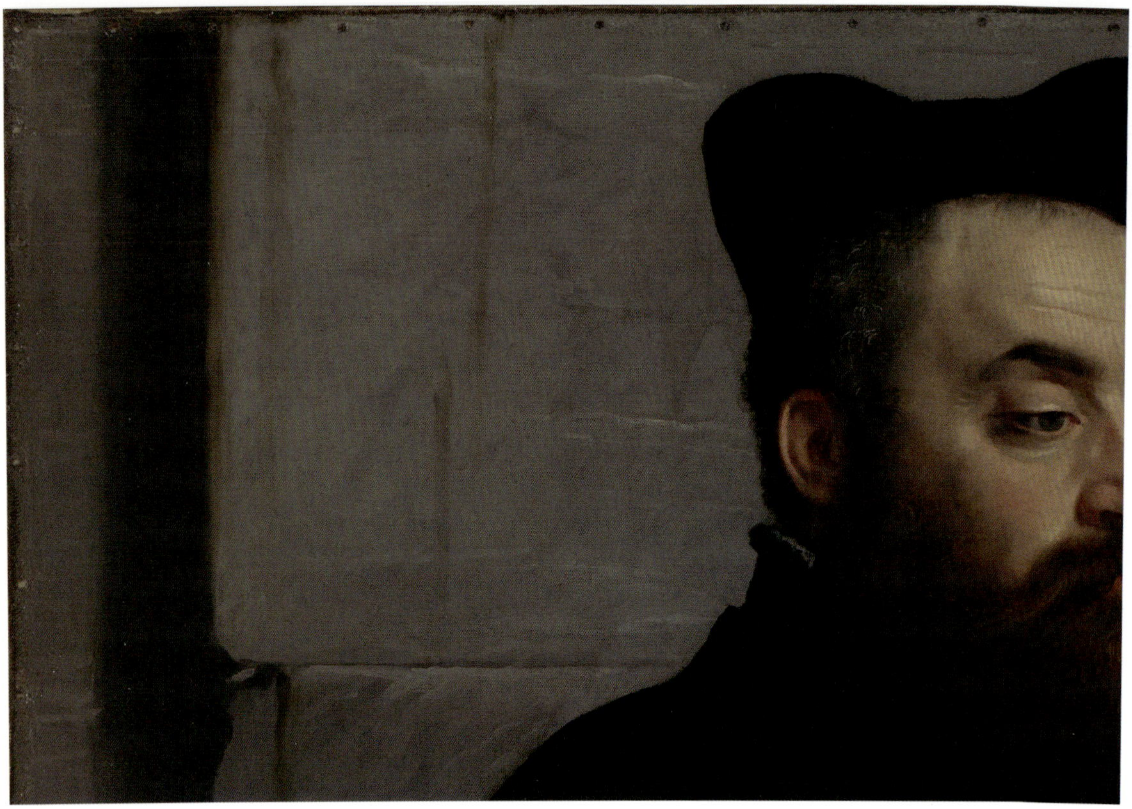

Fig. 4.5. Detail from Giovanni Battista Moroni, *Canon Ludovico di Terzi*, c. 1559–60. Oil on canvas (101.5 × 82.7 cm). National Gallery, London. Bought, 1876 (NG1024).

of white pigment and a binder, which reduced the absorbency of the canvas. The gesso ground was then primed with another layer of drying oil combined with pigmentation. This additional underlayer of colored priming (called "mestica," discussed in chapter 1) provided the foundation from which Moroni could work up the picture's chromatic tone and texture.

Technical analysis conducted by scientists at the National Gallery in London has shown that Moroni's mestica tends to consist of thick brown layers made up of yellow and red earths, manganese black, and lead white.[17] In his portrait of Canon Ludovico di Terzi (1559–60), the colored priming shows through many of the tacking holes on the picture's four sides (fig. 4.5).[18] Mestica added chromatic depth to the gray background and assisted Moroni in describing the sitter's beard. The sixteenth-century art theorist Giovanni Battista Armenini notably refers to this colored underlayer as a bed "to help other colors."[19] While brown underlayers were not uncommon, in Moroni's case it is significant that the color that will ultimately comprise the base note for the figure's hair begins by being spread across the whole wall surface. The restriction of this color to the head and face happens in a later step, when the wall is given its gray "outer skin."

Two other bust-length portraits exemplify how the mestica underlayer prepares for the figure's emergence from the wall. In the *Bust Portrait of a Young Man with an Inscription* (c. 1560), the creamy gray background wall consists of the brownish mestica base covered with a combination of manganese black, lead white, and verdigris (which imparts a greenish hue) (fig. 4.6).[20] Although they are made to resemble architectural structures, known for opacity and solidity, in their execution Moroni's gray backgrounds can more correctly be characterized as translucent veils. He does not use the gray background to seal off completely the brown priming layer. Instead, he applies the gray locally, as a type of filter. The gray layers cover the mestica only intermittently. In some places these chromatic base notes rise to the level of figural representation, while elsewhere they are submerged. At times being permitted to show through and at times being covered with the greenish-gray layer, the brownish mestica gives chromatic force to the young man's complexion, ruddy hair, and beard.[21] The layers of paint themselves play on the idea of protrusion and recession. Rather than moving into position in front of the wall, this figure emerges through it.

The gray background is thus more—or less—than a gray, hard wall. On close and extended looking, this background dissolves, becoming effervescent. The gray's indeterminate topography invites the viewer to look upon, across, and into the picture, and injects dynamism into an otherwise static portrait. The inscription that is mentioned in the painting's title, "dum spiritus hos reget artus" (as long as the spirit rules my limbs), from Virgil's *Aeneid* (4.336), proclaims the power of breath to animate the body.[22] In this painting, the dynamics of inhalation and exhalation are conferred upon the background, which acts as a gray mist or fog, tangibly enclosing yet ephemeral.

In the *Portrait of a Man with Raised Eyebrows* (c. 1570–75), the material makeup and physical application of the ground informs the appearance and affect of the sitter (fig. 4.7).[23] As in the case of the *Young Man with an Inscription,* the brownness in the mestica brings the wall's grayness closer to the chromatic composition of flesh and hair. The overlay of color facilitates the description of not only the sitter's skin and beard but also the hair at his temples, which passes from chestnut brown to gray. The supposedly nondescript intermediate zone that is the gray background brings the painting's superstrate and substrate together in the service of portraying likeness.

The effect of this convergence recalls an important distinction developed in the theory of portraiture in the Renaissance. The physician and writer on art Giulio Mancini asserted that there were two types of portraits. The first was what he called "il ritratto semplice" (the simple portrait), a mere transcription, which "expresses nothing more than the dimension, proportion, and resemblance of the thing it imitates." The second was what Mancini called "il ritratto con azione et espressione d'affetto" (the portrait with action and the expression of passion), which depicts the movement of emotion.[24]

In *Portrait of a Man with Raised Eyebrows,* the background joins the face in conveying psychic movement. This front layer acts like a curtain that, when lifted, reveals a place further inside, as in a stage set. The veil pulled back offers a glimpse into Moroni's working process. Backgrounds are often

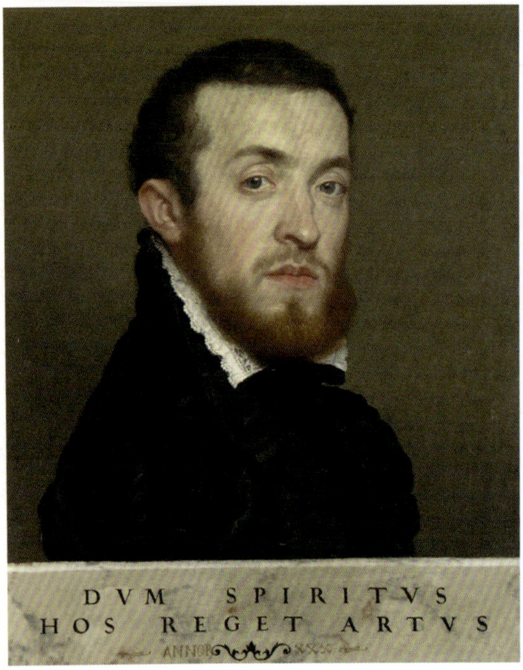

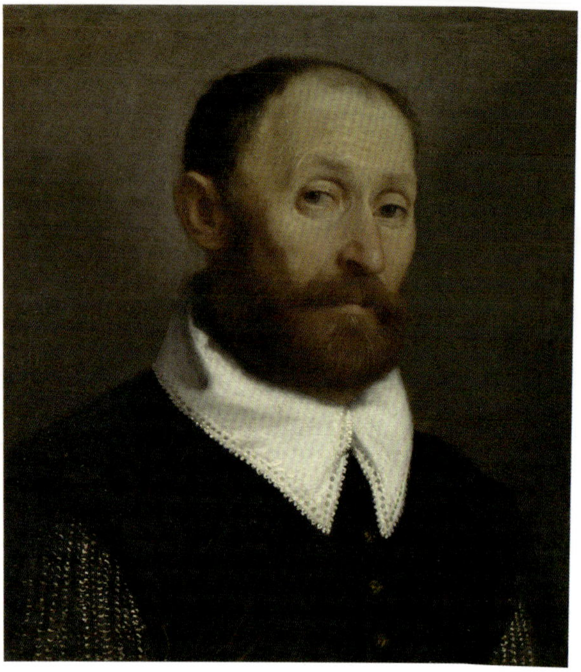

painted first, and the figure with its details of the face is left in reserve. This follows a sequence from the illusionistic "back" to "front." In this picture, however, Moroni displays his tendency to wait until late in the painting process to finish the gray background, so that it must be made to stop just short of the outer limits of the sitter.[25] As a result, the brown underlayer that sits beneath the gray background emerges as a narrow margin limning the sitter's ears, shoulders, and broad white collar. This is also the reason for the gap between figure and ground in *Young Man with an Inscription*.

In *Man with Raised Eyebrows*, one could imagine that the figure's gesture of surprise is a reaction to Moroni's final act of swiftly laying in the ground. Presumably, the sitter widens his eyes to express surprise or skepticism at a remark just uttered, by the artist or another person in the room. But one is tempted to imagine it could also be surprise and skepticism at what he feels: the brush that lightly sweeps his collar as it completes his image (here we are reminded that *tocco*, or touch, refers to brushwork). Although the raised eyebrow in fact was painted first, the gesture corresponds to the spontaneous body movements involved in painting. The face comes to express the artist's *prestezza*, the handling of the brush, which is paradoxically both rough and dexterous.

(LEFT)
Fig. 4.6. Giovanni Battista Moroni, *Bust Portrait of a Young Man with an Inscription*, c. 1560. Oil on canvas (47.2 × 39.8 cm). National Gallery, London. Layard Bequest, 1916 (NG3129).

(RIGHT)
Fig. 4.7. Giovanni Battista Moroni, *Portrait of a Man with Raised Eyebrows*, c. 1570–75. Oil on canvas (45.7 × 37.8 cm). National Gallery, London. Layard Bequest, 1916 (NG3128).

Finishing the coloring of a painting, according to Armenini, involved a process of continual returning apparent in Moroni's technique. To complete the work, the painter should go back and "retouch, blend, shade, and give relief." These finishing touches must be applied until "each and every part, and the whole together" satisfy. "Nor does one ever stop over the smallest detail."[26] While these recommendations resonate with Moroni's gray background, he departs from them, in that the different parts of the picture do not cohere into a harmonious unity. Instead, the picture thereby exercises action and acknowledges that action.

GRAY THEORY

While largely monochromatic, Moroni's gray grounds are thus not monolithic, homogeneous, or unvaried. In its ability to oscillate between brilliance and dullness, gray has an uncertain position on the chromatic scale. In the vernacular of Renaissance Italy, different words grasped gray's chromatic range: *bigio* (dull gray), *grigio* (ashy), *pardo* (from the pelt of the leopard), *cinereo* (ash-colored), *plumbeo* (lead), *berretino* (brown-gray). Meanwhile, gray could also unfold a spectrum of political, economic, and religious connotations. In fifteenth-century Florence, the Bigi (the Grays), as they were called, were a faction whose color reflected their wavering loyalties: they were partisans of the Medici and at the same time sympathetic to the anti-Medicean Dominican preacher Girolamo Savonarola, who railed against Florence's first family in his sermons.[27] While for the Bigi, gray symbolized a contrasting set of alliances, for religious orders, the color represented the virtues of restraint, self-abnegation, and withdrawal from the world. Mendicant Franciscans adhering to their vow of poverty wore humble robes that were a brown-gray.[28] Girls cloistered in Florence's many convents had in their wardrobes a gray cloth also called *bigio*. Nuns wore a heavy and coarse wool called *ceneritio*, which expressed "their supposedly more intense state of humility and mortification."[29]

True gray, however, was also a prestigious color. It was difficult to achieve in the process of dyeing silks and other valuable fabrics, so that Renaissance treatises on sericulture pay close attention to rare shades such as *berettino inzuccarato* (sugared gray), *argentino* (silver gray), and *cinerino* (delicate ash).[30] Otherwise, the color gray could be attained in the form of expensive materials such as fur. The word *vaio* (vair or miniver) referred to the color of squirrel fur, a variegated white, blueish, and gray, as well as the pattern that resulted when pelts were stitched together.[31] Vair adorned the clothing of aristocratic patrons and appeared in representations of kings, or of their demise. In a fifteenth-century French translation of Boccaccio, an illuminated miniature portrays Clytemnestra on the verge of assassinating her husband Agamemnon (fig. 4.8). She has trapped the Mycenaean king in a sumptuous cloak lined with gray vair fur. At the same moment, Aegisthus, tonsured and in the guise of a gray robed friar, raises his club to strike and kill.[32] The contrast between aristocratic wealth and the semblance of mendicant poverty takes the form of a violent confrontation between shades of gray.

A compressed discussion in sixteenth-century art theoretical literature that specifically describes the color gray occurs in Raffaello Borghini's

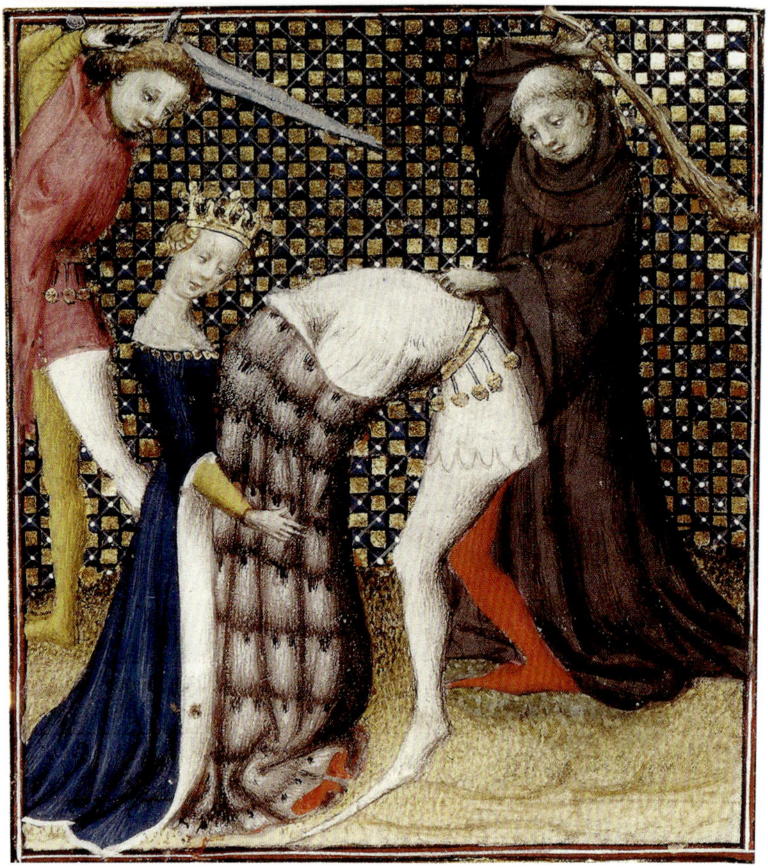

dialogue *Il riposo* (1584).[33] To explain the significance of different colors, the speaker states that he will follow the opinion of thinkers such as Aristotle but will also mention how colors are understood according to "common use," specifically, in heraldry. Playing on the double meaning of *campo* as a shield and terrain of debate, the speaker declares that these explanations will enable "painters in painting and gentlemen in making devices and liveries [to] have a larger field on which they can unfold their concepts." He describes the many kinds of gray in terms of different affective states. Dark gray indicates hope and patience, while "grays closer to white signify poverty, enmity, and desperation." A gray tending toward purple violet symbolizes the "hope of love" and "toil gladly undertaken." When marked with small dots, bright gray indicates "patience in contrary things, and suffering without pain." Gray "the color of ashes" indicates "troubles leading to death." Gray approaching black indicates transitions: "hope for one's thoughts, fear together with hope, and joyfulness turned into grief." Silver gray is also equivocal, meaning either "humility [or having] been deceived."[34]

Fig. 4.8. Maître des Clères Femmes, "The Assassination of Agamemnon." Parchment. From Giovanni Boccaccio, *De Claris mulieribus, traduction anonyme en français Livre des femmes nobles et renommées*, 1403. BnF Ms. Français 598, fol. 49v. Département des manuscrits, Bibliothèque nationale de France, Paris.

Borghini was following a long tradition of discerning the meanings of colors in heraldic devices. Already in the 1480s, an anonymous treatise

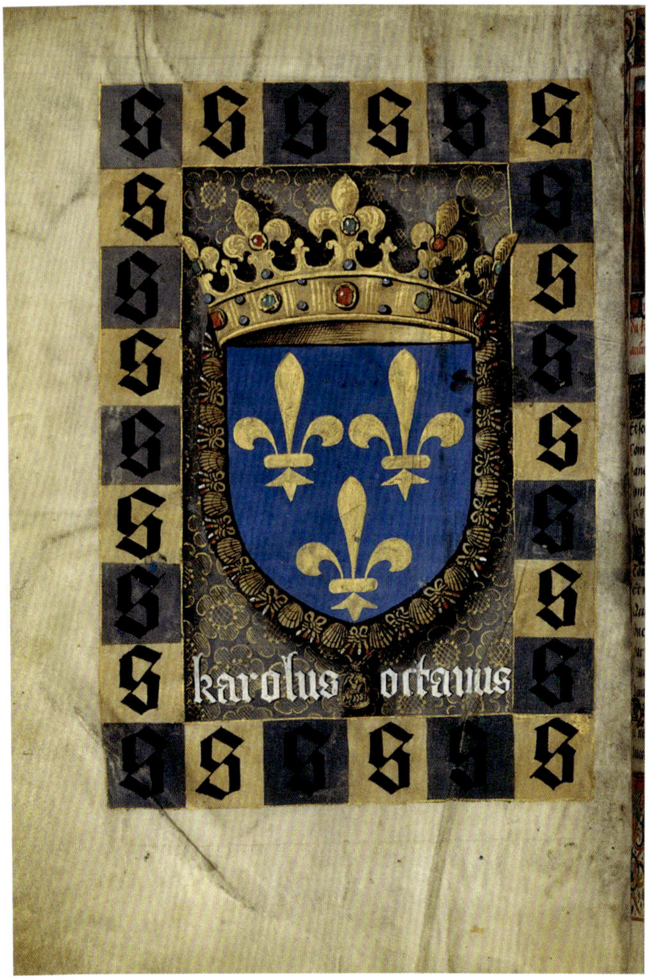

entitled *Le blason des couleurs en armes, livrées et devises* stated that when juxtaposed with white and black, gray on a shield is especially beautiful. The combination signifies "well-tempered hope." Gray was incorporated into the heraldic devices of rulers including Jean de Berry, Phillip the Good, King Charles VIII, and René d'Anjou (fig. 4.9). During his decades-long captivity in England after the battle of Agincourt (1415), Charles d'Orléans wrote a poem where gray expresses his desire and expectation to return to France: "Il vit en bonne Espérance / Puisqu'il est vetu en gris" (He lives in good hope / since he is dressed in gray).[35] Neither Borghini nor other writers on heraldry link the symbolism of colors used in crests and shields to specific paintings. How to apply this system to works of art remains an open question. Nevertheless, the period association of gray with patience and hope—a connection that strikes the modern reader as strange given gray's predominantly somber associations today—could certainly have lent the gray walls in Moroni's paintings connotations that have now become obscure.

Fig. 4.9. Circle of the Maître de Jacques de Besançon and Jean Bourdichon, "Shield with the Coat of Arms of France." Parchment. From Martial d'Auvergne, *Vigils of Charles VII* (*Vigiles de Charles VII*), c. 1484–85. BnF Ms. Français 5054, fol. Bv. Département des manuscrits, Bibliothèque nationale de France, Paris.

GOLD AND GRAY

As argued in chapter 2, the field of gold ground stages a dialectic between making and representing, material and illusion, flatness and depth, light and shade. This ground, which is achieved through the application of metallic leaf that is then stippled and pounced, differs substantively from Moroni's gray backgrounds, which are rendered through the layering and mixing of pigments suspended in oil. Despite this disparity in material and technique, the aesthetic effects of these grounds—gold and gray—overlap. Gold ground demonstrates a mimetic potential in the evanescent forms that the viewer must infer from the surface. In their collection on the color gray, Magdalena Bushart and Gregor Wedekind argue that gray ground offers an "experimental chromatic field for the painter to engage in a form finding process[; . . .] gray plumbs the depths of the potential and the boundary of the representational function of image/s."[36] By eschewing a chromatic portrayal of the world, works of art in gray invite reflection on the artistic process and passages between different media. This is especially the case in the field of chiaroscuro, or monochrome fresco painting, in which the painter deploys gray to simulate sculptural relief within a pictorial framework (fig. 4.10).

Chiaroscuro painting was placed on a building's exterior and courtyard walls. North of the Alps, chiaroscuro painting was referred to from the sixteenth century onward as "Grau in Grau"—gray in gray. In Vasari's description, material grounds (*campi*) moistened and prepared with potter's clay were then painted with tones from black to white, with the effect that dark tones recede and light tones come forward.[37] When chiaroscuro is expertly done, the play between figure and ground on these painted walls achieves clarity at a great viewing distance, so that the decorated building seems to "jump out" in urban space. Monochrome was the only fresco decoration Serlio deemed appropriate for facades, as coloring on walls risked breaking up the coherence and structure of architectural order.[38]

In Vasari's words, such painting made facades appear "to be built of marble or stone, with the decorative groups actually carved in relief." Vasari recognized that monochrome painting often served a civic function, especially in the medium of ephemeral architecture such as triumphal arches "erected on the occasion of the entrance of princes into the city, and of processions, or in the apparatus for fêtes and plays."[39] As in architectural friezes—horizontal bands that contain sculptural relief—monochrome decoration featured tightly compacted figures acting out narrative scenes within an illusionistic architectural framework. The gray grounds in Moroni's portraits can be conceived as elongating the intervals between chiaroscuro's figural forms so that gray background areas act as illusionistic walls within the fictive space of the picture. While chiaroscuro presents a community of significant figures, in his portraits, Moroni considers a single, prominent figure in isolation. Notably, a much later local source (Antonio Tassi's *Le Vite de' pittori, scultori e archittetti Bergamaschi*, 1793) reports Moroni to have executed

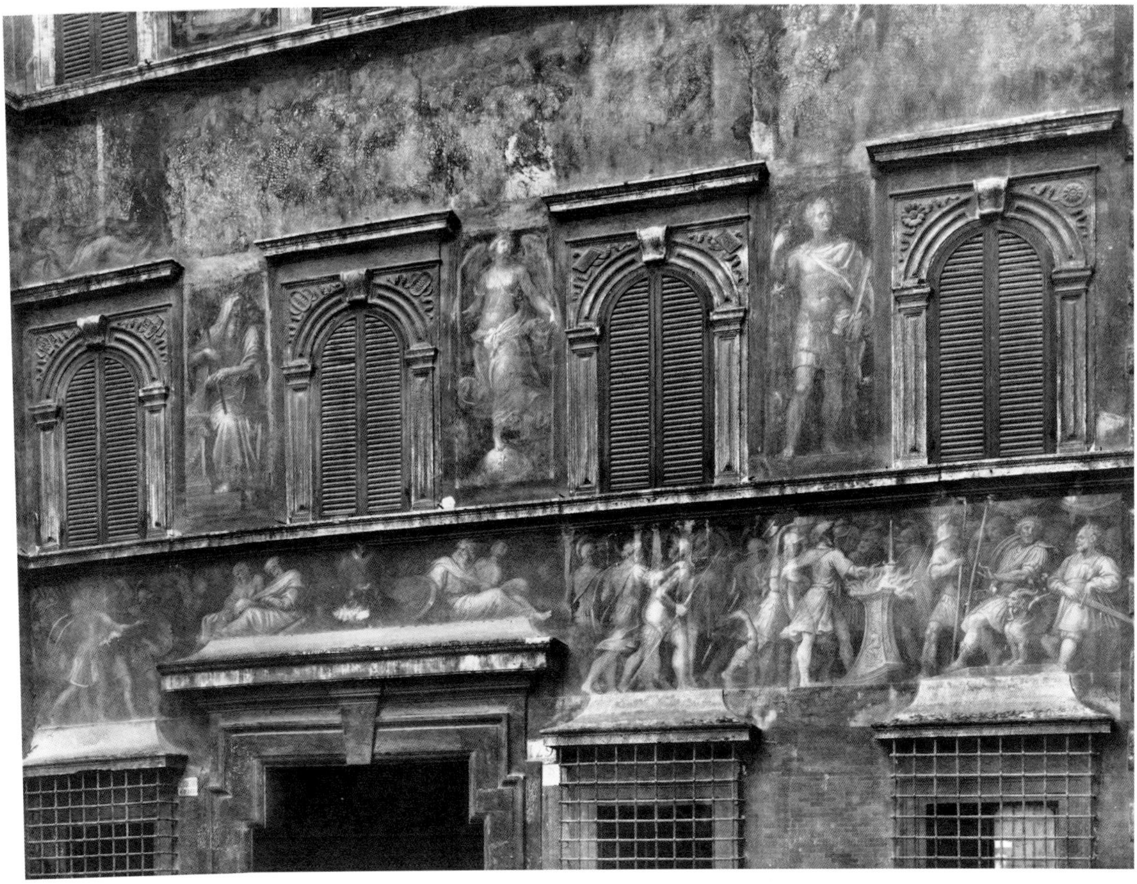

several works featuring architectural decoration in fresco—some passages of which were possibly in chiaroscuro—on public facades and interior spaces in his native town of Albino.[40]

Hence, while at first glance Moroni's gray grounds seem to present a monochromatic stone wall as a plane against which the colored figure appears, upon closer looking, it becomes possible to understand Moroni's sitters as articulations of the wall: they are joined to the ground's illusionistic surface and they emerge from its material depth.

EMINENCE GRISE

Painters before Moroni—including his teacher Moretto, whose work we will discuss below—also used gray ground to investigate the overlaps and distinctions between painting and adjacent arts such as sculpture and architecture. In Parmigianino's *Portrait of a Collector*, dated to before 1524, gray ground gives rise to the relief sculpture of Mars, Venus, and Cupid (fig. 4.11).[41] Beneath and above the relief, an abandoned delineation of an archway can be discerned. The idea for the background seems to have unfolded over the course of

Fig. 4.10. Polidoro da Caravaggio and Maturino da Firenze, *Episodes from a Roman History*, 1520–27. Fresco. Palazzo Ricci, Rome.

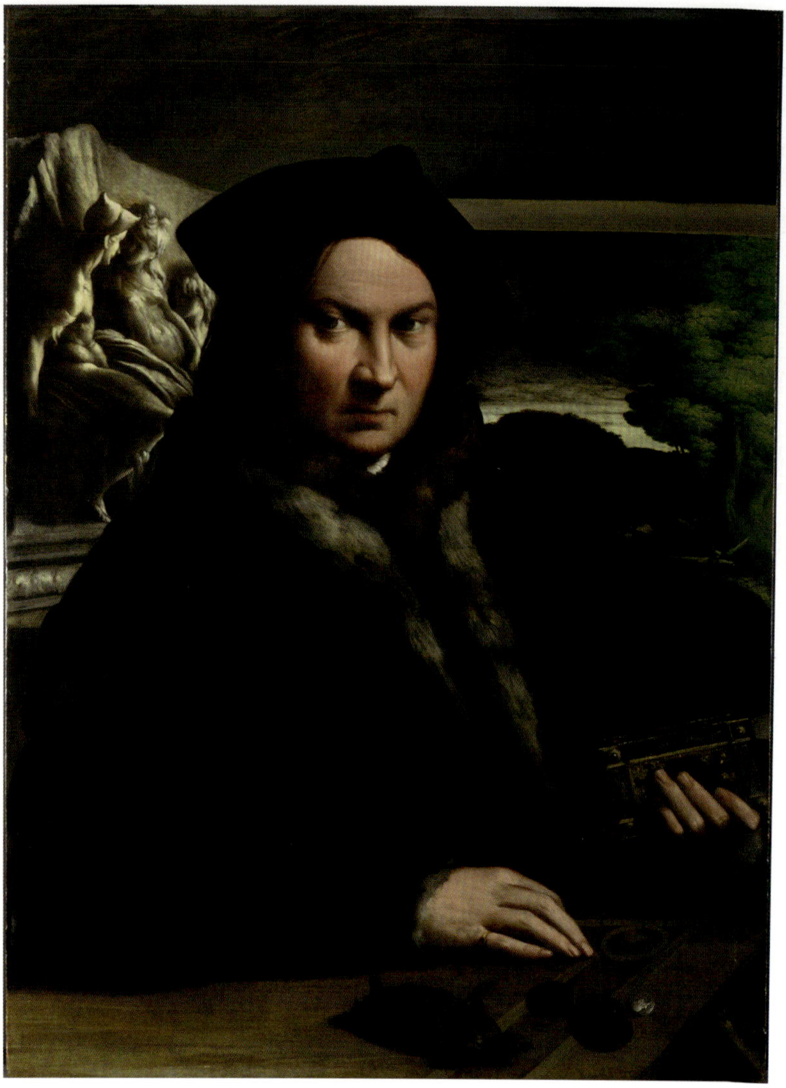

Fig. 4.11. Parmigianino, *Portrait of a Collector*, c. 1523. Oil on panel (89.5 × 63.8 cm). National Gallery, London. Bought, 1977 (NG6441).

painting.[42] As the painting's technical report states, the relief was most likely "painted to complete the background."[43] The relief is placed at a disjointed angle with a landscape painting, which also doubles as a distant view outdoors. The play between light and darkness sets the effects of relief and spatial recession at odds: the sculpture protrudes, while the painting recedes; the human figure serves as the hinge between the two modalities.

Both sculpture and landscape in Parmigianino's portrait seem continuous with the gray wall, so that the distinctions and transitions between these zones are difficult to grasp. The confrontation between the different media and subject matter creates an "epistemological spark." In the relief, the near kiss between Venus and Mars would seem to emphasize touch, while the green tree in the painting underscores the faculty of vision. The relief, for all of its physicality, appears colorless, while the tree, for all its greenness,

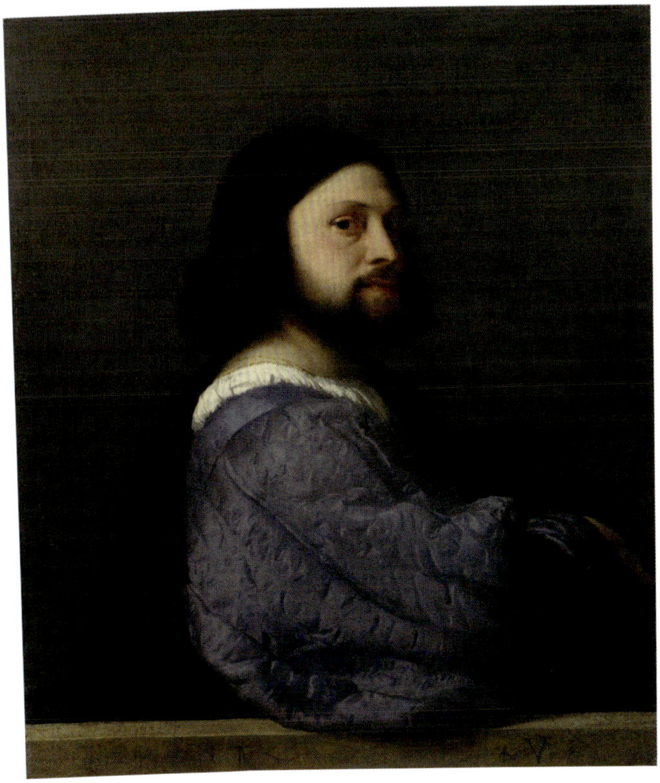

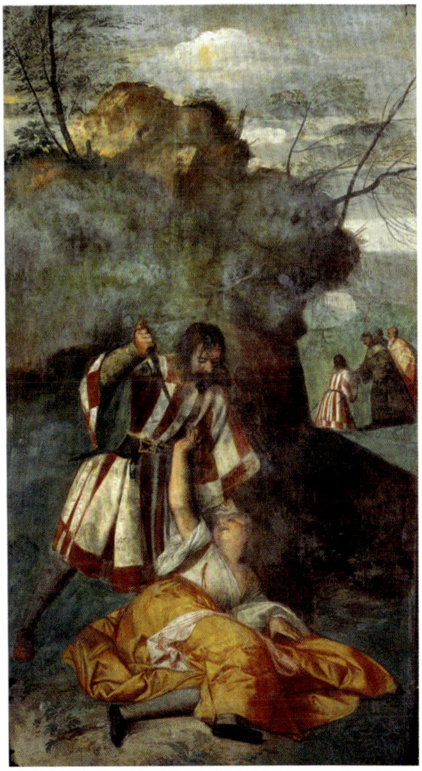

appears flat. In between, we are presented with the fleshiness of the collector's cheeks, the glint of his eyes, and the tactility of his fur collar. The question posed by this picture might be, "Which one comes closer to life?" or else, "Through which one do we know the world more truly?"

Gray produces a zone of interrogation that questions the distinctions between space and nonspace, between somewhere and nowhere. A second example is Titian's *Man with a Quilted Sleeve*, perhaps a portrait of the Venetian aristocrat Gerolamo Barbarigo, dated to around 1510 (fig. 4.12). The painting's most projecting components include the sitter's gaze, the texture of the cloth, and the parapet inscribed with Titian's initials, "T.V."[44] Yet also compelling is the portrait's gray ground. The somber tone was composed of layers of lead white and lamp black, to which was added a brownish yellow earth pigment to convey warmth.[45] We might perceive this zone as a solid wall. Less than a year before he executed the portrait, Titian was engaged in painting scenes from the life of Saint Anthony of Padua in fresco on the walls of a confraternity meeting house. The artist built up and modeled the intonaco, or underlying wet plaster, so that certain passages on the wall's surface would protrude as far as two inches in relief. [46] In the scene showing the *Miracle of the Jealous Husband*, the raised plaster preparation around the wife's outstretched arm casts shadows around itself (fig. 4.13). Titian's incorporation of the relief technique within the painting, Maria Loh observes,

(LEFT)
Fig. 4.12. Titian, *Man with a Quilted Sleeve*, c. 1510. Oil on canvas (81.2 × 66.3 cm). National Gallery, London. Bought, 1904 (NG1944).

(RIGHT)
Fig. 4.13. Titian, *Miracle of the Jealous Husband*, 1511. Fresco (340 × 185 cm). Scuola del Santo, Padua.

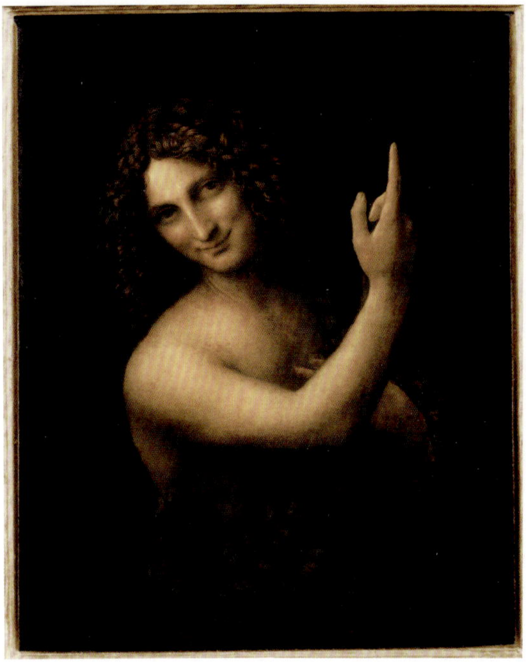

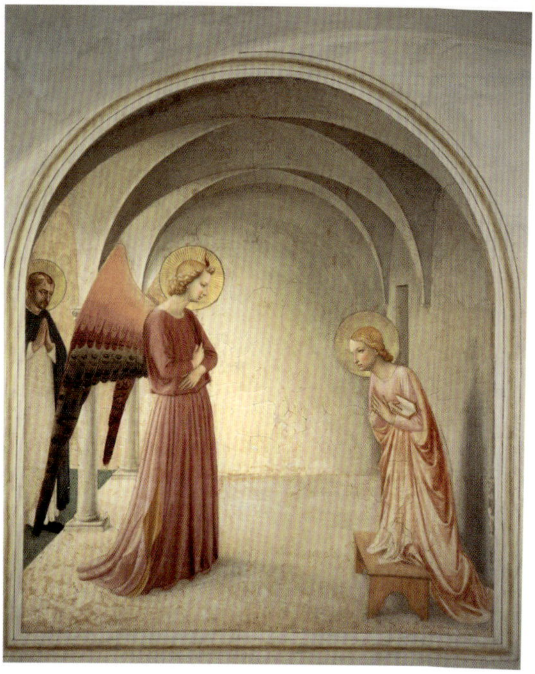

underscores the scene's dramatic force: "it is as if the foreshortened body of the wife is literally trying to break free from the site of her death—kicking, pushing, and punching out into the viewer's space on the other side of the picture plane."[47]

First, Titian worked with the physical substance of the wall to create an effect of dimensionality in these frescoes; and then second, in the portrait, he painted a gray area that has a more indeterminate physicality. While the gray ground in the *Man with a Quilted Sleeve* has been read as a fluctuating atmosphere or place of shadows, it might also have evoked for some viewers the physical canvas support with a prepared ground.[48] More than a mere foil, this gray ground has a consistency. It holds the figure while remaining undefinable.

The "in-betweenness" of gray grounds makes them negligible, and yet captivating. Two significant pictorial antecedents can be imagined as positioned at either end of the chromatic spectrum in which gray occupies a middle spread. First, there is *sfumato*: in his image *Saint John the Baptist* (c. 1513–16), Leonardo blurs edges and contours so that we perceive the figure obscured as if it were surrounded by veils of smoke (fig. 4.14). When contending with this hazy darkness, our eyes dilate. In this condition of dimness (and with enlarged pupils), the viewer is obliged to take a slower pace in contemplating the image of the saint pointing toward heaven.[49] At the other extreme is the sudden brightness of Fra Angelico's austere fresco of the *Annunciation* (1440–45), the occasion when Gabriel announces to Mary that she will conceive the Christ Child (fig. 4.15). Even her shadow, which

(LEFT)
Fig. 4.14. Leonardo da Vinci, *Saint John the Baptist*, 1513–15. Oil on panel (69 × 57 cm). Musée du Louvre, Paris.

(RIGHT)
Fig. 4.15. Fra Angelico, *Annunciation with Saint Peter Martyr*, c. 1440–45. Fresco (176 × 148 cm). Convento di San Marco, Florence.

is clearly cast on the wall, shows the Virgin has been illuminated by the angel's radiance: the message has been delivered. Clarity is a feature of this painting, with respect both to the legibility of the narrative event and to the scene's visibility.[50]

Gray grounds position a painting in between these extremes of obscurity and clarity. This position can be understood with regard to narrative, as well as in relation to the picture's temporality. One could consider gray grounds as representing a moment when the smoke in Leonardo's paintings begins to lift, so that it still contains the figure but also leaves room for it to stay or go. It is the moment before light floods the friar's cell and arrests the angel in the room. In a similar way, Moroni's gray grounds contain, without fully grasping, the figured self.

ARCHITECTURE AND ARTICULATION

Moroni gently disturbs the layers of paint that enclose the figure. He stirs them up to grant access to the interiority of his otherwise reserved sitters, who project outward from imposing walls. I have described the interplay between architecture and figure in these works as "contingent containment." One of Moroni's most common schemas consists of the figure—either full- or half-length—standing on a stone pavement and placed against a wall adorned with columns and niches, often in ruins.[51] In fact, Moroni descended from a long line of architects and engineers. His ancestors in the fourteenth and fifteenth centuries were charged with the maintenance and expansion of fortifications and castles in the Veneto. Moroni's father Francesco was active as an architect and stonemason. Girolamo Tiraboschi has substantiated and unearthed notarial records that document the elder Moroni's engagement to renovate a Carmelite convent in their hometown of Albino. Francesco also oversaw the construction of a palace, positioned on a rocky spur, for the aristocratic Lodrone family in Bondone, near Brescia. Contracts indicate that Francesco also undertook the tutelage of apprentices who sought to learn the arts of building and carpentry.[52]

In addition, the younger Moroni's teacher, Moretto, often positioned architectural backgrounds in his paintings. Buildings set the scene in his altarpieces, narrative cycles, and portraits. As Carlo Zani has pointed out, Moretto drew architectural motifs from a number of sources, among them local landmarks in Brescia, prints of narrative scenes by Albrecht Dürer, and contemporary architecture erected in the Veneto. The *Dinner in the House of Simon the Pharisee* features columns, pilasters, and architectural ornamentation found on the Palazzo Pompei in Verona and the portal of the Palazzo Conti in Vicenza. According to Zani, Moretto incorporated architecture in his paintings as an "instrument of spatial investigation."[53] But more than this, Moretto's architecture acts to reproduce and amplify the posture of the figures. The arch in one of Moretto's best-known works, *Portrait of a Man* (1526), has been aptly described as "answering the curve of the [sitter's] shoulders, participating in the sweep of the pose."[54] This painting is known as the earliest full-length and life-size portrait that survives from the Renaissance. It offers a prime example of how a painter can use architectural elements—base, pedestal, and column—to form an exoskeletal unit that encloses the figure and reinforces its stance. The body thereby achieves a mode of representation that extends it beyond its corporeal confines.

Compared to Moretto, Moroni employed fewer buildings in his work. From the temples, loggias, and towers in his teacher's oeuvre, Moroni seems to have extracted the gray wall chiefly as a vehicle to explore and clarify the analogies between body and building. In Moretto's portrait, the vertical architectural elements contrast with the flexion and softness that are evident throughout the sitter's body. However, instead of bending, Moroni's figures take on the rigid vertical stance of the wall. While the figures are often inscrutable, many of these paintings also contain mottoes or inscriptions. I therefore argue that these works meditate on *articulation*, in the sense of the formation of utterance from inchoate sound, or the emergence of form from a formless expanse. Articulation can also refer to jointedness: the body's joints grant its limbs mobility while binding their parts. In the body of the painting, wall and sitter are like anatomical parts that come together at a joint. But joints can also snap out of place.[55]

NAILED TO THE WALL

A portrait dated 1560 features the Spanish aristocrat Don Gabriel de la Cueva y Girón (1525–71) (fig. 4.16).[56] The many aristocratic appendages to his name recall Oliver Goldsmith's quip about "a Spanish nobleman with more titles than shirts." Gabriel was the fifth Duke of Alburquerque, Count of Ledesma and Hulema, the second Marquis of Cuéllar, Grandee of Spain "de la primera clase y antiguedad," viceroy of Navarre, knight of the Order of Alcántara, and commander of Santivanez.[57] After the portrait's completion, he served as governor and commander general of the State of Milan from 1564 until his death in 1571. The precise conditions under which the portrait was commissioned remain unknown. It is also unclear where it was originally hung. A distinct possibility is an apartment in the royal ducal palace in Milan, where Don Gabriel resided during his tenure as the representative of the Spanish crown. A seventeenth-century description of the palace, Giacomo Torre's *Il ritratto di Milano* (1674), describes a later portrait of Don Gabriel, alongside images of his predecessors and successors, displayed in a portico in the palace of the governor general.[58]

Despite Don Gabriel's aristocratic epithets, Moroni does not picture him in the format of the official Spanish state portrait, which often showed the sitter full-length, alongside titles, coats of arms, and insignia of knighthoods. Later in the seventeenth century, the codified portrait of Hapsburg nobility would become an instrument to deify the ruler.[59] Instead of allegory, Moroni pursues articulation. Rather than abbreviate the inherent complexity of the self through the insertion of symbolic devices, the artist pursues a deceptively simpler operation: he allows the emergence of a likeness that itself functions to express, or nearly express, some of the sitter's significant attributes. This emergence of depicted interiority is itself a central phenomenon of the Renaissance picture. In these pictures, Moroni both cultivates this effect and guards against it through the relationship between figure and wall.

In articulating Don Gabriel's figure, Moroni draws a series of analogies between his body and the structure of the wall. If put into words, these analogies might read, "Thigh is to hip as plinth is to ledge; spine is to elbow as pilaster is to niche." The wall offers an abstracted version of the body, while the figure incarnates the wall. Renaissance architectural theorists, in emulation of the ancients, described building construction in terms of anatomical parts made out of different types of tissue, which work together to perform a function: the formation of an angle, the enclosure of space, the carrying of weight. Alberti writes in *De re aedificatoria* that a cornerstone should "extend into the adjoining wall like the elbow joint of an arm" (3:7). A wall constructed from stacked stone "would be equivalent to a wall made entirely out of 'ribs or bones.'" (3:8).[60] Prescribing methods for vault construction, he states that "we should imitate Nature throughout, that is, bind together the bones and interweave flesh with nerves running along every possible section" (3:14).[61] Meanwhile, anatomical treatises likened the skeleton to architecture. Vesalius, in his *On the Fabric of the Human Body* (1543), stated that some bones are "like bastions, defense walls, and ramparts, affording natural protection."[62]

Moroni brings these metaphors into his use of architectural structures to enclose and extend bodies in portraiture. Stance moves beyond the figure and reverberates in the surrounding architectural field. Just as Alberti imagines a building as having flesh and nerves, Moroni brings life into solid architecture, introducing flexion into immobile structures. In the portrait of Don Gabriel, as we have seen in previous portraits, the brownness in the gray approaches the coloring of flesh and hair. At the same time, a shimmering or scintillation occurs such that cool tones in the gray ground correspond with the sitter's pale blue eyes. Optically, he seems bound to the wall with his eyes, as if they were a pair of nails. Conversely, the gray ground, which is designed to appear occluded by the figure, becomes momentarily visible through the figure's ocular apertures. Uncannily, the wall looks back at the viewer.

Las paredes tienen ojos—the walls have eyes. This *refranero*, or popular saying, is attested in early seventeenth-century sermons and plays, though its usage may have begun long before.[63] According to the *Diccionario de autoridades* (1737), the expression warns that evil deeds conducted in secret will not go unpunished.[64] Materially, Gabriel's eyes may not be constituted by a gray layer lying under the skin—just as the gray wall does not in fact extend behind the figure. Even so, Moroni is certainly positing portraiture as constituted through the protrusion or extrusion of the picture's underlying layers. Moroni perforates the figure to allow the wall's gaze to rise to the surface.[65]

The adage written on the plinth develops the linkage between figure and wall. It reads, "AQUI ESTO SIN TEMOR / Y DELA MVERTE / NO HE PAVOR" (I am here without fear, and of death I have no dread). As Rosalie Colie noted, such adages in emblematic pictures work as "thematic punctuation," summing up "a mass of experience in one charged phrase."[66] Possibly a family motto, the adage might also refer to Don Gabriel's fortitude in the political, military, and ecclesiastical conflicts he mediated as viceroy of Navarre and later on, as governor general of Milan.[67] In the specific context of the portrait, however, the adage articulates the affective register of his stance.

Spanish assigns two verbs, *ser* and *estar*, to express "to be." *Ser* derives from the Latin *esse* (to be) and *sedere* (to sit), while *estar* comes from *stare* (to stand). Hence, while *ser* indicates existence or essence, *estar* describes dynamic states of being. According to Juan Carlos Scannone, while *ser* is the territory of stable identity, *estar* "has a more local and circumstantial sense, where it signifies being firm (upright), but ready to begin moving."[68] These nuances bear directly on our understanding of Don Gabriel's motto. He not only asserts his fearlessness; he "stands" fearless in the face of death. His interior stance is given voice through the dynamic notion of being conveyed through the adage's use of *estar*.

But *estar* also signals the potential of impeding movement. The figure, prepared to act, can snap out of place. It seems that Don Gabriel could extract himself at any moment from the stationary wall and draw his sword. In this three-quarter-length portrait, his hand and wrist, reinforced by the handle of the sword, do the work that is normally reserved for feet: that is, it demonstrates the stable tectonics of a figure that is nonetheless prepared to act. The portrait therefore signals an imminent detachment of figure from wall and, consequently, the breaking down of analogies between body and building. The dynamic between body, plinth, and motto thus underscores the tension between articulation—the joining together of the figure, its enunciated stance, and the vertical wall—and impeding movement—the fragmentation of the whole, which will occur at an implied future moment when the body detaches from the wall.

In turn, the portrait moves from simulation (the rendering of outer likeness) to dissimulation (the disguise of inner being). It makes an analogy between the sitter's aristocratic standing, his physical stance, and a stalwart affective stance. The motto appears to grant access to Don Gabriel's interiority. But at the same time, it guards him, concealing his emotional life. To deny fear is to deny affect. We encounter the adage on an empty pedestal, where we imagine Don Gabriel might have stood as a sculpture, an image of fearlessness. He seems to have stepped off the pedestal and now leans against it, pausing to contemplate his relationship to his motto. Like the skeleton in Vesalius's anatomy, whose motto reads, "VIVITVR INGENIO, / CÆTERA MORTIS ERVNT" (Genius lives on, all else is mortal), and who is simultaneously student and cadaver, Don Gabriel descends from his pedestal to enter a reflexive dimension of selfhood (fig. 4.17).[69]

Meanwhile, his costume is a reservoir of material sensuousness, in the rippling layers of slashed sleeves and the codpiece peeking out beneath the doublet. The difference between this graspable material presence and the subject's inner being briefly appears, if only in flashes, before coalescing into the artifice of the portrait. The portrait allows a glimpse of the variance between visible tactility and interiority, the apertures that are the eyes and their encasement in the sitter's stoic face. Yet in the end, we see nothing but a wall, an impervious defensive enclosure. The seventeenth-century Spanish theologian Baltasar Gracián remarked that "where there is a solid foundation (fondo), secrets can be kept profound (profundo): there are spacious cellars where things of moment may be hid."[70] In this wordplay, depth of ground holds emotion in reserve. There is a movement toward interiority, and then interiority is revoked: figure becomes wall.

SECRETION

In the *Portrait of a Gentleman* (*The Unknown Poet*) (1560), Moroni pursues a variation on the analogy between body, architecture, and affect (fig. 4.18).[71] As in the portrait of Don Gabriel, the composition of the body corresponds to that of the wall. The gentleman's upright posture echoes the verticality of the gray stone pilaster and strip of brickwork; the hip coincides with the pedestal; even the bending of the joints in the fingers and wrist emphasize the molding's profile. In the position of the fingers, we are reminded that articulation joins many rigid pieces into a structure that itself is capable of curvature.

Yet the gray ground also lays bare the weak links in this chain of associations. The wall, open to the sky, is exposed to the elements and exhibits signs of wear and weathering. These converge with the poet's face and body. Calligraphic cracks in the stone approach the bravura of script. Alluding, perhaps, to the elemental forces at work in the poet's mind, clefts point to the sitter's eyes and brow. Water stains running down the pilaster follow the length of his trunk. They stream from the cracks next to his eyes, like falling tears, or else like blood flowing down the body's central arteries along the length of his body. The jagged edges of the bricks mirror the poet's profile, his high forehead and prominent nose.

The wall alludes to architecture recent in Moroni's time that juxtaposed brickwork with plain pilasters, some of which would have been constructed from a local gray stone such as macigno. In his *L'idea dell'architettura universale* (1615), the architect Vincenzo Scamozzi writes that the inhabitants near Padua use this variety of stone "to make almost all of their foundations and also large walls and *legamento rustico* [bonding material for bricks and stone]."[72] The etymological link between this word and "ligament" as connective tissue is worth noting. The pairing of stone revetment over brick, a type of stone skin over clay flesh, is widespread in mid-sixteenth-century architecture, especially on the facades of northern Italian churches. One such example is the funerary chapel in Milan known as the Mausoleo

→

Fig. 4.16. Giovanni Battista Moroni, *Gabriel de la Cueva*, 1560. Oil on canvas (114.5 × 90.8 cm). Gemäldegalerie der Staatliche Museen zu Berlin.

→ →

Fig. 4.17. Andreas Vesalius, "Humani corporis ossium caeteris quas sustinent partibus liberorum suaque sede positorum ex letere delineatio." Woodcut (38.7 × 26 cm). From *De humani corporis fabrica*, 1543.

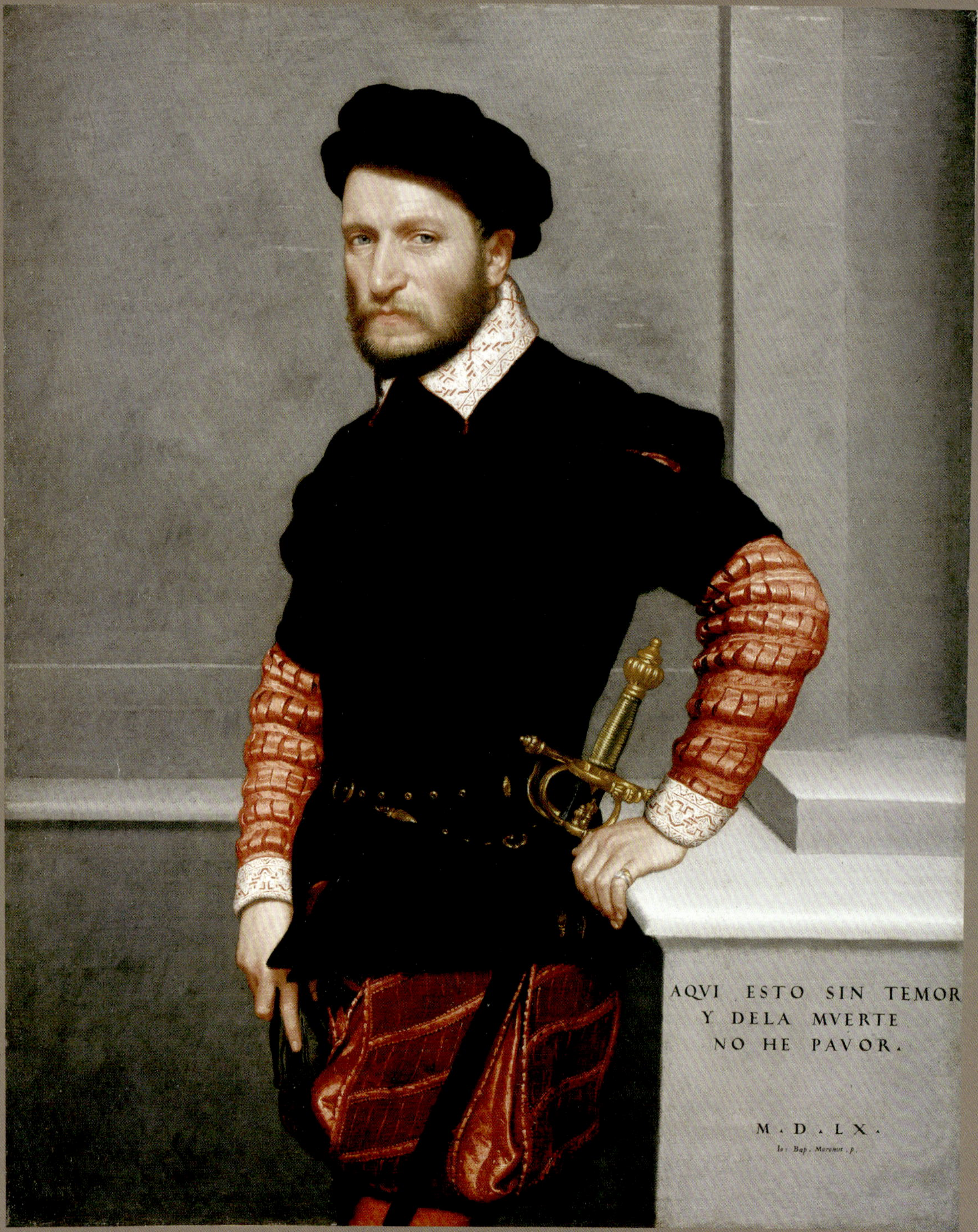
AQVI ESTO SIN TEMOR
Y DELA MVERTE
NO HE PAVOR.
M.D.LX.

HVMANI CORPORIS OSSIVM CAETERIS QVAS SVSTINENT PARTIBVS LIBERORVM, SVAQVE SEDE POSITORVM EX *latere delineatio.*

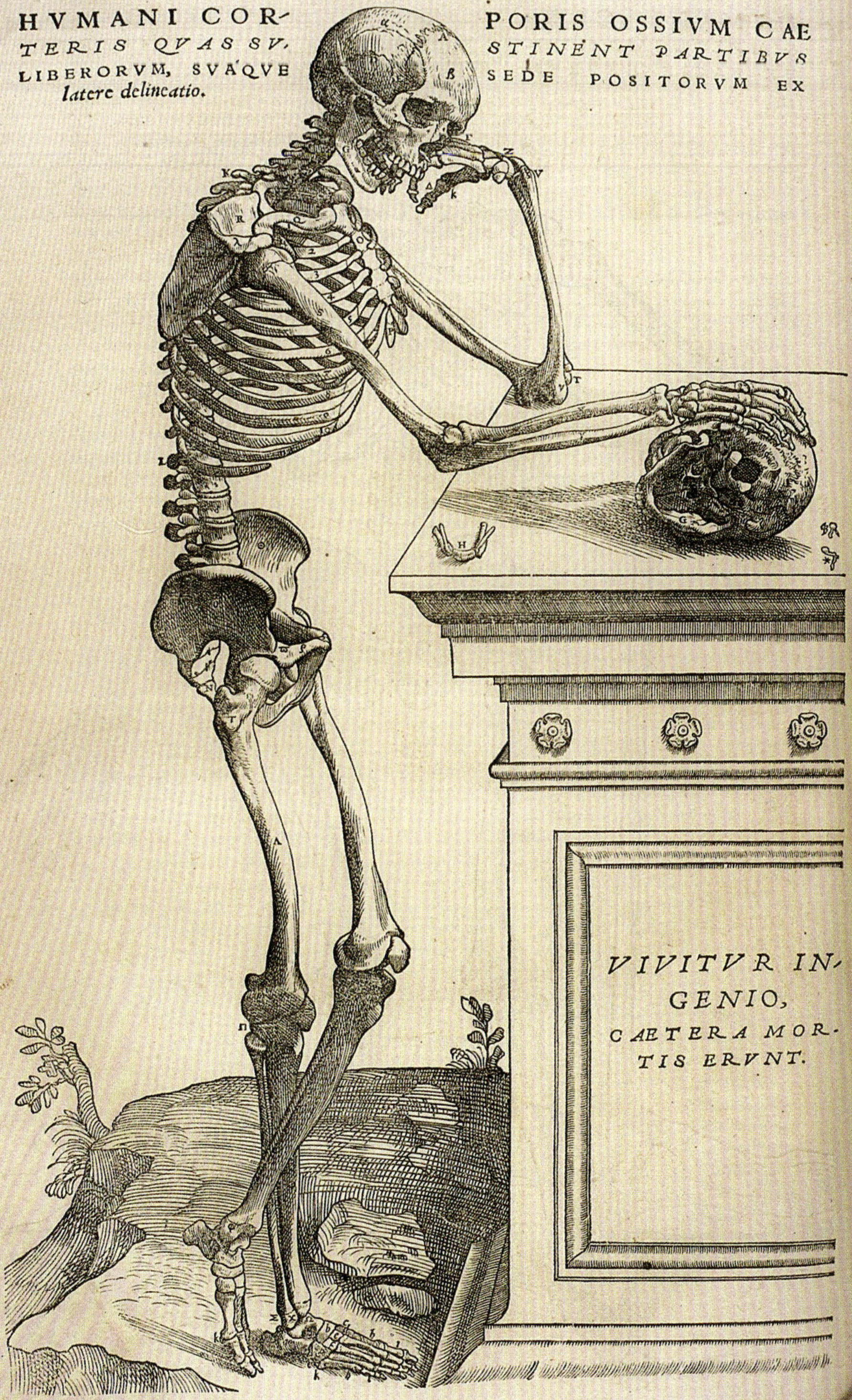

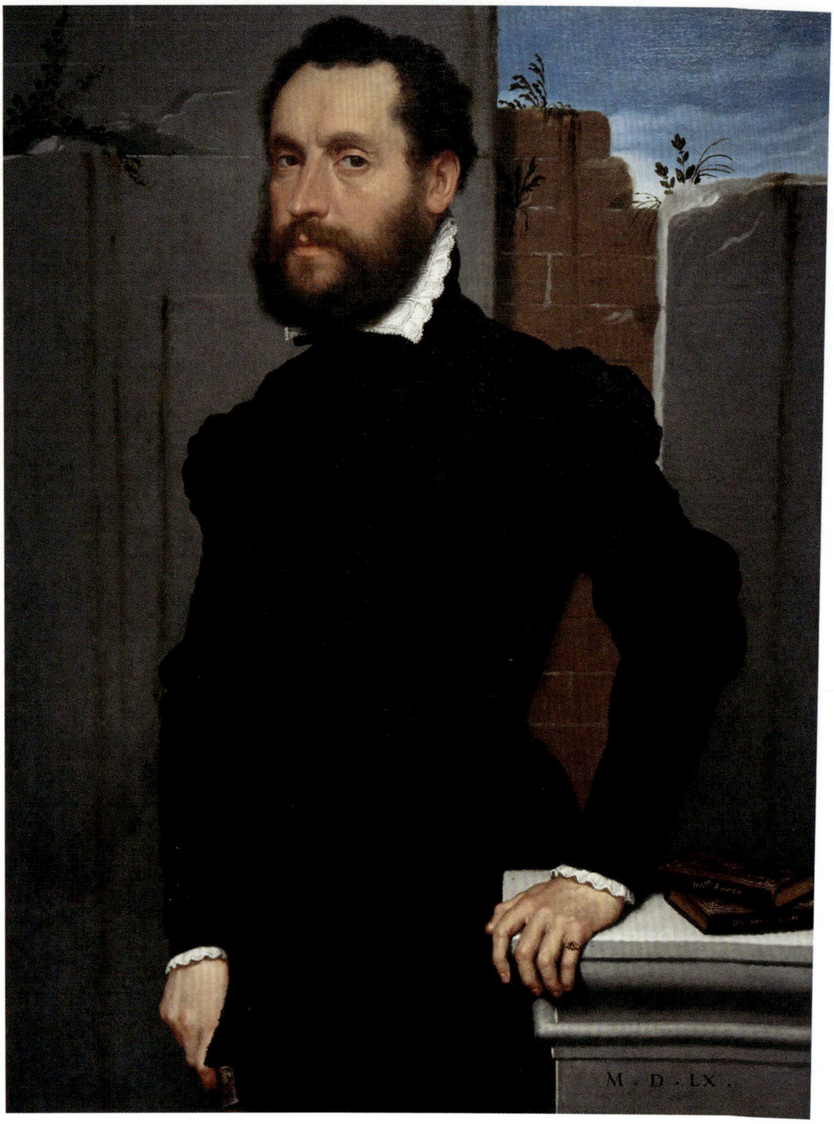

Fig. 4.18. Giovanni Battista Moroni, *The Unknown Poet*, 1560. Oil on canvas (106 × 80 cm). Pinacoteca Tosio Martinengo, Brescia.

Trivulzio, designed by Bramantino in 1512. Its facade pairs stone pilasters composed of white granite and Ornavasso marble, in the Tuscan order, against brick (fig. 4.19).[73] In *The Unknown Poet*, Moroni's similar pairing of brick and ashlar stone presents architecture in the process of decay. Renaissance architects were keenly aware that their buildings were subject to *tempus edax*—devouring time, the teeth of transience.[74] Alberti frequently commented on architecture's vulnerability to the elements. He described how walls might crack and fall apart, how their "bones" might "break." Stone, like wood, could split and warp on account of unseen "abscesses and pockets of decayed matter, which eventually swell up."[75] Weathering eventually turns architectural exteriors, which we often take as exemplars of solid

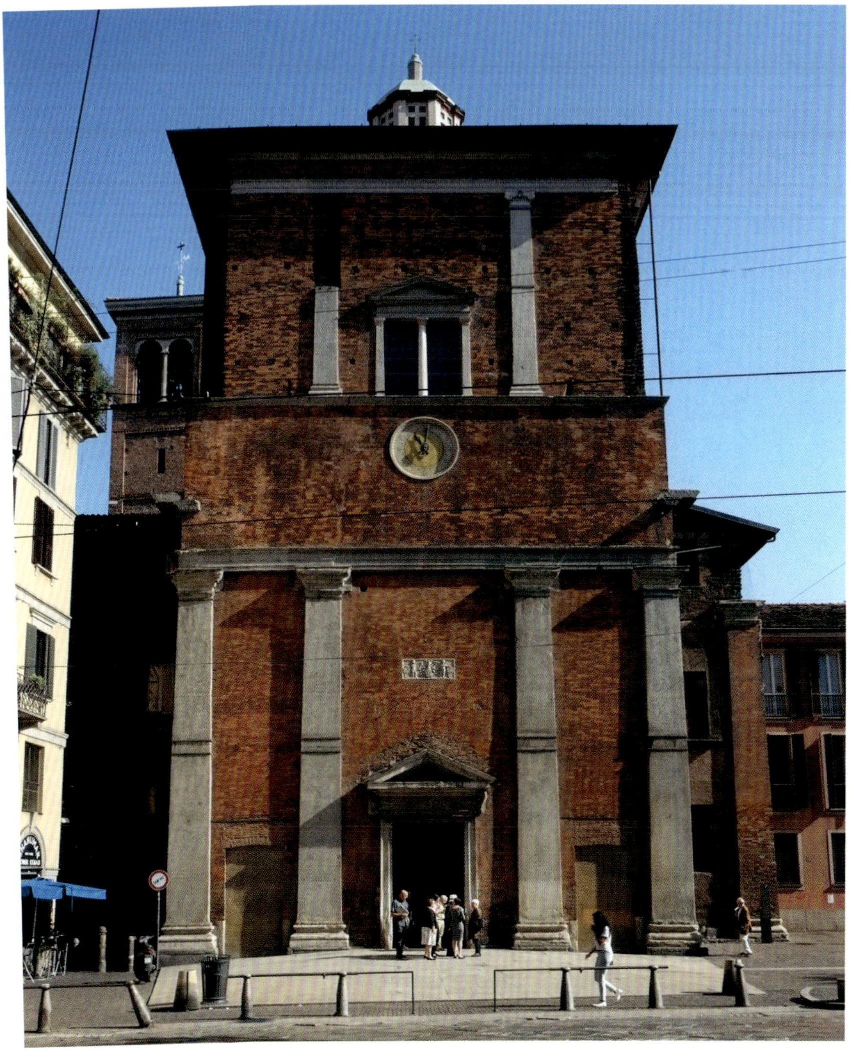

immutability, into their opposite, sites of evident decay. In these paintings, Moroni therefore juxtaposes two modalities or scales of time: the decay of the building, which happens gradually, makes the temporary wholeness of the living body appear even more transitory.

There is an irony to weathering. When buildings weather, their fragmentary nature recalls the process of their being built, brick by brick. Wind and weather erase one surface and expose another that had been concealed in the depths of a building's structure.[76] In *The Unknown Poet*, the phenomenon of weathering has affective force. It suggests the potential release of deposits—not material, but emotional. The poet has at his side books that contend with the mutability of love and friendship. On the spine of the one he holds in his hand we can make out the word "Affetti" (passions). This book, which is barely visible at the bottom edge of the picture behind the

Fig. 4.19. Bartolomeo Suardi, called Bramantino, Trivulzio Mausoleum, begun 1512. Milan.

flap of the poet's cloak, has been identified as a sixteenth-century commentary on Galen's "anatomy of the soul" in his writings on the passions, among them anger, greed, and gluttony.[77] In this case, the ruined architecture may refer to the instability and unbridled energy of the soul, which the ancient physician describes. The sitter's stoic expression, by contrast, exhibits the mastery of those passions whose vices the books surrounding him describe.[78]

The identity of the sitter is therefore perhaps less likely a poet, who would contend with his passions in verse, and more probably a natural philosopher, who would study such a commentary on the soul. As with Gabriel's motto about fearlessness, it also seems significant here that the emotional realm is banished from the medium of painting into language. The books might be about "Affetti," but we aren't reading them: we are looking at a picture where this one word just barely manages to appear. Yes, the passions are mastered, the walls are plastered; but there are seeping abscesses inside. The passions are displaced from the figure and instead inhabit the gray ground. The wall intimates the presence and forces of affect, while preventing their full exposure.

OUT OF JOINT

In the *Portrait of Count Faustino Avogadro* (c. 1555–60), a Bergamasco aristocrat, the ground takes part in anticipating the movement of the figure at the same time as this movement is impaired (fig. 4.20).[79] The customary layer of yellow-brown mestica provides the chromatic base for the lines of damp that streak the wall. These irregular marks created by nature pair themselves incongruously with Faustino's attire and face. In their color and shape, the streaks form a visual analogy with the edges of the chain mail, the golden thread that bisects the feathers, and the beard outlining his face. In spite of these resonances, the figure is "out of joint" with the ground.[80] The aristocrat is dislocated from his proper palatial setting. Just as cracks in the wall seemed to emanate from the eyes and forehead of the "Poet," here the curve of a crack follows the curve of the plumage in Faustino's hat. The feathers are light, airy, fluffy, whereas the wall is heavy, hard, flat. However, the decorative feathers seem to recruit the wall and its marks into performing a decorative function. The crack, another line created by nature, connects Faustino to the wall yet at the same time calls attention to the artifice of this ruin.

The bottom half of the portrait, specifically the floor, lays bare the mechanics of bodily disassembly and impairment. Faustino is not identical to the organism inhabiting his skin. Instead, his stance incorporates fragments that lie beyond the self. Pieces of armor are scattered on the ground: to the left, a cuirass, collar, and a left gauntlet; to the right, gear to protect the upper leg and knee, which, in its horizontal position and its hinging, visually echoes Faustino's elbow.[81] The elements of stance are broken apart to show themselves as components. Of course, when assembled, these pieces make up part of the jousting kit that creates what has been described by

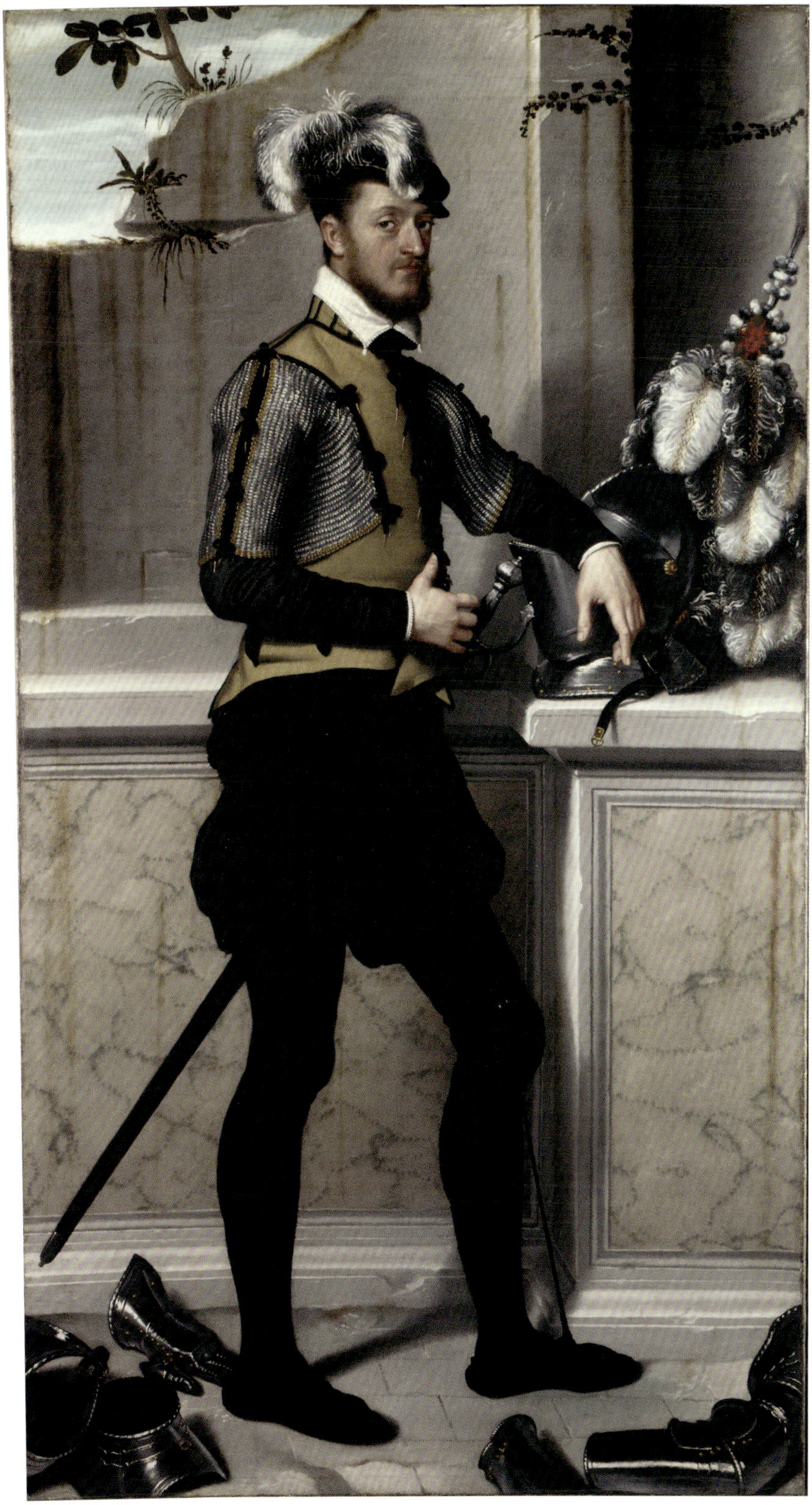

Fig. 4.20. Giovanni Battista Moroni, *Faustino Avogadro (The Knight with the Wounded Foot)*, c. 1555–60. Oil on canvas (202.3 × 106.5 cm). National Gallery, London. Bought, 1876 (NG1022).

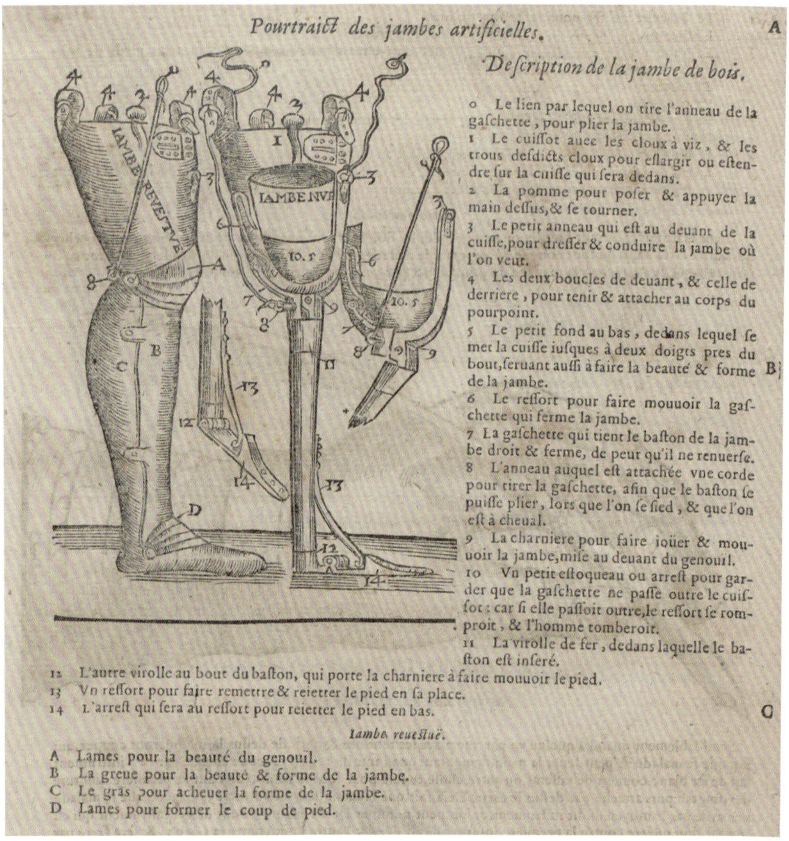

Victor Stoichita as the prince's "second skin."[82] Armor was an impermeable corporeal layer or exoskeleton characterized by durable, shiny materials embossed and engraved with figures. A mirror of war, this metallic encasement offered up the prince's body to the scrutiny of the spectator during ceremonial occasions, such as festivals and parades. Armor reinforces the body even as it conceals. It is "a simulacrum that is inhabited."[83] Armor in portraiture could be considered to represent an intermediate step between the softness of the body and the obdurate encasement that is the wall.

Moroni decomposes this simulacrum. The armor that surrounds Faustino comprises a broken metallic frame, which for the time being reveals the body that it normally encloses and protects. The edges of the picture plane slice through the breastplate and greave, stressing their status as pieces. Period treatises described how the knight ought to master the process of assembling and disassembling his armor, piece by piece. Gonzalo Fernández de Oviedo y Valdés, a sixteenth-century Spanish historian, states that "the man-at-arms, or jouster, starts arming himself from the feet to the head." When he begins to disarm, he continues, "the first thing he does is to take off the helm." When donning armor, he begins with the spurs, continuing upward until he is ready to mount the horse.[84] Other manuals detail how to

Fig. 4. 21. Grégoire Huret, "Portrait des jambes artificielles" (Illustration of prosthetic legs). From Ambroise Paré, *Les œuvres d'Ambroise Paré, conseiller et premier chirurgien du Roy*, 1641. BnF FOL-S-953. Département Arsenal, Bibliothèque nationale de France, Paris.

position each piece in such a way as to ensure comfort and flexibility along with protection. The stakes were high, since a loose attachment during a joust could make the difference between life and death.[85]

Even after having removed his armor, Faustino's stance is enmeshed with technics through the principle of contiguity, the moment when physical proximity facilitates a transfer of meaning. The gauntlet lies next to the foot, linking the limb to a metallic casing. The shadow asserts the physicality of Faustino's figure. Its very intangibility, however, calls attention to the implements propping up his stance, either visually or physically. The sword, which normally acts as a prosthetic extension of the arm, here takes on the role of an additional leg. Most remarkably, Moroni has depicted Faustino with a leg brace.

In a forthcoming study on Renaissance prosthetics, John Gagné has studied this brace, which can be associated with other supportive devices described in sixteenth-century surgical manuals.[86] Ambroise Paré illustrates one such example in his surgical manual *La maniere de traicter les playes* (1552) (fig. 4.21). A flexible metal bar (indicated with the number 13) "closes the triangle" between the shin and the foot piece. In Faustino's device, a twisted silk cord attached to a cuff below his knee connects to another cuff encircling his shoe. This device most likely addressed Faustino's "foot-drop," an impaired ability to lift the toes, resulting in a foot that drags while walking.[87] The twisted cord would lift Faustino's foot as he takes a step. Rather than drooping, like the limp hand pictured above, or trailing, like the streaks of damp, the foot, thanks to the brace, can take a firm step.

Moroni's portrait of Faustino shows us the mechanistic "underworkings" behind the figure's stance. The helmet has been removed to show the face (after tournaments, jousters would lift up their visors to reveal their identities); armor is discarded to show the doublet beneath; cracks and stains on the wall reveal the passage of time and processes of nature. Blue veins in the marble, surging around Faustino's legs, allude to the circulation of blood, only faintly suggested in his hands above. Likewise, the brace points to the distribution of weight and flexion needed for gait. The brace underscores the contingency of stance, looking back on the picture's composite nature. It is the joint on which the portrait stands. Moroni offers a different answer to the riddle posed by the Sphinx: "What is that which has one voice and yet becomes four-footed and two-footed and three-footed?" Like Oedipus, the tragic king with maimed limbs, Faustino prompts us to imagine a notion of human stance that goes beyond the normative figure standing alone on his own two feet on the ground.

ARRESTED TIME

We are now better equipped to return to the *Man in Pink* (fig. 4.22) and understand the compositional force Moroni has invested in the supposedly plain foil of gray ground that the gray wall comprises. In this full-length portrait,

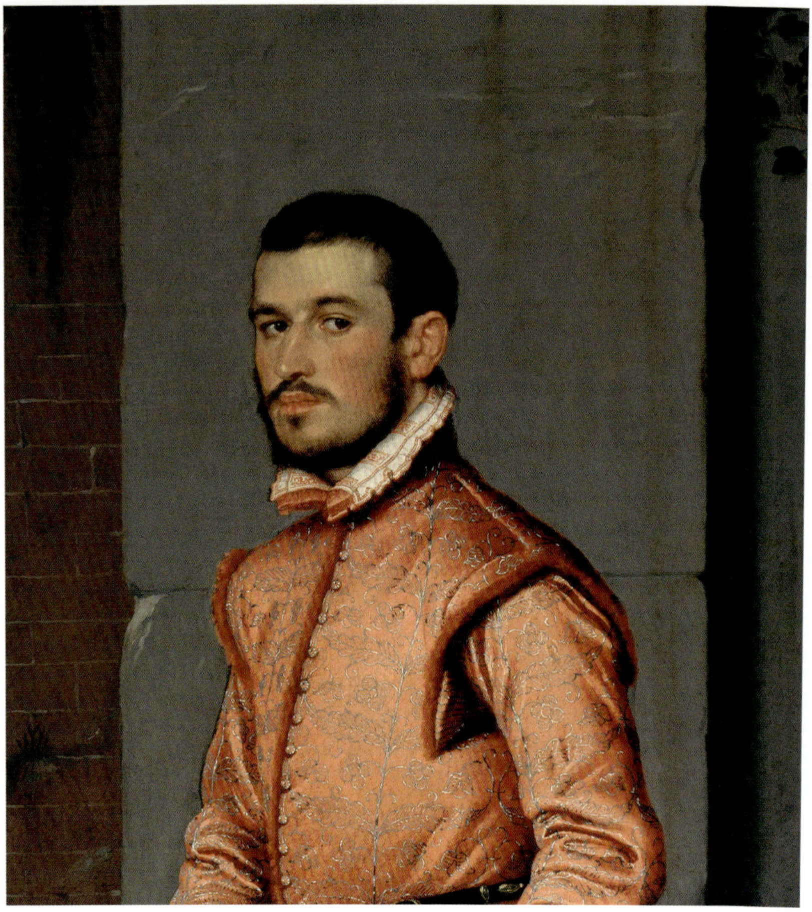

Fig. 4.22. Detail from Giovanni Battista Moroni, *Portrait of Giovanni Gerolamo Grumelli (The Man in Pink)*, 1560. Oil on canvas (216 × 123 cm). Fondazione Museo di Palazzo Moroni, Bergamo. Lucretia Moroni Collection.

groundwork signals modes of embodiment and narrative that digress from and supplement the purely figural. The coloring of the wall, the depiction of decay, and the insertion of objects propose a particular idea of portraiture that addresses the interiority of the sitter obliquely, by means of articulation and impending movement—that is, the joining together or separation of the body and its surroundings. Put another way, the ground implies embodiment. Figural attributes are displaced from the subject's person and undergo transformation through symbolism, poetic allusion, disintegration, and displacement.

The alternation of warm pink and cool gray occurs on both a micro and a macro level in the picture, such that body and building intertwine. Pilasters of gray stone project from the elevation of pinkish bricks. Joining and fusing the bricks are layers of gray *legamento*, mortar paste. Meanwhile, delicate silver thread delineates the stems, leaves, and flowers that course throughout Grumelli's magnificent pink silk costume. Italian Renaissance authors use the verb *arrossire*—to redden—to describe the ripening of figs, the inflaming of passions, or blushing in embarrassment.[88] This *arrossamento* seems to be in progress in Grumelli's face. It could be said that the flush in

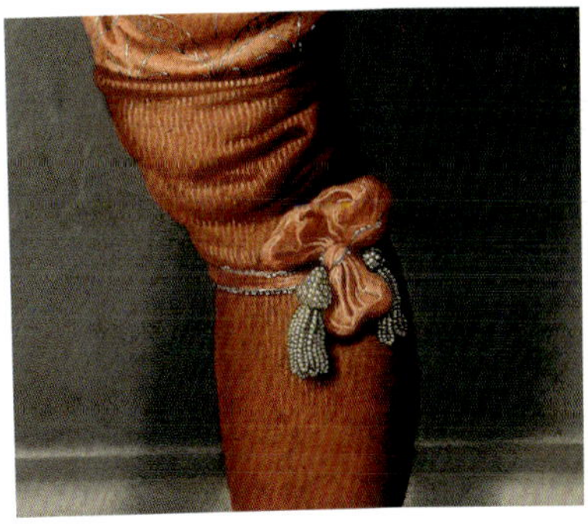

his cheeks rises from his pink jacket through the vessels of the stems of the plants embroidered on it. Like that of the *Man with the Raised Eyebrows*, Grumelli's body is caught at the moment of a reflex action, between sensation and conscious response. His flushed face could allude to his upcoming marriage: the festivities took place the year after the portrait was completed, in 1561.[89] Another possible reference to his nuptials are the beadwork knots on his garters (the expression "to tie the knot" appears in *Romeo and Juliet* [4.2.24] and was in use already centuries before).[90] Here the knot, the soft joint, literally ties the colors pink and gray together (fig. 4.23).

The motif of pink and gray emphasizes the contrast between warm flesh and cold stone. The chromatic motif also alludes to landmarks in the cities where Moroni lived and worked. In Bergamo the Baptistery and Bartolommeo Colleoni's commemorative chapel,[91] and in Brescia the Monte Vecchio di Pietà, Santa Maria de' Miracoli, and the Mausoleo Martinengo (fig. 4.24)[92] all exhibit patterns of pink and gray, which are created from different varieties of sandstone, limestone, and marble extracted from quarries relatively nearby. Localities in northern Lombardy, such as Musso, Nembro, and Saltrio, provided stones with varying shades of gray, while Rosso Verona marble was the source of red and pinks.[93] Some of these monuments are memorials, as if the pink stone, alluding to the flesh and the flush of life, keeps the memory of the individual alive; and some are churches and sites of burial. In connection with this, we might think of the Stone of Unction, the highly venerated slab on which the body of Christ was placed and prepared for burial. It was believed that the stone, *breccia corallina*, which featured blotches of red and white, had absorbed Christ's blood and the Virgin Mary's tears. Fragments thought to come from the slab were worn by pious Christians as necklace pendants. Devotion confronted real flesh (of the wearer's body) and metaphoric flesh (in the form of colored stone).[94]

A city can be thought to have a "local color" (or "colors"), a distinctive palette for its people and buildings.[95] Ancient architectural theorists defined the city in terms of two concepts: the first was *urbs*, the built environment. The second was *civitas*, the citizenry who lived inside a city's houses, worshipped in its churches, and were protected within its walls.[96] The pink and gray characters in Moroni's paintings, the *civitas*, incarnate the *urbs*, and seem to be formed from the same stone. Looking at the characteristic buildings of Bergamo, we notice how pink and gray alternate in bands and grids. The banding or checkering of these two colors, in and between figure and ground, occurs in a more pronounced way in Moroni's work than in other paintings of the period in which pink and gray form a significant chromatic

Fig. 4.23. Detail from Giovanni Battista Moroni, *Portrait of Giovanni Gerolamo Grumelli (The Man in Pink)*, 1560. Oil on canvas (216 × 123 cm). Fondazione Museo di Palazzo Moroni, Bergamo. Lucretia Moroni Collection.

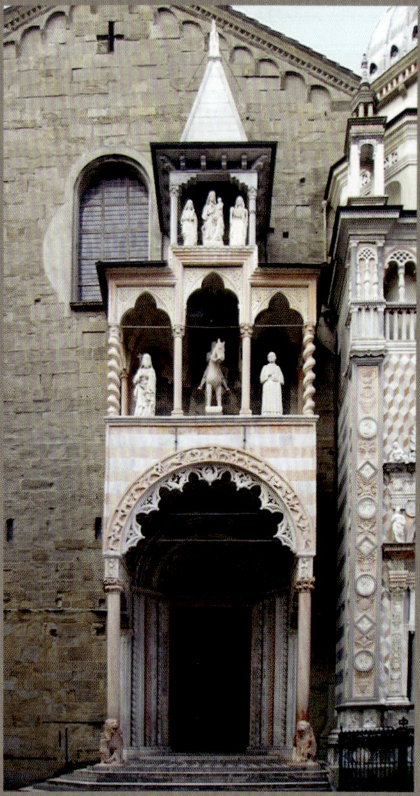
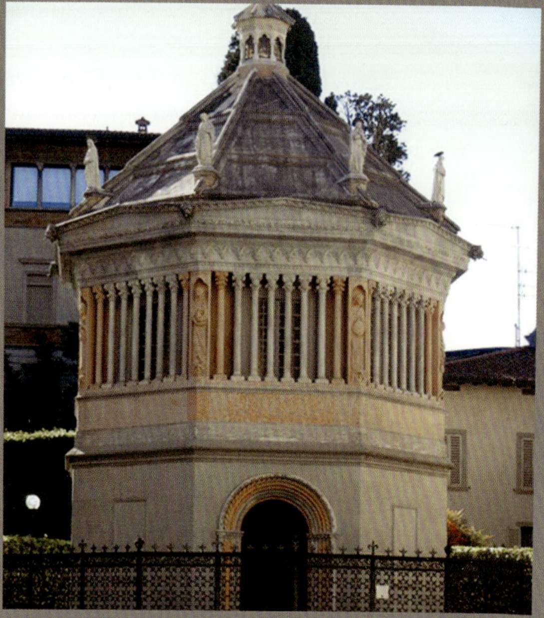
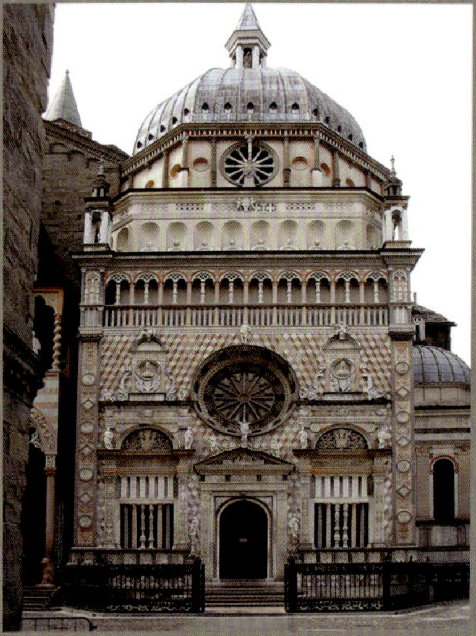
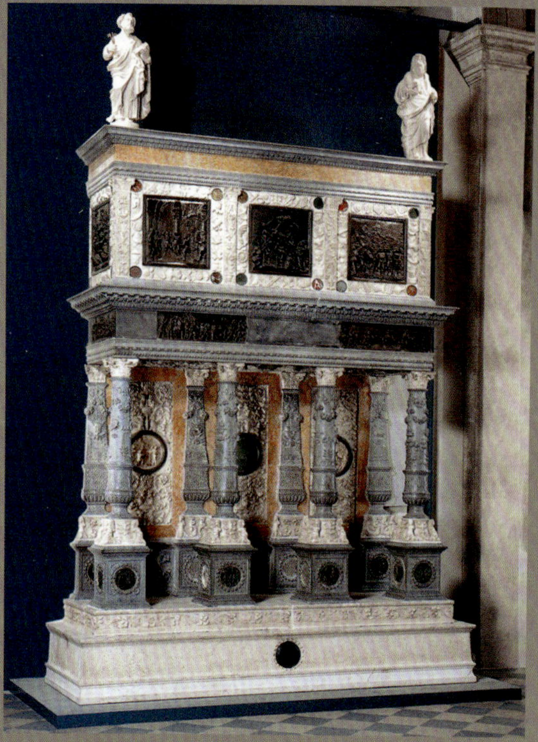

motif. Pink and gray, bodies and buildings, the arts of painting and architecture interlock. They work together to imagine a civic existence arising between the walls of a city that itself is colored by its particular location. Identity is grounded in geography, whose lithic components are unearthed and displayed.

But is the self ever anchored? The mark of the figured self is its containment by the wall. In the portrait of Grumelli, the figure's containment is contingent. He stands against a scene of decay. The pilasters and wall are chipped and stained. The niche is crumbling away, exposed and overgrown with plants. There, a lone foot remains of what was once a heroic sculpture. Its torso has tumbled to the ground. The ground has cracked and is accumulating clouds of dust. The portrait dramatizes transition, or the passage between different states of being. The relief depicted in the painting reflects on this concern. We see a key episode in the life of the prophet Elijah and his follower Elisha (fig. 4.25). 2 Kings 2:11 recounts, "[B]ehold a fiery chariot, and fiery horses parted them both asunder: and Elias [Elijah] went up by a whirlwind into heaven." Moroni depicts Elijah in his chariot, surrounded by a pinwheel of billowing flames. He confers his mantle, the symbol of prophetic succession, upon his follower Elisha, who kneels below.[97]

The motto under the relief, as in the portrait of Don Gabriel, is written in Spanish, attesting to the close ties between Bergamo and Spanish-controlled Milan: "Mas el çaguero que el primero" (It is better to be last than the first). In modern Spanish, *çaguero* would be spelled *zaguero*: while today the word is used for defenders on a soccer team—players such as Gerard Piqué or Sergio Ramos—in medieval and early modern Spanish, *zaguero* often refers to soldiers who took up the rear.[98] Scholars have interpreted the motto and the relief as commenting on circumstances in the subject's life. Grumelli was the second, not the first husband of Isotta Brembati, whom he was to marry in 1561, one year after the portrait's completion. Moroni painted Isotta herself at least twice.[99] Hence Grumelli would be the erotic victor over Isotta's first husband.[100] Grumelli is "más"—more. As the first ones fall, the followers rise.

The principle of transition also operates in the organization of figure and wall. Grumelli's sword, which is floating unsupported in the air, makes an explicit connection between the monochromatic relief and his vibrant costume. The flames surrounding Elijah's chariot, also defying gravity, imply the color red. One might imagine, then, that the sword conveys the red of the flames from the colorless relief and transfers it to Grumelli's costume with its florid ornament and codpiece, framed by his hands where the coursing of blood is visible. His cheeks then also inflame, to signal the triumph

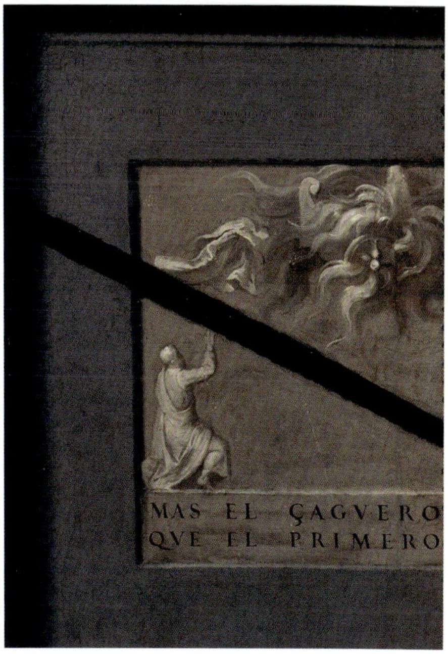

←

Fig. 4.24. Montage showing monuments in Bergamo and Brescia using the polychromatic motifs of pink, white, and gray. Clockwise from upper left: Giovanni da Campione, Porch of the Red Lions, 1353, Basilica di Santa Maria Maggiore, Bergamo; Giovanni da Campione, Baptistery, 1340, Bergamo; Gasparo Cairano and Bernardino dalle Croci, Martinengo Mausoleum, 1503–18, Museo di Santa Giulia, Brescia; Giovanni Antonio Amedeo, Colleoni Chapel, 1472–76, Bergamo.

(ABOVE)

Fig. 4.25. Detail from Giovanni Battista Moroni, *Portrait of Giovanni Gerolamo Grumelli (The Man in Pink)*, 1560. Oil on canvas (216 × 123 cm). Fondazione Museo di Palazzo Moroni, Bergamo. Lucretia Moroni Collection.

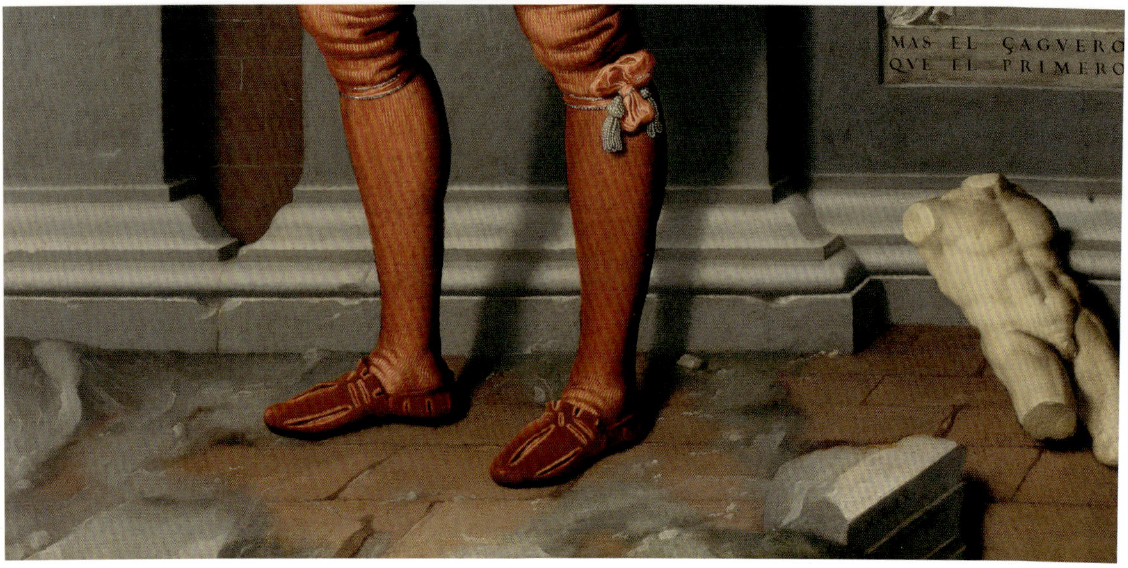

of youthful vigor. Figure draws vitality from ground. The subject's attribute effects this displacement of color and transfer of meaning.

Grumelli's sword cuts across the illusionistic relief right above Elisha's hand, which is raised to catch Elijah's mantle. The diagonal splits the scene, causing the transfer of prophetic office to exist in a state of indefinite suspension. Elisha will forever be awaiting the prophet's cloak, perpetually hanging in the air. This might seem to call into question Grumelli's identity as successor. But we could look at it in another way. While Grumelli is surrounded by signs of decay, for him at least the aging process has been arrested. The gray wall encloses him, yet its ruined state shows that this containment can only be temporary. The sword is an instrument that inserts a pause in this transience, cuts through it. The Italian expression "ritagliarsi del tempo," to take some time, is literally formulated as "to cut out some time for yourself."

Finally, we might ask ourselves what happens when Grumelli takes a step, drawing his sword away from the relief. At that point, the prophetic succession will be underway. Elisha will continue Elijah's miraculous deeds. The knot has been tied. As time consumes him, Grumelli himself will eventually resemble the statue in the empty niche, the contours of the body only intimated by the network of ivy or the cut of an empty costume. His body will be a fragment of itself, like the torso that seems to have slid to the ground. He will resemble the dust that surrounds his feet, the sediments of time, which Monika Wagner has described as "the ultimate entropic material" (fig. 4.26).[101] He will become what painting always was, since its inception: a shadow of a beloved, cast against a gray plane. The wall becomes a monument. It energizes the picture as the site of remembrance, the figure's second and occluded self.

Fig. 4.26. Detail from Giovanni Battista Moroni, *Portrait of Giovanni Gerolamo Grumelli (The Man in Pink)*, 1560. Oil on canvas (216 × 123 cm). Fondazione Museo di Palazzo Moroni, Bergamo. Lucretia Moroni Collection.

★

Moroni's figures adopt different stances, which manifest through the body's contact with the "circum"-stances afforded through the wall as ground. This relationship between figure and ground flips back and forth between articulation and impending movement: distinct parts of the body connect; body connects to ground; interiority is displaced onto an external surface that can be read and interpreted; then also, these connections are broken when the painting evokes the figure's potential to ambulate. The wall does not only serve, therefore, to commemorate the figure through the transcription of shadow, as in Pliny's myth of the Corinthian maiden. When mestica becomes skin, or the gray wall becomes eyes, when metal encasement is likened to a disassembled skeleton, or pinkish stone to flesh, the painting is conceived as a layering of veils or anatomical tissues from which a solid form protrudes and becomes a figure. This anatomical wall offers "contingent containment": the enclosure of the body is fated to fall away as the depicted figure is shown to occupy a depicted pose only temporarily before the viewer. Structure is contingent, the body is mobile, and ground is ready—prepared to indicate narrative action. The anatomical qualities of Moroni's gray grounds, their portrayal of figural presence, affect, locomotion that nonetheless remains latent, confront the more fundamental issue of the movement of the figure—its positioning, disappearance, and restitution—in Renaissance art and art historical scholarship. How might the process of forming a figure and semantic plentitude emerge in a ground normally thought to be empty and negative? As the following chapter will show, figuration can be translated across the pictorial field, even emerging in spaces that appear totally dark.

5

Transumption: Echoes in the Darkness

imāgō, ~inis, *f.* [. . .] **1** A representation in art of a person or a thing, picture, likeness, image. **2** A death-mask of an ancestor. **b** (usu. pl., as representing noble ancestry). **3** A reflection in a mirror or sim. **b** a reflection of sound, echo.

***Oxford Latin Dictionary*, ed. P.G.W. Glare, s.v. "imago"**

UNNAMEABLE DARKNESS

Louis Marin characterizes his 1977 book *To Destroy Painting* as "a journey through paintings" that "transforms images into discourse." The subjective nature of these translations, he acknowledges, might be enough "to annoy the most benevolent reader."[1] To render this transit from painting to prose more legible, Marin announces that he will make explicit use of those linguistic instruments that aid reading and sense-making. To characterize Caravaggio's black backgrounds, he cites a series of dictionary entries, beginning with the Latin *arca*:

> *Arca*: 1/ coffre—armoire—cassette; 2/ cercueil; 3/ prison étroite, cellule; 4/ citerne, réservoir; 5/ borne de délimitation.
>
> *Arcanus, a, um* (arca): 1/ discret, sûr (poet.) arcana box (Ovide): nuit discrete; 2/ cache, secret, mystérieux.
>
> *Arceo, ui, ere* (cf. arca, arx, grec arkeô) tr: 1/ contenir, enfermer, retenire: flumina, Ciceron, *Nat.* 2, 152, maintenir les fleuves dans leurs lits; 2/ tenir éloigné, détourner, écarter.[2]

Caravaggio's black fields, the lexical excerpt suggests, are like a money chest, a coffin, prison cell, or cistern; they are subtle, arcane, and secret; they contain, keep away, and prevent approach. They turn away, divert, and push away. Operative is the association to the "arc of the covenant," something hermetically sealed due to the power of its contents, the shrouding of

Detail, Figure 5.14

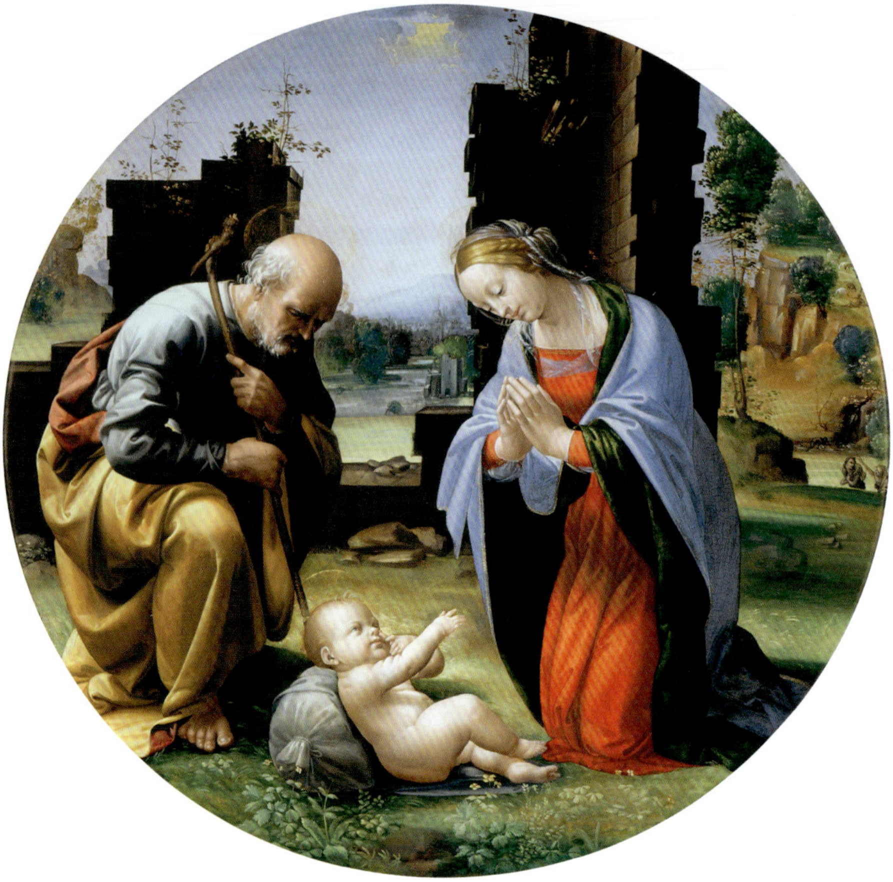

scripture in ritual. Marin asks, "What does black hold?" and answers with a contradiction of sorts: "It creates a distance. It divides and separates."[3] Caravaggio's grounds, expansive fields of darkness that modulate between rich browns and blacks, might therefore be likened to a gap within a closed receptacle, a hole contained inside a box. For Daniel Arasse, Marin's erstwhile thesis advisee and interlocutor, such spaces of omission in the picture have the capacity to bring out the affective dimension of the art historical enterprise. "I choose as an object of study to write or to speak about painting," Arasse declares, "which is exactly what escapes writing and speaking." The interval of darkened emptiness between figures transforms painting, the object of study, into "an object of desire." Darkness does not equal either representation or lack thereof; it is rather an evasion. This turning away elicits what Arasse calls the "verbal process" (in the senses of both procedure and trial), a coupling of interrogation and longing.[4]

Fig. 5.1. Baccio della Porta, called Fra Bartolomeo, *Adoration of the Child*, c. 1490. Tempera on panel (diameter 89 cm). Galleria Borghese, Rome.

In the tradition of the Renaissance picture, the interval between figures could often be occupied by landscape backgrounds: these afforded views of a distant horizon toward which the gaze was intended to wander until it could come to rest. In Fra Bartolomeo's tondo of the Holy Family, for instance, the viewer's attention is directed not only toward the Christ Child on the ground; complementing this portrayal of the Redeemer are landscape views, which break through the walls of the ruined building symbolizing the Old Dispensation (fig. 5.1). The contour implicit in the tondo format bounds negative space, as the fragmented rock walls bound the distant sky. In Caravaggio's paintings, darkened backgrounds initiate a mode of viewing that allows no access to a space in the distance; instead, the viewer's gaze is led into darkness. Those dark spaces contain latent presences that are felt as ready to emerge.

NARCISSUS

Narcissus, a work often though not definitely attributed to Caravaggio, depicts the beautiful youth attempting to embrace his own image in the pool.[5] According to the myth, the kneeling figure falls and passes into its reflection, closing the circuit of solipsistic desire. In the painting, glimmering streaks of white paint, which describe the water's edge, cut the picture almost in half. To articulate parts of the figure, such as the contours of the face and hair, the artist left portions of the material ground exposed, as though anticipating the figure's eventual convergence with the ground. The highlighted cheekbone and nose leave the ocular socket in deep darkness. "The eye, the organ at the very heart of the myth," Rossella Vodret observes, "is both emphasized and obscured."[6] The part of the ground comprised by the reflection on the water's surface, a passage that takes up almost half of the painting, in its obscurity is the counterpart to Narcissus's eye because it is the object of his gaze. In chapter 1, this ground as plane was posited as one of the primal sites of painting. It is a context that originates figuration and reinforces the desire to possess it, no matter how fleetingly. The reflective ground in the painting seems to arrest time: in Ovid's version of the myth (*Metamorphoses* 3.418–19), Narcissus is described as being spellbound (*adstupet*) and motionless (*immotus*) before his reflection, which is itself compared to an immobile object, a statue hewn from Parian marble. This reflective and still ground also prefigures the fate that will befall Narcissus after his death and transformation into a flower. "Even when he had been received into infernal abodes [postquam est inferna sede receptus], he kept on gazing on his image in the Stygian pool."

The painting's background unfolds a further dimension of temporality that has rarely received commentary. It is possible to read the darkness behind Narcissus's shoulders as a space of anteriority, the time that came *before* the moment portrayed in the picture. For according to the myth, in order to behold himself, Narcissus must first turn away from Echo. Compacted into this dark space in the painting is a narrative sequence where figures move into and out of view amidst a forest setting as they address one another in a dialogue that spans interrogation, incomprehensibility, frustration, disappearance, and death. Narcissus, addressing the figure that is Echo, asks, "equis adest?" (Is anyone here?), to which Echo answers, "adest" (is here, is here, is here). In turn, Narcissus addresses his own reflection, which also remains mute. While Kaja Silverman has attended to these dimensions of volte-face in Ovid's tale, it is also instructive to think about what has been left behind in the background, what voices still occupy it.[7]

Ovid introduces Narcissus by describing him as a youth who "had reached his sixteenth year and might seem boy or man." Many youths desired him, as did many maidens. Echo, originally "a nymph of resounding speech" (vocalis nymphe [. . .] resonabilis) becomes a paramour of Zeus and is punished by Hera, who curtails her vocal powers by condemning her to repeat whatever is said to her. Echo falls in love with Narcissus upon first seeing him. Her heart burns for him, and she "follows him by stealth" (sequitur vestigia furtim). The longing of the invisible nymph in the forest is likened to a torch, an instrument of night pursuit and metaphor of passion: "the more she followed, the more she burned by a nearer flame; as when quick-burning sulphur, smeared round the tops of torches, catches fire from another fire brought near." She longs to approach Narcissus but cannot address him. It is at this point that Narcissus cries, "Is anyone here?" to which Echo can only respond "[is] here." The youth then looks around him: "He sent forth his gaze in all directions." He looks behind him yet sees no one coming. To assist her words, Echo comes out of the forest in the hope of encircling his neck in her arms. Emphasizing Narcissus's rejection of Echo's advances by repeating the word for escape, Ovid remarks that the youth "fled and fleeing says, 'Hands off! Embrace me not!' " (ille fugit fugiensque 'manus conplexibus aufer! ante' ait). After eluding the embraces of Echo as well as those of other maidens and youths, Narcissus turns toward his own image in the ill-fated pool: "Here the youth, worn by the chase and the heat, lies down."

The act of turning away, through its repetition in biblical and classical mythology, becomes a trope or metaphor that associates the background setting with past time. Lot's wife disobeys the commandment not to turn back and look at the city of Sodom as it is consumed by flames. She becomes a pillar of salt (Genesis 19). Although ordered by Hades not to look back as he rescues Euridice, Orpheus cannot resist the temptation and consigns his lover to the underworld. Both of these characters turn away from what lies ahead in turning toward what lies behind them, or what is in the past—which has been forbidden. The consequences of this momentary act become irreversible. In Caravaggio's rendering of the Narcissus myth, the trope of turning away, like the drawing of a curtain, reveals the dark background, representing "that which I refuse to behold." Haunting the upper edges of the picture's dark ground is the condemned nymph who answers with a fractured voice.

ECHO AS RESONANT GROUND

In his classic account *The Figure of Echo* (1981), the American poet John Hollander explored how echo's mythical origins inform the use of refrain, rhyme, and assonance in Renaissance poetry. The term "echo," Hollander reminds us, "is used figuratively to indicate a musical or linguistic repetition, usually of a short utterance or the terminal portion of a longer one." He adds that "the repeated sound is not only contingent upon the first, but in some way a qualified version of it." While analyzing echo as a fragmentation of poetic form, Hollander called attention to the *place* of echo. Woodlands, rocky landscapes, antique ruins, and especially caves are "complex conformations of reflecting surfaces." These "intricate interiors of stone and masonry" bring forth "serial echoes—echoes themselves reechoed—as well as diverse direct flections from various distances." Such subterranean chambers produce "delays in return, scattering, and proliferation," the effect of a "lurking and invisible vocal presence." The cave, seemingly deprived of human presence, emerges as a place of inquiry. There is only a small step from "Where are you hiding?" to "Echo, where are *you* hiding?" The cave, writes Hollander, "hides both body and disembodied voice."[8]

The mythological figure of Echo is concealed in the background or underground. From classical sources to their interpretations in Renaissance texts, the myth of Echo establishes a precedent for an understanding of ground as containing fragments of a body that, while concealed, remain poignantly resonant. An episode in the ancient Greek pastoral romance *Daphnis and Chloe* (3.23) places the two titular lovers next to the sea, listening to the songs of fishermen as they row. Coming beneath a promontory, the mariners enter "a flexuous, horned, hollow bay." Their voices resonate and multiply, producing a "shrill sound as into an organ." Since this is her first experience of an echo, Chloe asks Daphnis "whether there were [another] sea beyond the promontory and another ship did pass by there, and whether they were other mariners that had sung the same song." Amused, Daphnis recounts the tale of Echo: she was a beautiful woodland nymph and excelled in music, singing and dancing with the Muses, who taught her "to play on the hautboy and the pipe, to strike lyre, to touch the lute."[9] Refusing the advances of mortal men or divine beings, such as Pan, Echo embraces virginity, a fatal choice. George Thornley's 1657 translation of *Daphnis and Chloe* narrates the consequences of Echo's decision in a horrific image of dismemberment: "Pan [. . .] takes occasion to be angry at the maid, and to envy her music because he could not come at her beauty. Therefore, he sends a madness among the shepherds [. . .] and they tore her all to pieces and flung about them all over the earth her yet singing limbs. The Earth in observance of the Nymphs buried them all, preserving to them still their music property, and they by an everlasting sentence and decree of the Muses breathe out a voice."[10]

Echo's body had been given to music-making and dance—her fingers plucked strings; her feet took steps in rhythm. Now disembodied, her limbs continue to flex and strum, her wrists rattling and shaking instruments beneath the earth. Annibale Caro's translation into Italian (before 1538) accentuates the image of Echo's dismemberment and the haphazard scattering of her limbs. In his alliterative rendering, the shepherds and goatherds "scerparono e sbranaron tutta"—mangle and tear her completely asunder. While Echo is still singing, "they dispersed pieces of her across the earth" (ne sparsero i pezzi per tutta la terra). The ground, customary location of repose and silence, becomes a subterranean sonic chamber through which Echo's music resounds. Now invisible, she is still audible, though any melodic flow is broken into pieces. The narrative framing device of this story in which the myth of Echo emerges—the scene of Daphnis and Chloe listening to the fishermen's songs—likewise conceives the repeated sounds as each uttered by a separate voice. The phenomenon of echo provokes the shepherdess to cast doubt on what is visible in and of itself, to imagine other coves containing other bodies.[11]

In the locus classicus of Echo's story, Ovid's *Metamorphoses* (3.339–401), the poet's diction enacts while describing the nymph's vanishing and condition of invisibility. Madly in love with, yet rejected by, the handsome Narcissus, Echo "lurks in the woods," the verb *latet*, etymologically related to "latency," accentuating the condition of concealment. Shamefaced, Echo covers herself with foliage ("pundibundaque frondibus ora protegit"). Literally meaning "to cover over" or "hide in front," the verb *protegere* conveys the image of Echo bending the branches of the trees to conceal herself, her eyes peering through the openings between the leaves. From nestling her among the trees, Ovid then takes Echo inside the earth: "from now on, she lives in lonely caves" (solis ex illo vivit in antris). Assuming habitation in a hollow place beneath ground, Echo thus comes to embody the previously suggested state of latency.

Having removed her not only from Narcissus but from human company in general, the poet describes the process by which Echo becomes physically removed from herself and assumes a state of disembodiment. Her sleepless cares "waste away her miserable body" (extenuant corpus miserabile). It is interesting to note that Ovid's selection of the verb *extenuare* to describe Echo's disappearing body resonates with ancient accounts of painters executing fine and thin brushstrokes. Pliny describes Apelles's brushwork as "lineam [. . .] summae tenuitatis" (*Nat. hist.* 35.81–83; a line of the utmost subtlety). Through the process implicit in "extenuant," Echo takes on the gaunt linear form of the trees among which she hides. Then also "thinness wrinkles her skin" (adducitque cutem macies). All moisture leaves her body, disappearing "in aere"—into her invisible surroundings. In the last stage of the nymph's dematerialization, her body merges with the forest. Along with her voice, Echo's bones remain ("vox tantum atque ossa supersunt"). Finally, these bones themselves transform into "a figure of stone" (figuram lapis). The device of indirect speech—"ferunt" (they say)—is used to express this final transformation. Ovid removes the reader from the scene of Echo's fable by degrees, just as Echo herself was removed, first from Narcissus and, eventually, from her own corporeal envelope.

Echo moves from being a character in a fable to a poetic device that fragments utterance into parts that eventually die away. Sixteenth-century renderings of the Ovidian myth continue to portray the nymph's body degenerating into bones, stones, and dust, which merge with terrestrial and subterranean surroundings. In his widely diffused and frequently reprinted translation of Ovid, first published in part in 1553, Giovanni Andrea dell'Anguillara portrays Echo reacting to Narcissus's rejection by mutilating herself.[12] She beats and scratches herself (3.157; "si batte, e graffia"), actions that prefigure the eventual disintegration of her body. Such is her desire for Narcissus that flames consume her, reducing her flesh to ashes and dust (3.158; E tanto consumando al corpo noce, / che la carne si fa cenere e polve). Her bones turn to hard stones, which in turn also disappear, leaving Echo only her voice. Instead of simply stating, as Ovid did, that Echo lives alone in caves, Anguillara positions the disembodied nymph deeper in the earth. She inhabits "some cavernous grotto" (qualche grotto cavernosa), at times responding when addressed. Ludovico Dolce's version of *Metamorphoses*, entitled *Trasformationi*, also first published in 1553 and reprinted through the 1560s, emphasizes Echo's consolidation with her surroundings (Canto 6, 69r). Spurned by Narcissus, Echo hides herself in "the great forest," which is dark and thick" (la gran Selva è oscura e folta.) Her mourning ever intensifying, her body transforms into "a dry hard rock" (un duro sasso asciutto). Ultimately, she avoids living in the mountains, residing and responding "nel piano," that is to say, in a valley. In Dolce's account, Echo is literally placed in the ground.[13]

Another writer fascinated with Echo was Giambattista Marino, the famed Neapolitan poet who befriended Caravaggio during the artist's first years in Rome, in the 1590s, when the *Narcissus* painting was also produced.[14] In his lyric entitled "Eco," first published in 1614, Marino imagines her movement among solitary caverns and grottos.[15] The poet uses prepositions—"in," "among," "through"—to indicate the effort of determining the nymph's location, which by definition is always temporary. Assuming the guise of Pan, the woodland god whose advances Echo rejected, the speaker both describes the nymph's tragic fate and invokes her presence in order to lament his unrequited love. Pan remarks that just as he has fled the sun and world, Echo "flees from people and light." She is "the soul of the woods, citizen of the shadows" who pursues her beloved Narcissus "among the dark dwellings of the beasts." Echo herself laments, nestled "between the opaque and dark shadows, removed from hope and joy." While the nymph's location in the dark sylvan landscape is indeterminate, her auditory presence expands. As Pan declares, "The dark and black air of this hidden cave resounds today of your profound sorrow." From identifying Echo's movement in, among, and between the trees of the forest, Marino moves to a language of definition and direct address. Echo is ultimately "the invisible image, the inhabitant of inhospitable harrowing shadows." The tension between felt presence and invisibility is so intolerable that Pan doubts the very pretext motivating his desire to locate, much less address Echo. Calling her "illusory daughter of air and speech," the speaker declares the futility of lyric description, as if he were turning away from his subject and from poetry itself: "I see you are nothing" (ben veggio che sei nulla).[16]

TRANSUMPTIVE GROUND

Hollander sees in Echo's unseen existence a mythographic counterpart for a particular mode of poetic allusion, namely metalepsis (literally "jumping over" in Greek), also Latinized in English as "transumption." If metaphor involves the transfer of attributes from one entity to another, then transumption entails, as Hollander puts it, the "movement from one trope to another, which operates through one or more middle terms of figuration." In transumption, these middle terms are alluded to in their very suppression, such that Hollander can describe the figure as "elusive and allusive."[17]

One literary instance of transumption cited by Hollander occurs in the description of a cave in *Aeneid* 1. 60. In this verse, Virgil recounts how Jupiter imprisons the winds of Aeolus in the depths of the earth: "sed pater omnipotens speluncis abdidit atris" (the father omnipotent hid them in gloomy caverns). Glossing this line of verse in *De copia* (1514), Erasmus stated that the figure of transumption occurs "when we proceed by steps to that which we wish to express, as: he hid in dark caves. For the connotation is of black caves, from black obscure, and from this finally, extreme depth." The German humanist Johannes Susenbrotus in his handbook of rhetorical figures *Epitome troporvm* (1542) offered a succinct resume of the trope: "gloomy means black; black, shadowy; and shadowy, deep" (atris: nigrae enim intelliguntur, ex nigris tenebrosae, et per hoc in praeceps profundae).[18] Richard Sherry in *A Treatise of Schemes and Tropes* (1550) writes (and rhymes), "By blacke is understand ful of darkenes and consequently stepe down and very depe."[19] Italian handbooks of rhetoric often seized on the expression *spelunca atra* (gloomy cavern) to illustrate arrival at concealed meaning. Bartolomeo Cavalcanti in *La retorica* (1559) associates transumption with procession by intervals, as though walking on a terraced path. The trope "leads us to what [is] meant, almost by degrees, the half step to another serving us only to give us a path, so that we can pass through." Likewise, if in "speaking of the deepest crag [profondissima balza], one called it black; by which word we first will understand darkness, and by means of this we will pass to the intended meaning of depth." Interpreting transumption involves descending into the depths of the earth to retrieve the transumed ideas that lurk in shadowed profundity.[20]

Of course, these writers seized on the image of the cave to demonstrate metalepsis (the elision of "depth," its replacement with "darkness") because the cave itself instantiates elision: through a gap or breach, meaning enters or escapes. Recalling our discussion of the Frick Bellini in chapter 3, we can now observe that Francis's gaping mouth as well as the cave beside him opens itself to the process of inquiry and sense-making. As can be read in Leonardo's famous report of the fear and fascination that he felt on coming to a cavern's dark entrance, the obscurity and implicit depth contained in hollow forms invite a mode of viewing that conjoins the visual with the interrogative—"What is there?" or "What else is there?"

Hollander's passage from Echo to transumption—from the mythological figure to the rhetorical figure—allows us to conceive of ground in terms that go beyond what we have said about it thus far. It becomes evident that groundwork can operate as a painterly procedure whose purpose is paradoxically to reveal itself as cloaking or hiding something else. By preventing us from seeing inside, the cave in turn elicits our act of inquiry by asking, "What is inside of me?" The mystery of the cave heightens, even dares the viewer to activate, the hermeneutic faculty. As Dolce suggested in his version of Echo's fate, the nymph comes to reside "nel piano": here, the flat and featureless ground becomes a figure of latent figuration. Broadly speaking, this transumptive ground provides the foundation for a way of reading, looking, and thinking that works through implication, not indication. The classical rhetoricians' accounts of metalepsis, in fact, give an overly rational sense of what this figure of speech can do. In their schema, one adjective replaces another, but they do not catalyze the subject-verb relationship, where a substantive and action transform one another. The effect of metalepsis can be much more fantastic and inventive than they suggest. The singing fragments of Echo's body do not belong to a rationalist interpretive mode. They are not easily inserted into the pictorial narrative, and for that reason, they inhabit the darkness.

THE DARKENED ROOM AND THE AFTERMATH OF VISUALITY

Giulio Mancini, physician to Pope Urban VIII and an art connoisseur well acquainted with Caravaggio and his art, authored a series of manuscripts collectively known as *Considerazioni sulla pittura*, which were written and compiled largely from 1619 to 1624 although they were edited, circulated, and annotated in many different versions.[21] Cited and read by subsequent writers on art such as Giovanni Baglione, Giovanni Battista Bellori, and Filippo Baldinucci, the *Considerazioni* identifies the salient visual characteristics of Caravaggio and his followers and places those attributes in a taxonomy of historically based style. Paintings from Caravaggio's "school," Mancini writes, attained heightened contrasts between "very bright highlights and very dark shadows" (i chiari e l'ombre molto chiare e molto oscure). To visualize the effect, he encourages readers to imagine an architectural interior "with concentrated light, coming from on high without reflections, as if it were through a window in a room with walls colored black."[22] Introduced by the conditional form "come sarebbe," this description supposedly of Caravaggio's atelier is hypothetical, not indicative. Mancini momentarily absents the figure from the space of walls "colored black," or as one version of the manuscript specifies, "walls covered with black colored things," presumably stretches of cloth.[23] He writes that this scenography effects figuration by producing accentuated chromatic contrasts ("in this way [. . .] the lights and shadows [are] very bright and deep"). In art historical reception, Mancini's statement regarding the room is conventionally taken to attest that Caravaggio and his school did in fact paint with a single light source in a room with black walls, because the hypothetical is embedded in a longer passage about painting from nature or "il vero."

Caravaggio's paintings do not depict a black-painted room. And yet, the image of the darkened studio would be reiterated by other period voices. Giovanni Pietro Bellori, a critic whose remarks about Caravaggio's darkness will be treated more fully toward the end of this chapter, states that the artist "discovered a way to ground [his figures] amidst the dark atmosphere of an enclosed room."[24] Bellori here deploys the charged critical term *campire* (to ground), which can designate the application of a preparatory layer of paint and the positioning of figures in a composition. Hence, what Mancini interpreted as copying from life proves, in Bellori's understanding, to be an imagined mise-en-scène. However, one of Caravaggio's biographers, Joachim Sandrart, who was well acquainted with the artist's work and clientele, stated that "to better bring out the effects of relief and natural roundness, [Caravaggio] used dark vaults or shadowed rooms which had one source of light from above, so that the light falling on the model made strong shadows and so emphasized the effects of relief."[25] Sandrart's statements, along with historical documents—such as a legal complaint from 1603 attesting that Caravaggio was sued by his landlady for having broken the ceiling of his apartment, perhaps in seeking to illuminate his models from above—continue to fuel scholarly debate, particularly in respect to the artist's use of the camera obscura, mirrors, and other optical instruments to produce his intense chiaroscuro effects.[26] Yet what period critics and modern art historical scholarship fail to acknowledge—almost willfully so—is the imaginative function of Caravaggio's black grounds.[27] In this way, the darkened grounds are made into sites of negation or emptiness, lacking in any deeper significance.

Instead of inferring a mimetic relationship between Caravaggio's paintings and his physical surroundings, we might also place the conceit of the darkened room in relation to myths, tropes, and theories of the wall as pictorial ground. The wall excludes and indicates the absent figure through the traced shadow of the lover; the wall absorbs the figure, as in the cases of Saint Francis on La Verna and of Echo herself; and the wall articulates the figure by likening body to architectural elevation and by expressing the inner life of the sitter on the wall's surface. In these situations, a lesser or greater degree of tactile connection between figure and ground charges the ground with meaning. Enclosed and dark, though pierced with light, Caravaggio's *camera rinchiusa* gives rise to the anticipation of tactility, though never its complete fulfillment. Here we might recall Ovid's metaphor that describes Echo as she draws near but cannot grasp Narcissus: in Ovid's image, the fire jumps from torch to torch though the torches do not touch. As in the figure of metalepsis, the flame skips across, leaving an interval of darkness between points of warmth and brightness. The myth of Echo clears a way to approach, even understand, Caravaggio's ground as a place of interrogation that dramatizes darkness as the inception or aftermath of visuality. In this dark space, the figure once was. Though it is now absent, it will return.

There is a concrete technical dimension to this idea. To supplement his brush underdrawings, Caravaggio incised figural contours in the imprimatura and other preparatory layers, often for the purpose marking off areas of darkness in the composition. These lines describe the outlines of figures and of shadows themselves, also in order to delineate the fall of shadows on the body.[28] Hence, Caravaggio incised contours around shadows as if the shadows themselves were bodies. Even though those lines would often, though not always, remain invisible, his process in a certain sense thus involved tracking and confining the location of obscurity.[29] Like Narcissus asking, "Where are you?" the beholder of Caravaggio's paintings is tasked with locating the figure, at the same time as the figure eludes the viewer's grasp. Likewise, in the literary sources we have analyzed, the viewer passes through the roles of Pan, Echo, and Narcissus: there is a desiring pursuit, an evasion of contact, a turning away that instead turns toward a place of perpetual suspension.

ISTORIA

In Caravaggio's oeuvre, the case of the *istoria*, or narrative painting involving a complex, multifigured composition, only heightens the viewer's difficulty with orientation. Lorenzo Pericolo has called this effect "the poetics of dislocation."[30] In his *Considerazioni*, after imagining the studio setup we have discussed above, Mancini asks the reader to imagine a group of models attempting to enact a dramatic scene when they are squeezed into the dark room with one light source. Painting directly from this cramped assembly would result in abrupt transitions in pose and expression. The issue of visibility, or rather invisibility, would result in narrative incoherence. "It is impossible," Mancini categorically declares, "to put in *one* room a *multitude* of people acting out a story with that light coming in from a *single* window."[31] The numeration here is significant. There is the container (one darkened room), its contents (a multitude), and the means to see those contents (light from one window). Instead of "Who is there?" Caravaggio's approach to the istoria compels the viewer to ask, "Who *else* is there?"

The next sentence in the passage groups together a set of compositional possibilities that nonetheless do not fit together. The chiaroscuro scheme makes it impossible to unify in one picture "one who laughs or one who cries, or one who pretends to walk and one who remains still to be copied." The conjunctions, or rather disjunctions, in Mancini's language, marked by the series "or . . . or . . . and," can be thought of as standing in for the intervals of darkness between figures in unrelated poses that convey movements of the soul (the emotions of laughter and weeping) as well as those of the body (strolling vs. standing still). The dark ground, Mancini suggests, impinges on the delineation of a context. These figures' relationships with one another are difficult to discern, and therefore, the viewer is hindered in connecting and comprehending expressions and movements that underlie narrative goals. The obscure picture is therefore unintelligible.

By Renaissance standards, the unsuitability of Caravaggio's method to the istoria effectively prevents him from realizing a painter's greatest ambition. Approximately thirty years before Mancini's *Considerazioni*, Giovanni Battista Armenini published a treatise that declares, "There is no doubt at all that the greatest enterprise which can be undertaken by an excellent painter, through which his every concept [concetto] must be explained, is truly the istoria." To realize an istoria, two conditions must be met. First, the subject must be of a certain quality, such that the painter "can compose in it the most diverse elements." Second, the physical space given to the painter must be sufficiently "capacious and large so that it can properly contain the invention he wishes to give form." Elaborating this second condition, Armenini states that "in such an ample and spacious ground [in così ampio e spazioso campo], the judicious man can strive with ease, and show and express with all the forces of his mind everything he knows and possesses." In the field of the picture, the painter can show his worth (*adoperarsi*), place something visible before the spectator (*mostrare*), and manifest his idea with clarity (*esprimere*). Those who understand will judge an artist's merit by means of these narrative paintings ("si fa sopra di così fatte imprese giudizio del valor").[32]

It is on this basis that Mancini asserts the importance of a discernible setting in a pictorial narrative. In the seventh section of the treatise, which itself does not address Caravaggio, Mancini states that figures in an istoria should contribute to the portrayal of action. In conceiving this, the painter ought first to consider the site and place of the figure ("prima si considera il sito e il luogo"). The chief protagonist should be immediately recognizable in relation to the setting where the events unfold. Mancini cites as an example the fresco in the Vatican apartments depicting the Battle of the Milvian Bridge: Raphael (and his assistants, notably Giulio Romano) placed the rival Roman emperors Constantine and Maxentius "nel luogo più principale e visto" (in the main and most visible location): the former, triumphant, is mounted on a horse above a chaotic jumble of soldiers, horses, and armor; the latter, defeated, is supine in the Tiber.[33]

In the Renaissance picture, ground conventionally acts as a kind of attribute: it extends from the figure and receives properties of the figure's identity. The direction can also be reversed: in Mancini's understanding, the viewer is intended to read the personhood of Maxentius by a centripetal process whereby the figure draws his identity, in part, from his immersion in the setting of the Tiber. What Mancini calls the "sito scenico" (scenic site), that is, an accurate historical setting, is fundamental to the depiction of narrative action. For instance, the Fall of Simon Magus, a scene depicting the plummet of a false prophet pretending to be the Son of God, should be depicted where it actually occurred in Rome, in the area near the Theater of Marcellus. Meanwhile, Mancini censures certain works of Jacopo Bassano—who will become the subject in the next section—and Flemish artists because they give the chief protagonist too marginal a position in their paintings.[34] For example, instead of placing Christ in the foreground in a Nativity scene, these paintings would insert the Savior deep in the background. In Mancini's opinion, the correct treatment of setting, by enabling the viewer to recognize the protagonist and identify his or her role in the unfolding narrative, determines the success of the composition.

Mancini accords importance to setting across genres. Frances Gage has observed that the task of regarding the different zones of landscape painting for him demanded varying degrees of exertion. In the foreground, the viewer would be required to look at detail and color of botanical and zoological specimens with the acuity of a naturalist. By degrees, Mancini states, "with greater or lesser action, terminating and finishing," the eye would gradually achieve a state of repose in beholding the backgrounds. "La vista vien ad essere finita in questa quiete" (vision comes to be sated in this quiet), he writes.[35] Given the significance that he attributes to grounds and backgrounds in the viewer's comprehension and pace of viewing, it is no wonder that he censures dark grounds in Caravaggio's istorie. Darkened settings conceal, either wholly or partially, the piano and campo, which ought to be particular and appropriate to a given figure. The image of the enclosed room, which Mancini and other Renaissance critics assumed was the site of origination for dark grounds, can be understood as dramatizing these authors' sense of constriction when they were confronted by these paintings. It is as though the atelier were sealed, deprived of space and air, the lone window offering the sole possibility to exit. Because of their expectation of an "ampio e spazioso campo," these critics fail to appreciate another possibility: namely, that the darkness conceals a profundity, a tunnel that yields onto the imaginative depths of the picture.

A BAPTISM INTO DARKNESS

In Jacopo Bassano's late works, which are often characterized as important precursors to Caravaggio's tenebrist compositions, dark grounds contain more than what they show. In *The Baptism of Christ* (c. 1590), which Bassano left unfinished though it would be prized for generations by the artist's heirs, he displaces the viewer's expectations of a certain type of ground and background (fig. 5.2).[36] Baptisms in Renaissance altarpieces often portray Christ, front and center, standing in the River Jordan; the depiction of water is an occasion to represent reflections and distortions in perception. These paintings' backgrounds show sunlit landscapes, some of which extend into distant views specific to the painting's place of display. Piero della Francesca's *Baptism*, dated to after 1437, forges a number of links between its background and the topography of the location for which the altarpiece was made: mountains pictured in the distance feature gray swaths of paint that refer to *genga*—a sedimentary lime and clay rock characteristic of the eastern Tuscan terrain of Sansepolcro.[37] Cima da Conegliano's baptismal scenes, in their backgrounds, feature fortified hilltop towns in the Veneto, including fantastical or idealized elaborations of the town—Conegliano—from which the artist's name derives.[38] This blending of the site of the River Jordan with local topography corresponds to the importance of correct and comprehensible settings which Mancini would later call for in his treatise. Bassano's background, however, does not present a luminous landscape setting that refers to a specific ambient in the Veneto. Instead, a dark ground, multilayered and multireferential, spreads over the picture. The artist's handling of paint and distinctive approach to the subject matter instigate the "Echo effect": when faced with the dark ground, viewers are prodded to ask, "Where is this?" and "When is this?"

After preparing the twill canvas support with a layer of calcium carbonate and drying oil, Bassano applied a dark priming layer containing a "carbon-based black," with coal as the probable source. In their study of the *Baptism*'s condition and reception, Andrea Bayer, Michael Gallagher, and Silvia Centeno observe that rather than generating an overall effect of flat and dark opacity, the coal in the priming layer interacts through refraction with the lighter color of the material preparation and canvas support below.[39] The resultant field of darkness modulates between rich browns and blacks. It provides the foundation for the obscurity that pervades the picture, from the dark water of the Jordan below to the dark sky above. In addition, the coal-based paint layer also contrasts with brighter pigments that describe bodily forms and light effects. The dark ground functions as a stage for the artist's swift brushstrokes and abbreviated application of paint.

In his insightful reading of the image, Paolo Berdini stated that "darkness does not hide things: it conditions viewing."[40] Our eyes adjust to darkness. On the basis of the analysis above of transumption, one might also say that darkness does hide things, *in order to condition* viewing. That is, to behold dark ground is to unearth subsumed figures or events that, while seemingly negated or obscured, remain latent and resonant. As Berdini noted, the darkness of field in Bassano's painting, along with Christ's bent-over posture and anguished facial expression, transpose the baptism in the River Jordan to Mount Calvary and the Passion. As Christ approaches his death, Luke 23:44–45 recounts, "there was darkness all over the earth" and "the sun was darkened." Bassano painted *The Crucifixion* (c. 1575), on a black slate tablet, which anticipates the darkening of the sky as the Passion narrative unfolds.[41] At the same time, the slate support disjoins figures and attributes from one another, inserting intervals of darkness between the scene's participants and props (fig. 5.3). In pulling apart the composition, black ground transforms the narrative image of the Crucifixion into a variant of the Arma Christi, an arrangement of discrete emblematic symbols and scenes recounting Christ's

→

Fig. 5.2. Jacopo Bassano, called Jacopo da Ponte, *The Baptism of Christ*, c. 1590. Oil on canvas (191 × 160.3 cm). Metropolitan Museum of Art, New York. Partial and Promised Gift of Mr. and Mrs. Mark Fisch, 2012 (2012.99).

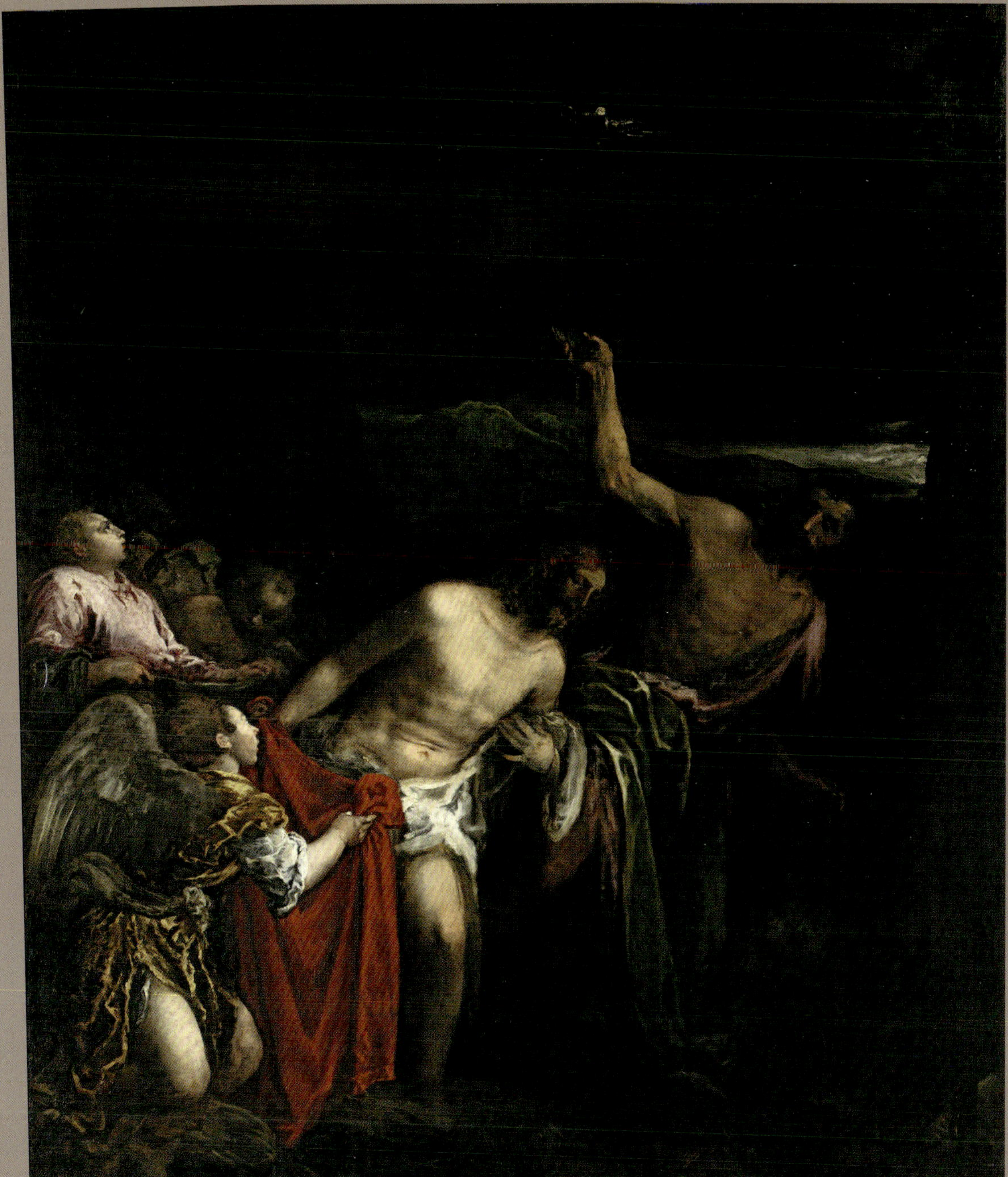

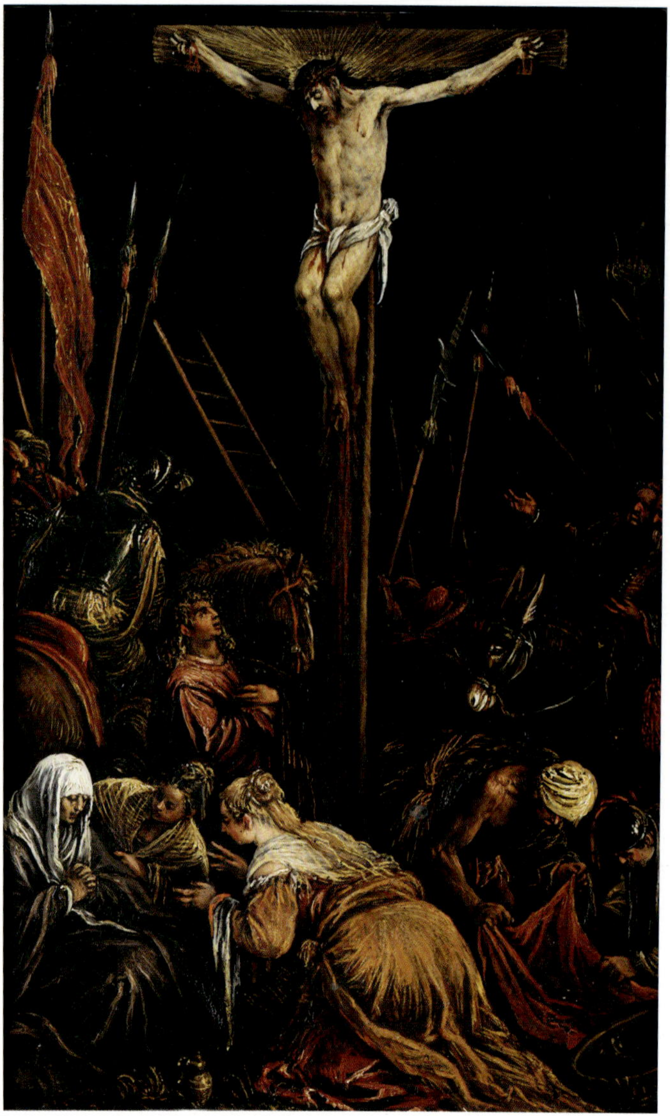

Fig. 5.3. Jacopo Bassano, called Jacopo da Ponte, *Calvary*, c. 1575. Oil on slate (49.4 × 29.8 cm). Museu Nacional d'Art de Catalunya, Barcelona.

suffering.[42] Yet Bassano also deployed dark grounds to present nocturnal renditions of conventionally daylit scenes, an adaptation that would enable a scene to move between multiple narrative registers. Berdini further observed that a verse in the book of Romans (6:3) accounts for the nocturnal rendition of *The Baptism of Christ*: Saint Paul asks, "Know you not that all we, who are baptized in Christ Jesus, are baptized in his death [in morte ipsius]?" The obscuration of the ground allows for slippage in the sequence of events constituting Christ's life, at the same time as it engulfs the succession of artistic precedents, which in sixteenth-century art theory emerges as a nascent history of art. Darkness is a field where events, Christological and art historical, are placed underground, awaiting excavation and retrieval.

NARRATING THROUGH CHIAROSCURO

In his two versions of *The Supper at Emmaus*, Caravaggio exploits darkened ground's capacity to pass through, allude to, and signify a series of narrative moments. Implication, rather than direct portrayal, defines his compositional strategy. Regarding Caravaggio's chiaroscuro, Todd Olson observes that "radical tonal disjunction elicits a rupture between perceived surface and void, undercutting the seamless continuity of planar surface to member, member to body, and body to composition."[43] I would like to examine how darkened grounds disrupt, hollow out, and thereby also enrich this latter category, namely, composition. In the Emmaus paintings under discussion, darkened settings encroach on the action of the figures themselves and act as a medium through which past events have been subsumed and future events are presaged.

The effects of chromatic contrast, discontinuous action, and the contingency of vision in these paintings can also be found in the text on which the subject matter is based, the Gospel according to Saint Luke, chapter 24.[44] The Evangelist recounts that women of Galilee, having prepared spices to embalm the body of Christ, visit the sepulcher three days after the Crucifixion. The stone sealing the entrance to the tomb is rolled back. On entering, they discover Christ's body is missing. Though the sepulcher is not described, its depth and darkness are implied by what the women of Galilee encounter: standing inside the tomb are two men "in shining apparel." Terrified, the women "bowed down their countenance towards the ground." The men, associated by some commentators with Moses and Elijah, rhetorically ask and declare, "Why seek you the living with the dead? He is not here, but is risen." They then ask the women to recall "how he spoke unto you [. . .] Saying: The Son of man must be delivered into the hands of sinful men, and be crucified, and the third day rise again." Returning from the tomb, the women announce the miraculous event to the apostles, who are incredulous: "these words seemed to them as idle tales." Yet among them Peter, "rising up," runs to the sepulcher, "and stooping down, he saw the linen cloths laid by themselves; and went away wondering in himself at that which was come to pass."

These opening verses of Luke 24 consist mainly of narrative action. "It came to pass," a stock phrase that recurs throughout the Bible, including the Gospel of Luke, connects a sequence of events while advancing it.[45] The repetition of "and" at the beginning of almost every verse continues to propel the action.[46] A trace of description is also released through the act of reading that follows the trail of figural movement. The characters' actions of arriving at the cave, going inside it, and returning to the outdoors allude to an alternation of settings. Although these backgrounds are not described, the details of the surroundings emerge from what else is present in the text. In imagining the story, the readers (or listeners) bring qualities of setting, such as a dark interior, to a story in which characters go inside a cave. Caravaggio would later visualize this alternation in settings as shifts from bright to dark to bright again, through the use of chiaroscuro within a single image. In his paintings, narrative sequence structures the depiction of a scene, and imbues the setting with foreknowledge.

The Vulgate Latin describes the two men as standing in the tomb "in veste fulgenti." The verb *fulgere* means to glow, flame, or flash, as in the phrase *astra fulgens*, a shining star. Yet here radiance shines below the sky, inside the earth. This first moment of description is significant. The cave, through association, comes to be understood as dark, and therefore deep. The women's action of turning their faces to the ground ("et declinarent vultum in terram") also suggests shielding their eyes from illumination. Then, "et regressae a monumento" (and having returned from the tomb) implies a subsequent transition from darkness back to light. The ocular experience of passing between extremes of darkness and illumination is alluded to in the text in the manner of transumption. The recipients of the text, be they readers or listeners, must provide something from their own experiences to re-create the story. In his own case, Caravaggio provides the chiaroscuro technique in order to bring forward that which is alluded to but remains absent in the text.

In Hollander's analysis, the cave as a sonic chamber gives rise to a literal echo, while the repetitions in biblical prose are what he would consider metaphorical echoes. In the Gospel of Luke, what has been witnessed in the cave sets off a series of echoes that reverberate beyond the resonating chamber of the tomb and return to their site of origin. These consist of declaration ("He is not here"), recollection ("Remember how he spoke unto you"), reportage ("they told all these things"), fabulation ("idle tales"), confirmation ("stooping down, he saw") and self-interrogation ("[Peter] went away wondering"). These echoes consist of actual, mental, and remembered utterances. They are acts of representation for the purpose of cognition or communication to an audience. Like Echo, Christ at this point in the narrative assumes a linguistic form while his physical location remains unknown. But while in the case of Echo the mythological nymph is herself the person answering, Christ's speech is assumed by a chorus of interlocutors who repeat, so as to amplify or question, the key terms of his death, absence, and resurrection.

Hence, in the cave, Christ transforms from a somatic to a verbal presence. Later in Luke 24, the once dematerialized divine presence briefly reemerges, only to vanish again immediately. This occurs at another location, which is often visualized as an architectural interior. The narrative of the chapter, according to biblical scholar John Drury, "is carefully structured to hold a tension between ignorance and recognition, confusion and clarity."[47] Likewise, it can be said that in this narrative, the settings that support these dialectics of obscurity and realization are the cave and architectural interior. They provide a surrounding structure of invisibility and visibility, as the narrative provides the route from one to the other. Luke recounts that two men, one of whom is identified by the name Cleophas, travel from Jerusalem to Emmaus. They discuss what occurred at the tomb—echoes from the cave reverberate in the mouths of the two wayfarers. In the course of their journey, the two men are joined by Christ. Though he is reintroduced at this point in the narrative as an incarnate physical figure, he remains unrecognized; the moment of nonsight or nonrecognition is described with a powerfully tactile figure of speech: "But their eyes *were held*, that they should not know him" (24:16; oculi autem illorum *tenebantur* ne eum agnoscerent). Now on the road to Emmaus, the space of the cave that physically holds, contains, and conceals closes over the apostles' eyes.

Unaware of the fellow traveler's identity—they ask him "Art thou only a stranger to Jerusalem, and hast not known the things that have been done there in these days?" (24:18)—the two men recount to Christ the story of his own life, thereby compressing into six verses his beginnings, teachings, crucifixion, and resurrection. In the town of Emmaus, the obscurity of nightfall contrasts with the clarity of realization: "it is toward evening, and the day is now far spent" (24:29), says one of the men. Gathered with his companions at a table, Christ breaks and blesses the bread. As if the tearing apart of bread coincides with the shattering of illusion, the two men suddenly understand: "And their eyes were opened, and they knew him"; Christ then immediately disappears: "and he vanished out of their sight" (24:31). But a few verses later, he appears to the apostles back in Jerusalem, and in revealing himself to them, contrasts his embodiment with his previous evanescence: "See my hands and feet, that it is I myself; handle, and see: for a spirit hath not flesh and bones, as you see me to have" (24:39). Caravaggio's chiaroscuro approach fills in the transumed part of the biblical text where characters pass between states of extreme brightness and darkness. It also becomes possible to say that his chiaroscuro addresses movement in the text from visibility and corporeal presence to invisibility and physical absence / spiritual presence.

EMMAUS I: THE BREAKING OF BREAD

The moment in which Christ is recognized, immediately before he disappears, is depicted in both versions of *The Supper at Emmaus* painted by Caravaggio. The first version (at the National Gallery of Art in London) was executed in 1601 (fig. 5.4)[48] A document notes that on January 7, 1602, 150 scudi were disbursed to "Michel Angelo da Caravaggio pittore" for "il Quadro de N[ostro] S[ignore] in fractione panis" (the painting of Our Savior [in the act of] breaking bread). The entry was registered by Ciriaco Mattei in his own hand. Research into Mattei's account books confirms that the Roman nobleman had hosted Caravaggio in his residence and commissioned two other paintings by the artist.[49] The phrase "in fractione panis" in Mattei's record of payment was also used to describe Caravaggio's second version of the subject (in the Pinacoteca di Brera, Milan) (fig. 5. 9). Executed in 1606, five years after the first version, and then dispatched for sale, the painting appears in a 1624 inventory of the art collection of the papal treasurer, Marchese Costanzo Patrizi.[50] This collection was overseen by the Cavaliere d'Arpino (Giuseppe Cesari), the prominent

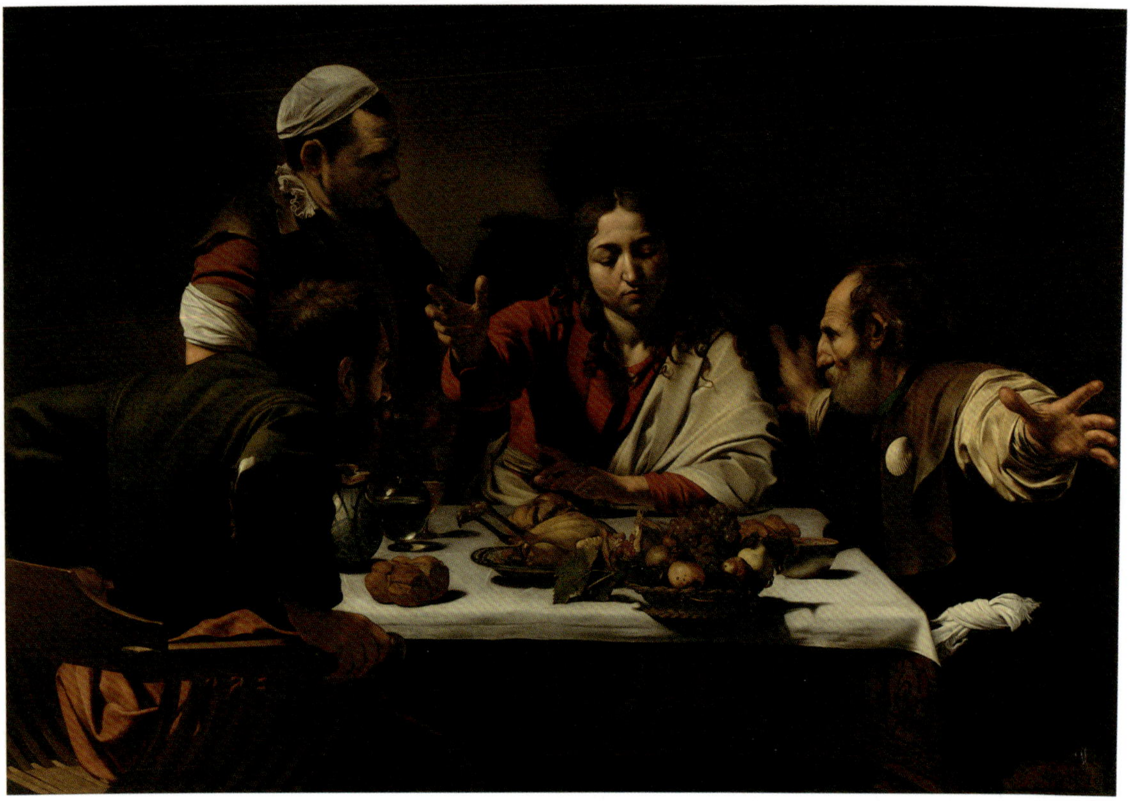

Fig. 5.4. Caravaggio, *Supper at Emmaus*, 1601. Oil and tempera on canvas (141 × 196.2 cm). National Gallery, London. Presented by the Hon. George Vernon, 1839 (NG172).

Roman artist in whose workshop Caravaggio once served for several months as an apprentice. The inventory of Patrizi's collection reads, "nella Galleria [. . .] un altro Quadro grande di una Cena q[uan]d[o] cognoverunt eum in fractione panis di mano del Caravaggio" (in the Gallery [. . .] another large painting of a Supper when they recognized him in the act of breaking bread by the hand of Caravaggio).[51] Derived from the Vulgate text (Luke 24:30; "panem [. . .] fregit"), the phrase "in fractione panis" denotes the fissure and rupture of the sacramental bread.[52] Yet "fractione" also alludes to Caravaggio's composition, in which he breaks opens and breaks up the picture to release the power of signification. In the London picture, it is as though crevices and hollows in the bread constitute in miniature the previous setting, the cavern of the miraculous resurrection, where shadows, fragmented shapes, and forms of interrogation echo, resound, and scatter.

The effect of darkness arises from the foundational strata of the London *Supper at Emmaus*. In accordance with the artist's technique at this point in his career, the painting's material ground was applied on a plain-weave linen canvas and consists of a reddish-brown imprimatura of earth pigments, calcite, and lead white. This ground layer was left exposed in several areas of the painting. These include the contours around the hair and outstretched arm of the figure to the right; the passage between the seated figure's

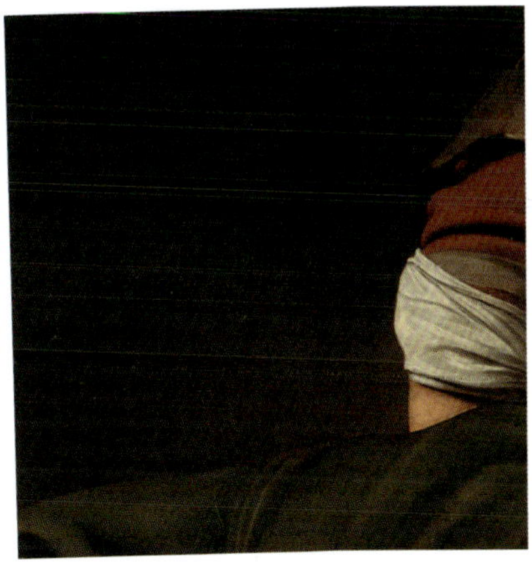

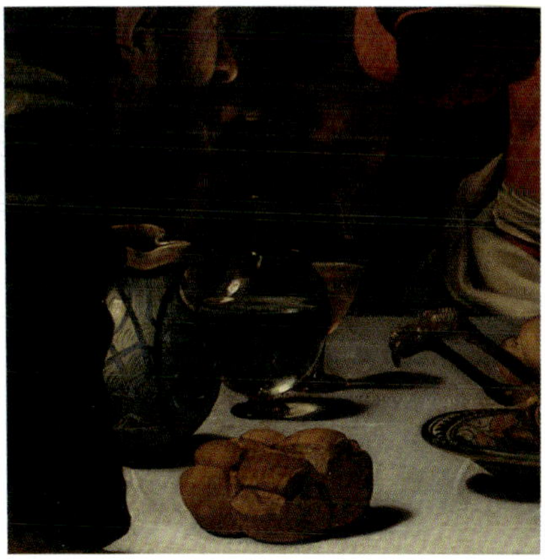

green jacket sleeve and the darkened background wall; the pattern in the carpet draped over the table in the foreground; and the shadowed bases of the goblet and glass resting on the table (fig. 5.5; fig. 5.6).[53] To the naked eye, then, portions of the ground merge with the shadows cast against the background wall. While the practice was not uncommon in sixteenth- and seventeenth-century Italian painting, Caravaggio's tendency to disclose and exploit the material ground was distinctive enough to bear mention by one period commentator: "he left the imprimatura of the canvas for the middle tones."[54] In the London *Supper at Emmaus*, the ground also appears to have enabled Caravaggio to conceive of the contrast between bright and dark in terms of opacity and transparency: beneath the brighter colors, the darker ground layer blocks the passage of light, thereby intensifying the opacity and visual effect of flatness of the upper layers of paint. By contrast, when it lies beneath thin layers of translucent darker paint, the relatively lighter ground makes these dark areas appear deeper and more luminous. Having said this, it is important to acknowledge that the tonality of grounds might exaggerate tenebrist effects over time, since with age, oil paint tends to become more transparent.[55]

Even so, Caravaggio's stratified approach to tenebrism creates an effect of transparency and depth of darkness that strikingly resembles water and recalls Narcissus's pool. Layering enables the material ground and illusionistic background to work metaleptically. In other words, darkness comes into view and achieves semantic force through implication. This implication can be spatial: the dark areas on both edges of the painting indicate the presence of a wall that extends above and to the sides of the picture plane. Then also, it can be narrative and figural: the shadow at the center of the painting, ostensibly cast by the innkeeper standing beside Jesus, amounts to "a sort of dark aureole[, . . .] an unfitting, looming, and distorted silhouette of Christ himself."[56] So observes Pericolo, who unearths how previous scholars have sought to make sense of this "dark aureole" (fig. 5.7). Roberto Longhi called it an "almost caricatural shadow" that served as "a first element of dramatic

(LEFT)
Fig. 5.5. Caravaggio, detail of reddish-brown imprimatura passages left exposed from the *Supper at Emmaus*, 1601. Oil and tempera on canvas (141 × 196.2 cm). National Gallery, London. Presented by the Hon. George Vernon, 1839 (NG172).

(RIGHT)
Fig. 5.6. Caravaggio, detail of reddish-brown imprimatura passages beneath goblets from the *Supper at Emmaus*, 1601. Oil and tempera on canvas (141 × 196.2 cm). National Gallery, London. Presented by the Hon. George Vernon, 1839 (NG172).

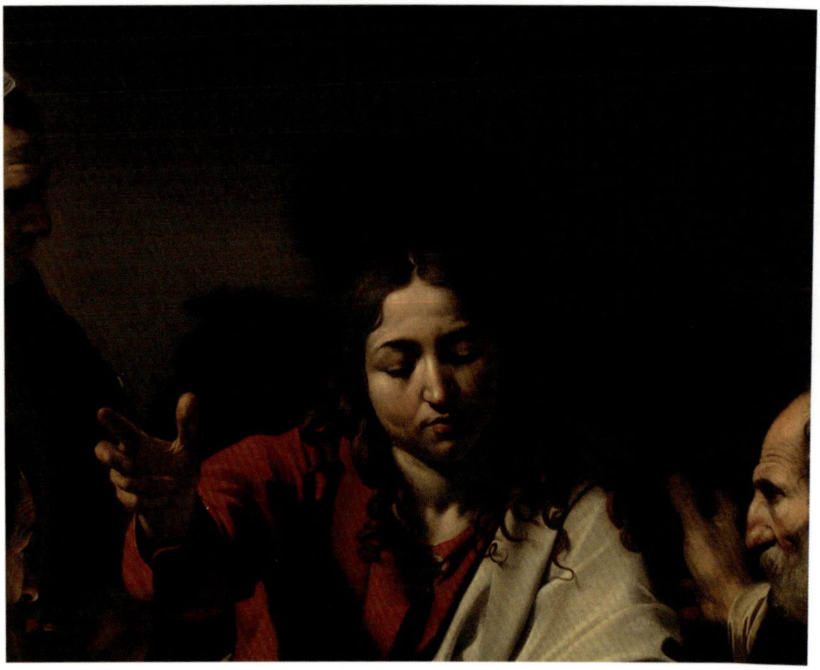

Fig. 5.7. Detail from Caravaggio, *Supper at Emmaus*, 1601. Oil and tempera on canvas (141 × 196.2 cm). National Gallery, London. Presented by the Hon. George Vernon, 1839 (NG172).

inflection." Charles Scribner credits Walter Liedtke with the observation that the innkeeper's shadow creates "a dark, 'negative' halo in the form of a foreshortened disc." The contrast between the dark halo and Christ's fully illuminated face provide "a clear indication of the metaphysical qualities of Caravaggio's chiaroscuro." Finally, according to Catherine Puglisi, the cast shadows in the painting have multiple functions: "to reaffirm the corporeality of forms, to project a halo shape on the wall above Christ's head, and to imply the transient nature of the moment represented." For, as Puglisi remarks, in the instant following this theophany—the manifestation of the divine in the human world—Christ disappears.[57]

The shadow cast behind Christ also creates a seemingly unpassable strait, disrupting the company, in the senses of togetherness and eucharistic bread-sharing (*com*, "with"; *panis*, "bread"). The right hand of the bald apostle seated closest to Christ, Pericolo notes, "gropes for a contact never to be achieved."[58] Christ appears set back, as though engulfed by an invisible niche. An evident point of reference for Caravaggio's rendering of Christ and this withdrawn positioning was Leonardo's *Last Supper*. In turn, the remote figure of Leonardo's Christ, crowned with a segmental pediment doubling as halo, also recalls the triangular format, static bearing, and downcast facial expression in terracotta busts produced in the workshop of Leonardo's teacher, Verrocchio. As a boundary that dramatizes the interval between Christ and the grasping apostle, Caravaggio's darkened ground evokes another of Verrocchio's sculptures, *Doubting Thomas* (1483) (fig. 5.8).[59] Much as the apostle reaches out in the London picture, Thomas approaches but

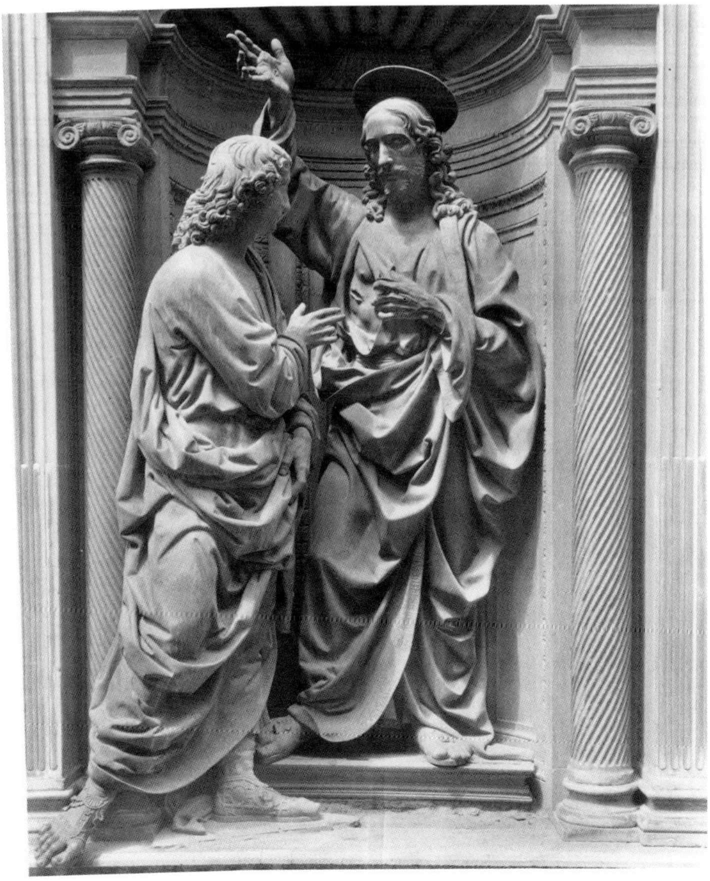

does not touch Christ as he displays his wounds. The interval between the two bronze figures positioned inside the niche enacts a pause, the moment before disbelief becomes belief. (John 20:24–29). In both this sculpture and Caravaggio's painting, the idea of a gap is used to represent visually a moment in time; specifically, a charged moment before everything changes. The semantic force of implication stems from the temporal gap. In myths and their visual renderings, darkness and emptiness in those gaps or intervals become tropes that, by permitting the passage of language and sense-making through vacant space, translate voids into meaning, absence into desire. An absence will become a presence, just as the physical body of Christ is a presence that will become an absence. As Echo burns for Narcissus (*Metamorphoses* 3.373; "The more she followed him, the hotter did she burn"), the apostles' hearts burn while Christ discusses scripture (Luke 24:32). The fugitive beloved inflames the feeling of longing.

As writers such as Mancini suggested even in Caravaggio's own time, the critical characteristics of his paintings include the interior setting, the isolated light source, fragmentation of bodies, a reduction in the scale of action, and a disorientation of the viewer that makes this action hard to read.

Fig. 5.8. Andrea del Verrocchio, *Doubting Thomas*, 1466–83. Bronze (height 230 cm). Orsanmichele, Florence.

The figure of transumption, as an abstraction of Echo's latent presence, allows us to unearth the impacted layers of narrative moments and allusions to figuration and setting that are deposited in the darkened ground. In the London picture, the darkness in the material ground and background refer to the surrounding narrative and its elements: the empty tomb; the absent figure of Christ; his anonymity on the road to Emmaus; the time of evening after the day's journey; and most crucially, the cascade of moments before, during, and directly after Christ's theophany. This whole sequence becomes concentrated into, and is released by, one of its parts; that is, the depiction of the moment at the supper table. The dark ground allows the creation of a concentrated fragment, the viewing of which triggers or releases the whole sequence in the viewer's mind. In this respect, we are also reminded of painting's mythical origins as a shadow on the wall. The Corinthian maiden embraces the outline of her lover after he has departed, as if in a symbolic retrieval of the past. Yet in the moment following that depicted in the *Supper at Emmaus*, both Christ's physical presence and his shadow disappear, leaving a background of charged emptiness. While the figures in the painting, according to the Gospel, enact epiphanic surprise at recognizing Christ (Luke 24:31; "And their eyes were opened"), the darkened ground refers to the tenuity of grasping that which has been recognized but will also immediately be revoked from view.[60]

EMMAUS II: DARKNESS AND DISAPPEARANCE

With its obstructed views and displaced points of focus, Caravaggio's second version of the Emmaus story, probably executed in 1605–6, is also characterized by spatial disjointedness (fig. 5.9).[61] The younger apostle has his back turned to us, his right hand barely visible in the darkness. The apostle to the left of Christ is seen only in a diminished profile, the rotated pitcher next to him both glazed and darkened. Half of Christ's face is cloaked in shadow. Ironically, the most discernable figures are peripheral characters, the innkeeper and serving woman, who appear unaware of what is going on in the scene.[62] Their bodies are fragmented: the innkeeper's shoulder is blocked by the apostle's face; and the serving woman's body is reduced to a skeletal half-length figure, a partial cut of flesh like the symbolic rack of lamb she holds in her serving bowl. The innkeeper and serving woman, unaware of Christ's identity, stand in contrast to the apostles, whose surprised gesticulations convey their recognition of the stranger. The inclusion of such witnesses and their varied responses in biblical scenes, Mitchell Merback argues, posits recognition as the turn from ignorance to knowledge, and from knowledge to introspection and self-knowledge.[63] And yet, the second Emmaus picture's prominent areas of black ground act to insert a temporal wedge in between these epistemic turns, effectively slowing down any sudden epiphanic revelation. As Merback observes, "transformative experience often lags behind revelation; the past-anchored self resists the challenge of the new."[64] This temporal effect of slowing down revelation

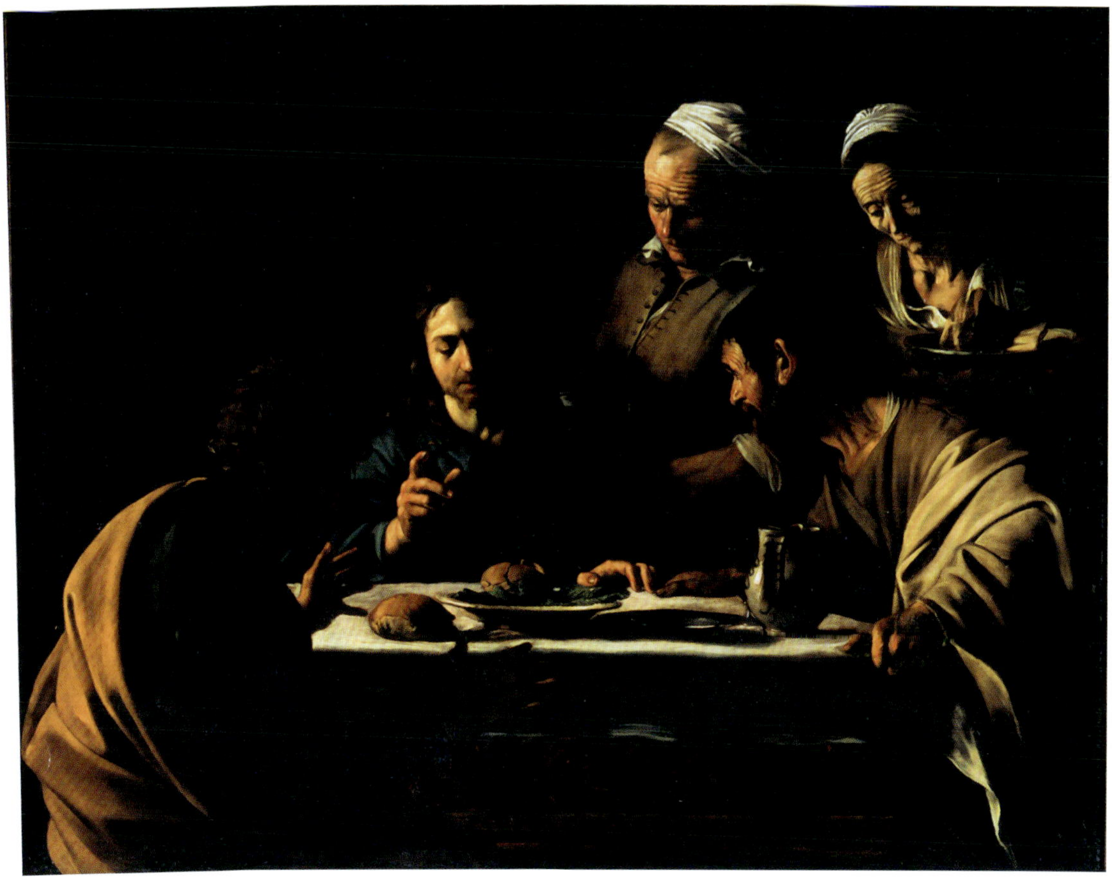

Fig. 5.9. Caravaggio, *Supper at Emmaus*, 1606. Oil on canvas (141 × 175 cm). Pinacoteca di Brera, Milan.

could well be contrasted with a temporality of the instant as seen in the first Emmaus picture, where action is frozen.

In the second version, it is as if the characters are waiting. This effect of deceleration to the point of narrative suspension is anchored in Caravaggio's technique. Using abbreviated and shaky brushstrokes, the artist thinly painted the outer perimeter of the figural group on a layer of black paint superimposed on the material preparation. The ocher cloak and crown of hair of the apostle sitting with his back turned, the edges of Christ's hair and face, and portions of the innkeeper's figure therefore emerge from darkness instead of being defined by it (fig. 5.10). Renaissance art theorists defined contour as a linear element sealing off figure from ground.[65] In his earlier work, as was described previously, Caravaggio used contour to define areas of shadow as if to grant them bodily presence. In the second Emmaus painting, as in his later work overall, Caravaggio seems to have further modified contour's shape and function. By enlarging the width and placement of figural outline, he transformed it into a type of flexible shadow that wraps around, across, and through the arrangement of figures, as if weaving them into the ground. Contours are not exclusively the property of

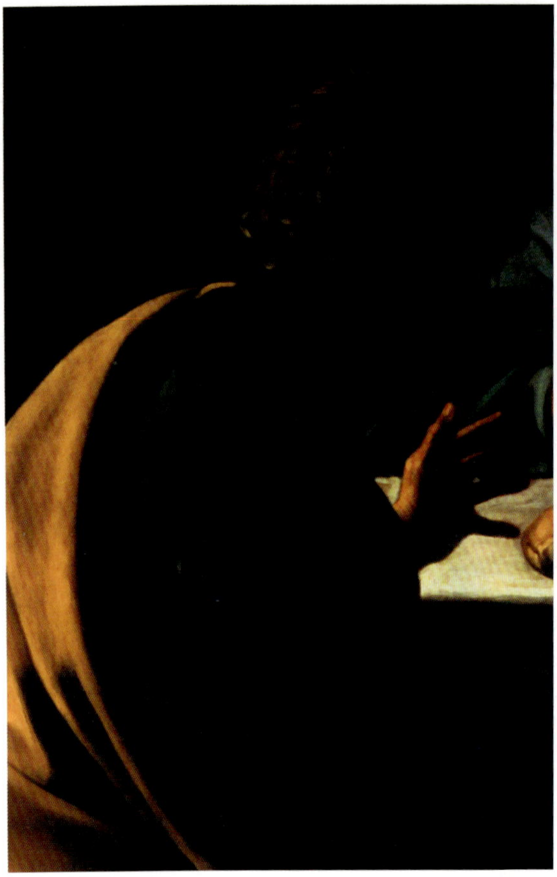

the positive space—they also bound the ground. On a perceptual level, then, the way in which these figures seem to come forth into view from obscurity, rather than simply projecting forward in space, acts to diminish the speed of this narrative, which, in fact, is predicated on sudden revelation: "And their eyes were opened, and they knew him: and he vanished out of their sight" (Luke 24:31).

Pericolo has demonstrated that Caravaggio's calibration of lights and dark in this version of the Emmaus scene took the medium of print as a significant point of reference. An engraving of the episode, which was executed toward the end of the sixteenth century by Aegidius Sadeler II after Pietro Candido (Pieter de Witte), also shows the apostle from behind and a sparse tabletop of empty plates (fig. 5.11).[66] A dense network of lines describes the apostle's darkened figure—his hair, torso, and hand. Along with the sides of the tablecloth, they contrast with the white of the candle's flame, which stands out against the obscure architectural background.

This engagement with print raises the possibility of correlating painterly groundwork with the groundwork operative in engravings. As previously stated, Caravaggio frequently incised lines freehand directly into the still moist and pliable imprimatura of a painting using a stylus or other pointed instrument. Though the purpose of these incisions remains a topic of considerable debate, a strong possibility is that they served as provisional indications to guide the artist while painting from the live model.[67] In printmaking, the "raised ground," the worked area or the field that has been scored and scratched, holds ink and becomes dark. In some respects, the black background expanse of Caravaggio's paintings resembles the face of the printing plate after having been covered in ink and before being wiped and inserted into the press. We might therefore say that the black ground of his paintings anticipates the eruption of delineated form.

It is notable that, in defining his categories of *disegno*, Mancini correlated the darkened backgrounds in prints, drawings, and paintings while distinguishing these media in their ability to convey distance (*lontananze*), darkness (*obscurità*), and light (*lume*). Pen ink, lapis, charcoal, and the cut in a print (which either leaves a form or carves it out) are "varie specie subalterne" (various subordinate species) of painting, which Mancini specifically defines as "the imitation of things found in this world."[68] In later passages, the correlation between darkness and distance is also discussed in respect

Fig. 5.10. Caravaggio, detail of imprimatura visible around crown of apostle's hair from the *Supper at Emmaus*, 1606. Oil on canvas (141 × 175 cm). Pinacoteca di Brera, Milan.

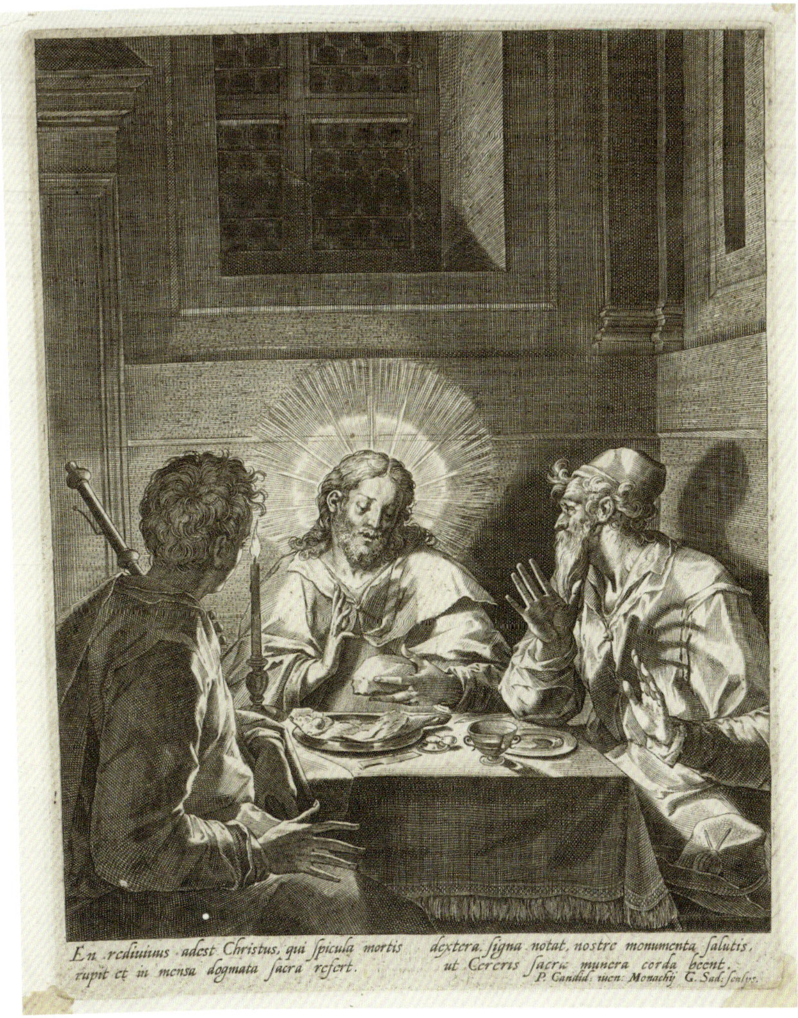

Fig. 5.11. Aegidius Sadeler II after Peter de Witte, *Christ at Emmaus*, c. 1588–97. Engraving (24.4 × 18.2 cm). British Museum, London.

to a wide variety of media and materials, including mosaic, intarsia, and oil paint. In paintings on stone, such as slate (*pietra di paragone*), the black lithic surface stands in for the shadows of the painting.[69] In identifying darkened ground as a common denominator across media, Mancini implies that art making begins from something and somewhere. This place of origination, while concealed, is nonetheless present in its latency. In the Milan *Supper at Emmaus*, ground as place of origination also carries a narrative charge as a point of conclusion, since it foreshadows Christ's sudden disappearance into darkness.

While the form of the background wall is more clearly implied in the London picture, the Milan picture sets the dinner scene against a shallow plane, a field of darkness that would seem to stretch out indefinitely behind and around the group. (Yet in light of the practice of enclosing Caravaggio's chiaroscuro paintings with gilt ornamental frames, the viewer then as now

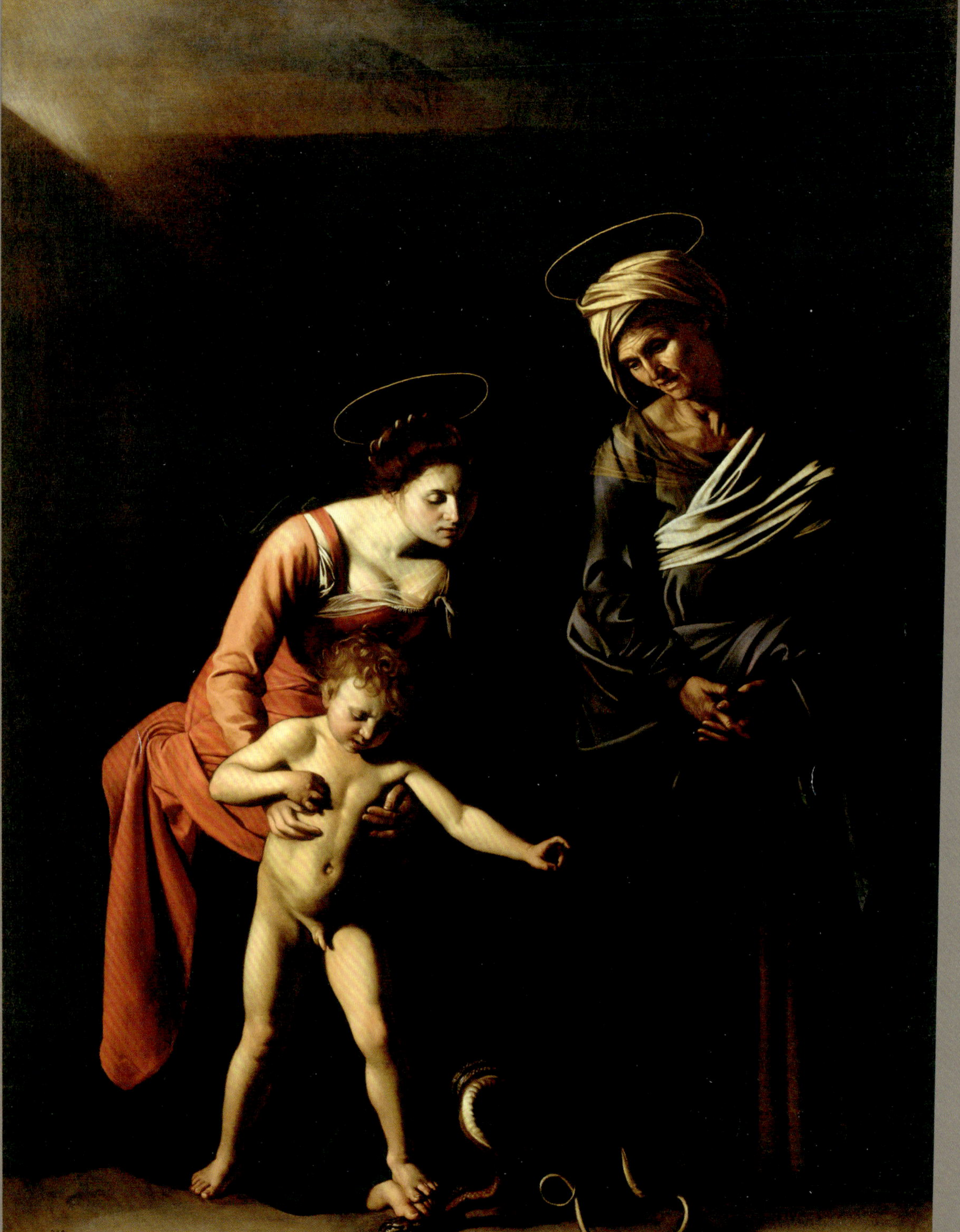

would have been asked to consider this area of darkness as bounded and defined.)[70] In establishing the background's spatial and semantic parameters, the artist effected a transfer between figure and ground, objects and bodies, foreground and background. The bread roll's craggy lines resemble the fissures in a human skull and echo, on a compressed scale, the irregular triangular shape of the figures. To be sure, "in fractione panis," the subject of the painting as stated in period inventories, refers to the blessing and breaking of bread as an analogy for communal partaking of Christ's body. In Caravaggio's painting, however, the fragmented loaf of bread functions not only as a eucharistic object of ingestion: its form signals outward, toward the jagged edges of the triangular group of bodies, and beyond them, to the picture overall, which is split into figuration on one side of the divide and emptiness on the other. As we have said, this emptiness breaks open a space charged with narrative potential.

The absence of figuration in the upper corner of the image and its association with a key narrative moment was developed in the *Madonna dei Palafrenieri* (1606), which was painted several months before the second version of the Emmaus scene (fig. 5.12). This monumental work had been destined for display in the nave of the Basilica of St. Peter's, specifically on the altar allotted to the confraternity of the papal grooms (known as the Palafrenieri), whose patron was Saint Anne.[71] Shortly after its installation in St. Peter's, the altarpiece was removed from display, for reasons that remain a subject of scholarly debate: explanations range from the artist's indecorous representation of sacred characters, the confraternity's loss of rights to its altar in the basilica, and Cardinal Scipione Borghese's desire to acquire the work for his personal art collection.[72]

A complex allegorical image that harks back to northern Italian prototypes, the altarpiece has been read in light of period theological interpretations of Genesis 3:15, which predicts the fate of the serpent in the Garden of Eden ("it shall bruise thy head, and thou shalt bruise his heel"). During the Counter-Reformation, it was debated whether the verse in Genesis prophesied the respective roles that Christ and Mary played in the annihilation of original sin. A papal bull of 1569 regarding the rosary countermanded Protestant arguments precluding the Virgin's role, stating that Christ "by her seed has crushed the head of the twisted serpent."[73] It has been argued that Caravaggio accordingly portrayed Virgin and Child both stepping on the snake, which represents evil in general as well as Lutheran heresy.[74] As the 1569 bull declared, due to the prayers of the faithful, "[t]he darkness of heresy began to be dispelled, and the light of the Catholic faith to be revealed."[75]

As in the Milan *Supper at Emmaus*, Caravaggio divided his composition along a transverse diagonal: the figures stand in the area below the space that is left bare above. Consisting primarily of clay earth pigments, the typical reddish-brown material ground is intermittently visible throughout the surface of the picture.[76] The ground shows through in part due to abrasions inflicted in previous restoration campaigns, though in an undamaged state

←

Fig. 5.12. Caravaggio, *Madonna and Child with Saint Anne* (*Madonna dei Palafrenieri*), c. 1605–6. Oil on canvas (292 × 211 cm). Galleria Borghese, Rome.

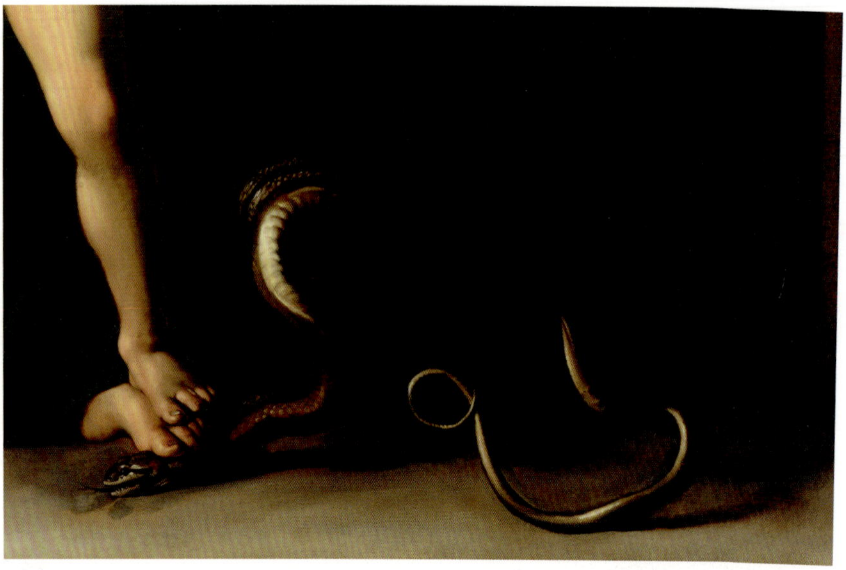

Fig. 5.13. Detail from Caravaggio, *Madonna and Child with Saint Anne* (*Madonna dei Palafrenieri*), c. 1605–6. Oil on canvas (292 × 211 cm). Galleria Borghese, Rome.

this preparatory underlayer would give warmth to the darkened background, which is composed of red lead, charcoal and bone blacks, and verdigris.[77] From the picture's bottom edge, bands progressing from lead white and yellow to ocher to darker grays and black describe the transitions from highlighted foreground—the site of action—to background. Above, broad brushstrokes of paler paint indicate the light streaming into the interior.

Caravaggio here uses color to correlate the upper part of the high space and the floor below. Both draw from a similar palette of lead white, yellows, and warm brownish grays, which help define the upper and lower edges of the picture. Likewise, dark paint passes through the setting, figures, and demonic antagonist to signal a flow of force, action, and reaction: the background's obscurity is reiterated in the shadow cast by the Christ Child's fist clenched against his chest—the site of his future side wound. The shadow of his uncircumcised sex, symbol of incarnate divinity, takes on the adversarial guise of a reptilian head profile and tail (fig. 5.13). These abstracted serpentine shadow forms descend, accelerate, and culminate in the writhing snake, evoking Augustine's description of Satan as "mobile with twisting coils" (*City of God* 14.11).[78]

The darkened background therefore can be seen as initiating a transfer from diffused shadow to compact line, suggestion to form. Meanwhile, it breaks the figural group apart. This compositional decision carries significant theological implications, by setting Anne, symbol of Grace, apart from the Virgin and Child; the interval therefore disintegrates the *metterza*—the visual portrayal of Child, Virgin, and Anne, *terza* (third), as an interlocked entity. In distancing this family unit, Caravaggio displaces the focus of attention to the snake writhing on the ground. In this picture, the darkened background initiates a mode of viewing that is not directed beyond, into the distance, but

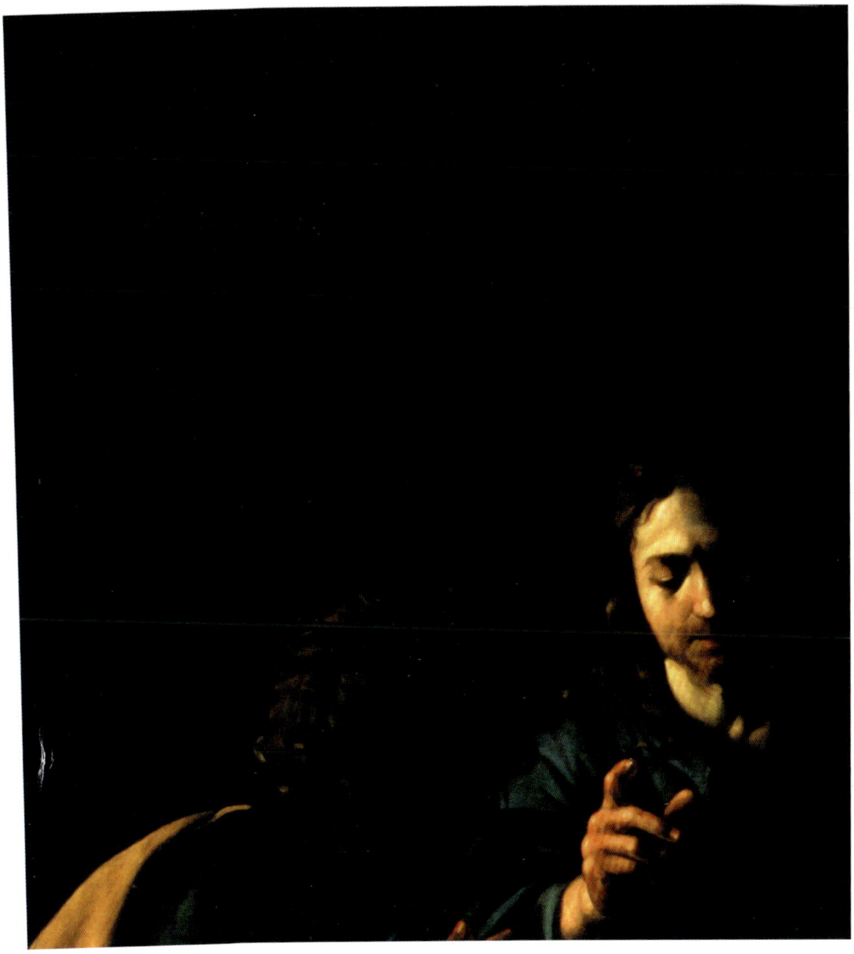

down below, where snake and ground meet to signal the effects of weight, pressure, and spontaneous reflex. This direction of the gaze dropping downward toward the piano, which is also seen in the *Narcissus*, where the youth gazes downward toward his fatal reflection, replaces the conventional direction outward, toward the horizon and lontani. The painting's subject matter dramatizes the artist's concern with downward movement, which takes as its visual goal the painting's ground plane.

In the Milan *Supper at Emmaus,* narrative action is removed from the group of figures, where action appears suspended, and is transferred to the supposedly empty background, which interweaves and wraps around the figures. Pericolo likens the permeating darkness that occupies the painting's left side to "the vehicle of his [Christ's] divine disappearance" (fig. 5.14).[79] Darkness seems already to be enacting this disappearance upon the apostle to Christ's right, whose darkened form merges with the space above it. Hence, darkness is not only the ground from which forms originate. Nor does it refer, as in the case of the Corinthian maiden who embraces the traced the

Fig. 5.14. Detail from Caravaggio, *Supper at Emmaus*, 1606. Oil on canvas (141 × 175 cm). Pinacoteca di Brera, Milan.

profile of her lover, to a time in the past when the being represented by the shadow was there. Instead, the black ground alludes to Christ's future disappearance. When the shadow comes to be there, Christ's body will dissolve into the ground. Just as a reflection (or print) inverts left and right, this dark background reverses the sequence of events. Whereas shadows in the cave refer to what has already happened ("He has risen"), this black void is proleptic. Caravaggio employs the ground to compress the episodes of sequential narration: the dark ground will come to occupy and engulf the space where Christ now is.[80]

Black space offers the scene a spatial "out" (for Christ to exit the physical world) and a temporal "and then . . ." (the moment when he vanishes). The composition's uneasy conjoining of figures and emptiness points to the Emmaus story's melding of an "afterward" and an "already": after he vanishes, the disciples discover that Christ was already there.[81] It could be said that the areas of black ground in this painting contain the presence that becomes still more present through his absence. The black ground is thus best understood not as a void bereft of meaning but rather as a type of pocket or receptacle: this cavity conceals and contains; it provides an enclosure to receive the transfer of figuration that takes place between the human form (significantly, Christ's form) and its surroundings. Therein lies the temporal hold that Caravaggio's paintings have on the viewer. While seeming to depict a single moment, that very instant is enfolded, or immerses itself, into a larger narrative that is made simultaneous through the vehicle of groundwork. Olson observes that in his narratives, Caravaggio was more attuned to duration rather than to plot.[82] The single moment is shown to contain or be immersed in the medium of a number of moments.

BLACKNESS AS REFRAIN

In *Le vite de' pittori, scultori e architetti moderni* (1672), a series of artists' biographies written by the antiquarian and critic Giovanni Pietro Bellori, the blackness in Caravaggio's paintings exerts a gravitational pull.[83] As Bellori sets out to describe the artist's relationship with the artistic past, his dialogue with contemporaries and students, and even his physical body and appearance, the writing is recurringly drawn toward the phenomenon of blackness.[84] A refrain, Hollander reminds us, "may emphasize or reinforce emotion or meaning by catching up, echoing, and elaborating a crucial image or theme." In Bellori's text, the refrain of blackness serves to reinforce the dismissal of Caravaggio's later work at the same time as it calls attention to what more is present in this very blackness that the author refuses to address.

As his biography begins, Bellori approvingly notes the artist's initial rapport with the coloring of Renaissance Venetian painting. Implicitly likening these early stages of stylistic progression to a journey, the critic states that Caravaggio adopted Giorgione "as a guide [iscorta] in imitation." These early works are "sweet, direct"—and as if a dark curtain then appears at the edges of the critic's field of vision, "without those shadows that he used later on." The spatial metaphor of the journey modulates into a temporal sequence in which a promising "before" ("l'opere sue prime") precedes a misguided "after" ("ch'egli usò poi").[85] The biography follows Caravaggio's travels from Lombardy to Venice and eventually Rome. There the artist executes works in which Bellori detects "the first brushstrokes [. . .] with tempered darkness" (li primi tratti del pennello [. . .] con oscurità temperati).[86] The two paintings purchased by Cardinal del Monte display Caravaggio's "beginning [. . .] to intensify the darks" (cominciando [. . .] ad ingagliardire gli oscuri).[87] In his use of the verb *ingagliardire* (embolden), it is apparent that Bellori understood Caravaggio's darkness as informed by the physical qualities of vigor and energy.

Darkness also reverberates in the public and ecclesiastical spaces where Caravaggio's paintings are displayed. Referring to the two lateral narrative scenes from the life of Saint Matthew in the church of San Luigi dei Francesi in Rome, Bellori observes that "the darkness of the chapel and of the color make it impossible to see these two pictures." Earlier in this passage, he singles out the darkness of the background ("obscurità del campo") of *Saint Matthew and the Angel*, the chapel's altarpiece. Darkness in the chapel overtakes darkness in the pictures, such that, as Bellori puts it, obscurities in effect "remove [them] from sight" (tolgono [. . .] alla vista).[88]

Caravaggio eventually became "more famous every day because the coloring he was introducing [. . .] became boldly dark and black." As Bellori specifies in the following clause, the artist, through "making considerable use of black" (servendosi assai del nero), was able to bring bodily forms into relief.[89] Intense chiaroscuro eventually became the hallmark of Caravaggio's style, so much so that "he never showed his figures in open daylight." As if to underscore the presence of darkened grounds in Caravaggio's paintings, Bellori categorically states in another passage that the artist never painted "clear, sky-blue air" (aria turchina e chiara).[90] Instead, he continues, the artist "found a way to ground [the figures] amidst the dark atmosphere of an enclosed room" (trovò una maniera di campirle entro l'aria bruna d'una camera rinchiusa). According to the opinion of older established artists, Bellori says, Caravaggio "did not know how to come out of the cellars" (non sapeva uscir fuori dalle cantine).

In this figure of speech there is a metaphoric—if not mimetic—transfer of darkness from the physical space of the atelier to pictorial ground.[91] Recall that Mancini and other period critics seized upon blackness in order to find fault with Caravaggio, whose realism was otherwise considered to be very advanced. In Bellori's statement, "the cellars" are not only dark and black; the phrase alludes to something unmentionable that is buried, stored, or concealed in those subterranean chambers. By literalizing Caravaggio's grounds as mimetic while repeatedly calling out their blackness, Bellori seems to want to repress any possible associations (such as latent figural presence and its reverberations) in the artist's darkened grounds, but without acknowledging that repression. It is as though Caravaggio's period critics say compulsively, covering their eyes, "There's nothing here, it's just black walls."

This refusal to acknowledge that which is concealed returns us to the myth of Echo and her horrific dismemberment: "they tore her all to pieces and flung about them all over the earth her yet singing limbs." The story of Daphnis and Chloe embeds this gruesome tale within the comic story of seafarers whose echoing voices reverberate against the walls of sea coves. In a piece entitled "Beneath the Foundations," Hans Blumenberg considers how such narrative devices of superimposition conceal, yet imply. In his analysis, the sure foundation of a building site (*Baugrund*) is "a privileged metaphor of modernity," a notion predicated on the assumed surmounting of the past. Looking down into the ground instead of up toward the heavens—as Catholic congregations were told, "sursum corda" (lift up your hearts)—the modern viewer is compelled to contemplate the ground in which the foundation is planted, in contrast to the uppermost layer, which seeks to overcome and move beyond it. Blumenberg develops and applies the image of the obscuring foundation to the levels of remembering and forgetting in history. He writes, "[J]ust as myth narrates which monstrosities have been overcome and which have been forever exorcised, the insertion of the old idols into new foundations combines being allowed to forget with the easing memory of what has been sunk. Nothing grows forth or upward from it; everything lies upon and over it in order to use weight and cunning to fight against it rising up." Like these foundations, blackness as a trope of Caravaggio's groundwork covers yet is supported by "old idols"—images that have been sequestered. Through repeated use, blackness is made to stand in for and stand for other things. The artist's critics insist on the literality of blackness when, in fact, Caravaggio's use of these colors referred to collectively as "black" serves to access areas of meaning that are traditionally the domain of metaphor. As Marin suggested through his lexical entry *Arca* (see the beginning of this chapter), black grounds enclose and contain, turn away and divert attention, overpass and recall.

★

In conclusion to this chapter, it can be said that black ground brings another space into the picture that is not a mimetic space; it also introduces a different awareness of narrative time. Black ground functions as an interval to introduce a pause in action, in order to dilate "the moment before everything changed" and then also implicitly evoke "the moment after." Additionally, black ground has been shown to be a pocket that contains the latency of a figural presence, the effects of Echo, who is felt and heard but not seen. This multilayered temporal awareness enfolds and extends the istoria beyond the depiction of a moment, or sequence of moments, to a mode of representation in which memory and anticipation exist in tension with one another, so that the viewer is held in suspense. This retelling of dramatic action that takes place within the confines of the picture then also becomes implicated with an art historical narrative that takes place beyond the frame.

The streams of this story originate in the headwaters of gold ground and meet the sea of chiaroscuro's darkness, while bringing along and depositing at intermediate points the sediment of landscape views and gray grounds. This narrative can be recursive, in its recollecting and culminating the tropes of groundwork, its doubling back on them. When the bend of the river becomes acute, islands of distinct approaches to groundwork can form. Then, there is the delta, where, at the point closest to its destination, the water fans into multiple rivers. The transumptive dark ground, in skipping over a repertoire of accumulated effects, collects and refers to them indirectly. Caravaggio's groundwork presented a critical point in this cursus, whose ensuing flood of darkness gave rise to the need to confront, although not able to resolve, groundwork's theoretical complexities.

Conclusion: The Fugitive Ground

The Renaissance picture is commonly understood as a mode of art making that is premised on the naturalistic rendering of the human figure or figures, who are often in the course of acting out a narrative while embedded in a convincing, illusionistic surrounding. In this book, I have advocated reorganizing our conventional art historical protocols, which place paramount importance on the figure, by first approaching the Renaissance picture through the complex and unstable stratigraphy of the ground. When regarded collectively, grounds can constitute an art historical narrative that charts a progression from the gold ground of the Trecento to the darkened grounds of the early Seicento. And yet, when we attempt to posit a sequence of pictorial events that moves from brightness to darkness, glimmering surface to shadowy depths, the strands in that sequence interlace. Michel Serres, in his book *Rome: The Book of Foundations* (1983/1991), describes history with the striking image of a "knot of different times," a dense cluster where civilizations from the past overlap and intertwine.[1] Similarly, ground has a complex history; its manifestations initiate a set of unexpected analogical procedures that unexpectedly come together as they move across art historical time. The potentiality of gold ground is less surpassed than subsumed: the demands placed on the viewer to make out and make sense of the fluctuation between diaphanous figures and auriferous fields are reformulated when the ground is transmuted to feature distant views, a fissured rock face, a masonry wall, or even gold ground's presumed antithesis, the tenebrist interior, where figuration echoes in seemingly empty spaces. While groundwork changes its appearance, its function, to enter into semantic exchange with the figure, is consistent over time. The analysis of this function thus calls into question the autonomy of figuration in Renaissance art historiography.

Critics and art historians writing at the time are relatively reticent when it comes to ground. In order to generate and free up language about the ground, or let the ground itself produce discourse, I have largely relied on formalist approaches, which implement the dynamic between close looking, writing and rewriting, and referral to historically anchored sources (and their blind spots) as primary mediators between artwork and art historian.[2] The method practiced here does not intend either to reify or to refute these artworks' formal structures.[3] Instead, this book aims to uncover and undo art history's analytic hierarchy between figure and ground, between the picture's focal point and its edges, by showing how each passes into or imparts its characteristics to the other. By positing the contingency of the figure, the ground establishes the picture's logic; the ground also often ruptures the visual field as a basic condition of temporality and narrative action. Groundwork stretches the boundaries of representation by referring to ground's materiality and instability; by asserting ground's indeterminate location at the same time as it prompts the viewer to ask, "Where?" It could be argued that the instability of ground is itself mimetic (and not only representational), in that it models what it introduces: the variable of movement from an unexpected source (the secure foundation) in contradistinction to a static theorization of the visual arts. This problematic contributes to the picture's liveliness and semantic excess.

Groundwork also becomes a structuring metaphor, a way into the picture that moves from the first layer that the artist puts down to something that is represented in the picture as "underneath" or "out there." In the first instance, groundwork denotes the necessary task of artists' laying down the picture's physical foundation, which extends from support to priming. To look at groundwork in this way is also to insert the historical figure of the Renaissance artist in a locality; to reconstruct that artist's interaction with the physical world, the acquisition and use of its materials. Groundwork can thus generate proof about social and historical circumstances through the painting's status as artefact. Then, in its connection to these primary acts of making, groundwork expresses artistic potency. Groundwork's impingement upon or disruption of the figure can therefore also be seen as the artist's open-ended interrogation of figural givens.

To speak about grounds, be they concealed beneath the surface or placed underfoot or in the distance, is to acknowledge that there exist modes of artistic thinking that are not completely accessible, or at least not present to view, after the first or even subsequent glances. Ground represses, just as it has been repressed. Hence metaphor and myth—short and long linguistic forms that bring to articulation concepts that resist formation—offer a way of speaking about groundwork, which operates not only by defining distinct (or overlapping) areas within the Renaissance picture but, more importantly, by alluding to, anticipating, or suspending figural action. Groundwork opens up and expands the "when" of the istoria, such that a moment or sequence of moments can swell to include imagined pasts and possible futures. Ground anticipates the coming of the figure, and, less optimistically, its disappearance and engulfment.

I see this elasticity between figure and ground dramatized in the ancient Roman grammarian Hyginus's account of how the allegorical figure Cura conceived, shaped, and sought to name the first human.[4] Cura—whose name can be translated as "care," "concern," or even "worry," the condition she personifies—catches sight of a patch of muddy clay as she crosses a river. With her hands she takes up the wet and pliant material. "Cogitabunda" (thinking/thoughtful), Cura begins to fashion a human form. By pondering the ground, Cura's *première pensée*—an artist's "first thought" expressed through a rough sketch—quickens even before she lays her fingers on the moist clay. After shaping the figure, she reflects, "Cura was thinking to herself what she had done" (deliberat secum quidnam fecisset). The phrase parallels the refrain in Genesis, when God creates and then contemplates his creation: "And God saw that it was good." In between moments of making come intervals of pause and observation whereby the divine artist becomes the first viewer.[5] The ground reflects back the maker's work.

Interrupting Cura's meditation on her handiwork, Jupiter arrives on the scene. Cura asks him whether he might impart spirit to the inert human form. This he easily does. Having seen the muddy figure come to life, Cura decides to give it her own name. Jupiter objects, protesting that it should be named after himself. Amidst this quarrel arises Tellus Mater—Mother Earth. She counters that the figure should bear her name because she gave it her own body ("quandoquidem corpus suum praebuisset"). The three disputants appeal to Saturn, who announces the following judgment:

> You, Jupiter, since you have given spirit, take the soul after death; Tellus, since she provided the body, should receive the body. Cura, since she first fashioned him, let her possess him as long as he is alive; but since there is a dispute over the name, let him be called "Homo," since he appears to have been made from humus. (*Fabulae* 220)[6]

Death will cleave the human into halves, a physical entity resting in the earth and a spirit ascending to the sky. Yet the final sentence in Saturn's decree conjoins two distinct questions. The first relates to custody: "Who will possess and be responsible for the human during its life span?" The second relates to naming: "What should this creature be called?" These legal and philological questions seek to define the fundamental nature of the human. The pliability between *homo* (human being) and its cognate *humus* (earth) mimics the material pliability of the wet mud in Cura's hands. As she squishes and molds the clay into a body, figure comes into being. Humus births homo. Like the biblical figure of Adam, whose name was interpreted by Talmudic commentators as deriving from the ancient Hebrew *adamah* (earth), the human draws on the ground for its nominal description and ontological status. Adam, in turn, names the animals on the earth, thereby extending the scope of divine creation.[7] The terms of the relationship between figure and ground resist separation, and therefore definition. The name encodes the inseparability of figure and ground as permanent during the human life span. Saturn's decree is explicit, but it is far from comprehensive, leaving room for uncertainty, even unease—or care—about figure's derivation from and eventual return to the ground.

In his reading of the myth in *Care Crosses the River* (*Die Sorge geht über den Fluss*, 1987), Hans Blumenberg identifies in Hyginus's recounting of the fable an "irritating" lacuna, which to him suggests that an essential kernel has been cut from "the heart of the myth." How did Cura come to picture the shape of the human she molded with her hands? And why is she initially portrayed crossing the river? After all, she could just as well have been walking along its banks when she came on the patch of muddy clay.[8] In answering this question, Blumenberg concludes that Cura sees her own reflection in the river as she crosses its depths. It is the sight of her own form that impels her to take up the earth and fashion the first mortal being in her image. Therefore, Cura is allowed to keep the human for its life span, not because she fabricated the human race but instead "because the human was made in her image and likeness, and thus partakes in her being."[9]

Blumenberg here alludes to Alberti's identification of Narcissus as the first painter. Alberti asks, "What is painting but the act of embracing by means of art the surface of the pool?"[10] Narcissus, while lying on the ground, glimpses his own reflection in the fatal pool, and, in other readings, plunges into its depths to meet his avatar. In linking Cura with Narcissus, Blumenberg associates the tale with Gnostic cosmology, which identifies narcissistic concern as the fundamental impediment to human spiritual ascent. We might even say, citing Pierre Hadot's essay on Plotinus, that Cura and Narcissus in their acts of creative or contemplative self-regard are sunk "in the dark depths hostile to the intellect."[11] In seeking to give it her name, Cura conceives the human as her protégé, bound forever out of obligation to its creator. And yet, the human will eventually elude Cura's grip. The materiality of the figure—the source of its identity in the ground—makes it elusive. Its condition is transience. The picture's ground itself reflects the desire for a distant beyond, all the while being firmly planted in a beneath. The reciprocity between ground and figure may not be immediately evident, but as the human's name reveals, figure is always also humus. Is this, in part, why a dispute arises about the naming of Care's creation?[12]

In his analysis of Hyginus, the literary scholar John Hamilton writes that "the fable that began with creation ends with the designation of a name, with the determination of a species."[13] Yet the philological debate is etiological and ontological too. Figure's point of origination moves between the (alleged) reflection on the surface of the river and the banks containing it, a slippage that points to the fundamental paradox of the picture as both surface phenomenon and accretion of layers. In showing how the figure is informed, inflected, disrupted by the ground beneath and surrounding it, groundwork proposes a selfhood that is accidental and incidental. The instability of the ground, its capacity to fissure and tendency to erupt, dissolve, or transform, fundamentally challenges the integrity of the figure. Naming the "human" obscures differentiation between ground and figure at the same time as it alludes to the infinite other beings contained in the mud, in a state of potentiality, that await Jupiter's breath.

While the ground is foundational, it is fugitive. Though we know it is beneath our feet, it seems to rise by receding into the distance. If the myths discussed in this book point to ground as a condition of painting's physical inception and theoretical contemplation, then the Cura myth speaks perhaps to the transience of any ownership of the ground—via looking, holding, or language. Vasari's definition of painting as a contour that seals off the figure *from* the ground can be seen as an ideological act of security (derived from *sine cura*, or "without care") whose effects can only ever be temporary. In other words, figuration is an attempt to give a name that is not "humus" to the figure. But the line of defense is porous and breachable. Figure derives from ground and ground receives the figure. Figure and ground pass in and through each other. Such reciprocity is the achievement of a composition, and more generally, the work of art itself. In the demonstration of ground's continual interplay with figure, ground is ultimately shown to abscond; always *there*, it is ultimately elusive.

Acknowledgments

The notion of a single author monograph seems misguided when one considers just how much scholarly writing depends on the support and encouragement of friends, colleagues, and institutions. This book had its inception as a research project at the University of Zurich, where Wolfgang Brückle, Roger Fayet, Mateusz Kapustka, and, especially, Tristan Weddigen provided a congenial environment for the germination of this project. The Center of Advanced Study in the Visual Arts (then "CASVA," now "The Center") was the ideal setting to develop the book in relation to the collections of the National Gallery. I am grateful to former dean Elizabeth Cropper, associate deans Peter Lukehart and Therese O'Malley, and staff members Danielle Horetsky, Jen Rokoski, Helen Tangires, and the late Elizabeth Kielpinski. While in Washington, DC, I had the benefit of airing hypotheses about groundwork with Al Acres, Charles Dempsey, Seth Estrin, Aaron Hyman, Hagi Kenaan, Estelle Lingo, Giancarla Periti, Lisa Pon, Susannah Rutherglen, Elizabeth Walmsley, and Michelle Wang. To Klaus Krüger and Peter Geimer, codirectors of the research group Bildevidenz at the Freie Universität Berlin and to Tristan Weddigen and Tanja Michalsky, codirectors of the Biblioteca Hertziana—Max Planck Institute for Art History, thank you for inviting me to be a fellow at your respective institutions. I had the great fortune of presenting initial portions of this project as the Tomás Harris Visiting Professor at UCL-London. Mechtild Fend, Tamar Garb, Anna Kim, Allison Stielau, Alison Wright, and particularly Rose Marie San Juan made my brief residency memorable and stimulating. My initial thoughts on Bellini were first presented at the University of Hamburg and later appeared in preliminary form in *Steinformen: Materialität, Qualität, Imitation*, edited by Isabella Augart, Maurice Saß, and Iris Wenderholm (Berlin: De Gruyter, 2019). A film essay on Bellini's backgrounds, *The Desert and the Lagoon* (2021) was the result of a fruitful collaboration with Amelia Saul. Angela Vanhaelen and Bronwen Wilson provoked me to consider the "worldliness" of gold grounds as part of their special issue *Making Worlds: Art, Materiality, and Early Modern Globalization*, *Journal of Early Modern History* 23, nos 2–3 (May 2019). Aimee

Ng invited me to take a closer look at the paintings of Moroni, and I would like to thank her and Xavier Solomon for the Frick Collection's openness and generous dialogue. I was able to bring this project closer to completion thanks to a fellowship at Villa I Tatti—the Harvard University Center for Italian Renaissance Studies. Warm thanks to Alina Payne, who has been an invaluable interlocutor, reader, and friend since my graduate school days, and the I Tatti staff, especially Susan Bates, Patrizia Cerella, Angela Lees, and Michael Rocke. In Florence, I benefited from conversations with Roberto Bazzuoli, Francesca Borgo, Nicola Courtright, Francesca Frantappiè, Ludovica Galeazzo, Christine Göttler, Peggy Haines, Patricia Falguières, Pauline Lafille, Ivan Lupić, Scott Nethersole, Wolfram Pichler, Patricia Rubin, and Lucia Simonato. Lorenzo Pericolo shared portions of his work on Caravaggio when access to libraries was challenging. I had the great luck to weather lockdown with Brian Bregge, Byron Hamman, Nelda Ferace, and Putt Ferace at San Martino a Mensola, while the presence of Alina Payne and Mark Peploe across the way and Sarah Guérin and Nick Hermann up the hill in Settignano was especially comforting.

I am lucky to have generous colleagues at Penn and have gained a great deal from extended exchanges with Mauro Calcagno, Eva del Soldato, David Eng, Robert Ousterhout, Brian Rose, Larry Silver, Ann Kuttner, Kaja Silverman, and Gwendolyn DuBois Shaw. Thank you to Karen Redrobe for conversations about Barbara Johnson and André Bazin. Shira Brisman commented on substantial portions of the text, while André Dombrowski has provided feedback on every stage of this project from its inception. I've had also had the privilege of discussing the contents of this book in seminars and would like to acknowledge the graduate student participants for their engagement in extended sessions of close reading and looking.

Thanks also go to friends and colleagues elsewhere, including Nate Bench, Makeda Best, Giancarlo Casale, Stephen Campbell, Leslie Geddes, Darlene Jackson, Charles Kang, Peter Karol, Eleanor Kim, Megan Luke, Alexander Nagel, Yamit Rachman-Schrire, Libby Saylor, and Edward Wouk. Special thanks, too, to Estelle Lingo, Stuart Lingo, Maria Loh, and Nicola Suthor for discussing dimensions of groundwork over the years with insight and generosity. At Princeton University Press, I am grateful to Michelle Komie, who has supported this project for almost a decade, as well as to Kenneth Guay, Terri O'Prey, and Steven Sears. Francis Eaves copyedited the manuscript with multilingual finesse and David Luljak prepared the index.

I owe a special debt of gratitude to Elizabeth Tucker, *lectrice* extraordinaire, whose intelligence, creativity, and rigor have informed every page of this text. I thank her warmly. Thanks are due too to my immediate family, Won Soon Kim, Sue Ann Kim, and Adrian Lewis, and my uncles Dr. Chang-Kun Lee and Dr. Chang-Nam Lee for supporting my education. Finally, this book is dedicated to Ivan Drpić, with whom I am never adrift.

Notes

INTRODUCTION

1 Vasari 1550, vol. 2, 555–56 (my emphasis); Elkins 1998, 78–128; Cole 2014, ix. On the undoing of the body through violent imagery, see Nethersole 2018.

2 My thanks to Peter Karol for suggesting this turn of phrase.

3 *OED*, s.v. "ground"; Kenaan 2007.

4 Arasse 1999.

5 It is in this sense that one of the characters in Shakespeare's *Romeo and Juliet* exclaims that the quarrel between the Montagues and Capulets is "the true *ground* of all these piteous woes." Or when David Hume in his *An Enquiry Concerning Human Understanding* (1748) criticizes those who practice "obscurity in the profound and abstract philosophy" and charges that they who are "unable to defend themselves on fair *ground* raise intangling brambles to cover and protect their weakness" (1.11).

6 Schapiro 1972–73, 9.

7 In the domain of architecture, this was called *area*, which the artist and humanist Leon Battista Alberti defined as "the precisely limited and defined section of the overall locality for future building" (*De re aedificatoria* 1.7).

8 Burioni 2011, 956.

9 Pind 2014.

10 Wood 1993, 60; Iversen 2005.

11 Steinberg 1996, 220; Danti 2002.

12 Masheck 1991, 37; Anne Friedberg and Hubert Damisch would claim that perspective is an "epistemological model," which generates knowledge about a given represented object. I also think that perspective acts as a "disciplinary" model, nourishing perceptions about different art historical fields. Friedberg 2006; Damisch 1994b; Iversen and Melville 2010; Fore 2012, 16.

13 Notwithstanding, on the relationship between perspective and iconography such as the Annunciation in Renaissance painting, see Holmes 2003; Holmes 2004.

14 Johnson 1998, 267. See also Lewis 2020 for a recent account that stresses the politically oriented and submerged aspects of ground in contemporary art.

15 Cole 2014, ix; Hollanda 2013, 179–80.

16 Wharton 1905, 174.

17 Beuys-Wurmbach 1977, 35–37; Gramm 1912.

18 Stumpel 1988; Puttfarken 2000, 97–122; Boehm and Burioni 2012, 11–28.

19 Ledderose 2012.

20 Cranston 2010, 12.

21 Koerner 2016.

22 Flyvbjerg 2006; Arasse 1992, 13; Nietzsche 1996, 125.

23 Suthor 2018, 195.

24 Levy 2015.

25 Levine 2015, 24–35.

26 Chambers 2020.

27 Levine 2015.

28 For a recent reassessment of Baxandall's conception of language as both limiting and enabling analytical instrument, see Mack and Williams 2015.

29 Wood 2019, 292.

30 Greenberg 1960; Arnheim 1966; Wollheim 1987; Damisch 1993; Neuner 2009; Bois 1990. For a discussion of these various theories, see Pichler and Ubl 2014, 136–213.

31 Lajer-Burchart and Graw 2016.

32 Morrison 2020.

33 Insightful accounts of this approach can be found in Rzepińska 1986; Sapir 2012.

34 Kosellek 2018.

I. WORDS FOR GROUNDS

1 McHam 2013, 232–33; Pliny, *Natural History* 35.15, 35.43, 37.5–6; Ovid, *Metamorphoses* 3.342; Alberti 1973, 46; Alberti 2011b, 45–46.

2 Kris and Kurz 1979; Krüger 2013.

3 Blumenberg 2020, 174.

4 Ibid., 176.

5 Ibid., 236.

6 Stoichita 1997; Wolf 1998; Bettini 1999; Pfisterer 2001; Kenaan 2006; Damisch 2010; Loh 2015.

7 Cecchi 1998; De Girolami Cheney 2006; Loh 2015, 230–31; Seifertova 2007; Lohff 2015; Nygren 2017.

8 Dunkerton and Spring 1998; Nadolny 2010; Cerasuolo 2017, 190–91, 238–45; Baldinucci 1681, s.v. "mestica."

9 Huth 1967, 64; Nadolny 2010.

10 O'Malley 2005, 80; Broecke 2015, 138–39.

11 Bomford et al. 1989, 1–26; Dunkerton 1991, 155; Hendy and Lucas 1968; Skaug 2008a; Broecke 2015, 150–58.

12 Hendy and Lucas 1968; Dunkerton and Spring 1998. The humanist Pietro Bembo opens one of his most famous sonnets (*Rime*, 5) with the phrase "Crin d'oro crespe e d'ambra tersa e pura" (Curly hair of gold and of pure,

bright amber). Most likely one of a pair of sonnets Bembo sent to Lucrezia Borgia in 1503, the poem continues by praising the radiant though distant beauty of his beloved, describing her eyes as "clearer than the sun," her teeth like pearls, her hands like ivory. The gesso ground in Palma's *Blonde Woman* does groundwork, enabling the painting's mimetic aims to render illuminated and idealized female beauty. See Cropper 1976; Pozzi 1984; Rylands 1992, 94, 208; Bembo 2008, 17–21.

13 Dunkerton 1991, 161–64; Skaug 2008a; Skaug 2008b.

14 Boschini 1966, 711–12.

15 Neuner 2017.

16 Dunkerton and Spring 1998, 121.

17 Cerasuolo 2017, 243.

18 Hochmann 2015, 121–22; Berrie 1994; Berrie and Fisher 1993; Rothe and Carr 1998, 60; Humfrey and Lucco 1998, 170–74.

19 Suthor 2010.

20 Dunkerton and Spring 1998, 122–23; Dunkerton and Spring 2015, 29–30; Cerasuolo 2017, 100–114.

21 Stumpel 1988, 231–32.

22 Barbaro 1584, 405–8.

23 Lugli 2019.

24 Stumpel 1988, 231–32; Barbaro 1584, 405–8; Bagnoli et al. 2003, 208–18; Tripps 2008, 115–18.

25 Clark 2002, 135–36.

26 Goffen 2003.

27 Clark 2002; Koerner 2016, 272–73.

28 Clark 2002, 135–36.

29 Summers 2003.

30 Alberti 1973, 41; Alberti 2011b, 42; Stumpel 1990, 218–22.

31 We might also imagine the effect of beholding the *Annunciation*'s grid ground through a physical grid, a metal lattice, as did cloistered Clarissan nuns from the church's adjoining convent, who viewed the work through a grille from the raised gallery at the church's opposite end. As Beth Mulvaney has observed regarding these paintings' representation of space, "the repeated emphasis on open and closed, inside and outside, intact and penetrated found in the shutters speaks to the many carefully circumscribed boundaries that defined and confined the lives of these women." Alongside these tensions, the grid in the pictorial field capacitates viewers to measure the Annunciation, enfolding them in the event's location and moment. Mulvaney 2015, 118

32 Bätschmann 2008, 123–27; Howard 2004; Fogolari 1908.

33 In addition to conceiving itself as ground as plane (*piano*) extending laterally, the checkerboard pavement also prompts reflection on the vectors of height and depth in the picture. In so doing, the grid broaches the compositional effects and narrative import of levitation and profundity. One passage in the *Trattato di architettura* (1461–64) written by the architect and theorist Filarete makes a striking analogy between drawing, digging, and raising. "When you wish to build a building," the speaker instructs, "it is necessary to prepare the things needed for its construction. When they are prepared, the foundations are dug, and then arrangements are made for walling up." The same is true for laying out a pavement. "As it is necessary to have a site in order to build and to dig the foundations," he continues, "so too we will first make the site in which we wish to make our drawing. First of all our site must be a plane that is made by rule. Then the things drawn here will also be according to rule and measure." The ground plane is likened to a building site where a masonry base will be laid below, and walls will rise above. Or as Quintilian noted in the *Institutio oratio* 1, "invisible foundations support the visible parts of the work" (ut operam fastigial spectantur, latent fundamenta). The pavement provides the framework under which and over which the artist can erect or burrow. Filarete 1972, 191; Stumpel 1990, 218–22; Damisch 2010, 309.

34 Banks 1978, 7–43; Arnheim 1977; Tardito 1990; Marinelli 1996; Cassegrain 1999–2000.

35 Hogarth 1753, 112.

36 Merleau-Ponty 1993, 93.

37 Marin 2001, 253; Rosand 1983, 104; Goffen 1975; Christiansen 2008, 27–28, 42–48, 50–55; Krüger 2014. Note as well that the parapet also alludes to the physical and tactile dimensions of this devotion. The horizontal ledge echoes and draws attention to the molded profile of the picture's bottom edge. The actual frame, gessoed, applied with bole, and burnished with water gilding bears traces of burns in the wood, suggesting that candles were once lit before it.

38 Loh 2019, 16.

39 Loh reads Titian's personal motto as a proclamation that both "painting and sculpture join forces to defeat the mortal body of nature." The parapet posits the presence of an audience to behold the artist's triumph in the agon between art and nature. Loh 2019, 24.

40 Goffen 1975; Rosand 1983, 104.

41 Stone 2012; Rand 1983; Marin 1989; Marin 2001. A background can also receive lines of narrative or explanatory inscription as it does in a later work such as Philippe de Champaigne's *Ex voto* of 1662. Here background serves as both wall in the Parisian convent of Port-Royal and "grayboard" on which the lengthy inscription, added after the completion of the painting, recounts the illness and cure of the painter's daughter, as well as the artist's donation of the painting itself.

42 Falciani and Natali 2010, 8–9.

43 Fehrenbach 2018, 113.

44 Stumpel 1988, 230; Crusca 1612, s.v. "piano"; Vasari

1550, vol. 1, 15; Sorte 1960, 297–98; Gombrich 1966; Blass-Simmen 2015.

45 Stumpel 1988; Burioni 2012, 95–99.

46 Stumpel 1988; Vasari 1550, vol. 1, 71; Vasari 1907, 208–9.

47 Stumpel 1990, 220–21; Burioni 2012.

48 Stumpel 1998, 222–24; Franklin 2003, 137–41.

49 Kim 2014, 130–35; Gombrich 1966; Puttfarken 2000, 108–10; Baxandall 1972, 17–27; Wiemers 1996, 183–228; Milanesi 1887; Wood 1993, 63–78; Colby 2008; Drpić 2016, 143–44.

50 Marmugi 1984, 166–73; Brown and Van Nimmen 2005, 15–16; Meyer zur Capellen and Falcucci 2011.

51 Marmugi 1984, 166–73; Gusmeroli 2017. Evans sees the residence as a project designed for intimate domesticity, where "the latent structure of inhabited space burst through the confines of classical planning in architecture." See Evans 1997, 55–91.

52 Nixdorff 1999; Endres, Wittmann, and Wolf 2005; Weddigen 2015.

53 Shearman 1984; Elet 2016. Artefacts of sixteenth-century home furnishing, these linen-covered windows transported the biblical scene centuries forward to the here and now. That the painting exemplifies the type of works Renaissance merchants hung in their often sparse domestic interiors—and perhaps in close proximity to a window itself—would only have emphasized the sense of familiarity. Brown and Van Nimmen 2005, 16.

2. POSSIBILITY: ANGELS IN THE GROUND

1 Burckhardt 1860, 280–82; Burckhardt 1878, 285. On Burckhardt's borrowing of the formulation "The Discovery of the World and of Man" from Jules Michelet, see Febvre 1973, 261ff.

2 Burckhardt 2000, 44–45 (my emphasis): "das Altarblatt, jetzt voellig vom Goldgrund losgesprochen (mit einzelnen seltenen Ausnahmen bei Mariotto Albertinelli), ist die Geburtsstaette der wahren Luft und der wahren Wolken in der Malerei gewesen, ja auch die Landschaft ist nur hier zu einem so schoenen und feierlichen Dasein gelangt." Immanuel Kant understood *Dasein*, literally meaning "being there," in a dynamic sense. As opposed to *Nichtsein* (nonbeing), *Dasein* is synonymous with the real and actual (*wirklich*). David 2014.

3 Burckhardt groups Francia along with other artists such as Cosimo Tura, Stefano da Ferrara, and Lorenzo Costa who place the Virgin Mary on a throne that reveals, through an opening in the steps, a landscape view. Burckhardt 2000, 45: "Welche Eifer hat zB: die Schule von Ferrara bethaetigt, als sie sogar die Marienthrone frei auf Stuetzen schweben liess, um unter denselben noch einen landschaftlichen Ausblick zu gewinnen."

4 Meyer 1882, 54: "Ins Museum bin zu später / Stunde heut ich noch gegangen, / Wo die Heilgen, wo die Beter / Auf den goldnen Gründen prangen. / Dann durchs Feld bin ich geschritten / Heißer Abendglut entgegen, / Sah, die heut das Korn geschnitten, / Garben auf die Wagen legen." Notably in his first version of the poem, Meyer described the painting as having a pale background. For discussion of the various versions of Meyer's poem and its relation to a realist aesthetic, see Stockinger 2010, 105–7.

5 For historiographic discussions of gold ground, see Zaunschirm 2012; Schwarz 2012. For recent treatments of gold grounds in medieval and early Renaissance art, see Wenderholm 2005; Beyer 2008, 187–201; Rudolph 2011; Degler and Wenderholm 2016; Drpić forthcoming.

6 Riegl 1985, 12–13; Riegl 1901, 8: "Der Goldgrund der byzantinischen Mosaiken hingegen, der den Hintergrund im allgemeinen ausschliesst und damit zunaechst einen Rueckschritt zu bezeichen scheint, ist nicht mehr Grundebene, sonder idealer Raumgrund, welche die abendlaendischen Voelker in der Folge mit realen Dingen bevoelkern und in die unendliche Tiefe ausdehnen konnten."

7 Lange 1901, 145: "En udelukkende symbolsk Betydning har Guldglansen i Helgenglorien, der jo er som en udskaaret Del af en hel Guldgrund, det vil sige af den himmelske Glans, der følger de hellige ogsaa paa Jorden som Betegnelse af deres Værdighed. Dog har Guldgrunden i Middelalderens Kunst ikke alene Betydning af Empyreet i en stor Mængde Tilfælde træder den i Stedet for den jordiske Luft idet de enkelte Ting og Figurer paa Billedet ere malede med naturlige Farver medens alt det som den senere Kunst vilde male som Luft er gengivet ved Forgyldning."

8 Florenskij 1988, 138: "Aber es gibt nicht nur eine sichtbare Welt—und sei es für den vergeistigten Blick—, sondern auch eine unsichtbare, die Göttliche Gnade, die wie geschmolzenes Metall in vergöttlichter Realität dahinströmt."

9 Spengler 1926, 248. Note also the implications Spengler draws from the gradual disappearance of gold ground: "When 'natural' backgrounds, with their blue-green heavens, far horizons and depth perspective, began to appear in early Gothic, they had at first the appearance of something profane and worldly. The change of dogma that they implied was, if not acknowledged, at any rate felt, witness the tapestry backgrounds with which the real depth of space was covered up by a pious awe that disguised what it dared not exhibit."

10 Schöne 1954, 25; Braunfels 1950; Franses 2003.

11 Claussen 2007.

12 Gombrich 1935, 67: "Dann wäre eine weitere

Eigenschaft der Goldfarbe deutlicher hervorgetreten, die der Autor nur streift und auf die O. Pächt den Referenten aufmerksam gemacht hat: daß sie nämlich im eigentlichen Sinne des Wortes keine Farbe ist, den Farben des Spektrums gleichwertig, sondern Materie, Metall, d. h. eben: Gold."

13 Gombrich 1935, 61: "Denn während B. und andere den außernatürlichen wirklichkeitsfremden Charakter des Goldgrundes im Bilde eindringlich schildern, dürfen wir auch, polar dazu, seine Dinghaftigkeit betonen."

14 Beer 1983.

15 Dunlop 2009.

16 Benjaminsen and Berge 2004; Nixon, Guerra, and Rehren 2011; Guérin 2018.

17 Gomez 2018; Cuoq 1985.

18 Grosjean 1978. On the map's deployment of figural and iconographic conventions to portray Mansa Musa, see Massing 2007; Thissen-Lorenz 2014.

19 Schwarz 2012, 36.

20 Cassin 2014b.

21 Agamben 2017, 37–38.

22 Kemp 1997, 84–90; Ames-Lewis 2000, 177; Löhr 2008; Broecke 2015.

23 Löhr 2008, 159.

24 Broecke 2015, 166–67: "Come si può mettere d'oro con verdeterra in tavola"; "Ancora secondo che usavano gli antichi puoi fare"; 168: "E se vedi che l'oro non sia in tutto accostato all'acqua, togli un poco di bambagia nuova, e leggieri quanto puoi al mondo, calca il detto oro"; 168–69: "acciò che sempre vadia risparmiando l'oro, il più che puoi facendone masserizia, e cuoprendo con fazzuoli bianchi quell'oro che hai mettudo"; 171–72: "Egli è vero che di verno tu puoi mettere d'oro quanto vuoi, essendo il tempo umido e morbido, e non alido."

25 Broecke 2015, 174.

26 Goldthwaite 2009, 312, 325, 385, 344–45.

27 Lucchi 2009.

28 Goldthwaite 2009, 555. On documents attesting to Antonio's activity as a goldbeater and his rental of a bottega near the Parte Guelfa, see Cecchi 2005, 18–19.

29 Sachs 2009, 64–65.

30 For a succinct discussion of the gold leaf application process and its role in period contracts, see O'Malley 2005, 49–64.

31 Sachs 2009, 64–65.

32 Broecke 2015, 174.

33 O'Malley 2005, 56–57.

34 Broecke 2015, 172. The emphasis on artists' need to understand the environmental conditions in which they work continues in the writings of Giorgio Vasari, notably in the *Introduction to the Three Arts of Design* that precede the better-known biographies. In the case of incorporating colors in fresco painting, for instance, Vasari aligns the awareness of material properties, moisture, and rates of evaporation with the all-important faculty of judgment. One needs, he declares, "a hand that is dexterous, resolute, and rapid, but most of all a sound and perfect judgment." Whereas while wet on the wall "the colors show up in one fashion," he points out, "afterwards when dry they are no longer the same." Well-executed *buon fresco* "when exposed to the air [. . .] throws off all impurities, water does not penetrate it, and it resists anything that would injure it." Vasari 1907, 221–22.

35 On the concept of "pictorial intelligence," defined as "a deep engagement with how pictures work, how they produce (or, at times, frustrate) meaning," see Lobel 2014, 5, 56.

36 On "stickiness," see Gell 1998, 80–86. On this media overlap, see Auld 1986; Mack 2002; Curatola 2006; Spallanzani 2007; Nagel 2011; Kim 2016.

37 Ward 1993, 71–94; Spallanzani 2010. I am grateful to Marianne Shreve Simpson for her suggestions on this point.

38 Notably the same or comparable language ("brunire," "camosciare," "granire") is found in Cellini's treatise on goldsmithery. For a translation and explanation of these technical terms, see Cellini 1898, 147–64.

39 Broecke 2015, 174–75.

40 Weppelmann 2008; Eclercy 2007.

41 Broecke 2015, 175.

42 Ibid., 176.

43 On the canonical status of the altarpiece in art historical narratives, see Christiansen 2005, 11–40.

44 MacGregor and Freschi 2005.

45 On the irregular and diffused lighting effects in the altarpiece, see the entry authored by Mauro Minardi in Laureati and Mochi Onori 2006, 148–49.

46 The following remarks on the patronage, display, condition, and iconography on the panel draw from Christiansen 1982, 5, 83–84; De Marchi 1992, 50–51, 90, no. 27; Marcelli 2005, 49–64; and the entries by Andrea De Marchi and Vittoria Garibaldi in Laureati and Mochi Onori 2006, 94–97.

47 De Marchi 2004.

48 Marcelli 2005, 61–64

49 Broecke 2015, 195.

50 Steingräber 1969; Alexander 1993–94, 27–36, 377–80.

51 On these techniques, see Graves 1926; Gay 1887–1928, vol. 1: 536, 620, 716, 782, 785, 796; vol. 2: 192, 355, 247, 250; Lightbown 1978, 75–82.

52 French Gothic manuscript illumination might have provided another cross reference. Several of the figural groups in the triptych recall compositions in *Très Riches Heures du Duc de Berry*. Notably, Arnold, the youngest of the Limbourg Brothers, is documented in 1417 as serving as an apprentice to a goldsmith in Nijmegen. See Alexander 1993–94.

53 Collareta 2006.
54 This too is further complicated by the fact that what we see is, in fact, a type of backward relief or relief in reverse, given that the forms that seem to project out into space are due to cavities in the ground.
55 As voiced later by the sixteenth-century painter and art writer Giovanni Battista Armenini in his exposition on the different kinds and distinctions of colors. See Armenini 1977, 186. The relation between opus punctorium and grisaille painting could be further explored in relation to Cennino's remarks, in chapter 31 of the *Libro*, about painting figures in lead white on a prepared paper support. See Schäffner 2009, 81–88, 131–46; Schüppel and Brückle 2008.
56 Tizio 1998.
57 The work was also mentioned in passing by Bartholomaeus Facius in his *De viris illustribus* (1456): "His is a work in the Piazza at Siena, again the Mother Mary holding the Christ in her lap as if she would wrap him round with fine linen. John the Baptist, the Apostles Peter and Paul, and Christopher carrying Christ on his shoulder are here done with art so admirable that it seems to be reproducing also even the motion and action of the body." (Eius est opus Senis in foro, eadem Maria mater Christum itidem puerum grémio tenens, tenui linteo ilium velare cupienti adsimilis, Iohannes Baptista, Petrus ac Paulus Apostoli et Christoforus Christum humero sustinens, mirabili arte, ita ut ipsos quoque corporis motus ac gestus representare videatur.) Baxandall 1964, 100–101.
58 For documents pertaining to the commission, discovered to have been overseen by Jacopo della Quercia, see Fattorini 2010.
59 Laureati and Mochi Onori 2006, 46–47.
60 Tizio 1998, 178. On this passage, see De Marchi 2004, 29–30 and his remarks in Laureati and Mochi Onori 2006, 94–95.
61 Tizio later mentions how Gentile da Fabriano's painting in the Campo was destined for a public audience celebrating the election of Cardinal Antonio Casini attending the Council of Siena (1423–24). See Tizio 1998, 182; Fattorini 2010, 158.
62 Alberti 2011b, 72. I have slightly modified Sinisgalli's translation.
63 Schwarz 2012, 29.
64 Gill 2014, 24.
65 Aquinas 1911, 310–24. This issue brings to mind Protestant apologists who ridiculed Thomas Aquinas for supposedly asking how many angels can dance on the point of a needle. On the origin and afterlife of this question imputed to medieval scholastics, see Harrison 2016.
66 Aquinas 1911, 320–23.
67 For a comparable observation, see Marcelli 2005, 61: "I volti di Maria o del Bambino nella pala di Perugia sono diventati materiali, carne e pelle plasmate e sforiate dal sole e dalle ombre, così come tutta la parte restante della tavola è stata il frutto di una lucida alchimia di tecniche e materiali."
68 Kessler 2000, 53–58, 39–47; Tilghman 2016, 168–69.
69 Verbal and substantive instances of the word, searchable through the online version of the text (http://fonti-sa.sns.it/index.php) include: "incarnare" (4), "incarnassi" (1), "incarnata" (1), "incarnata" (1), "incarnato" (1), "incarnazione" (23), "incarnazioni" (14).
70 In Book 7 of Dante's *Paradiso*, Beatrice explains why humankind could only be saved through the death of Christ: "All other means fell short of justice / save that the Son of God / should humble Himself by becoming flesh [non fosse umilïato ad incarnarsi]."
71 Laureati and Mochi Onori 2006, 112–13.
72 See Steinberg 1996, 24 where he refers to Gentile da Fabriano's altarpiece *Madonna and Child with Saints Nicholas and Catherine* (c. 1400, Berlin, Gemäldegalerie) as representative of the growing convention to expose Christ's sex.
73 On the character's preoccupation with gold, called "the spiritualism of your present-day societies," see Pasco 1980.
74 Marx 1993, 642. Marx paraphrases Alexander Anderson, *The Recent Commercial Distress* (London, 1847), 4: "Capital is divided by some into two different kinds—fixed and floating; that is, fixed to the soil such as houses, lands [. . .]. Floating capital is all sorts of goods and commodities floating about for exchange or consumption such as [. . .] furniture, tools. But the distinction into fixed and floating is more apparent than real. Gold is fixed capital properly so called, although there is nothing under the sun so floating perhaps; it yields an annual return as interest the same as land yields[; . . .] it is only floating capital as far as it is consumed for gilding and other purposes in art or manufacture for the sake of its beauty or other useful quality without reference to its value."
75 Denis Possot, *Le voyage de la Terre Sainte. Composé par maître Denis Possot et achevé par messire Charles Philippe, seigneur de Champarmoy et de Grandchamp, 1532*, ed. Charles Schefer (Paris, 1890), 87: "On ne prent monnoye ne or sinon que icelluy du coing de Venise; mais l'or estranger, on le prent au poix et la monnoye non. Et portasmes de l'or et de la monnoye de Venise de secque jusques oultre la Terre Saincte." Cited and discussed in Chareyron 2005, 38.

3. METAMORPHOSIS: ROCKLAND, FISSURE, MARSHLAND, CAVE

1 Vasari 1568, vol. 1, 119 (my emphasis): "*sopra una lastra piana e pulita* con un sasso un poco appuntato ritraeva una pecora di naturale." Kim 2014, 64–65.
2 Vasari 1996, vol. 1, 742; Vasari 1568, vol. 2, 85.
3 Burckhardt 2000, 44–45.

4 On Raphael's pictorial variety, see Kim 2014, 130–33; R. Williams 2017, 23–27.

5 Pearson 2011, 5.

6 Bachelard 1964, 202.

7 See chapter 1.

8 Baker-Bates and Calvillo 2018.

9 Preimesberger 2011, 51; Calvillo 2013, especially 486–77; Cerasuolo 2017, 260–71.

10 Nygren 2017.

11 For the letter, written by the papal courtier Vittorio Soranzo to Pietro Bembo, see Bembo 1985, 110v; Hirst 1981, 124–25; Baker-Bates 2018.

12 Nygren 2020 142–44.

13 Kim 2013, 24–26. According to the Central File Report of the Getty Museum, the collection's *Portrait of Pope Clement VII* (c. 1531), painted by Sebastiano del Piombo, was executed on a ⅜-inch [1 cm]-thick piece of slate weighing 67.5 [30.6 kg] (a total of 97 lb [44 kg] when combined with its support) and features a 3-inch [7.6 cm] break on the lower right hand corner.

14 Mancini 1956, 20–21: "Che veramente queste pitture mi par che di gioie diventin vetro, anzi che, quasi invidioso, l'huomo gli toglie la lor perpetuità; e di ciò a questi giorni se n'è visto essempio che una miniatura fatta dal Ligozza in una pietra paragone nel cascare è andata in pezzi."

15 Cennino, writing several generations after Giotto, remarked in his artists' manual that "if you want to become skillful at mountains so that they appear real, take some big stones which are craggy but not smooth and copy them from life" (*Libro*, ch. 88). He further recommends putting in the lights and darks "as your system dictates." Not only does Cennino advocate studying and painting from nature; he also observes that nature's deformations—typical of large, craggy rocks as opposed to smooth ones—provide the occasion for the artist to create chiaroscuro gradations and represent a surface of irregular visual incident. Broecke 2015, 125; Tripps 2008, 110.

16 Scholarship on the panel is enormous, and informative and insightful contributions other than those discussed elsewhere in this chapter include Meiss 1964; Fletcher 1972; Fleming 1982; Grave 2004; Lugli 2009.

17 Among the most significant discoveries made by Rutherglen and Hale is Bellini's "unusually muted treatment of the stigmata." Instead of making the signs of Christ's wounds on Francis's body immediately visible and discernible from a distance, the artist placed the discreet blot of red paint on the saint's left hand in an area of shadow, thereby subtly cloaking the mark of blood; and at his right hand, Bellini extended the width and length of the saint's sleeve such that the furling brown habit would draw attention away from another restrained red blot on the palm. Microscopic analysis also revealed that Bellini placed a further wound on Francis's foot, though this blot has abraded over time. The artist never included a wound in Francis's side, which is conventionally signaled through a tear in the saint's habit. By showing the cloth as untorn, Bellini alludes to the presence of the wound without showing it. Bellini's restrained depiction of the stigmata is consonant with Francis's desire to hide these wounds out of humility. What is more, the red marks on Francis's body would be rendered invisible when Bellini's painting was viewed from afar. "The artist hints at the ineffable and unknowable nature of these sacred wounds," Rutherglen and Hale state, "capturing the essence of Francis both in his corporeal martyrdom and spiritual wholeness." Rutherglen and Hale 2015b, 94.

18 Pächt 2003, 232.

19 Rutherglen and Hale 2015a, 170.

20 Reinforcing the joins between the panels are butterfly inserts, which date from the painting's inception. To the far left and right, two vertical battens, one located near the leaning tree, the other near the trellis, further stabilize the panel's support. See Rutherglen and Hale 2015b, 84, 87, 96, 105, 110.

21 Spengler 1926, 248.

22 Blass-Simmen 2015, 88.

23 Koschorke 1990, 54 as cited in Blass-Simmen 2015, 88, 91 n. 36. On the endurance of supposedly obsolete media, see Lehmann 2015.

24 Broecke 2015, 89–92; Bucklow 2009, 43–74; Sframeli et al. 2015.

25 Rutherglen and Hale 2015b, 98–106.

26 Dunkerton 2004, 211; Volpin and Lazzarini 1994, 32, 34.

27 Nagel and Wood 2010, 335–45.

28 Rutherglen and Hale 2015a, 181.

29 Habig 1973, 1449.

30 Tripps 2008.

31 Suthor 2010.

32 Rutherglen and Hale 2015b, 98.

33 Eberhart 2004, 16.

34 Chastel 1978.

35 Brisman 2016, 120.

36 Such rugged geological forms opening up faraway distance stand in contrast to other types of framing instruments in Bellini's oeuvre, such as the oft-cited and discussed Pesaro Altarpiece. In that work, he drew on the cleavage of stone to delineate the sharp and polished marble frame inlaid with colored disks. Echoing the altarpiece's rectilinear gilded frame, the illusionistic framing device within the picture encases the view of the distant landscape and serves as architectonic ornamentation for the figures of the Virgin and Christ. Within the field of this frame, the towers of the citadel that successively punctuate the ascending curtain wall, reiterate the form of Mary's crown, thereby underscoring the honorific theme of the Virgin's

Coronation. Wilson 1977, 145–50, 160–80; Wright 2019, 114.

37 See Brown 1983, 11 in reference to Brown 1971; Rutherglen 2015, 48.

38 Bonaventure of Bagnoregio 1995, 889–90: "Unde cum secundum exigentiam locorum et temporum alienae condescendisset procurandae saluti, inquietationibus derelictis turbarum, solitudinis secreta petebat locumque quietis, quo liberius Domino vacans, extergeret, si quid pulveris sibi ex conversatione hominum adhaesisset. Biennio itaque antequam spiritum redderet caelo, divina providentia duce, post labores multimodos perductus est in locum excelsum seorsum, qui dicitur Mons Alvernae." Bonaventure of Bagnoregio 2000, 630.

39 For the theological reading of Francis as pillar of the church, see Rutherglen and Hale 2015b, 90.

40 Grig 2012, 133. In fifteenth- and sixteenth-century prints and painting, Jerome is frequently shown as being surrounded by visual depictions of his epistles, in addition to open books and other pieces of writing. These scholarly attributes not only figure him as a translator and Doctor of the Church. The medium of the written word on paper registers viewers' affective proximity to, and physical and historical distance from, the saint. See Brisman 2016, 115–27.

41 Barausse 2008, 347–48: "el quale [Giovanni Bellini] mi rispoxe [. . .] che, piazendo a vostra signoria illustrissima, lo faria la nostra Donna con el Puto, eziam el san Ioan Batista et qualche lontani et altra fantaxia che molto più se achomoderia a ditto Quadro et che molto staria meglio." Cited and discussed in Blass-Simmen 2015, 79. On Isabella d'Este's collection as display and reflection on selfhood, see Campbell 2004a.

42 Speroni 1560, 22: "Questa vostra ragione è simile molto alle dipinture, lequali noi volgarmente appelliamo lontani; ove sono paesi, per lequale si vedono caminare alcune picciole figurette, che paiono huomini; ma sottilmente considerate, non hanno parte alcuna, che a membro di huomo si rassomigli." Cited and discussed in Blass-Simmen 2015, 80.

43 Bembo 1987–93, vol. 1: 201. For further bibliography and discussion of the letter, see Brown 2004, 284, 299 (no. 114); Grave 2004, 85–86; Aurenhammer 2013, 225–26; Brown 2013. Note that Bembo's comments are only reportedly Bellini's and were made in response to the complex exigencies and protracted discussions surrounding a commission in Isabella's private study in Mantua. See Campbell 2004a, 56–57.

44 In a series of lectures delivered in 1967–68 at the University of Vienna, Pächt considered the Renaissance Venetian artist a proponent of "the arrested gaze" (der stillgestellete Blick): the viewer's absorption in a work's optical appearance seen from a situated distance. In circumspect opposition to Pächt's notion of the "arrested gaze," Hans Aurenhammer sees in Bellini's work an interest in a wandering, even distracted approach to looking, which displaces and distributes the gaze throughout the image. Pächt 2003, 12; Aurenhammer 2013.

45 Hammond 2002; Hammond 2007; Di Vito 2015.

46 Acres 2006, 24.

47 Janson 1994. For Carolyn Wilson's most recent assessment of the Pesaro Altarpiece, see Wilson 2019.

48 In another devotional painting by Mantegna that figures *Christ as Suffering Redeemer* (c. 1495–1500), the background makes the connection between quarry and future time even more explicit: stonemasons measure and sculpt the Arma Christi directly beneath Mount Calvary: inserted in the ground above are three empty crosses that await the bodies of the condemned. Arnold Hauser has furthermore argued that Mantegna's scenes of excavation are more than simply proleptic devotional scenes. The statue being hewn in the quarry is a symbol of paganism in classical antiquity. The sculpture, however, is yet unfinished. Propped up against the side of the rock wall, it anticipates its future on top of a column for idol-worship, a positioning which will eventually be toppled. Idolatry's future demise is already inscribed during the act of the idol's creation. Mantegna's groundwork signals the tense of the future perfect, actions that will already have been done. At the same time, the process of working in stone befits the discursive and ongoing rhetoric against paganism. The battle with heathenism takes place in the continuous present, since it must be waged again and again. Hauser 2003.

49 Agamben 2020, 20.

50 Connell 1988.

51 Suthor 2010.

52 Ackerman 1990; Alpers 1996.

53 Spencer 1970; Goy 2006, 136–39; Schofield and Ceriani Sebregondi 2006–7.

54 Serlio 2001, 459–512.

55 Alberti 1988, 74.

56 Rosenberg 2001; Branagan 2006.

57 Alberti 1988, 328. Discussed in Dal Prete 2018, 430–31.

58 For commentary on the specific terms in this passage, see Vitruvius 1983, 77–79. On the reception of Vitruvius in the Venetian cultural ambient, see D'Evelyn 2012.

59 Cesariano 2002, 19–20; Kim 2014, 49.

60 Bonaventure, *Legenda Maior* 8.11: "We should have the greatest reverence, therefore, for St. Francis' loving compassion which had such wonderful charm that it could bring savage animals into subjection and tame the beasts of the forest, training those which were tame already and claiming obedience from those which had rebelled against fallen mankind." Cited and discussed in Sorrell 1988, 51.

61 In sculpture of the period, such as in a relief of *Saint Jerome in the Wilderness* (1470; Metropolitan Museum of

Art, New York, 2001.593), attributed variously to Benedetto da Maiano or his master Antonio Rossellino, the fracture of stone literally creates the rocky crevices in the wilderness where the saint performs his act of penance. See Wardropper 2011, 23–25.

62 Rutherglen 2015, 33; Rutherglen and Hale 2015b, 123.

63 Luz 2005, 563–64.

64 Drpić 2008, 232–33.

65 My thanks to Shira Brisman for these observations.

66 Corbo 1988, 59–61, 64–66, 415–19.

67 Rachman-Schrire 2019.

68 On the *Itinerarium Antonini Placentini*, see Antoninus of Piacenza 1965, 163; Wilkinson 1977, 83; Rachmann-Schrire 2019, 47.

69 See Rutherglen and Hale 2015b, 112–14, which associates the spout with the miracle of Francis quenching the thirst of a poor man, or in a more allegorical vein, as an allusion to the artist's creativity, given the signature on the cartellino placed nearby.

70 Theoderich of Würzburg 2016, 168.

71 Rachman-Schrire 2012; Rachman-Schrire 2019, 49.

72 Fabri 1843–49, vol. 2: 299, as cited and discussed in Rachmann-Schrire 2019, 49.

73 The text directly above the miniature which continues on the following leaf reads: "E dicando cossì ello passò, e de presente la cina delo Templo se fendé perfine allo fondamento, e la terra se avrì e le prede se spezone e li monumenti se aprino e molti sancti corpi che erano morti resuscitono e insiveno deli monumenti e dreto la resurrection de Yesù veneno in la citade de Yerusalem e apariteno a molti." See Vitale-Brovarone 1987, vol. 1: 203 and vol 2: 119v.

74 Pratesi and Sabatelli, 1958, 223–24: "E fra l'altre fu una volta in quella quaresima, che uscendo un dì santo Francesco della cella in fervore di spirito e andando ivi assai presso a stare in orazione in una tomba d' un sasso cavato, della quale insino giù a terra è una grandissima altezza e orribile e pauroso precipizio, subitamente viene il demonio, con tempesta e con rovinìo grandissimo, in forma terribile, e percuotelo per sospignerlo quindi giuso. Di che santo Francesco non avendo dove fuggire e non potendo soffrire l'aspetto crudelissimo del demonio, di subito si rivolse con le mani e col viso e con tutto il corpo al sasso e raccomandossi a Dio, brancolando colle mani se a cosa nessuna si potesse appigliare. Ma come piacque a Dio, il quale non lascia mai tentare li servi suoi più che possano portare, subitamente per miracolo il sasso, al quale egli s' accostò, si cavò secondo la forma del corpo suo e sì lo ricevette in sè, a modo come s'egli avesse messe le mani e 'l viso in una cera liquida, così nel detto sasso s'improntò la forma delle mani e de viso di santo Francesco; e così aiutato da Dio, scampò dinanzi al demonio."

75 Conigliello 1999. Curated by Ginger Hammer, the exhibition "Heavenly Earth: Images of Saint Francis at La Verna" at the National Gallery of Art, Washington, DC (February 25—July 8, 2018) displayed how Ligozzi's print included an overslip to show the guard railing later erected to protect visitors. See Hammer 2018.

76 Collegium S. Bonaventurae 1885, 164.

77 Ubertino da Casale 2001, 190.

78 Rutherglen and Hale 2015b, 97–98, 111.

79 Zorach 2011.

80 Rutherglen and Hale 2015b, 98.

81 Ibid., 120–21.

82 On the early Franciscan presence in the Holy Land, see Golubovich 1913: 412–23; Lemmens 1925; Pringle 1993–2009; Jotischky 2016.

83 See Habig 1973, 1438.

84 Pratesi and Sabatelli 1958, 218–19: "Ivi a pochi dì, istandosi santo Francesco allato alla detta cella e considerando la disposizione del monte e meravigliandosi delle grandissime fessure e aperture di sassi grandissimi, si puose in orazione; e allora gli fu rivelato da Dio che quelle fessure così maravigliose erano state fatte miracolosamente, nell'ora della passione di Cristo, quando, secondo che dice il Vangelista, le pietre si spezzarono. E questo volle Iddio che singularmente appresse in su quel monte della Vernia, perché quivi si dovea rinnovare la passione del nostro Signore Gesù Cristo, nell'anima sua per amore e compassione, e nel corpo suo per impressione delle sacre sante Istimate. Avuta ch'ebbe santo Francesco quella rivelazione, immantanente si rinchiude in cella e tutto si ricoglie in sé medesimo e sì si dispone attendere al misterio di questa rivelazione. E d'allora inanzi santo Francesco per la continova orazione cominciò ad assaggiare più spesso la dolcezza della divina contemplazione, per la quale egli ispesse volte era sì ratto in Dio, che corporalmente egli era veduto da' compagni elevato di terra e ratto fuori di sè." See also Augart 2019.

85 Hui 2016.

86 Bätschmann 2008, 119–22. The Berlin panel uses the same method of constructing the support with three poplar panels as the Frick painting, though the Berlin painting is flipped by ninety degrees, thereby suggesting that Bellini may have purchased the panels wholesale. See Rutherglen and Hale 2015b.

87 For discussion of Leonardo's statement, see Ackerman 1980, 30.

88 Rutherglen and Hale 2015b, 87–88.

89 Bailey 2018, 83.

90 Zorzi 1961; Fletcher 1972; Fletcher 1981; Michiel 2000; Schmitter 1997, 27–37; Schmitter 2003; Lauber 2007.

91 Hochmann 1999, 1181; Cranston 2019, 49.

92 Hochmann 1999, 1181–83; Schmitter 2003, 564–65.

93 Rutherglen 2015, 49–55.

94 For readings of *paese* as the wilderness, see Belting 2014; Cranston 2019, 49.

95 Lauber 2015.
96 Bonaventure of Bagnoregio 2000, 592. As cited and discussed in Lavin 2007, 235.
97 Lavin 2007, 236–38.
98 Ibid., 243.
99 For the bull of Pope Pius II, dated September 9, 1460, see Lavin 2007, 249.
100 Szafran 2015; Rutherglen 2016.
101 My thanks to Karen Redrobe for this observation.
102 In addition to possibly alluding to the marshy environment of San Francesco del Deserto, the aqueous setting might also allude to the miracle whereby Francis salved a poor man's thirst with water produced from a rock. Rutherglen and Hale 2015b, 112.
103 Barry 2020, 64–65, 137–38.
104 Geddes 2020, 130–32.
105 Pincus 2008; Brown 2013. Though postdating Bellini's painting by more than a decade, Bembo's verse cites and comments on such classical authorities as Hesiod, Empedocles, Lucretius, and Seneca, whose texts were in circulation in early fifteenth-century Italy. See G. Williams 2017, 255–68.
106 Bembo 2005, 239.
107 For an inventive application of Warburg's notion of the *Pathosformel*, see Lingo 2009.
108 Pincus 2008.
109 Suthor 2010.

4. ARTICULATION: WALLED FIGURES, FIGURED WALLS

1 Leonardo da Vinci 1883, 134.
2 On the materiality of the screen in contemporary visual culture, see Bruno 2014.
3 For the most recent bibliography on the portrait, see Ng, Facchinetti, and Galansino 2019.
4 Anonymous 1999, 530.
5 Gregori 1979, 224, 274; Humfrey 2000, 28, 29, 64; Penny 2004, 195: the artist's "carefully graded greys provide a perfect foil for the complexions of his sitters."
6 For early modern readings of this passage, see Kim 2014, 50.
7 Vitruvius 1983, 77–78.
8 Romano 1987, 171–78; Wulfram 2001, 94–132; Di Stefano 2012, 31; Cesariano 2002, 18–21; Rykwert 1972, 10–20.
9 Alberti 1988, 3; Alberti 1966, 9: "Fuere qui dicerent aquam aut ignem praebuisse principia, quibus effectum sit, ut hominum coetus celebrarentur. Nobis vero tecti parietisque utilitatem atque necessitate spectantibus ad homines conciliandos atque una continendos maiorem in modum valuisse nimirum persuadebitur."
10 Rykwert 1972, 116.
11 Alberti's treatise is recorded as being in the inventory of Francesco Ricchino, a Brescian artist with whom Moroni painted the Chapel of the Sacrament in the church of Santa Maria Assunta in Romano di Lombardia in 1565. See Fiori 2016a, 212, 215, 217.
12 Rykwert 1972, 116–17.
13 Serlio 1996, 372–73.
14 Palladio 1997, 13–17.
15 This was Moroni's preferred painting support, and he worked throughout his career with a variety of weaves including herringbone and tabby, and, later on, heavier twill weaves.
16 Penny 2004, 196.
17 Ibid.
18 Penny 2004, 224–25; Bomford 1979, 39–40.
19 Cerasuolo 2017, 243.
20 Penny 2004, 228–31; Ng, Facchinetti, and Galansino 2019, 96–99.
21 Biow 2015.
22 In the sixteenth century, the motto stood for a declaration of loyalty to Catholic sovereignty, given that the phrase was often found on the reverse of coins and medals featuring an allegorical figure of religion. See Penny 2004, 228; Rossi 2015–16. The inscription may also demonstrate a commitment to the sitter's marital intentions. The awkward execution of the parapet as well as the difficult correspondence between the inscription and expression of the sitter has also raised doubts about the contemporaneity of the parapet and inscription with the portrait's original conception. See Ng, Facchinetti, and Galansino 2019, 99.
23 Penny 2004, 250–51.
24 Mancini 1956, 115.
25 Penny 2004, 196, 232, 250.
26 Armenini 1586, 195.
27 Jurdjevic 2002. For discussion of the Bigi as opposed to the Bianchi (anti-Medicean, pro-Savonarolan republicans), see Weinstein 2011, 127, 132, 227.
28 Pastoureau 2009, 109; Cusato 2015.
29 Frick 2002, 143. The virtues of gray also attained an allegorical register in poetry. In his longest poem, *Rime*, 67 (written before 1534), a paean to rural life and simplicity, Michelangelo describes how "merry Poverty" (la lieta Povertà) roams free in the woods, "clad in coarse gray cloth" (in panni rozzi e bigi), "free of obligations, cares, and quarrels." Saslow 1991, 163–70.
30 As they were in Giovan Andrea Corsuccio's treatise on silk, *Il vermicello dall seta* (1581), cited and discussed in Molà 2000. See also Pastoureau 2009, 106–10.
31 Newton 1999, 28, 66.
32 Buettner 1996, 27, 37, 67–68.
33 Leon Battista Alberti's treatise *On Painting* (1435), a much earlier work (discussed in chapter 1), offers a

definition of gray in natural historical terms. The four elements correspond to four principle colors: fire to red, air to blue, water to green, and earth to *cinereum* (an ash color). There is thus a philosophical and theological association of the color gray with flesh, mortality, and transience. Glossing Alberti's text in the vernacular, one sixteenth-century commentator wrote that "since the earth [terra] is the residue of all the elements, perhaps we are not wrong to say that all colors are called gray [bixi]." In his magisterial work *Color and Culture*, John Gage took these annotations to mean that for the early modern reader of Alberti, "all colors were thus seen to partake of grey: grey was the key to the tonal coherence of the pictorial composition." In fact, many colors, such as gold and ultramarine, just to name two of the most precious, derive from the earth's minerals. Hence the designations of other colors in Renaissance manuals with the terms "terra di nera," "terra di giallo," "terra di verde." In the early twentieth century, experiments in optical perception led to the development of the "gray scale," which identifies the brightness or darkness of a color as a quality separate from hue. This development gives force to Alberti's idea that all colors are to some degree variations of gray. Alberti 1960–73, vol. 3, 311. The passage from the manuscript in the Biblioteca Capitolare, Verona (Cod. CCLXXIII) reads "e perché la terra è feccia di tuti li elementi forsi non diremo male tuti i colori chiamarsi bixi come feccia de la terra." Cited and discussed in Gage 1993, 118. Recent work on the color has repeated this assertion, at times without citation, using it as a precedent for modern and contemporary art's preoccupation with the color in the work of Jasper Johns and Gerhard Richter. Guerin 2018, 31–33.

34 Borghini 2007, 148; Borghini 1584, 230: "Acciocché i pittori nel dipignere et i gentiluomini nel fare imprese e livree abbiano il campo più largo da poter ispiegare i concetti loro." Later early modern writers on art intermittently touch on gray. Entries for the color can be found in Baldinucci's dictionary *Vocabolario toscano dell'arte del disegno* (1681), whose pithy entries cross-reference one another or allude to natural materials. *Cenerognolo* is "a color similar to ashes." *Bigio* is a "color similar to cenerognolo." *Grigio* is "a color similar to a black bigio, that between it is mixed white," most often used to describe fur and feathers. Baldinucci 1681, s.v. "cenerognolo," "bigio," and "grigio."

35 Pastoureau 2009, 109.

36 Bushart and Wedekind 2016, xix.

37 Lehmann 2018, 23; Hara 2018.

38 As described in book 4, chapter 9: "On Decoration in the Form of Painting, both Outside and Inside Buildings." Serlio 2001, 378.

39 Vasari 1907, 240.

40 Tassi 1793, 164: "Molto operò nella sua terra d'Albino sopra tele, e muri a olio, e a fresco e si fece conoscere per pittore universale, e ciò si vede in una stanza dipinta in casa Spini nell anno 1549, essendovi in essa molti capricci alla chinese paesetti puttini ed animali diversi con molta grazia e leggiadria insieme ripartiti. Fece in altra stanza un gruppo di puttini che sostengono lo stemma gentilizio di quella casa, e sopra il palazzo della Misericordia d'Albino posto sulla piazza della Parrocchiale colori a fresco la Beata Vergine col Bambino fra le braccia con varj poveri intorno e con bellissime architetture." Much of this work is not extant, though traces of Moroni's architectural decoration in the Palazzo Spini (currently known as the Cà del Fatur) remain. See Facchinetti 2004, 288.

41 On the painting's spatial organization, see Vaccaro 2002, 192–93; Ekserdjian 2006, 121–24; Thimann 2006, 68–70; Rubin 2007, 44–45.

42 The painting presents, as has been astutely observed, "conceptually charged rather than logically constructed space." See Rubin 2007, 17.

43 The citation from the conservation dossier, written by Jo Kirby, appears in Rubin 2007, 44–45.

44 On the parapet as a narrator that interrupts the dialogue between sitter and beholder, see Cranston 2000, 37–44.

45 Dunkerton et al. 2013, 52–54.

46 Morosini 1999.

47 Loh 2019, 38–39.

48 Campbell 1990, 112–15.

49 Fehrenbach 2002.

50 Baxandall 1993; Hood 1993; Ahl 2008, 140.

51 An early assessment of this interrelation can be found in Lehndorff 1933, 22–24.

52 At least one archival source documents the elder Moroni's engagement to oversee the construction of a palace for the aristocratic Lodrone family in the vicinity of the northern Italian city of Brescia. Tiraboschi 2016, 23–25.

53 Zani 1988, 289–90.

54 Penny 2004, 154–58.

55 Garber 1997.

56 Ng, Facchinetti, and Galansino 2019, 120–27.

57 Fernández de Béthencourt 1920, 270–72.

58 For accounts of the palace in the sixteenth century, see Bascapè 1969; Álvarez-Ossorio Alvariño 2008; Torre 1674, 365. On the gallery of portraits of Spanish governors, see D'Amico 2012, 136; Manfrè and Mauro 2010–11, 108–10.

59 Falomir Faus 2008, 446–47.

60 Leatherbarrow 1993, 166–67.

61 Alberti 1988, 86.

62 Vesalius 1998, 1.

63 In relation to ground, the expression is a perhaps a variant on the saying "campus habet oculos" (the field has eyes), which appears in Heinrich Bebel's *Proverbia germanica* (1508). Bebel 1879, 34. "Las paredes tienen ojos" appears in

a gloss on Genesis 4, referring to Cain's deceit, in Juan de Luna, *Sermones de quaresma* (1609), 139.

64 Real Academia Epsañola 1737, s.v. "parede," 129–30.

65 Elsewhere in the gray expanse, wispy brushstrokes take on the aspect of distant clouds. They not only describe streaks on the wall, signs of wear and tear, but also align with Gabriel's facial features, as though wrinkles have escaped from his face to corrugate the wall.

66 Colie 1973, 33–35.

67 On Gabriel's use of other mottos, see Ng, Facchinetti, and Galansino 2019, 122.

68 Cassin 2014a, 1030–31; Scannone 1980, 38. Moroni might also be understood as envisioning the portrait as a sort of enlarged emblem. We are asked to traverse the actual and conceptual space around each of the elements (figure, wall, and adage) and build the connective tissues that makes them into an organic whole.

69 Kim 2011; Kusukawa 2012, 198–227.

70 Gracián 2011, 73: "Donde hay fondo están los secretos profundos, que hay grandes espacios y ensenadas donde se hunden las cosas de monta."

71 Facchinetti and Galansino 2014, 124.

72 As cited in Malkiel 2013, 111.

73 My thanks to Michael Waters for this example. On the facade's brick and stonework, see Stolfi 2005, 291.

74 Trachtenberg 2005, 126–28; Kim 2014, 88–89.

75 Alberti 1988, 70, 358.

76 Mostafavi and Leatherbarrow 1993.

77 Hankinson 1991. On the proposed identification of these books, see Facchinetti and Galansino 2014, 124.

78 Galen 1963, 104–5. Interestingly enough, the treatise deploys the figure of the architect to illustrate the type of individual capable of mastering the passions.

79 Ng, Facchinetti, and Galansino 2019, 188–93.

80 Garber 1997.

81 Penny 2004, 200–205.

82 Stoichita 2012; Quondam 2003.

83 Stoichita 2016.

84 Avalle-Arce 1974, 215. Cited and discussed in Fallows 2010, 136.

85 The armor pieces are also scattered on the ground like the ruins that inhabit the foregrounds of Moroni's other full-length portraits. And like ruins, pieces of armor assumed a contradictory physical existence. While prized as components of a larger whole, both ruins and armor are subject to the blows of fortune and the elements. See Penny 2004, 200–205.

86 Gagné forthcoming.

87 See Paré 1552, 68–71; Gagné 2018.

88 Crusca 1612, s.v. "arrossire." See also Ariosto, *Orlando furioso* 27.35: "Nel viso s'arrossì l'angel beato." In relation to shades of red, see Calli 1595, 23: "Se si pone per l'arrossirsi talhor è segno di modestia e talhor d'ira o di colpa."

89 Tiraboschi 2016, 104; Ng, Facchinetti, and Galansino 2019, 196–201.

90 On the use of knots (*nodus Herculaneus*) in ancient Roman bridal costume, see Hersch 2010, 109–12.

91 Kohl 2004, 115.

92 Terraroli 2011; Volta 2014.

93 For the names and origins of these stones, see Bresciani 1990, 29.

94 Drpić 2019.

95 The whiteness of cities built along the Dalmatian coast corresponded to Renaissance ideas about the ideal Renaissance city. Built from brilliant Istrian stone, these cities when seen from afar appeared like a thin white line, a horizon of utopian tranquility. See Payne 2014. For a contemporary view regarding the facades in Rome, see Sutcliffe 2013.

96 Kagan 2000.

97 Ng, Facchinetti, and Galansino 2019, 198–99.

98 The word derives from the Arabic *zaga* (or *sak*), meaning "the last one." My thanks to Michael Solomon for an explanation of this word's etymology and usage. See also Real Academia Epsañola 1737, s.v. "zaguero."

99 Ng, Facchinetti, and Galansino 2019, 82–85, 174–79.

100 He was also the second of three sons of Marcantonio Grumelli, the paterfamilias of a noble Bergamasco family.

101 Wagner 2013.

5. TRANSUMPTION: ECHOES IN THE DARKNESS

1 Marin 1977, 12; Marin quotes Stendhal here. Marin 1995, 1–2.

2 Marin 1977, 189.

3 Ibid.

4 Arasse 2006, 319–21. Wolfgang Kemp referred to such intervals as "the constitutive blank" inviting the affective and visual engagement of the viewer: Kemp 1985.

5 Koering 2014; Berger 2020.

6 Vodret 1998, 62.

7 Silverman 2010, 52–58.

8 Hollander 1981, 1–12.

9 Longus 2009, 128–31.

10 Hollander 1981, 7–8.

11 Caro 1982, 91–94.

12 Dell'Anguillara 2019, 89–97; Premoli 2005; Bucchi 2011.

13 Dolce 2013, 69.

14 Cropper 1991; Rosen 2013.

15 Marino 2012, 477–81.

16 In *La galeria* (1620), a collection of poems that render a series of paintings in verse, Marino describes a picture, *Saint Jerome in Penitence*, in which "solitary caverns" and "dark deserts" are the holy scholar's place of self-mortification and study. The only companion in his solitude is the figure of Echo, who responds to the many poundings of stone against his chest by reverberating his groans. And yet, she is invisible. Marino 2005, 176: "Solitarie caverne, ermi quercetin, / Frondosi horror, ombre deserte, e sole." In a description of a painting of Echo by Ventura Salimbeni, the speaker casts doubt on the ability for the nymph's voice to be painted. Marino 2005, 15.

17 Hollander 1981, 115–16.

18 Susenbrotus 1608, 11; Hollander 1981, 138–39.

19 Thomas Wilson in *The Arte of Rhetorique* (1553, 1560) reiterated, "Transumption is, when by degrees wee goe to that, whiche is to bee shewed. As thus: Suche a one lieth in a darke doungeon, now in speakyng of darkenesse, we vnderstande closenesse, by closenesse, we gather blacknesse, and by blacknesse, we iudge deepenesse." Hollander 1981, 141–46.

20 Cavalcanti 1559, 262: "Un altro modo di mutatione ci è il quale col nome greco si puo chiamare e Metalepsi, col Latino Transumptio. Questa è tale, che dalla parola presa, & tramutata ci conduce alla cosa significata, quasi per gradi, non ci servendo il grado di mezzo ad altro, che à darci la via, si che per quello passiamo: come se alcuno parlando d'una profondissima balza, la chiamasse nera; per la qual parola intenderemo prima oscura, e per mezzo di questa passeremo all' inteso significato di profonda."

21 Mancini 1956; Hess 1968; Maccherini 1997; Maccherini 2004; Olson 2005; Gage 2008; Sparti 2008; Gage 2016.

22 Mancini 1956, 108–9. The entire passage reads, "Proprio di questa scuola è di lumeggiar con lume unito che venghi d'alto senza reflessi, come sarebbe in una stanza da una fenestra con le pariete colorite di negro, che così, havendo i chiari e l'ombre molto chiare e molto oscure, vengono a dar rilievo alla pittura, ma però con modo non naturale, nè fatto, nè pensato da altro secolo o pittori più antichi, come Raffaelo, Titiano, Correggio et altri. Questa schola in questo modo d'operare è molto osservante del vero, che sempre lo tien davanti mentre ch'opera; fa bene una figura sola, ma nella compositione dell'historia et esplicar affetto, pendendo questo dall'immagination e non dall'osservanza della cosa, per ritrar il vero che tengon sempre avanti, non mi par che vi vagliano, essendo impossibil di mettere in una stanza una moltitudine d'huomini che rappresentili l'historia con quel lume d'una fenestra sola, et haver un che rida o pianga o faccia atto di/ camminare e stia fermo per lasciarsi copiare, e così poi le lor figure, ancorchè habbin forza, mancano di moto e d'affetti, di gratia, che sta in quell'atto d'operare come si dirà."

23 Mancini 1956, 108.

24 Bellori 1976, 217: "ma trovò una maniera di campirle entro l'aria bruna d'una camera rinchiusa, pigliando un lume alto che scendeva a piombo sopra la parte principale del corpo, e lasciando il rimanente in ombra a fine di recar forza con veemenza di chiaro e di oscuro."

25 Sandrart 1675, 189: "Damit er aber auch die vollkommene Rondirung und natürliche Erhebung desto bäßer herfür bringen möchte/ bediente er sich fleißig dunkler Gewölber/ oder anderer finsterer Zimmer/ die von oben her ein einiges kleines Liecht hatten/ damit die Finsterniß dem auf das model fallenden Liecht/ durch starke Schatten/ seine Macht lassen/ und darmit eine hoch-erhobene Rundirung verursachen möchte."

26 Lapucci 2005; Varriano 2006, 8–15; Ebert-Schifferer 2018.

27 Nevenka Kroschewski has termed this the "*camera rinchiusa* topos": the idea of the artist painting in a room comparable to a camera obscura should be understood more as a paradigmatic image rather than testimony from his atelier. The fact that the darkened room has become a topos in art historical scholarship wishing to reconstruct Caravaggio's painting practice may be attributed to Mancini's skill in the art of rhetoric. Kroschewski 2002, 43–49.

28 Ebert-Schifferer 2012, 253.

29 For a recent assessment of these incisions, see Vodret 2016, 27–41.

30 Pericolo 2011, 3–13.

31 Mancini 1956, 108–9 (my emphasis).

32 Armenini 1586, 25–39; Armenini 1977, 200–201.

33 Mancini 1956, 117.

34 Ibid. In *Striking the Rock* (c. 1675, Louvre, INV 429), attributed to the Bassano studio, Moses—the protagonist—is inserted deep in the background, a small figure discernible by his illuminated "horns," while Israelites and the animals, depicted on a significantly larger scale, gather water in the foreground.

35 Mancini 1956, 114, 317, as discussed in Gage 2008, 1193–98.

36 Berdini 1997, 115–20.

37 Lavin 1981, 19–20; Silver 2013, 29–32; Banker 2014, 10–16.

38 Villa 2010, 112–15; Villa 2013, 24–63.

39 Bayer, Gallagher, and Centeno 2013.

40 Berdini 1997, 116–20.

41 Brown and Marini 1993, 308–9; Berdini 1997, 155–61.

42 See, for example, Lorenzo Lotto's panel featuring the Arma Christi painted over a black background. Strehlke and Israëls 2015, 391–96.

43 Olson 2014, 75.

44 Pericolo 2011, 265–95; Sapir 2012, 136–41; Suthor 2018, 65–91.

45 Drury 1987, 418–20.

46 Bovon 2012, 345.

47 Drury 1987, 422.

48 Gregori 1985, 308–10; Bell 1993, 106; Amendola 2014, 231.

49 Cappelletti and Testa 1994, 40–41, 104–5; Vodret 1995. Note that the painting is simply entitled *The Supper of Emmaus* in the Borghese 1693 inventory, the collection into which the painting eventually entered. Della Pergola 1964, 453: "261) Sotto al cornicione accanto a detti un quadro grande con la Cena di Emaus in tela del N° 1 con la cornice intagliata e dorata del *Caravaggi*."

50 For the biographical circumstances under which Caravaggio executed the painting in Paliano on the estate of the Colonna family, and comparative accounts of these two works, see Maderna and Pacia 2009.

51 For the inventory, see Spezzaferro 1983; Pedrocchi 2000.

52 "In fractione panis" also appears as a titular inscription in prints of the period, as in Pieter de Jode II's print of the subject, after Erasmus Quellinus, dated within the range of 1616–74. London, The British Museum, R,2.113.

53 Keith 1998.

54 Bellori mentions this, albeit in relation to *The Beheading of Saint John the Baptist* (1608). Keith 1998, 39: "lasciò in mezze tinte l'imprimatura della tela." For an overview of Caravaggio's approach to grounds, see De Ruggieri 2016, Puglisi 1998, 373.

55 Keith 1998, 39; Taylor 2015.

56 Pericolo 2011, 284.

57 Scribner 1977, 376 n. 10; Puglisi 1998, 213. As cited and discussed in Pericolo 2011, 284.

58 Pericolo 2011, 280.

59 Ibid., 461 n. 38; Kanter 2018, 88–90; Neilson 2019.

60 Merback 2014.

61 Gregori 2009.

62 Pericolo 2011, 271–75; Gregori 1985, 306.

63 Merback 2014, 311.

64 Ibid., 293.

65 See discussion in chapter 1.

66 Pericolo 2011, 292–93.

67 Vodret Adamo 2010, 27–40.

68 Mancini 1956, 13.

69 Ibid., 15–21.

70 February 27, 1624, Inventory of Marchese Costanzo Patrizi, Rome: "In the Gallery [. . .] Another large painting of a Supper when they came to know him in the breaking of the bread by Caravaggio with a frame touched in gold, 300 scudi" (Nella Galleria [. . .] Un altro quadro grande di una Cena q[uan]do congnosceru[n]t eum in fractione panis di mano del Caravaggio con cornice tocca d'oro scudi trecento 300). See Gregori 1985, 308; Amendola 2014.

71 Rice 1997, 43–45.

72 Calvesi 1998.

73 Tomassetti 1862, 774–75.

74 Spezzaferro 1974.

75 Tomassetti 1862, 774–75.

76 On the composition of the mestica layer, see Cardinali 2016.

77 Coliva 1998, 81–82, 86–95.

78 Calvesi 1998, 37.

79 Pericolo 2011, 295.

80 A precedent for this elliptical narrative mode can be seen in scenes on the reverse of Duccio's *Maestà* altarpiece. As Gervase Rosser has recently noted, the artist frequently deployed the motif of the open or half-open door, often looking onto a black void, to allude to arrival, presence, and disappearance. In the *Annunciation of the Death of the Virgin*, the angel enters the bedchamber to inform Mary of her impending death, an event foreshadowed through voids visible through the open doors. In Duccio's own version of the Emmaus story, Christ seems to blend into the gold ground as the two travelers turn around to greet their new companion. The road to the city leads to an open gate, which instead of opening onto views of an urban fabric become portals of darkness and invisibility. The precedents and successors of these examples provide transhistorical examples for the narrative potential of emptiness. Rosser 2012, 491.

81 Combet-Galland and Smyth-Florentin 1993, 323. Cited in Bovon 2012, 368.

82 Olson 2014, 17.

83 Spezzaferro 2000; Sabbatino 2004; Bellori 2018, 81–115.

84 Sohm 2002; Olson 2008; Stone 2012.

85 Bellori 1976, 212–13; Bellori 2005, 179.

86 Bellori 1976, 216; Bellori 2005, 180.

87 Bellori 1976, 217; Bellori 2005, 180.

88 Bellori 1976, 220–21; Bellori 2005, 181.

89 Bellori 2018, 106.

90 Bellori 1976, 229: "Non si trova però che egli usasse cinabri né azzurri nelle sue figure; e se pure tal volta li avesse adoperati, li ammorzava, dicendo ch'erano il veleno delle tinte; non dirò dell'aria turchina e chiara, ch'egli non colorì mai nell'istorie, anzi usò sempre il campo e 'l fondo nero; e 'l nero nelle carni, restringendo in poche parti la forza del lume." A case in point is the *Rest on the Flight to Egypt* (1595–96), a work that Bellori describes in terms of the characters who are positioned at the center, on the left, or on the right of the picture. Passed over in silence is the foothold of rocky soil on the left, a symbol of Joseph's earthly nature, and on the right, the grayish-blue sky behind the divine figures of Christ and Mary. Substituting the palm trees typical for this subject matter is a vista that evokes the banks of the Tiber and the hills of the Roman Campagna. Calvesi 2010, 34–31; Vodret Adamo 2010, 40–41.

91 Bellori 2018, 89; Ebert-Schifferer 2018.

CONCLUSION: THE FUGITIVE GROUND

1 Serres 1991, 268.

2 On this and related approaches, see Davis 2011.

3 Levine 2015, 31.

4 For the Latin text, see Marshall 2002, 171–72; Grant 1960, 157–58.

5 On the artist as the first viewer, see Silverman forthcoming.

6 Translated modified from Hamilton 2013, 3.

7 Houtman 2016.

8 Blumenberg 2010, 140.

9 Ibid., 141.

10 See chapter 1.

11 Hadot 1993, 9–10.

12 In the allegory of Cura, the human, before being given its name by Saturn, is repeatedly referred to by the demonstrative pronouns *ei* and *cui*, or "it" (as in "to give it spirit"; "to name it"). The constant pointing out of *it* makes the creature's lack of a name all the more acute and the need to bestow one all the more urgent.

13 Hamilton 2013, 3.

Bibliography

Ackerman, James S. 1990. *The Villa: Form and Ideology of Country Houses*. London: Thames and Hudson.

———. 1980. "On Early Renaissance Color Theory and Practice." *Studies in Italian Art and Architecture: 15th through 18th Centuries* 35: 11–44.

Acres, Alfred. 2006. "Elsewhere in Early Netherlandish Painting." In *Tributes in Honor of James H. Marrow*, edited by Jeffrey F. Hamburger and Anne S. Korteweg, 23–33. Turnhout: Brepols.

Adam, Jean-Pierre. 2009. *Roman Building: Materials and Techniques*. New York: Routledge.

Adama von Scheltema, F. 1946. "Das Problem des Grundes in der Geschichte der Kunst." *Geistige Welt: Vierteljahresschrift für Kultur- und Geisteswissenschaften* 1: 16–27.

Agamben, Giorgio. 2020. *Creation and Anarchy: The Work of Art and the Religion of Capitalism*. Translated by Adam Kotsko. Stanford: Stanford University Press.

———. 2017. "What is the Act of Creation?" In Agamben, *The Fire and the Tale*, translated by Lorenzo Chiesa, 33–56. Stanford: Stanford University Press.

Ahl, Diane Cole. 2008. *Fra Angelico*. London: Phaidon.

Alberti, Leon Battista. 2011a. *De pictura (redazione volgare)*. Edited by Lucia Bertolini. Florence: Edizioni Polistampa.

———. 2011b. *Leon Battista Alberti: On Painting*. Edited by Rocco Sinisgalli. Cambridge: Cambridge University Press.

———. 1988. *On the Art of Building in Ten Books*. Translated by Joseph Rykwert, Neil Leach, and Robert Tavernor. Cambridge, MA: MIT Press.

———. 1973. *Della pittura*. In Alberti 1960–73, vol. 3: 5–108. Bari: Laterza.

———. 1966. *L'architettura (De re aedificatoria)*. Edited and translated [into Italian] by Giovanni Orlandi, with an introduction by Paolo Portoghesi. 2 vols. Milan: Edizioni Il Polifilo.

———. 1960–73. *Opere volgari*. Edited by Cecil Grayson. 3 vols. Bari: Laterza.

Alexander, Jonathan J. G. 1993–94. "A Metalwork Triptych of the Passion of Christ in the Metropolitan Museum, New York." *Wiener Jahrbuck für Kunstgeschichte* 46/47: 27–36, 377–80.

Alpers, Paul J. 1996. *What is Pastoral?* Chicago: University of Chicago Press.

Álvarez-Ossorio Alvariño, Antonio. 2008. "La corte de los gobernadores del Estado de Milán." In *Studi in memoria di Cesare Mozzarelli*, vol. 1: 421–62. Milan: Vita e Pensiero.

Amendola, Adriano. 2014. "The Necessity of Frames." In *Display of Art in the Roman Palace, 1550–1750*, edited by Gail Feigenbaum with Francesco Freddolini, 231–33. Los Angeles: Getty Research Institute.

Ames-Lewis, Francis. 2000. *The Intellectual Life of the Early Renaissance Artist*. New Haven: Yale University Press.

Anonymous. 1999. "The Sacred Exchange between Saint Francis and Lady Poverty (1237–1239)." In *Francis of Assisi: Early Documents*, edited by Regis J. Armstrong, J. A. Wayne Hellmann, and William J. Short, vol. 1: 523–56. New York: New City Press.

Antoninus of Piacenza. 1965. *Itinerarium*. Edited by Peter Geyer. In *Itineraria et alia geographica. Itineraria hierosolymitana. Itineraria romana. Geographica*, edited by P. Geyer, O. Cuntz, A. Franceschini, R.Weber, L. Bieler, J. Fraipont, and F. Glorie, vol 1 (Corpus Christianorum Series Latina 175): 129–53, 157–74. Turnhout: Brepols.

Aquinas, Thomas. 1922. The Summa Theologica *of St. Thomas Aquinas. Literally Translated by Fathers of the Dominican Province*. 2nd revised edn, part 1, vols 2–3 (QQ. 27–74). London: Burns Oates & Washbourne.

Arasse, Daniel. 2006. *Histoire de peintures*. Paris: Gallimard.

———. 1999. *L'Annonciation italienne: Une histoire de perspective*. Paris: Hazan.

———. 1992. *Le détail: Pour une histoire rapprochée de la peinture*. Paris: Flammarion.

Armenini, Giovanni Battista. 1977. *On the True Precepts of the Art of Painting*. Edited and translated by Edward J. Olszewski. New York: Burt Franklin.

———. 1973. *De' veri precetti della pittura*, = *Scritti d'arte del Cinquecento*, edited by Paola Barocchi, vol. 3. Milan: Riccardo Ricciardi.

———. 1586. *De' veri precetti della pittura*. Ravenna: F. Tebaldini.

Armstrong, Carol. 2002. *Manet Manette*. New Haven: Yale University Press.

Arnheim, Rudolf. 1977. "Perception of Perspective Pictorial Space from Different Viewing Points." *Leonardo* 10: 283–88.

———. 1966. *Toward a Psychology of Art*. Berkeley: University of California Press.

Arquillo Torres, Francisco, and David Arquillo-Avilés. 2011. "El tenebrismo como recurso técnico y concepto estético." *Temas de estética y arte* 25: 180–204.

Auerbach, Erich. 1984. *Scenes from the Drama of European*

Literature. Minneapolis: University of Minnesota Press.

Augart, Isabella. 2019. "Luoghi aspri: Stone and Solitude in Trecento Painting." In Augart, Saß, and Wenderholm 2019, 25–44.

Augart, Isabella, Maurice Saß, and Iris Wenderholm, eds. 2019. *Steinformen: Materialität, Qualität, Imitation*. Berlin: De Gruyter.

Auld, Sylvia. 1986. "Kuficising Inscriptions in the Work of Gentile da Fabriano." *Oriental Art* 3: 246–65.

Aurenhammer, Hans. 2017. "Berge in der Lagune: die Entdeckung der Landschaft in der venezianischen Renaissancemalerei (1450–1520)." In *"Wie sonst nirgendwo . . .": Venedig zwischen Topographie und Utopie*, edited by Barbara Kuhn, 93–135. Würzburg: Königshausen & Neumann.

———. 2013. "Reflexionen des Sehens in Gemälden Giovanis Bellinis." In *Mobile Eyes*, edited by David Ganz and Stefan Neuner, 199–240. Paderborn: Wilhelm Fink.

Avagnina, Maria Elisa. 1993. "The Pictorial Technique of Jacopo Bassano as Discussed in the Early Sources." In *Jacopo Bassano, c. 1510–1592*, edited by Beverly Louise Brown and Paola Marini, 233–46. Fort Worth: Kimball Art Museum.

Avalle-Arce, Juan Bautista. 1974. *Las memorias de Gonzalo Fernández de Oviedo*. Vol. 1. Chapel Hill: University of North Carolina Press.

Bachelard, Gaston. 1964. *The Poetics of Space*. Boston: Beacon Press.

Bagnoli, Alessandro, Roberto Bartalini, Luciano Bellosi, and Michel Laclotte, eds. 2003. *Duccio: Alle origini della pittura senese*. Milan: Silvana.

Bailey, Douglass W. 2018. *Breaking the Surface: An Art/Archaeology of Prehistoric Architecture*. Oxford: Oxford University Press.

Baker-Bates, Piers. 2018. "'Uno nuovo modo di colorire in pietra': Technical Experimentation in the Art of Sebastiano del Piombo." In Baker-Bates and Calvillo 2018, 47–73. Leiden: Brill.

Baker-Bates, Piers, and Elena Calvillo, eds. 2018. *Almost Eternal: Painting on Stone and Material Innovation in Early Modern Europe*. Leiden: Brill.

Baldinucci, Filippo. 1681. *Vocabolario toscano dell'arte del disegno*. Florence: Santi Franchi.

Banker, James R. 2014. *Piero della Francesca: Artist and Man*. Oxford: Oxford University Press.

Banks, Elaine. 1978. "Tintoretto's Religious Imagery of the 1560s." PhD diss., Princeton University.

Barausse, Manuela. 2008. "Giovanni Bellini: I documenti." In *Giovanni Bellini*, edited by M. Lucco and G.C.F. Villa, 327–59. Milan: Silvana.

Barbaro, Daniel. 1584. *I dieci libri dell'architettura*. Venice: Francesco de' Franceschi.

Barkan, Leonard. 1991. *Transuming Passion: Ganymede and the Erotics of Humanism*. Stanford: Stanford University Press.

Barry, Fabio. 2020. *Painting in Stone: Architecture and the Poetics of Marble from Antiquity to the Age of Enlightenment*. New Haven: Yale University Press.

Bartoloni, Gilda, and Piera Bocci Pacini. 2003. "The Importance of Etruscan Antiquity in the Tuscan Renaissance." In *The Rediscovery of Antiquity: The Role of the Artist*, edited by Jane Fejfer, Tobias Fische-Hansen, and Annette Rathje, 449–79. Copenhagen: Museum Tusculanum Press.

Bascapè, Giacomo C. 1969. *Il "Regio Ducal Palazzo" di Milano: Dai Visconti ad oggi*. Milan: Banca populare di Milano.

Baskins, Cristelle. 1993. "Echoing Narcissus in Alberti's *Della Pittura*." *Oxford Art Journal* 16: 25–33.

Bätschmann, Oskar. 2008. *Giovanni Bellini*. Translated by Ian Pepper. London: Reaktion Books.

Baxandall, Michael. 1993. "Pictorially Enforced Signification: St. Antonius, Fra Angelico and the Annunciation." In *Hülle und Fülle*, edited by Andreas Beyer, Vittorio Lampugnani, and Gunter Schweikhart, 31–39. Alfter: VDG.

———. 1972. *Painting and Experience in Fifteenth-Century Italy*. Oxford: Oxford University Press.

———. 1971. *Giotto and the Orators: Humanist Observers of Painting in Italy and the Discovery of Pictorial Composition*. Oxford: Clarendon Press

———. 1964. "Bartholomaeus Facius on Painting: A Fifteenth-Century Manuscript of the *De Viris Illustribus*." *Journal of the Warburg and Courtauld Institutes* 27: 90–107.

Bayer, Andrea, Michael Gallagher, and Silvia Centeno. 2013. "Jacopo Bassano's *Baptism of Christ*." *Artibus et Historiae* 34: 83–103.

Bazin, André. 2005. "An Aesthetic of Reality: Neorealism." In Bazin, *What is Cinema?*, translated by Hugh Gray, vol. 2: 16–40. Berkeley: University of California Press.

Bebel, Heinrich. 1879. *Heinrich Bebel's* Proverbia germanica. Edited by Willem H. D. Suringar. Leiden: Brill.

Beer, Ellen J. 1983. "Marginalien zum Thema Goldgrund." *Zeitschrift für Kunstgeschichte* 46: 271–86.

Bell, Janis. 1995. "Light and Color in Caravaggio's *Supper at Emmaus*." *Artibus et Historiae* 16: 139–70.

———. 1993. "Some Seventeenth-Century Appraisals of Caravaggio's Coloring." *Artibus et Historiae* 27: 103–29.

Bellori, Giovanni Pietro. 2018. *Das Leben des Michelangelo Merisi da Caravaggio*. Edited by Valeska von Rosen. Göttingen: Wallstein Verlag.

———. 2005. *The Lives of the Modern Painters, Sculptors, and Architects*. Translated by Alice Sedgwick Wohl. Cambridge: Cambridge University Press.

———. 1976. *Le vite de' pittori, scultori e architetti moderni*. Edited by Evelina Borea. Turin: Einaudi.

Belting, Hans. 2014. "St. Jerome in Venice: Giovanni Bellini and the Dream of Solitary Life." *I Tatti Studies in the Italian Renaissance* 17: 5–33.

Belting, Hans, and Christiane Kruse. 1994. *Die Erfindung des Gemäldes: Das erste Jahrhundert der niederländischen Malerei*. Munich: Hirmer.

Bembo, Pietro. 2008. *Le rime*. Edited by Andrea Donnini. Rome: Salerno.

———. 2005. *Lyric Poetry: Etna*. Edited and translated by Mary P. Chatfield. Cambridge, MA: Harvard University Press.

———. 1987–93. *Lettere*. Edited by Ernesto Travi. 4 vols. Bologna: Commissione per i testi di lingua.

———. 1985. *Lettere da diversi re e principi e cardinali e altri uomini dotti a mons. Pietro Bembo scritte*. Edited by Daria Perocco. Sala Bolognese: Arnaldo Forni.

Benjaminsen, Tor A. and Gunnvor Berge. 2004. "Myths of Timbuktu: From African El Dorado to Desertification." *International Journal of Political Economy* 34: 31–59.

Berdini, Paolo. 1997. *The Religious Art of Jacopo Bassano: Painting as Visual Exegesis*. Cambridge: Cambridge University Press.

Berger, Susanna. 2020. "From Narcissus to Narcosis." *Art History* 43: 2–28.

Berrie, Barbara H. 1994. "A Note on the Imprimatura in Two of Dosso Dossi's Paintings." *Journal of the American Institute for Conservation* 33: 307–13.

Berrie, Barbara H. and Sarah L. Fisher. 1993. "A Technical Investigation of the Materials and Methods of Dosso Dossi." In *Preprints from the 10th Triennial Meeting Washington, DC, USA, 22–27 August 1993*, edited by Janet Bridgland, 70–74. Paris: ICOM Committee for Conservation.

Berzock, Kathleen Bickford, ed. 2019. *Caravans of Gold, Fragments in Time: Art, Culture, and Exchange Across Medieval Saharan Africa*. Princeton: Princeton University Press.

Bettini, Maurizio. 1999. *The Portrait of the Lover*. Translated by Laura Gibbs. Berkeley: University of California Press.

Beuys-Wurmbach, Eva. 1977. *Die Landschaften in den Hintergründen der Gemälde Leonardos*. 2nd ed. Munich: Schellmann & Klüser.

Beyer, Andreas and Guillaume Cassegrain, eds. 2015. *Mouvement. Bewegung: Über die dynamische Potenziale der Kunst*. Berlin: Deutscher Kunstverlag.

Beyer, Vera. 2008. *Rahmenbestimmungen: Funktionen von Rahmen bei Goya, Velázquez, van Eyck und Degas*. Paderborn: Wilhelm Fink.

Biow, Douglas. 2015. *On the Importance of Being an Individual in Renaissance Italy: Men, Their Professions, and Their Beards*. Philadelphia: University of Pennsylvania Press.

Bjornerud, Marcia. 2018. *Timefulness: How Thinking Like a Geologist Can Help Save the World*. Princeton: Princeton University Press.

Blass-Simmen, Brigit. 2015. " 'Qualche lontani': Distance and Transcendence in the Art of Giovanni Bellini." In *Examining Giovanni Bellini: An Art "More Human and More Divine"*, edited by Carolyn C. Wilson, 77–92. Turnhout: Brepols.

Blum, Gerd. 2015. *Fenestra prospectiva. Architektonisch inszenierte Ausblicke: Alberti, Palladio, Agucchi*. Berlin: De Gruyter.

Blumenberg, Hans. 2020. "Observations Drawn from Metaphors (1971)." In *History, Metaphors, Fables: A Hans Blumenberg Reader*, edited by Hannes Bajohr, Florian Fuchs, and Joe Paul Kroll, 209–38. Ithaca: Cornell University Press.

———. 2010. *Care Crosses the River*. Translated by John Fleming. Stanford: Stanford University Press.

———. 1987. *Die Sorge geht über den Fluss*. Frankfurt am Main: Suhrkamp.

Blumenröder, Sabine. 2002. "Andrea Mantegna's Grisaille Paintings: Colour Metamorphosis as a Metaphor for History." In *Symbols of Time in the History of Art*, edited by Christian Heck and Kristen Lippincott, 41–55. Turnhout: Brepols.

Bodart, Diane. 2009. "Le reflet et l'éclat: Jeux de l'envers dans la peinture vénitienne du XVIe siècle." In *Titien, Tintoret, Véronèse . . . Rivalités à Venise*, edited by J. Habert and V. Delieuvin, 216–59. Paris: Hazan.

Boehm, Gottfried and Matteo Burioni, eds. 2012. *Der Grund: Das Feld des Sichtbaren*. Paderborn: Wilhelm Fink.

Bois, Yve-Alain. 1990. *Painting as Model*. Cambridge, MA: MIT Press.

Bolland, Andrea. 2014. "Artifice and Stability in Late Mantegna." *Art History* 37: 352–75.

Bomford, David. 1979. "Moroni's 'Canon Ludovico di Terzi': An Unlined Sixteenth-Century Painting." *National Gallery Technical Bulletin* 3: 34–42

Bomford, David, Jill Dunkerton, Dillian Gordon, and Ashok Roy. 1989. *Art in the Making: Italian Painting before 1400*. London: National Gallery.

Bonadeo, Alessia. 2003. *Mito e natura allo specchio: L'eco nel pensiero greco e latino*. Pisa: ETS.

Bonaventure of Bagnoregio. 2000. "The Legends and Sermons about Saint Francis by Bonaventure of Bagnoregio (1255–1267)." In *Francis of Assisi: Early Documents*, edited by Regis J. Armstrong, J. A. Wayne Hellmann, and William J. Short, vol. 2: 495–717. New York: New City Press.

———. 1995. "Legenda maior sancti Francisci." In *Fontes Franciscani*, edited by Enrico Menestò and Stefano Brufani, 777–922. Assisi: Edizioni Porziuncola.

Borghini, Raffaello. 2007. *Il riposo*. Translated by Lloyd H. Ellis. Toronto: University of Toronto Press.

———. 1584. *Il riposo*. Florence: Giorgio Marescotti.

Borys, Ann Marie. 2014. *Vincenzo Scamozzi and the Chorography of Early Modern Architecture*. Burlington: Ashgate.

Boschini, Marco. 1966. *La carta del navegar pitoresco*, edited by Anna Pallucchini. Venice: Istituto per la collaborazione culturale.

Bovon, François. 2012. *Luke 3: A Commentary on the Gospel of Luke 19:28–24:53*. Translated by James Crouch. Minneapolis: Fortress Press.

Braham, Allan. 1978. *Giovanni Battista Moroni: 400th Anniversary Exhibition*. London: National Gallery.

Branagan, David. 2006. "Geology and the Artists of the Fifteenth and Sixteenth Centuries, Mainly Florentine." *Geological Society of America Special Paper* 411: 31–42.

Braunfels, Wolfgang. 1979. *Nimbus und Goldgrund: Wege zur Kunstgeschichte, 1949–1975*. Mittenwald: Mäander.

———. 1950. "Nimbus und Goldgrund." *Das Muenster* 3: 321–34.

Bredekamp, Horst. 2016. "Galilei's Spiral Scribbles, Campanella and Fludd." In *What Reason Promises: Essays on Reason, Nature and History*, edited by Wendy Doniger, Peter Galison, and Susan Neiman, 110–16. Berlin: De Gruyter.

———. 1993. *Antikensehnsucht und Maschinenglauben: Die Geschichte der Kunstkammer und die Zukunft der Kunstgeschichte*. Berlin: Klaus Wagenbach.

Bresciani, Efrem, ed. 1990. *Cappella Colleoni in Bergamo*. Bergamo: Lubrina.

Brisman, Shira. 2016. *Albrecht Dürer and the Epistolary Mode of Address*. Chicago: University of Chicago Press.

Broecke, Lara. 2015. *Cennino Cennini's* Il libro dell'arte. London: Archetype.

Brooks, Julian. 2007. *Taddeo and Federico Zuccaro: Artist-Brothers in Renaissance Rome*. Los Angeles: J. Paul Getty Museum.

Brown, Beverly Louise, and Paola Marini, eds. 1993. *Jacopo Bassano c. 1510–1592*. Fort Worth: Kimbell Art Museum.

Brown, Clifford M. 2004. "Digest of the Correspondence concerning the Paintings Commissioned for the *Studiolo* in the Castello (1496–1515)." In *The Cabinet of Eros*, edited by Stephen Campbell, 280–301. New Haven: Yale University Press.

Brown, David Alan. 2013. "Bembo and Bellini." In *Pietro Bembo e le arti*, edited by Guido Beltramini, Howard Burns, and Davide Gasparotto, 309–28. Venice: Marsilio.

Brown, David Alan, and Jane Van Nimmen. 2005. *Raphael and the Beautiful Banker: The Story of the Bindo Altoviti Portrait*. New Haven: Yale University Press.

Brown, Peter. 1983. "The Saint as Exemplar in Late Antiquity." *Representations* 2: 1–25.

———. 1971 "The Rise and Function of the Holy Man in Late Antiquity." *Journal of Roman Studies* 61: 80–101.

Bruno, Giuliana. 2014. *Surface: Matters of Aesthetics, Materiality, and Media*. Chicago: University of Chicago Press.

Bryson, Norman. 1990. *Looking at the Overlooked: Four Essays on Still Life Painting*. Cambridge, MA: Harvard University Press.

Bucchi, Gabriele. 2011. *Meraviglioso diletto: La traduzione poetica del Cinquecento e le* Metamorfosi *d'Ovidio di Giovanni Andrea dell'Anguillara*. Pisa: ETS.

Bucklow, Spike. 2009. *The Alchemy of Paint: Art, Science and Secrets from the Middle Ages*. London: Marion Boyars.

Buettner, Brigitte. 1996. *Boccaccio's "Des cleres et nobles femmes": Systems of Signification in an Illuminated Manuscript*. Seattle: University of Washington Press.

Burckhardt, Jacob. 2000. *Das Altarbild. Das Porträt in der Malerei: Die Sammler. Beiträge zur Kunstgeschichte von Italien*. Edited by Stella von Boch. Basel: Schwabe.

———. 1878. *The Civilisation of the Period of the Renaissance in Italy*. Translated by S.G.C. Middlemore. London: Kegan Paul & Co.

———. 1860. *Die Kultur der Renaissance in Italien: Ein Versuch*. Basel: Schweighauser.

Burioni, Matteo. 2012. "Grund und *campo*: Die Metaphorik des Bildgrundes in der frühen Neuzeit oder: Paolo Uccellos *Schlacht von San Romano*." In Boehm and Burioni 2012, 95–150. Paderborn: Wilhelm Fink.

———. 2011. "Der Künstler als Champion Kunsttheoretische Figuren des Grundes in der frühen Neuzeit." In *Departure for Modern Europe: A Handbook of Early Modern Philosophy (1400–1700)*, edited by Hubertus Busche, 954–68. Munich: Felix Meiner.

Bushart, Magdalena, and Gregor Wedekind, eds. 2016. *Die Farbe Grau*. Berlin: De Gruyter.

Calli, Antonio. 1595. *Discorso de' colori d'Antonio Calli*. Padua: Lorenzo Pasquati.

Calvesi, Maurizio. 2010. "Riposo durante la fuga in Egitto." In *Caravaggio*, edited by Claudio Strinati, 34–41 Milan: Skira.

———. 1998. "Tanto contenta di mirar sua figlia." In *La Madonna dei Palafrenieri di Caravaggio nella collezione di Scipione Borghese*, edited by Anna Coliva, 33–50. Venice: Marsilio.

Calvillo, Elena. 2013. "Authoritative Copies and Divine Originals: Lucretian Metaphor, Painting on Stone and the Problem of Originality in Michelangelo's Rome." *Renaissance Quarterly* 66: 453–508.

Campbell, Lorne. 1990. *Renaissance Portraits: European Portrait-Painting in the 14th, 15th, and 16th Centuries*. New Haven: Yale University Press.

Campbell, Stephen. 2020. *Andrea Mantegna: Humanist Aesthetics, Faith, and the Force of Images*. Turnhout: Brepols.

———. 2015. "On the Importance of Crivelli." In *Ornament*

and Illusion: Carlo Crivelli of Venice, edited by Stephen Campbell, 10–37. London: Paul Holberton.

———. 2004a. *The Cabinet of Eros: Renaissance Mythological Painting and the Studiolo of Isabella d'Este*. New Haven: Yale University Press.

———. 2004b. "Counter Reformation Polemic and Mannerist Counter-Aesthetics: Bronzino's *Martyrdom of St. Lawrence* in San Lorenzo." *RES* 46: 98–119.

Cappelletti, Francesca, and Laura Testa. 1994. *Il trattenimento di virtuosi: Le collezioni seicentesche di quadri nei Palazzi Mattei di Roma*. Rome: Argos.

Capriotti, Giuseppe. 2013. *Le Trasformationi di Lodovico Dolce: Il rinascimento ovidiano di Giovanni Antonio Rusconi*. Ancona: Affinità Elettive.

Cardinali, Marco. 2016. "Painting Technique." In *Caravaggio, opere a Roma: Tecnica e stile / Works in Rome: Technique and Style*, edited by Rossella Vodret, Giorgio Leone, Marco Cardinali, Maria Beatrice De Ruggieri, and Giulia Silvia Ghia, vol. 2 (*Schede / Entries*), 557–61. Milan: Silvana.

Caro, Annibale. 1982. *Gli amori pastorali di Dafni e di Cloe di Longo sofista*. Edited by Luigi Silori. Rome: Salerno.

Cassegrain, Guillaume. 1999–2000. "Le miracle de la surface: Véronèse, Tintoret et l'espace visionnaire." *Bulletin de l'Association des historiens de l'art italien* 6: 15–22.

Cassin, Barbara, ed. 2014a. *Dictionary of Untranslatables: A Philosophical Lexicon*. Translated by Seven Rendall, Christian Hubert, Jeffrey Mehlman, Nathaniel Stein, and Michael Syrotinski. Translation edited by Emily Apter, Jacques Lezra, and Michael Wood. Princeton: Princeton University Press.

———. 2014b. "*Dunamis*, *energeia*, *entelecheia*, and the Aristotelian Definition of Motion." In Cassin 2014a, 344–45.

Cavalcanti, Bartolomeo. 1559. *La retorica di M. Bartolomeo Cavalcanti*. Venice: Gabriel Giolito de' Ferrari.

Cecchi, Alessandro. 2005. *Botticelli*. Milan: Motta.

———. 1998. "Le case del Vasari ad Arezzo e Firenze." In *Case di artisti in Toscana*, edited by Roberto Paolo Ciardi, 29–77. Milan: Pizzi.

Cellini, Benvenuto. 1898. *The Treatises of Benvenuto Cellini on Goldsmithing and Sculpture*. Translated by C. R. Ashbee. London: E. Arnold.

Cerasuolo, Angela. 2017. *Literature and Artistic Practice in Sixteenth-Century Italy*. Translated by Helen Glanville. Leiden: Brill.

———. 2012. "Approfondimenti su Sebastiano del Piombo a Capodimonte." *Konsthistorisk tidskrift / Journal of Art History* 81: 254–61.

Ceriana, Matteo. 2006–7. "La pala di San Zeno: L'architettura reale e quella dipinta." *Annali di architettura* 18–19: 83–104, 249.

Cesariano, Cesare. 2002. *Vitruvio De Architectura: Libri II–IV. I materiali, i templi, gli ordini*. Edited by Alessandro Rovetta. Milan: Vita e Pensiero.

Chambers, Eddie. 2020. "It's Time to Share." *Colloquium, Panorama: Journal of the Association of Historians of American Art* 6. https://editions.lib.umn.edu/panorama

Chareyron, Nicole. 2005. *Pilgrims to Jerusalem in the Middle Ages*. Translated by W. Donald Wilson. New York: Columbia University Press.

Chastel, André. 1978. "Le tableau dans le tableau." In Chastel, *Fables, formes, figures*, 75–98. Paris: Flammarion.

Christiansen, Keith. 2013. "Bellini and the Meditational *poesia*." *Artibus et Historiae* 67: 9–20.

———. 2008. "Duccio and the Origins of Western Painting." *Metropolitan Museum of Art Bulletin* 66: 1–61.

———. 2006. "The Art of Gentile da Fabriano." In *Gentile da Fabriano and the Other Renaissance*, edited by Laura Laureati and Lorenza Mochi Onori, 19–52. Milan: Electa.

———. 2005. "*L'Adorazione dei Magi* di Gentile da Fabriano." In *Gentile da Fabriano agli Uffizi*, edited by Alessandro Cecchi, 11–40. Milan: Silvana.

———. 1982. *Gentile da Fabriano*. Ithaca: Cornell University Press.

Clark, T. J. 2018. *Heaven on Earth: Painting and the Life to Come*. London: Thames & Hudson.

———. 2002. "Painting at Ground Level." Tanner Lectures on Human Values, Princeton University.

———. 1982. "Clement Greenberg's Theory of Art." *Critical Inquiry* 9: 139–56.

Claussen, Peter Cornelius. 2007. "Goldgrund." *kritische berichte: Zeitschrift für Kunst- und Kulturwissenschaften* 35: 64–67.

Colby, Robert. 2008. "Dosso's Early Artistic Reputation and the Origins of Landscape Painting." *Papers of the British School at Rome* 76: 201–31, 357–60.

Cole, Michael W. 2014. *Leonardo, Michelangelo, and the Art of the Figure*. New Haven: Yale University Press.

Colie, Rosalie Littell. 1973. *The Resources of Kind: Genre-Theory in the Renaissance*. Berkeley: University of California Press.

Coliva, Anna, ed. 1998. La Madonna dei Palafrenieri *di Caravaggio nella collezione di Scipione Borghese*. Venice: Marsilio.

Collareta, Marco. 2006. "The Historian and the Technique: On the Role of Goldsmithery in Vasari's *Lives*." In *Sixteenth-Century Italian Art*, edited by Michael W. Cole, 291–300. Oxford: Wiley-Blackwell.

Collegium S. Bonaventurae, ed. 1885. *Analecta Franciscana, sive, Chronica aliaque varia documenta ad historiam fratrum minorum spectantia*. Vol. 4. Quaracchi: Ex Typographia Collegii S. Bonaventurae.

Combet-Galland, Corina, and Françoise Smyth-Florentin.

1993. "Le pain qui fait lever les Écritures: Emmaüs, Luc 24/13–35." *Études théologiques et religieuses* 68: 323–32.

Conigliello, Lucilla. 1999. *Le vedute del Sacro Monte della Verna: Jacopo Ligozzi pellegrino nei luoghi di Francesco*. Florence: Edizioni Polistampa.

Connell, Susan. 1988. *The Employment of Sculptors and Stonemasons in Venice in the Fifteenth Century*. New York: Garland.

Corbo, V. C. 1988. "Il Santo Sepolcro di Gerusalemme: Nova et vetera." *Liber Annuus* 38: 391–422.

Courtright, Nicola. 2003. *The Papacy and the Art of Reform in Sixteenth-Century Rome: Gregory XIII's Tower of the Winds in the Vatican*. Cambridge: Cambridge University Press.

Cranston, Jodi. 2019. *Green Worlds of Renaissance Venice*. University Park: Pennsylvania State University Press.

———. 2010. *The Muddied Mirror: Materiality and Figuration in Titian's Later Paintings*. University Park: Pennsylvania State University Press.

———. 2000. *The Poetics of Portraiture in the Italian Renaissance*. Cambridge: Cambridge University Press.

Cropper, Elizabeth. 1991. "The Petrifying Art: Marino's Poetry and Caravaggio." *Metropolitan Museum Journal*: 193–212.

———. 1976. "On Beautiful Women, Parmigianino, Petrarchismo, and the Vernacular Style." *Art Bulletin* 58: 374–94.

Crusca, Accademia della. 1612. *Vocabolario degli Accademici della Crusca*. Venice: G. Alberti.

Cuoq, Joseph M., ed. 1985. *Recueil des sources arabes concernant l'Afrique occidentale du VIIIe au XVIe siècle (Bilād Al-Sūdān)*. Paris: CNRS Éditions.

Curatola, Giovanni. 2006. "Venice's Textile and Carpet Trade." In *Venice and the Islamic World, 828—1797*, edited by Stefano Carboni, 204–11. New Haven: Yale University Press.

Cusato, Michael F. 2015. "*Cucullus non facit monachum*? The Controversy over the Franciscan Habit in the Early Fourteenth Century." In *Loyalty in the Middle Ages: Ideal and Practice of a Cross-Social Value*, edited by Jörg Sonntag and Coralie Zermatten, 361–403. Turnhout: Brepols.

D'Amico, Stefano. 2012. *Spanish Milan: A City within the Empire, 1535–1706*. New York: Palgrave Macmillan.

D'Evelyn, Margaret Muther. 2012. *Venice and Vitruvius: Reading Venice with Daniele Barbaro and Andrea Palladio*. New Haven: Yale University Press.

Dal Prete, Ivano. 2018. "The Ruins of the Earth: Learned Meteorology and Artisan Experience in Fifteenth-Century Italian Landscapes." *Nuncius* 33: 415–41.

Damisch, Hubert. 2014. "Dubuffet or the Reading of the World." Translated by Priya Wadhera, Kent Minturn, and Richard G. Elliot. *Art in Translation* 6: 299–316.

———. 2010. "The Inventor of Painting." *Oxford Art Journal* 33: 303–16.

———. 1994a. "Composer avec la peinture." *Faces: Journal d'architectures* 33: 39–42.

———. 1994b. *The Origin of Perspective*. Translated by John Goodman. Cambridge, MA: MIT Press.

———. 1993. "La peinture est un vrai trois." In *Fenêtre jaune cadmium, ou Les dessous de la peinture*, 275–305. Paris: Éditions du Seuil.

Danti, Cristina, ed. 2002. *La* Trinità *di Masaccio: Il restauro dell'anno duemila*. Florence: Edifir.

David, Pascal. 2014. "Dasein / Existenz." In Cassin 2014a, 195–200. Princeton: Princeton University Press.

Davis, Whitney. 2011. *A General Theory of Visual Culture*. Princeton: Princeton University Press.

De Girolami Cheney, Liana. 2006. *The Homes of Giorgio Vasari*. New York: Peter Lang.

———. 2017. "Giulia Lama: A Luminous Painter and a Tenebrist Poet." *Artibus et Historiae* 75: 225–52.

De Grummond, Nancy Thomson. 1975. "VV and Related Inscriptions in Giorgione, Titian, and Dürer." *Art Bulletin* 57: 346–56.

De Marchi, Andrea. 2004. "Interferenze possibili tra oreficeria e pittura nel Nord Italia, prima e dopo Gentile da Fabriano." *Annali della Scuola normale superiore di Pisa, Classe di lettere e filosofia* 15: 27–47.

———. 1992. *Gentile da Fabriano: un viaggio nella pittura italiana alla fine del gotico*. Milan: Federico Motta.

De Ruggieri, Maria Beatrice. 2016. "Caravaggio's Painting Technique: Compositional Processes and Material Structures." In *Caravaggio, opere a Roma: Tecnica e stile / Works in Rome: Technique and Style*, edited by Rossella Vodret, Giorgio Leone, Marco Cardinali, Maria Beatrice De Ruggieri, and Giulia Silvia Ghia, vol. 1 (*Saggi / Essays*), 89–131. Milan: Silvana.

Degler, Anna, and Iris Wenderholm. 2016. "Der Wert des Goldes—der Wert der Golde. Eine Einleitung." *Sonderband der Zeitschrift für Kunstgeschichte* 79: 443–60.

Dell'Anguillara, Giovanni Andrea. 2019. *Le* Metamorfosi *d'Ovidio, con le* Annotationi *di Giuseppe Orologi e gli* Argomenti *di Francesco Turchi*. Edited by Alessio Cotugno. Vol 1. Manziana: Vecchiarelli Editore.

Della Pergola, Paolo. 1964. "L'inventario Borghese del 1693 (II)." *Arte antica e moderna* 28: 451–67.

Di Stefano, Elisabetta. 2012. *Prologo al De re aedificatoria*. Pisa: ETS.

Di Vito, Mauro. 2015. "'Per lo quale ennallumini la nocte': il verbasco fiorito del *San Francesco che riceve le stimmate* di Giovanni Bellini alla Frick Collection ed altri appunti di storia naturale." In *Examining Giovanni Bellini: An Art "More Human and More Divine"*, edited by Carolyn C. Wilson, 113–25. Turnhout: Brepols.

Dini, Bruno. 1987. "Una manifattura di battiloro nel

Quattrocento." In *Tecnica e società nell'Italia dei secoli XII–XVI: Atti dell'undicesimo Convegno internazionale di studi (Pistoia 21–31 ottobre 1984)*, 83–111. Pistoia: Centro italiano di studi di storia e d'arte.

Dolce, Lodovico. 2013. *Le trasformationi di Lodovico Dolce: Il rinascimento ovidiano di Giovanni Antonio Rusconi*. Edited by Giuseppe Capriotti. Ancona: Affinità Elettive.

———. 2000. *Dolce's L'Aretino and Venetian Art Theory of the Cinquecento*. Edited and translated by Mark W. Roskill. Toronto: University of Toronto Press.

Drpić, Ivan. 2019. "Manuel I Komnenos and the Stone of Unction." *Byzantine and Modern Greek Studies* 43: 60–82.

———. 2016. *Epigram, Art, and Devotion in Later Byzantium*. Cambridge: Cambridge University Press.

———. 2008. "Art, Hesychasm, and Visual Exegesis: Parisinus Graecus 1242 Revisited." *Dumbarton Oaks Papers* 62: 217–47.

———. Forthcoming. "The Fictive Mosaics of Medieval Serbia." *Gesta* (2022).

Drury, John. 1987. "Luke." In *The Literary Guide to the Bible*, edited by Robert Alter and Frank Kermode, 418–39. Cambridge, MA: Harvard University Press.

Dunkerton, Jill. 2007. "Tintoretto's Painting Technique." In *Tintoretto*, edited by Miguel Falomir, 139–58. Madrid: Museo nacional del Prado.

———. 2004. "Bellini's Technique." In *The Cambridge Companion to Giovanni Bellini*, edited by Peter Humfrey, 195–225. Cambridge: Cambridge University Press.

———, ed. 1991. *Giotto to Dürer: Early Renaissance Painting in the National Gallery*. New Haven: Yale University Press.

Dunkerton, Jill, Susan Foister, and Nicholas Penny. 1999. *Dürer to Veronese: Sixteenth-Century Paintings in the National Gallery*. New Haven: Yale University Press.

Dunkerton, Jill, and Helen Howard. 2009. "Sebastiano del Piombo's *Raising of Lazarus*: A History of Change." *National Gallery Technical Bulletin* 30: 26–51.

Dunkerton, Jill, and Marika Spring. 2015. "Titian after 1540: Technique and Style in his Later Works." *National Gallery Technical Bulletin* 36: 6–39.

———. 1998. "The Development of Painting on Coloured Surfaces in Sixteenth-Century Italy." *Studies in Conservation* 43: 120–30.

Dunkerton, Jill, Marika Spring, Rachel Billinge, Kamilla Kalinina, Rachel Morrison, Gabriella Macaro, David Peggie, and Ashok Roy. 2013. "Titian's Painting Technique to c. 1540." *National Gallery Technical Bulletin* 34: 1–136. London: National Gallery.

Dunlop, Anne. 2015a. *Andrea del Castagno and the Limits of Painting*. London: Harvey Miller.

———. 2015b. "On the Origins of European Painting Materials, Real and Imagined." In *The Matter of Art: Materials, Practices, Cultural Logics, c. 1250–1750*, edited by Christy Anderson, Anne Dunlop, and Pamela H. Smith, 68–96. Manchester: Manchester University Press.

———. 2009. "Materials, Origins and the Nature of Early Italian Painting." In *Crossing Cultures: Conflict, Migration and Convergence*, edited by Jaynie Anderson, 472–76. Carlton, Vic.: Miegunyah Press.

Eberhart, Mark. 2004. *Why Things Break: Understanding the World by the Way It Comes Apart*. New York: Three Rivers Press.

Ebert-Schifferer, Sybille. 2018. "Caravaggio e la luce nell'atelier." In *Lumen, imago, pictura: la luce nella storia dell'ottica e nella rappresentazione visiva da Giotto a Caravaggio*, edited by Sybille Ebert-Schifferer, Pietro Roccasecca, and Andreas Thielemann, 39–64. Rome: De Luca.

———. 2012. *Caravaggio: The Artist and His Work*. Los Angeles: J. Paul Getty Museum.

Eclercy, Bastian. 2007. "'Granare'. Zur historischen Terminologie des Goldgrunddekors im Traktat des Cennino Cennini." *Mitteilungen des Kunsthistorischen Institutes in Florenz* 51: 539–54.

Edgell, G. H. 1913. "Architectural Backgrounds in the Series of *Scenes from the Life of San Bernardino* at Perugia." *American Journal of Archaeology* 8: 223–41.

Efal, Adi. 2016. *Figural Philology: Panofsky and the Science of Things*. London: Bloomsbury Academic.

Ekserdjian, David. 2006. *Parmigianino*. New Haven: Yale University Press.

Elet, Yvonne. 2020. "Stucco as Substrate and Surface in Quattrocento Florence (and Beyond)." In *The Art of Sculpture in Fifteenth-Century Italy*, edited by Amy R. Bloch and Daniel M. Zolli, 283–313. Cambridge: Cambridge University Press.

———. 2016. "Raphael and the Roads to Rome: Designing for Diplomatic Encounters at Villa Madama." *I Tatti Studies in the Italian Renaissance* 19: 143–75.

Elkins, James. 1998. *On Pictures and the Words that Fail Them*. Cambridge: Cambridge University Press.

———. 1994. *The Poetics of Perspective*. Ithaca: Cornell University Press.

Endres, Johannes, Barbara Wittmann, and Gerhard Wolf, eds. 2005. *Ikonologie des Zwischenraums: der Schleier als Medium und Metapher*. Paderborn: Wilhelm Fink.

Evans, Robin. 1997. *Translations from Drawing to Building and Other Essays*. London: Architectural Association.

Fabri, Felix. 1843–49. *Fratris Felicis Fabri Evagatorium in Terrae Sanctae, Arabiae et Egypti peregrinationem*. 3 vols. Stuttgart: Societatis Litterariae.

Facchinetti, Simone, ed. 2004. *Giovan Battista Moroni: Lo sguardo sulla realtà, 1560–1579*. Milan: Silvana.

Facchinetti, Simone, and Arturo Galansino. 2014. *Giovanni Battista Moroni*. London: Royal Academy of the Arts.

Falciani, Carlo, and Antonio Natali, eds. 2010. *Bronzino:*

Pittore e poeta alla corte dei Medici. Florence: Mandragora.

Fallows, Noel. 2010. *Jousting in Medieval and Renaissance Iberia*. Rochester, NY: Boydell & Brewer.

Falomir Faus, Miguel. 2008. "El retrato de corte." In *El retrato del Renacimiento*, edited by Miguel Falomir Faus, 109–23. Madrid: Museo nacional del Prado.

Fattorini, Gabriele. 2010. "Gentile da Fabriano, Jacopo della Quercia and Siena: The *Madonna dei banchetti*." *Burlington Magazine* 152 (1284): 152–61.

Febvre, Lucien Paul Victor. 1973. *A New Kind of History and Other Essays*. Edited by Peter Burke. New York: Harper & Row.

Fehrenbach, Frank. 2018. "Sfondare: Landschaft als Kraftraum." In *Kraft, Intensität, Energie: Zur Dynamik der Kunst*, edited by Frank Fehrenbach, Robert Felfe, and Karin Leonhard, 95–121. Berlin: De Gruyter.

———. 2002. "Der oszillierende Blick. Sfumato und die Optik des späten Leonardo." *Zeitschrift für Kunstgeschichte* 65: 522–44.

———. 1997. *Licht und Wasser: zur Dynamik naturphilosophischer Leitbilder im Werk Leonardo da Vincis*. Tübingen: E. Wasmuth.

Ferretti, Marco, Giolj Guidi, Pietro Moioli, Raffaele Scafè, and Claudio Seccaroni. 1991. "The Presence of Antimony in Some Grey Colours of Three Paintings by Correggio." *Studies in Conservation* 36: 235–39.

Ferretti, Marco, Giolj Guidi, and Claudio Seccaroni. 1991. "Analisi stratigrafiche al microscopio elettronico a scansione." In *La Danae e la pioggia d'oro: Un capolavoro di Antonio Allegri detto il Correggio restaurato*, edited by Maria Grazia Bernardini, 79–83. Rome: Multigrafica Editrice.

Filarete. 1972. *Trattato di Architettura*. Edited by Anna Maria Finoli and Liliana. Grassi: Edizioni Il Polifilo.

———. 1965. *Treatise on Architecture*. Translated by John R. Spencer. 2 vols. New Haven: Yale University Press.

Fiorenza, Giancarlo. 2008. *Dosso Dossi: Paintings of Myth, Magic, and the Antique*. University Park: Pennsylvania State University Press.

Fiori, Maria. 2016a. "Eclettismo di Francesco Ricchino, pittore, architetto, accademico e poeta nella Brescia di secondo Cinquecento." In *Brescia nel secondo Cinquecento: architettura, arte, e società*, edited by Filippo Piazza and Enrico Valseriati, 209–24. Brescia: Morcelliana.

———. 2016b. "Francesco Ricchino e il ritratto a Brescia a metà Cinquecento." *Nuovi Studi* 21: 87–112.

Fleming, John. 1982. *From Bonaventure to Bellini: An Essay in Franciscan Exegesis*. Princeton: Princeton University Press.

Fletcher, Jennifer. 1981. "Marcantonio Michiel, 'che ha veduto assai'." *Burlington Magazine* 123: 602–8.

———. 1972. "The Provenance of Bellini's Frick St. Francis." *Burlington Magazine* 114: 206, 209–15.

Florenskij, Pavel Aleksandrovič. 1988. *Die Ikonostase: Urbild und Grenzerlebnis im revolutionären Rußland*. Translated by Ulrich Werner. Stuttgart: Urachhaus.

Flyvbjerg, Bent. 2006. "Five Misunderstandings about Case-Study Research." *Qualitative Inquiry* 12: 219–45.

Fogolari, Gino. 1908. "Le portelle dell'organo di S. Maria dei Miracoli di Venezia." *Bollettino d'Arte* 11: 1–32.

Fore, Devin. 2012. *Realism after Modernism: The Rehumanization of Art and Literature*. Cambridge, MA: MIT Press.

Foucault, Michel. 2004. *La peinture de Manet*. Paris: Éditions du Seuil.

Frampton, Kenneth. 2009. "Museum as Palimpsest." In *Neues Museum Berlin*, edited by David Chipperfield Architects with Julian Harrap, 91–120. Cologne: W. König.

Fernández de Béthencourt, Francisco. 1920. *Historia genealógica y heráldica de la monarquía española, Casa Real y Grandes de España*. Vol. 10. Madrid: E. Teodoro.

Franklin, David. 2003. *The Art of Parmigianino*. New Haven: Yale University Press.

Franses, Rico. 2003. "When All That Is Gold Does Not Glitter: On the Strange History of Looking at Byzantine Art." In *Icon and Word: The Power of Images in Byzantium. Studies Presented to Robin Cormack*, edited by Antony Eastmond and Liz James, 13–24. Burlington: Ashgate.

Frick, Carole Collier. 2002. *Dressing Renaissance Florence: Families, Fortunes, and Fine Clothing*. Baltimore: Johns Hopkins University Press.

Friedberg, Anne. 2006. *The Virtual Window: From Alberti to Microsoft*. Cambridge, MA: MIT Press.

Frimmel, Theodor. 1907. "Bemerkungen zu Marc-Anton Michiels *Notizia d'opere di disegno*." *Blätter für Gemäldekunde* 3: 37–78.

Frinta, Mojmír S. 1981. "Raised Gilded Adornment of the Cypriot Icons, and the Occurrence of the Technique in the West." *Gesta* 20: 333–47.

Gage, Frances. 2016. *Painting as Medicine in Early Modern Rome: Giulio Mancini and the Efficacy of Art*. University Park: Pennsylvania State University Press.

———. 2008. "Exercise for Mind and Body: Giulio Mancini, Collecting, and the Beholding of Landscape Painting in the Seventeenth Century." *Renaissance Quarterly* 61: 1167–1207

Gage, John. 1993. *Color and Culture: Practice and Meaning from Antiquity to Abstraction*. Berkeley: University of California Press.

Gagné, John. 2018. "Emotional Attachments: Iron Hands, their Makers, and their Wearers, 1450–1600." In *Feeling Things*, edited by Sally Holloway, Stephanie Downes, and Sarah Randles. Oxford: Oxford University Press.

———. Forthcoming. "Bionic Renaissance: Half-Human/ist Traditions and the Body."

Galen. 1963. *Galen on the Passions and Errors of the Soul.* Translated by Paul W. Harkins. Columbus: Ohio State University Press.

Gamboni, Dario. 2002. *Potential Images: Ambiguity and Indeterminacy in Modern Art.* London: Reaktion Books.

Garber, Marjorie. 1997. "Out of Joint." In *The Body in Parts: Fantasies of Corporeality in Early Modern Europe*, edited by David Hillman and Carla Mazzio, 23–52. New York: Routledge.

Gay, Victor. 1887–1928. *Glossaire archéologique du Moyen Age et de la Renaissance.* Edited by H. Stein and M. Aubert. 2 vols. Paris: Librairie de la Société bibliographique.

Geddes, Leslie A. 2020. *Watermarks: Leonardo da Vinci and the Mastery of Nature.* Princeton: Princeton University Press.

Gell, Alfred. 1998. *Art and Agency: An Anthropological Theory.* Oxford: Clarendon Press.

Gély-Ghedira, Véronique. 2000. *La nostalgie du moi: Écho dans la littérature européenne.* Paris: Presses universitaires de France.

Gentili, Augusto. 2004. "Bellini and Landscape." In *The Cambridge Companion to Giovanni Bellini*, edited by Peter Humfrey, 167–81. Cambridge: Cambridge University Press.

Gill, Meredith J. 2014. *Angels and the Order of Heaven in Medieval and Renaissance Italy.* Cambridge: Cambridge University Press.

Giordano, Michael J. 2014. "Bronzino's Art of Emblazoning: The *Young Man with a Book, Lucrezia Panciatichi, Saint Bartholomew*, and *Laura Battiferri.*" In *Agnolo Bronzino*, edited by Liana De Girolami Cheney, 337–70. Washington, DC: New Academia Publishing.

Goffen, Rona. 2003. "Raphael's Designer Labels: From the Virgin Mary to *La Fornarina.*" *Artibus et Historiae* 24: 123–42.

———. 2001. "Signatures: Inscribing Identity in Italian Renaissance Art." *Viator* 32: 303–70.

———. 1975. "Icon and Vision: Giovanni Bellini's Half-Length Madonnas." *Art Bulletin* 57: 487–518.

Goldthwaite, Richard A. 2009. *The Economy of Renaissance Florence.* Baltimore: Johns Hopkins University Press.

Golubovich, Girolamo, ed. 1913. *Biblioteca bio-bibliografica della Terra Santa e dell' Oriente francescano.* Vol. 2. Florence: Collegio di S. Bonaventura.

Gombrich, Ernst. 1966. "The Renaissance Theory of Art and the Rise of Landscape." In Gombrich, *Norm and Form: Studies in the Art of the Renaissance*, 107–21. London: Phaidon.

———. 1935. "[Review of] *Entstehung und Bedeutung des Goldgrundes in der spätantiken Bildkomposition*, by Josef Bodonyi." *Kritische Berichte zur Kunstgeschichtlichen Literatur* 5: 65–76.

Gomez, Michael A. 2018. *African Dominion: A New History of Empire in Early and Medieval West Africa.* Princeton: Princeton University Press.

Goy, Richard J. 2006. *Building Renaissance Venice: Patrons, Architects, and Builders, c. 1430–1500.* New Haven: Yale University Press.

———. 1992. *The House of Gold: Building a Palace in Medieval Venice.* Cambridge: Cambridge University Press.

Gracián, Baltasar. 2011. *Oráculo manual y arte de prudencia.* Barcelona: Linkgua.

Gramm, Josef. 1912. *Die ideale Landschaft: Ihre Entstehung und Entwicklung.* Freiburg: Herdersche Verlagshandlung.

Grant, Mary, ed. 1960. *The Myths of Hyginus.* Lawrence: University of Kansas Press.

Grassi, Luigi, and Mario Pepe. 1978. *Dizionario della critica d'arte.* Vol. 2. Turin: UTET.

Grave, Johannes. 2004. *Landschaften der Meditation: Giovanni Bellinis Assoziationsräume.* Freiburg im Breisgau: Rombach.

Graves, Frances Marjorie. 1926. *Deux inventaires de la maison d'Orléans (1389 et 1408).* Paris: Champion.

Greenberg, Clement. 1993. "After Abstract Expressionism (1962)." In *The Collected Essays and Criticism*, edited by John O'Brian, 121–34. Chicago: University of Chicago Press.

———. 1960. "Modernist Painting." In *Forum Lectures.* Washington, DC: Voice of America.

Gregori, Mina. 2009. "Le due cene in Emmaus a confronto." In Maderna and Pacia 2009, 29–37. Milan: Electa.

———. 1985. "Caravaggio." In *The Age of Caravaggio*, edited by Keith Christiansen, 197–354. New York: Metropolitan Museum of Art.

———. 1979. *Giovan Battista Moroni: Tutte le opere.* Bergamo: Poligrafiche Bolis.

Grig, Lucy. 2012. "Deconstructing the Symbolic City: Jerome as Guide to Late Antique Rome." *Papers of the British School at Rome* 80: 125–43.

Grosjean, Georges, ed. 1978. *Mapamundi: The Catalan Atlas of the Year 1375.* Dietikon-Zurich: Urs Graf Verlag.

Guerin, Frances. 2018. *The Truth Is Always Grey: A History of Modernist Painting.* Minneapolis: University of Minnesota Press.

Guérin, Sarah M. 2018. "Golds Yellow, Red, and White: Gold, Copper, and Ivory in Trans-Saharan Trade." In *Caravans of Gold, Fragments in Time: Art, Culture, and Exchange across Medieval Saharan Africa*, edited by Kathleen Bickford Berzock, 175–201. Princeton: Princeton University Press.

Gusmeroli, Luisa. 2017. "Zur Restaurierung der *Madonna dell'Impannata.*" In *Raffael*, edited by Achim Gnann, 242–43. Munich: Hirmer.

Habig, Marion A., ed. 1973. *St. Francis of Assisi. Writings and Early Biographies: English Omnibus of the Sources for the Life of St. Francis*. Chicago: Franciscan Press.

Hadot, Pierre. 1993. *Plotinus, or The Simplicity of Vision*. Translated by Michael Chase. Chicago: University of Chicago Press.

Hamilton, John T. 2013. *Security: Politics, Humanity, and the Philology of Care*. Princeton: Princeton University Press.

Hammer, Ginger. 2018. "*The Sacred Mountain of La Verna*," National Gallery of Art, Washington, DC. https://www.nga.gov/features/description-sacred-mountain-la-verna.html#introduction

Hammond, Norman. 2007. "Bellini's Birds: Avifauna in the Frick *St. Francis*." *Burlington Magazine* 149: 36–38.

———. 2002. "Bellini's Ass: A Note on the Frick *St Francis*." *Burlington Magazine* 144: 24–26.

Hankinson, R. J. 1991. "Galen's Anatomy of the Soul." *Phronesis* 36: 197–233.

Hansen, Morten Steen. 2013. *In Michelangelo's Mirror: Perino del Vaga, Daniele da Volterra, Pellegrino Tibaldi*. University Park: Pennsylvania State University Press.

Hara, Mari Yoko. 2018. "Emphatic Presence: Architectural Chiaroscuro." In *Chiaroscuro als aesthetisches Prinzip: Kunst und Theorie des Helldunkels 1300–1550*, edited by Claudia Lehmann, Norberto Gramaccini, Johannes Rössler, and Thomas Dittelbach, 351–66. Berlin: De Gruyter.

Harcourt, Glenn. 1987 "Andreas Vesalius and the Anatomy of Antique Sculpture." *Representations* 17: 28–61.

Harrison, Peter. 2016. "Angels on Pinheads and Needles' Points." *Notes and Queries* 63: 45–47.

Harvey, J. R. 2013. *The Story of Black*. London: Reaktion Books.

Hauser, Andreas. 2003. "Andrea Mantegnas *Madonna delle cave*: Ein vulkanischer Christus als Quelle geistigen Lebens." *Georges-Bloch-Jahrbuch des Kunsthistorischen Instituts der Universität Zürich* 8: 79–109.

Hecht, Christian. 2003. *Die Glorie: Begriff, Thema, Bildelement in der europäischen Sakralkunst vom Mittelalter bis zum Ausgang des Barock*. Regensburg: Schnell & Steiner.

Hendy, Philip, and A. S. Lucas. 1968. "The Ground in Pictures." *Museum* 21: 245–76.

Hersch, K. K. 2010. *The Roman Wedding: Ritual and Meaning in Antiquity*. Cambridge: Cambridge University Press.

Hess, Jacob. 1968. "Note manciane." *Münchner Jahrbuch der bildenden Kunst* 19: 103–20.

Hills, Paul. 2006. "Titian's Veils." *Art History* 29: 771–95.

———. 1999. *Venetian Colour: Marble, Mosaic, Painting and Glass, 1250–1550*. New Haven: Yale University Press.

Hinds, Stephen. 2002. "Landscape with Figures: Aesthetics of Place in the Metamorphoses and Its Tradition." In *The Cambridge Companion to Ovid*, edited by Philip Hardie, 122–49. Cambridge: Cambridge University Press.

Hirst, Michael. 1981. *Sebastiano del Piombo*. Oxford: Clarendon Press.

Hirst, Michael, and Jill Dunkerton. 1994. *The Young Michelangelo*. London: National Gallery.

Hochmann, Michel. 2015. *Colorito: La technique des peintres vénitiens à la Renaissance*. Turnhout: Brepols.

———. 1999. "Marcantonio Michiel e la nascita della critica veneziana." In *La pittura nel Veneto: Il Cinquecento*, edited by Mauro Lucco, 1181–202. Milan: Electa.

Hogarth, William. 1753. *Analysis of Beauty*. London: J. Reeves.

Hollanda, Francisco de. 2013. *On Antique Painting*. University Park: Pennsylvania State University Press.

Hollander, John. 1981. *The Figure of Echo: A Mode of Allusion in Milton and After*. Berkeley: University of California Press.

Holmes, Megan. 2013. *The Miraculous Image in Renaissance Florence*. New Haven: Yale University Press.

———. 2004. "Copying Practices and Marketing Strategies in a Fifteenth-Century Florentine Painter's Workshop." In *Artistic Exchange and Cultural translation in the Italian Renaissance City*, edited by Stephen J. Campbell and Stephen J. Milner, 38–74. Cambridge: Cambridge University Press.

———. 2003. "Neri di Bicci and the Commodification of Artistic Values in Florentine Painting (1450–1500)." In *The Art Market in Italy*, edited by Marcello Fantoni, Louisa Matthew, and Sara F. Matthews-Grieco, 213–23. Modena: Panini.

Hommes, Margriet van Eikema. 2000–2001. "Discoloration or *Chiaroscuro*? An Interpretation of the Dark Areas in Raphael's *Transfiguration of Christ*." *Simiolus: Netherlands Quarterly for the History of Art* 28: 4–43.

Hood, William. 1993. Fra Angelico at San Marco. New Haven: Yale University Press.

Hope, Charles. 2000. "Composition in Italian Art Literature." In *Pictorial Composition from Medieval to Modern Art*, edited by Paul Taylor and François Quiviger, 27–44. London: Warburg Institute.

Houtman, Alberdina. 2016. "The Development of the Adamic Myth in Genesis Rabbah." In *Religious Stories in Transformation: Conflict, Revision and Reception*, edited by Alberdina Houtman, Tamar Kadari, Marcel Poorthuis, and Vered Tohar, 36–51. Leiden: Brill.

Howard, Deborah. 2004. "Bellini and Architecture." In *The Cambridge Companion to Giovanni Bellini*, edited by Peter Humfrey, 157–62. Cambridge: Cambridge University Press.

———. 2000. *Venice and the East: The Impact of the Islamic World on Venetian Architecture, 1100–1500*. New Haven and London: Yale University Press.

Hui, Andrew. 2016. *The Poetics of Ruins in Renaissance*

Literature. New York: Fordham University Press.
Hume, David. 1748. *An Enquiry concerning Human Understanding*. London: A. Millar.
Humfrey, Peter. 2000. *Giovanni Battista Moroni: Renaissance Portraitist*. Fort Worth: Kimbell Art Museum.
Humfrey, Peter, and Mauro Lucco, eds. 1998. *Dosso Dossi: Court Painter in Renaissance Ferrara*. New York: Metropolitan Museum of Art.
Huth, Hans. 1967. *Künstler und werkstatt der spätgotik*. Darmstadt: Wissenschaftliche Buchgesellschaft.
Iversen, Margaret. 2005. "The Discourse of Perspective in the Twentieth Century: Panofsky, Damisch, Lacan." *Oxford Art Journal* 28: 191–202.
Iversen, Margaret, and Stephen Melville. 2010. *Writing Art History: Disciplinary Departures*. Chicago: University of Chicago Press.
Jacobs, Fredrika Herman. 2005. *The Living Image in Renaissance Art*. Cambridge: Cambridge University Press.
Janson, Anthony F. 1994. "The Meaning of the Landscape in Bellini's *St. Francis in Ecstasy*." *Artibus et Historiae* 15: 41–54.
Johnson, Barbara. 1998. "Is Female to Male as Ground is to Figure?" In Johnson, *The Feminist Difference: Literature, Psychoanalysis, Race, and Gender*, 17–36. Cambridge, MA: Harvard University Press.
Jollet, Etienne. 2007. *La nature morte, ou, La place des choses: L'objet et son lieu dans l'art occidental*. Paris: Hazan.
Jotischky, Andrew. 2016. "The Franciscan Return to the Holy Land (1333) and Mt Sion: Pilgrimage and the Apostolic Mission." In *The Crusader World*, edited by Adrian Boas, 241–55. New York: Routledge.
Jung, Jacqueline E. 2010. "The Tactile and the Visionary: Notes on the Place of Sculpture in the Medieval Religious imagination." In *Looking Beyond: Visions, Dreams, and Insights in Medieval Art and History*, edited by Colum Hourihane, 203–40. Princeton: Princeton University Press.
Jurdjevic, Mark. 2002. "Machiavelli's Sketches of Francesco Valori and the Reconstruction of Florentine History." *Journal of the History of Ideas* 63: 185–206.
Kagan, Richard L. 2000. *Urban Images of the Hispanic World, 1493–1793*. New Haven: Yale University Press.
Kanter, Laurence B. 2018. *Leonardo: Discoveries from Verrocchio's Studio; Early Paintings and New Attributions*. New Haven: Yale University Press.
Keith, L. 1998. "Three Paintings by Caravaggio." *National Gallery Technical Bulletin* 19: 37–51.
Keith, L., and A. Roy. 1996. "Giampietrino, Boltraffio, and the Influence of Leonardo." *National Gallery Technical Bulletin* 17: 4–19.
Kelley, Justin L. 2020. *The Church of the Holy Sepulchre in Text and Archaeology*. Oxford: Archaeopress.
Kemp, Martin. 1997. *Behind the Picture: Art and Evidence in the Italian Renaissance*. New Haven: Yale University Press.
Kemp, Wolfgang. 1985. "Death at Work: A Case Study on Constitutive Blanks in Nineteenth-Century Painting." *Representations* 10: 102–23.
Kenaan, Hagi. 2007. "The Ground's Hidden Surface." *Wolkenkuckucksheim: International Journal of Architectural Theory* 12: 17–28.
———. 2006. "Tracing Shadows: Reflections on the Origins of Painting." In *Pictorial Languages and Their Meanings: Liber Amicorum in Honor of Nurith Kenaan-Kedar*, edited by Christine B. Verzar and Gil Fishhof, 17–28. Tel Aviv: Tel Aviv University.
Kessler, Herbert L. 2000. *Spiritual Seeing: Picturing God's Invisibility in Medieval Art*. Philadelphia: University of Pennsylvania Press.
Kim, David Young. 2016. "Lotto's Carpets: Materiality, Textiles, and Composition in Renaissance Painting." *Art Bulletin* 98: 181–212.
———. 2014. *The Traveling Artist in the Italian Renaissance: Geography, Mobility, and Style*. New Haven: Yale University Press.
———. 2013. "Why Weight? The Heaviness of Art and Narrative Force." In *Matters of Weight: Force, Gravity, and Aesthetics in the Early Modern Period*, edited by David Young Kim, 9–34. Emsdetten: Edition Imorde.
———. 2011. "The Horror of Mimesis." *Oxford Art Journal* 34: 335–53.
King, David. 2008. "The Meaning of Amputation in the *Chansons de geste*." *Symposium* 62: 35–51, 64.
Kirby, Jo, and Raymond White. 1996. "The Identification of Red Lake Pigment Dyestuffs and a Discussion of their Use." *National Gallery Technical Bulletin* 17: 56–80.
Koehne, Carl Ernst. 1979. "Vom Goldgrund zum Raumbild." *Die Kunst und das schoene Heim* 91: 725–29.
Koering, Jérémie. 2014. "Au miroir de Narcisse: La peinture de Caravage?" In *Poesis: Über das Tun in der Kunst*, edited by Andreas Beyer and Dario Gamboni, 95–108. Berlin: Deutscher Kunstverlag.
Koerner, Joseph Leo. 2016. *Bosch and Bruegel: From Enemy Painting to Everyday Life*. Princeton: Princeton University Press.
Kohl, Jeanette. 2004. *Fama und Virtus: Bartolomeo Colleonis Grabkapelle*. Berlin: Akademie Verlag.
Koschorke, Albrecht. 1990. *Die Geschichte des Horizonts: Grenze und Grenzüberschreitung in literarischen Landschaftsbildern*. Frankfurt am Main: Suhrkamp.
Koselleck, Reinhart. 2018. *Sediments of Time: On Possible Histories*. Edited by Sean Franzel and Stefan-Ludwig Hoffmann. Stanford: Stanford University Press.
Kris, Ernst, and Otto Kurz. 1979. *Legend, Myth, and Magic in the Image of the Artist: An Historical Experiment*. New Haven: Yale University Press.

Krischel, Roland. 2010. "The Inventory of the Venetian *Vendecolori* Jacopo de' Benedetti: The Non-Pigment Materials." In *Trade in Artists' Materials: Markets and Commerce in Europe to 1700*, edited by Jo Kirby, Susie Nash, and Joanna Cannon, 253–66. London: Archetype.

Kroschewski, Nevenka. 2002. *Über das allmähliche Verfertigen der Bilder: Neue Aspekte zu Caravaggio*. Munich: Scaneg.

Krüger, Klaus. 2014. "Andrea Mantegna: Painting's Mediality." *Art History* 37: 222–53.

Krüger, Steffen. 2013. "Die Legende vom Künstler als Propagandastrategie." In *Im Dienste des Ich*, edited by Steffen Krüger and Thomas Röske, 99–118. Vienna: Böhlau Verlag.

Kubovy, Michael. 1986. *The Psychology of Perspective and Renaissance Art*. Cambridge: Cambridge University Press.

Kusukawa, Sachiko. 2012. *Picturing the Book of Nature: Image, Text, and Argument in Sixteenth-Century Human Anatomy and Medical Botany*. Chicago: University of Chicago Press.

Lajer-Burchart, Ewa, and Isabelle Graw. 2016. *Painting Beyond Itself: The Medium in the Post-medium Condition*. Berlin: Sternberg Press.

Lakey, Christopher. 2015. "The Materiality of Light in Medieval Italian Painting." *English Language Notes* 53: 119–36.

Lange, Julius. 1901. "Et Blad af Koloritens Historie (1893)." In *Udvalgte skrifter af Julius Lange*, edited by Georg Brandes and P. Købke, 136–56. Copenhagen: Det Nordiske Forlag.

Lanzi, Luigi. 1968. *Storia pittorica della Italia dal Risorgimento delle Belle Arti fin presso al fine del XVIII secolo*. Edited by Martino Capucci. 4 vols. Florence: Sansoni.

Lapucci, Roberta. 2005. *Caravaggio e l'ottica: Perché bisogna saper vedere e osservare*. Edited by Mina Gregori. Florence: Rest & Art.

Lauber, Rosella. 2015. "'Finito et ricercato mirabilmente'. Per nuovi contributi sul *San Francesco nel deserto* di Giovanni Bellini, ora nella Frick Collection di New York." In *Examining Giovanni Bellini: An Art "More Human and More Divine,"* edited by Carolyn C. Wilson, 93–112. Turnhout: Brepols.

———. 2014. "'Gran forza et gran vivacità'. Per Antonello da Messina nel collezionismo veneziano rinascimentale attraverso le carte di Marcantonio Michiel." *Artibus et Historiae* 35: 171–96.

———. 2007. "'Et maxime in li occhi'. Per la descrizione delle opere d'arte in Marcantonio Michiel." In *Testi, immagini e filologia nel XVI secolo*, edited by Eliana Carrara and Silvia Ginzburg, 1–36. Pisa: Edizioni della Normale.

Laureati, Laura, and Lorenza Mochi Onori, eds. 2006. *Gentile da Fabriano and the Other Renaissance*. Milan: Electa.

Laurenza, Domenico 2012. *Art and Anatomy in Renaissance Italy: Images from a Scientific Revolution*. New Haven: Yale University Press.

Lavin, Marilyn Aronberg. 2007. "The Joy of St. Francis: Bellini's Panel in the Frick Collection." *Artibus et Historiae*: 231–56.

———. 1981. *Piero della Francesca's* Baptism of Christ. New Haven: Yale University Press.

Lazzarini, Elena. 2010. *Nudo, arte e decoro: Oscillazioni estetiche negli scritti d'arte del Cinquecento*. Pisa: Pacini.

Leatherbarrow, David. 1993. *The Roots of Architectural Invention: Site, Enclosure, Materials*. Cambridge: Cambridge University Press.

Lechi, Giacomo, Adriana Conconi Fedrigolli, and Piero Lechi. 2010. *La grande collezione: Le Gallerie Avogadro, Fenaroli-Avogadro, Maffei-Erizzo; storia e catalogo*. Brescia: Grafo.

Lechi, Isabella. 1995. "La collezione Avogadro di Brescia." *Arte Lombarda* 113/115: 170–80.

Lecoq, Anne-Marie. 1975. "'Finxit': Le peintre comme 'fictor' au XVIe siècle." *Bibliothèque d'Humanisme et Renaissance* 37: 225–43.

Ledderose, Lothar. 2012. "Der Bildgrund in Ostasien." In Boehm and Burioni 2012, 165–88. Paderborn: Wilhelm Fink.

Lehmann, Ann-Sophie. 2015. "The Matter of the Medium: Some Tools for an Art-Theoretical Interpretation of Materials." In *The Matter of Art: Materials, Practices, and Cultural Logics, c. 1250–1750*, edited by Christy Anderson, Anne Dunlop, and Pamela H. Smith, 21–41. Manchester: Manchester University Press.

Lehmann, Claudia. 2018. "*Chiaroscuro* as an Aesthetic Principle. The Art and Theory of *Chiaroscuro* in the Early Modern Period: An Introduction." In *Chiaroscuro als aesthetisches Prinzip: Kunst und Theorie des Helldunkels 1300–1550*, edited by Claudia Lehmann, Norberto Gramaccini, Johannes Rössler, and Thomas Dittelbach, 9–47. Berlin: De Gruyter.

Lehndorff, Gertrud. 1933. *Giovanni Battista Moroni: Der Porträtmaler von Bergamo*. Winterthur: Schoenenberger & Gall.

Leinkauf, Thomas. 2018. "Möglichkeit, Potential und Kraft (*possibilitas, potentia, potestas, virtus/vis*)." In *Kraft, Intensität, Energie*, edited by Frank Fehrenbach, Robert Felfe, and Karin Leonhard, 31–51. Berlin: De Gruyter.

Lemmens, Leonhard. 1925. *Die Franziskaner im heiligen Lande*. Münster: Aschendorff.

Leonardo da Vinci. 1939. *The Notebooks of Leonardo da Vinci*. Edited by Edward MacCurdy. New York: Reynal & Hitchcock.

———. 1914. *Trattato della pittura*. Edited by Angelo Borzelli. Lanciano: Carabba.

———. 1883. *The Literary Works of Leonardo da Vinci*. Edited by Jean Paul Richter. Vol. 1. London: S. Low.

Levine, Caroline. 2015. *Forms: Whole, Rhythm, Hierarchy, Network*. Princeton: Princeton University Press.

Levy, Evonne. 2015. *Baroque and the Political Language of Formalism (1845–1945): Burckhardt, Wölfflin, Gurlitt, Brinckmann, Sedlmayr*. Basel: Schwabe.

Lewis, Sarah Elizabeth. 2020. "Groundwork: Race and Aesthetics in the Era of Stand Your Ground Law." *Art Journal*, 79: 92–113.

Lightbown, R. W. 1978. *Secular Goldsmiths' Work in Medieval France: A History*. London: Society of Antiquaries.

Lingo, Estelle. 2019. "Baroque Visuality between Perspective and the Photograph." Paper presented at conference "Baroque to Neo-Baroque: Curves of an Art Historical Concept," Kunsthistorisches Institut in Florenz, Florence, Italy, June 4.

———. 2013. "Francesco Mochi's Balancing Act and the Prehistory of Bernini's *Four Rivers Fountain*." In *Matters of Weight: Force, Gravity and Aesthetics in the Early Modern Period*, edited by David Young Kim, 129–50. Berlin: Edition Imorde.

———. 2011. "Beyond the Fold: Drapery in Seventeenth-Century Sculptural Practice and Criticism." In *Unfolding the Textile Medium in Early Modern Art and Literature*, edited by Tristan Weddigen, 121–29. Emsdetten: Edition Imorde.

———. 2009. "Mochi's Edge." *Oxford Art Journal* 32: 1–16.

Lingo, Stuart. 2016. "Agnolo Bronzino's *Pygmalion* and the Statue and the Dawn of Art." *Art History* 39: 868–95.

———. 2015. "Looking Askance: Machiavelli, the Burlesque, and Bronzino's *Martyrdom of San Lorenzo*." *Rivista di letterature moderne e comparate* 68: 217–42.

———. 2013. "Raffaello Borghini and the Corpus of Florentine Art in an Age of Reform." In *The Sensuous in the Counter-Reformation Church*, edited by Marcia B. Hall and Tracy E. Cooper, 113–35. Cambridge: Cambridge University Press.

Little, Anna. 2007. "Le motif de l'escalier dans le développement de l'espace pictural moderne (Sienne, première moitié du XIVe siècle)." Translated [into French] by Laurence Debeque-Michel. *Ligeia* 73/76: 19–32.

Lobel, Michael. 2014. *John Sloan: Drawing on Illustration*. New Haven: Yale University Press.

Loh, Maria. 2019. *Titian's Touch: Art, Magic and Philosophy*. London: Reaktion Books.

———. 2015. *Still Lives: Death, Desire, and the Portrait of the Old Master*. Princeton: Princeton University Press.

———. 2007. *Titian Remade: Repetition and the Transformation of Early Modern Italian Art*. Los Angeles: Getty Research Institute.

Lohff, Johanna Beate. 2015. *Malerei auf Stein: Antonio Tempestas Bilder auf Stein im Kontext der Kunst- und Naturtheorie seiner Zeit*. Munich: Hirmer.

Löhr, Wolf-Dietrich. 2008. "'Disegnia sechondo che huoi': Cennino Cennini e la fantasia artistica." In *Grafie di immagini tra Quattrocento e Cinquecento*, edited by Marzia Faietti and Gerhard Wolf, 163–90. Venice: Marsilio.

Longus. 2019. *Daphnis and Chloe*. Edited by Ewen Bowie. Cambridge: Cambridge University Press.

———. 2009. *Daphnis and Chloe. Anthia and Habrocomes*. Edited and translated by Jeffrey Henderson. Cambridge, MA: Harvard University Press.

Lucchi, Piero. 2009. "L'arte dei 'tira' e 'battioro': Sulle tracce della 'mariégola' perduta." In *Con il legno e con l'oro: La Venezia artigiana degli intagliatori, battiloro e doratori*, edited by Giovanni Caniato, 199–206. Sommacampagna: Cierre Edizioni.

Lugli, Emanuele. 2019. *The Making of Measure and the Promise of Sameness*. Chicago: University of Chicago Press.

———. 2009. "Between Form and Representation: The Frick *St. Francis*." *Art History* 32: 21–51.

Lukes, Alexandra. 2019. "An Aesthetics of Discomfort: Nonsense, Madness, and the Limits of Translation." *Translation Studies* 12: 1–14.

Lunghi, Elvio. 2012. "Le prime immagini della Verna." In *Altro monte non ha più santo il mondo*, edited by Nicoletta Baldini, 137–58. Florence: Edizioni Studi Francescani.

Luz, Ulrich. 2005. *Matthew 21–28: A Commentary*. Minneapolis: Fortress Press.

Maccherini, Michele. 2004. "Ritratto di Giulio Mancini." In *Bernini dai Borghese ai Barberini: La cultura a Roma intorno agli anni venti*, edited by Olivier Bonfait and Anna Coliva, 47–57. Rome: De Luca.

———. 1997. "Caravaggio nel carteggio familiare di Giulio Mancini." *Prospettiva* 86: 71–92.

MacGregor, Nicola Ann, and Sandra Freschi. 2005. "Il restauro dell'Adorazione dei Magi." In *Gentile da Fabriano agli Uffizi*, edited by Alessandro Cecchi, 173–80. Milan: Silvana.

Mack, Peter, and Robert Williams, eds. 2015. *Michael Baxandall, Vision and the Work of Words*. New York: Routledge.

Mack, Rosamond E. 2002. *Bazaar to Piazza: Islamic Trade and Italian Art, 1300–1600*. Berkeley: University of California Press.

MacLennan, Douglas, and Laura Llewellyn. 2019. "Mapping Gold Leaf in Gentile da Fabriano's Paintings: A Case Study." *Burlington Magazine* 161: 988–89, 992–95.

MacLennan, Douglas, Laura Llewellyn, John K. Delaney, Kathryn A. Dooley, Catherine Schmidt-Patterson, Yvonne Szafran, and Karen Trentelman. 2019. "Visualizing and Measuring Gold Leaf in

Fourteenth- and Fifteenth-Century Italian Gold Ground Paintings Using Scanning Macro X-ray Fluorescence Spectroscopy: A New Tool for Advancing Art Historical Research." *Heritage Science* 7: 3, 5, 7–8.

Maderna, Valentina, and Amalia Pacia, eds. 2009. *Caravaggio ospita Caravaggio*. Milan: Electa.

Malkiel, David. 2013. *Stones Speak: Hebrew Tombstones from Padua, 1529–1862*. Leiden: Brill.

Mancini, Giulio. 1956. *Considerazioni sulla pittura*. Edited by Adriana Marucchi. Vol. 1. Rome: Accademia nazionale dei Lincei.

Manfrè, Valeria, and Ida Mauro. 2010–11. "Rievocazione dell'immaginario asburgico: Le serie dei ritratti di viceré e governatori nelle capitali dell'Italia spagnola." In *Ricerche sul '600 napoletano: Saggi e documenti 2010–2011*, edited by Giuseppe de Vito, 107–35. Naples: Arte'm.

Marcelli, Fabio. 2005. *Gentile da Fabriano*. Milan: Silvana.

Marin, Louis. 2001. "The Frame of Representation and Some of Its Figures." In *On Representation*, translated by Catherine Porter, 352–72. Stanford: Stanford University Press.

———. 1995. *To Destroy Painting*. Translated by Mette Hjort. Chicago: University of Chicago Press.

———. 1989. "The Order of Words and the Order of Things in Painting." *Visible Language* 23: 188–203.

———. 1977. *Détruire la peinture*. Paris : Galilée.

Marinelli, Sergio. 1996. *Il ritrovamento del corpo di san Marco di Jacopo Tintoretto*. Milan: TEA.

Marino, Giambattista. 2012. *La lira: 1614*. Edited by Luana Salvarani. Trento: La Finestra.

———. 2005. *La galeria*. Edited by Paganino Gaudenzi, Alessandra Ruffino, and Marzio Pieri. Trento: La Finestra.

Marmugi, Caterina, ed. 1984. *Raffaello a Firenze: Dipinti e disegni delle collezioni fiorentine*. Milan: Electa.

Marshall, Peter K., ed. 2002. *Hyginus <Mythographus>: Fabulae*. Berlin: Teubner.

Martin, Élisabeth. 2008. "Grounds on Canvas 1600–1640 in Various European Artistic Centres." In *Preparation for Painting: The Artist's Choice and Its Consequences*, edited by Joyce H. Townsend, Tiarna Doherty, Gunnar Heydenreich, and Jacqueline Ridge, 59–67. London: Archetype.

Marx, Karl. 1993. *Grundrisse: Foundations of the Critique of Political Economy (Rough Draft)*. Translated by Martin Nicolaus. New York: Penguin Books.

Marzi, M. G. 1996. "Dagli archivi fiorentini notizie sul collezionismo di ceramica apula nel XVI secolo." In *Venezia, l'archeologia e l'Europa: Congresso internazionale, Venezia 27–30 giugno 1994 (Rivista di Archeologia* Supplementi 17), 131–36. Rome: Giorgio Bretschneider.

Masheck, Joseph. 1991. "Alberti's 'Window': Art-Historiographic Notes on an Antimodernist Misprision." *Art Journal* 50: 34–41.

Massing, Jean Michel. 2007. "Observations and Beliefs: The World of the 'Catalan Atlas'." In *Studies in Imagery*, edited by Jean Michel Massing, vol. 2, 1–22. London: Pindar Press.

Matthew, Louisa C. 2002. "'Vendecolori a Venezia': The Reconstruction of a Profession." *Burlington Magazine* 144: 680–86.

———. 1998. "The Painter's Presence: Signatures in Venetian Renaissance Pictures." *Art Bulletin* 80: 616–48.

Matthew, Louisa C., and Barbara H. Berrie. 2010. "'Memoria de colori che bisognino torre a vinetia': Venice as a Centre for the Purchase of Painters' Colours." In *Trade in Artists' Materials*, edited by Jo Kirby Susie Nash, and Joanna Cannon, 245–52. London: Archetype.

McHam, Sarah Blake. 2017. "Voids Matter: Donatello's *Lamentation of Christ* in the Victoria and Albert Museum." *Artibus et Historiae*: 77–93.

———. 2013. *Pliny and the Artistic Culture of the Italian Renaissance: The Legacy of the Natural History*. New Haven: Yale University Press.

McPhee, John. 1981. *Basin and Range*. New York: Palgrave Macmillan.

McTighe, Sheila. 2020. *Representing from Life in Seventeenth-Century Italy*. Amsterdam: Amsterdam University Press.

Meiss, Millard. 1964. *Giovanni Bellini's St. Francis in the Frick Collection*. Princeton: Princeton University Press.

Melnikas, Anthony. 1975. *The Corpus of the Miniatures in the Manuscripts of Decretum Gratiani*. Rome: Libreria Ateneo Salesiano.

Merback, Mitchell B. 2014. "Recognitions: Theme and Metatheme in Hans Burgkmair the Elder's *Santa Croce in Gerusalemme* of 1504." *Art Bulletin* 96: 288–318.

Merleau-Ponty, Maurice. 1993. "Indirect Language and the Voices of Silence." In *The Merleau-Ponty Aesthetics Reader: Philosophy and Painting*, edited by Galen A. Johnson, 76–120. Evanston: Northwestern University Press.

Meyer, Conrad Ferdinand. 1882. *Gedichte*. Leipzig: H. Haessel.

Meyer zur Capellen, Jürg and Claudio Falcucci. 2011. *The* Portrait of Baldassare Castiglione *and the* Madonna dell'Impannata Northwick*: Two Studies on Raphael*. New York: Peter Lang.

Michiel, Marcantonio. 2000. *Notizia d'opere del disegno*. Edited by Cristina De Benedictis. Florence: Edifir.

Miedema, Hessel, and Bert Meijer. 1979. "The Introduction of Coloured Ground in Painting and Its Influence on Stylistic Development, with Particular Respect to Sixteenth-Century Netherlandish Art." *Storia dell'arte* 35: 79–98.

Milanesi, Gaetano. 1887. "Documenti inediti dell'arte

toscana dal XII al XVI secolo." *Il Buonarroti* 2 Ser. 3: 335–38.

Molà, Luca. 2000. *The Silk Industry of Renaissance Venice.* Baltimore: Johns Hopkins University Press.

Monfardini, Pierpaolo. 2000. "Supporti lignei e sistemi di struttura: Techniche di costruzione e interventi di restauro." In *Il color ritrovato: Bellini a Venezia*, edited by Rona Goffen and Giovanna Nepi Sciré, 168–74. Venice: Gallerie dell'Accademia.

Morosini, Sergio Rossetti. 1999. "New Findings in Titian's Fresco Technique at the Scuola del Santo in Padua." *Art Bulletin* 81: 163–64.

Morrison, Toni. 2020. "Playing in the Dark: Whiteness and the Literary Imagination." In *Racism in America: A Reader*, edited by Annette Gordon-Reed, 1–9. Cambridge, MA: Harvard University Press.

Mostafavi, Mohsen, and David Leatherbarrow. 1993. *On Weathering: The Life of Buildings in Time.* Cambridge, MA: MIT Press.

Mulvaney, Beth A. 2015. "Elevated Vision: Bellini's *Annunciation* and the Nuns at Santa Maria dei Miracoli." In *The World of St. Francis of Assisi*, edited by Bradley R. Franco and Beth A. Mulvaney, 100–120. Leiden: Brill.

Mussolin, Mauro. 2012. "Deserti e crudi sassi: mito, vita religiosa e architetture alla Verna dalle origini al primo Quattrocento." In *Altro monte non ha più santo il mondo*, edited by Nicoletta Baldini, 117–36. Florence: Edizioni Studi Francescani.

Nadolny, Jilleen. 2010. "European Documentary Sources before c. 1550 relating to Painting Grounds Applied to Wooden Supports: Translation and Terminology." In *Preparation for Painting: The Artist's Choice and its Consequences*, edited by Joyce H. Townsend, Tiarna Doherty, Gunnar Heydenreich, and Jacqueline Ridge, 1–13. London: Archetype.

———. 1999. "Some Observations on Northern European Metalbeaters and Metal Leaf in the Late Middle Ages." In *The Materials, Technology, and Art of Conservation: Studies in the Honor of Lawrence J. Majewski*, edited by Rebecca Anne Rushfield and Mary W. Ballard, 134–60. New York: Conservation Center of the Institute of Fine Arts, New York University.

Nagel, Alexander. 2011. "Twenty-five Notes on Pseudoscript in Italian Art." *RES: Anthropology and Aesthetics* 59/60: 229–48.

Nagel, Alexander, and Christopher S. Wood. 2010. *Anachronic Renaissance.* New York: Zone Books.

Nehlsen-von Stryk, Karin, and Dieter Nörr, eds. 1985. *Diritto comune, diritto commerciale, diritto veneziano.* Venice: Centro tedesco di studi veneziani.

Neilson, Christina. 2019. "Bridging Dimensions: Verrocchio's *Christ and Saint Thomas* as Absent Presence." In Neilson, *Practice and Theory in the Italian Renaissance Workshop: Verrocchio and the Epistemology of Making Art*, 118–51. Cambridge: Cambridge University Press.

Nethersole, Scott. 2018. *Art and Violence in Early Renaissance Florence.* New Haven: Yale University Press.

Neuner, Stefan. 2017. "Canvas." In *Textile Terms: A Glossary*, edited by Anna Roehl, Mateusz Kapustka, and Tristan Weddigen, 29–32. Emsdetten: Edition Imorde.

———. 2009. "Topologische Wendungen bei Jasper Johns." In *Topologie: Falten, Knoten, Netze, Stülpungen in Kunst und Theorie*, edited by Wolfram Pichler and Ralph Ubl, 235–94. Munich: Turia & Kant.

Newton, Stella Mary. 1999. *Fashion in the Age of the Black Prince: A Study of the Years 1340–1365.* Suffolk: Boydell & Brewer.

Ng, Aimee. 2019. "Moroni and the Invention of Portraiture" In Ng, Facchinetti, and Galansino 2019, 31–57.

Ng, Aimee, Simone Facchinetti, and Arturo Galansino, eds. 2019. *Moroni: The Riches of Renaissance Portraiture.* New York: Frick Collection.

Nietzsche, Friedrich. 1996. *Human, All Too Human: A Book for Free Spirits.* Translated by R. J. Hollingdale. Cambridge: Cambridge University Press.

Nixdorff, Heide. 1999. *Das textile Medium als Phänomen der Grenze, Begrenzung, Entgrenzung.* Berlin: Reimer.

Nixon, S., Maria Filomena Guerra, and Thilo Rehren. 2011. "New Light on the Early Islamic West African Gold Trade: Coin Moulds from Tadmekka, Mali." *Antiquity* 85: 1353–68.

Nygren, Christopher. 2020. *Titian's Icons: Tradition, Charisma, and Devotion in Renaissance Italy.* University Park: Pennsylvania State University Press.

———. 2017. "Titian's *Ecce Homo* on Slate: Stone, Oil, and the Transubstantiation of Painting." *Art Bulletin* 99: 36–66.

Olson, Todd. 2014. *Caravaggio's Pitiful Relics.* New Haven: Yale University Press.

———. 2008. "Striking Through the Artist's Body: Ekphrasis in Bellori's Life of Caravaggio." In *Editing the Image: Strategies in the Production and Reception of the Visual*, edited by Mark A. Cheetham, Elizabeth Legge, and Catherine M. Soussloff, 15–30. Toronto: University of Toronto Press.

———. 2005. "Caravaggio's Coroner: Forensic Medicine in Giulio Mancini's Art Criticism." *Oxford Art Journal* 28: 83–98.

O'Malley, Michelle. 2005. *The Business of Art: Contracts and the Commissioning Process in Renaissance Italy.* New Haven: Yale University Press.

O'Malley, Michelle, and Evelyn Welch, eds. 2007. *The Material Renaissance.* Manchester: Manchester University Press.

Oxford Latin Dictionary. 1968. Edited by P.W.G. Glare. Oxford: Clarendon Press.

Pächt, Otto. 2003. *Venetian Painting in the 15th Century: Jacopo, Gentile and Giovanni Bellini and Andrea Mantegna*. Translated by Fiona Elliott. London: Harvey Miller.

Palladio, Andrea. 1997. *The Four Books on Architecture*. Translated by Rovert Tavernor and Richard Schofield. Cambridge, MA: MIT Press.

Pardo, Mary. 1984. "Paolo Pino's *Dialogo di pittura*: A Translation with Commentary." PhD diss., University of Pittsburgh.

Parker, K. T. 1956. *Catalogue of the Collection of Drawings in the Ashmolean Museum*. Vol. 2: *Italian Schools*. Oxford: Clarendon Press.

Paré, Ambroise. 1552. *La maniere de traicter les playes faictes tant par hacquebutes, que par fleches, & les accidentz d'icelles*, [. . .]. Paris: Arnoul L'Angelié.

Parlato, Enrico. 2007. "Pietro Aretino ritratto da Sebastiano del Piombo, 'stupendissimamente' descritto da Giorgio Vasari: Metamorforsi delle identità aretiniane." In "In utrumque paratus": *Aretino e Arezzo, Aretino a Arezzo; In margine dal ritratto di Sebastiano del Piombo*, edited by Paolo Procaccioli, 207–25. Rome: Salerno.

Pasco, Allan H. 1980. "Descriptive Narration in Balzac's *Gobseck*." *Virginia Quarterly Review* 56: 99–108.

Passeri, Irma. 2015. "Gold Leaf in Early Coins and Gold Italian Paintings." In *The Matter of Art: Materials, Practices, Cultural Logics, c. 1250–1750*, edited by Christy Anderson, Anne Dunlop, and Pamela H. Smith, 97–118. Manchester: Manchester University Press.

Pastoureau, Michel. 2009. *Black: The History of a Color*. Translated by Jody Gladding. Princeton: Princeton University Press.

———. 1986. *Figures et couleurs: Études sur la symbolique et la sensibilité médiévales*. Paris: Léopard d'Or.

Payne, Alina. 2014. "The Thin White Line: Palladio, White Cities and the Adriatic Imagination." In *Dalmatia and the Mediterranean: Portable Archaeology and the Poetics of Influence*, edited by Alina Payne, 145–82. Leiden: Brill.

———. 2013. "Renaissance *sgraffito* Facades and the Circulation of Objects in the Mediterranean." In *Synergies in Visual Culture*, edited by Annette Hoffmann and Nicola Suthor, 229–41. Paderborn: Wilhelm Fink.

———. 1998. "Creativity and Bricolage in Architectural Literature of the Renaissance." *RES: Anthropology and Aesthetics*: 20–38.

Pearson, Caspar. 2011. "Philosophy Defeated: Truth and Vision in Leon Battista Alberti's *Momus*." *Oxford Art Journal* 34: 1–12.

Pedrocchi, Anna Maria. 2000. *Le stanze del tesoriere: La quadreria Patrizi; Cultura senese nella storia del collezionismo romano del Seicento*. Milan: Alcon.

Penny, Nicholas. 2004. *Paintings from Bergamo, Brescia, and Cremona*. Vol. 1 of Penney, *The Sixteenth Century Italian Paintings*. London: National Gallery.

Penny, Nicholas, Ashok Roy, and Marika Spring. 1996. "Veronese's Paintings in the National Gallery, Techniques and Materials: Part II." *National Gallery Technical Bulletin* 17: 32–55.

Pericolo, Lorenzo. 2011. *Caravaggio and Pictorial Narrative: Dislocating the Istoria in Early Modern Painting*. London: Harvey Miller.

———. 2009. "The Invisible Presence: Cut-In, Close-Up, and Off-Scene in Antonello da Messina's Palermo *Annunciate*." *Representations* 107: 1–29.

Perogalli, Carlo, and Giovanni Battista Sannazzaro. 1982. "Le architetture fortificate negli arazzi Trivulzio e nei dipinti del Bramantino." *Rassegna di studi e di notizie* 10: 305–57.

Peselmann, Veronica. 2020. *Der Grund der Malerei: Materialität im Prozess bei Corot und Courbet*. Berlin: Reimer.

Petrarca, Francesco. 1995. *Petrarch's Songbook:* Rerum Vulgarium Fragmenta; *A Verse Translation*. Translated by James Wyatt Cook, with and edition of the Italian text by Gianfranco Contini (Medieval & Renaissance Texts & Studies 151). Binghamton: Center for Medieval and Early Renaissance Studies, State University of New York at Binghamton.

Pfisterer, Ulrich. 2001. "Künstlerliebe: Der Narcissus-Mythos bei Leon Battista Alberti und die Aristoteles-Lektüre der Frührenaissance." *Zeitschrift für Kunstgeschichte* 64: 305–30.

Pfisterer, Ulrich, and Max Seidel. 2003. *Visuelle Topoi: Erfindung und tradiertes Wissen in den Künsten der italienischen Renaissance*. Berlin: Deutscher Kunstverlag.

Pianigiani, Ottorino. 1988. *Vocabolario etimologico della lingua italiana*. Genoa: I Dioscuri.

Pichler, Wolfram, and Ralph Ubl. 2014. *Bildtheorie zur Einführung*. Hamburg: Junius Verlag.

Pincus, Deborah. 2008. "Giovanni Bellini's Humanist Signature: Pietro Bembo, Aldus Manutius and Humanism in Early Sixteenth-Century Venice." *Artibus et Historiae* 29: 89–119.

Pind, Jörgen L. 2014. *Edgar Rubin and Psychology in Denmark: Figure and Ground*. Cham: Springer.

Pino, Paolo. 1960. "Dialogo di pittura di Messer Paolo Pino nuovamente dato in luce. In Vinegia, per Pavolo Gherardo MDXLVIII." In *Trattati d'arte del Cinquecento, fra manierismo e Controriforma*, edited by Paola Barocchi, 93–139. Bari: Laterza.

Plesters, J. 1980. "Tintoretto's Paintings in the National Gallery: Part II." *National Gallery Technical Bulletin* 4: 32–48.

Plesters, Rosa Joyce, and Lorenzo Lazzarini. 1996. "I materiali e la tecnica dei Tintoretto della Scuola di San

Rocco." In *Jacopo Tintoretto nel quarto centenario della morte*, edited by Paola Rossi and Lionello Puppi, 275–80. Padua: Il Poligrafo.

Poldi, Gianluca, and Giovanni Carlo Federico Villa. 2011. "Analisi scientifiche (*Elemosina di sant'Antonino*)." In *Lotto in Veneto*, edited by Gianluca Poldi and Giovanni C. F. Villa, 106–9. Milan: Silvana.

Politi, Adriano. 1615. *Dittionario toscano compendio del vocabolario della Crusca*. Venice: Gio. Guerigli & Francesco Bolzetta.

Potocnik, Michele, and Giovanni C. F. Villa, eds. 2013. *Il paesaggio di Cima: Da Conegliano ai monti di Endimione*. Cornuda: Antiga.

Pozzi, Giovanni. 1984. "Temi, topoi, stereotipi." In *Teoria e poesia*, edited by Alberto Asor Rosa, 391–436. Vol. 1 of *Letteratura italiana 3: Le forme del testo*. Turin: Einaudi.

Pratesi, R., and G. Sabatelli, eds. 1958. *I fioretti di san Francesco*. Florence: Salani Editore.

Preimesberger, Rudolf. 2011. *Paragons and Paragone: Van Eyck, Raphael, Michelangelo, Caravaggio, and Bernini*. Los Angeles: Getty Research Institute.

Premoli, Beatrice. 2005. *Giovanni Andrea dell'Anguillara: Accademico sdegnato ed etereo, 1517–1572*. Rome: Fondazione Marco Besso.

Preyer, Brenda. 2015. "Palazzo Tornabuoni in 1498: A Palace 'In Progress' and Its Interior Arrangement." *Mitteilungen des Kunsthistorischen Institutes in Florenz*, 57: 42–63.

Pringle, Denys. 1993–2009. *The Churches of the Crusader Kingdom of Jerusalem: A Corpus*. 4 vols. Cambridge: Cambridge University Press.

Puglisi, Catherine. 2019. Review of *Rencontres à Venise: Étrangers et Vénitiens dans l'art du XVIIe siècle*, edited by Linda Borean and Sefania Mason Rinaldi. *caa.reviews*. https://doi.org/10.3202/caa.reviews.2019.10

———. 1998. *Caravaggio*. London: Phaidon.

Puttfarken, Thomas. 2000. *The Discovery of Pictorial Composition: Theories of Visual Order in Painting, 1400–1800*. New Haven: Yale University Press.

Quondam, Amedeo. 2003. *Cavallo e cavaliere: L'armatura come seconda pelle del gentiluomo moderno*. Rome: Donzelli.

Racco, Tiffany A. 2016. "Darkness in a Positive Light: Negative Theology in Caravaggio's *Conversion of Saint Paul*." *Artibus et Historiae* 73: 285–98.

Rachman-Schrire, Yamit. 2019. "Christ's Side-Wound and Francis' Stigmatization at La-Verna: Reflections on the Rock of Golgotha." In Augart, Saß, and Wenderholm 2019, 45–58. Berlin: De Gruyter.

———. 2012. "Evagatorium in Terrae Sanctae [. . .]: Stones Telling the Story of Jerusalem." In *Jerusalem as Narrative Space / Erzählraum Jerusalem*, edited by Annette Hoffmann and Gerhard Wolf, 353–66. Leiden: Brill.

Rand Olan A., Jr. 1983. "Philippe de Champaigne and the *Ex-Voto* of 1662: A Historical Perspective." *Art Bulletin* 65: 78–93.

Real Academia Española. 1737. *Diccionario de Autoridades*. Madrid: Francisco del Hierro.

Reilly, Patricia L. 1992. "The Taming of the Blue: Writing Out Color in Italian Renaissance Theory." In *The Expanding Discourse: Feminism and Art History*, edited by Norma Broude and Mary D. Garrard, 86–99. New York: Routledge.

Rice, Louise. 1997. *The Altars and Altarpieces of New St. Peter's: Outfitting the Basilica, 1621–1666*. Cambridge: Cambridge University Press.

Riedmatten, Henri de. 2011. *Narcisse en eaux troubles: Francis Bacon, Bill Viola, Jeff Wall*. Rome: "L'Erma" di Bretschneider.

Riegl, Alois. 1985. *Late Roman Art Industry*. Translated by Rolf Winkes. Rome: Giorgio Bretschneider.

———. 1901. *Die Spätrömische kunst-Industrie nach den Funden in Österreich-Ungarn im zusammenhange mit der Gesammtentwicklung der bildenden Künste bei den Mittelmeervölkern*. Vol. 1. Vienna: K. K. Hof- und Staatsdruckerei.

Romano, Elisa. 1987. *La capanna e il tempio: Vitruvio o dell'-architettura*. Palermo: Palumbo.

Rosand, David. 1983. "The Portrait, the Courtier, and Death." In *Castiglione: The Ideal and the Real in Renaissance Culture*, edited by Robert W. Hanning and David Rosand, 91–130. New Haven: Yale University Press.

———. 1982. *Painting in Cinquecento Venice: Titian, Veronese, Tintoretto*. Cambridge: Cambridge University Press.

Rosen, Valeska von. 2013. "Caravaggio, Marino und ihre 'wahren Regeln': Zum Dialog der Malerei und Literatur um 1600." In *Barocke Bildkulturen*, edited by Rainer Stillers and Christiane Kruse, 307–33, 468, 478. Wiesbaden: Harrassowitz.

Rosenberg, Gary D. 2001. "An Artistic Perspective on the Continuity of Space and the Origin of Modern Geologic Thought." *Earth Sciences History* 20: 127–55.

Rosser, Gervase. 2012. "Beyond Naturalism in Art and Poetry: Duccio and Dante on the Road to Emmaus." *Art History* 35: 474–97.

Rossi, Francesco. 2015–16. "Sui ritratti 'spagnoli' di Giovanni Battista Moroni." *Bergomum* 109: 89–110.

Rothe, Andrea, and Dawson W. Carr. 1998. "The Technique of Dosso Dossi: Poetry with Paint." In *Dosso Dossi: Court Painter in Renaissance Ferrara*, edited by Peter Humfrey and Mauro Lucco, 55–64. New York: Metropolitan Museum of Art.

Rubin, James Henry. 1992. "The People's Hand: David's 'Unfinished' Backgrounds and Paradigms of Revolutionary Representation." In *L' art au temps de la*

Révolution française, edited by Robert Rosenblum, 19–34. Strasbourg: Société alsacienne pour le développement de l'histoire de l'art.

Rubin, Patricia L. 2007. *Portraits by the Artist as a Young Man: Parmigianino, ca. 1524*. Groningen: Gerson Lectures Foundation.

———. 2006. "Signposts of Invention: Artists' Signatures in Italian Renaissance Art." *Art History* 29: 563–99.

Rudolph, Pia. 2011. "Goldenes Mittelalter: Zur Verwendung von Gold im Hoch- und Spätmittelalter aus kunsthistorischer Sicht unter besonderer Berücksichtigung des Goldgrunds." In *Farbe im Mittelalter: Materialität, Medialität, Semantik*, edited by Ingrid Bennewitz and Andrea Schindler, vol. 1: 283–96. Berlin: Akademie Verlag.

Ruffini, Marco. 2011. "Alberti on the Surface." *California Italian Studies* 2. https://escholarship.org/uc/item/3pd1g732

Rutherglen, Susannah. 2016. "Painting at the Threshold: Pictures for Doors in Renaissance Venice." *Art Bulletin* 98: 438–65.

———. 2015. "The Desert and the City: Marcantonio Michiel and the Early History of St. Francis." In Rutherglen and Hale 2015a, 47–57. New York: Frick Collection.

Rutherglen, Susannah, and Charlotte Hale, eds. 2015a. *In a New Light: Giovanni Bellini's* St. Francis in the Desert. New York: Frick Collection.

———. 2015b. "*St. Francis in the Desert*: Technique and Meaning." In Rutherglen and Hale 2015a, 80–131. New York: Frick Collection.

Rykwert, Joseph. 1972. *On Adam's House in Paradise: The Idea of the Primitive Hut in Architectural History*. New York: Museum of Modern Art.

Rylands, Philip. 1992. *Palma Vecchio*. Cambridge: Cambridge University Press.

Rzepińska, Maria 1986. "Tenebrism in Baroque Painting and Its Ideological Background." *Artibus et Historiae* 7: 91–112.

Sabbatino, Pasquale. 2004. "La scrittura dell'arte nelle *Vite* di Bellori e la pittura di Caravaggio." In *Storia della lingua e storia dell'arte in Italia*, edited by Vittorio Casale and Paolo D'Achille, 257–74. Florence: Cesati.

Sachs, Hans. 2009. *A Sixteenth-Century Book of Trades: Das Ständebuch*. Translated by Theodore K. Rabb. Palo Alto: Society for the Promotion of Science and Scholarship.

Salter, Emma G. 1912. *Nature in Italian Art: A Study of Landscape Backgrounds from Giotto to Tintoretto*. London: Adam & Charles Black.

Sandrart, Joachim von. 1675. *Teutsche Academie der edlen Bau-, Bild- und Mahlerey-Künste*, vol. 2. Nuremberg: Bey J. von Sandrart.

Sapir, Itay. 2017. "Shadowy Realism." *Nuncius* 32: 640–57.

———. 2012. *Ténèbres sans leçons: Esthétique et épistémologie de la peinture ténébriste romaine 1595–1610*. New York: Peter Lang.

Saslow, James M. 1991. *The Poetry of Michelangelo*. New Haven: Yale University Press.

Saunders, David, and Jo Kirby. 1994. "Light-Induced Colour Changes in Red and Yellow Lake Pigments." *National Gallery Technical Bulletin* 15: 79–97.

Scannone, J. C. 1980. "Un nuevo punto de partida en la filosofia latinoamericana." *Stromata* 36: 25–47.

Schäffner, Almut. 2009. Terra verde*: Entwicklung und Bedeutung der monochromen Wandmalerei der italienischen Renaissance*. Weimar: VDG.

Schapiro, Meyer. 1972–73. "On Some Problems in the Semiotics of Visual Art: Field and Vehicle in Image-Signs." *Simiolus: Netherlands Quarterly for the History of Art* 6: 9–19.

Scharf, Friedhelm. 2001. *Der Freskenzyklus des Pellegrinaios in S. Maria della Scala zu Siena: Historienmalerei und Wirklichkeit in einem Hospital der Frührenaissance*. Hildesheim: Olms.

Schleier, Erich. 1991. "Savoldos *Magdalena* in der Berliner Gemäldegalerie: Zur Wiederstellung eines Meisterwerks der Brescianer Cinquecentomalerei." *Jahrbuch der Berliner Museen* 33: 135–47.

Schmitter, Monika Anne. 2003. "The Dating of Marcantonio Michiel's *Notizia* on Works of Art in Padua." *Burlington Magazine* 145: 564–71.

———. 1997. "The Display of Distinction: Art Collecting and Social Status in Early Sixteenth-Century Venice." PhD diss., University of Michigan.

Schofield, Richard V. and Giulia Ceriani Sebregondi. 2006–7. "Bartolomeo Bon, Filarete e le case di Francesco Sforza a Venezia." *Annali di architettura* 18/19: 9–51.

Schöne, Wolfgang. 1954. *Über das Licht in der Malerei*. Berlin: Gebr. Mann Verlag.

Schulz, Vera-Simone. 2016a. "Bild, Ding, Material: Nimben und Goldgründe italienischer Tafelmalerei in transkulturellen Perspektive." *Zeitschrift für Kunstgeschichte* 79: 508–41.

———. 2016b. "Intricate Letters and the Reification of Light: Prolegomena on the Pseudo-Inscribed Haloes in Giotto's *Madonna di San Giorgio alla Costa* and Masaccio's San Giovenale Triptych." *Mitteilungen des Kunsthistorischen Institutes in Florenz* 58: 59–93.

Schulze, Sebastian. 2015. *Metamorphosen des Echos: Lektüren der gehörten Stimme in Barock, Romantik und Gegenwart; Lektüren der gehörten Stimme in Barock, Romantik und Gegenwart*. Paderborn: Wilhelm Fink.

Schüppel, Katharina Christa, and Irene Brückle. 2008. "Zur Ästhetik des Monochromen um 1400: Zwei Zeichnungen Lorenzo Monacos aus der Sammlung des Berliner Kupferstichkabinetts." In *Fantasie und*

Handwerk: Cennino Cennini und die Tradition der toskanischen Malerei von Giotto bis Lorenzo Monaco, edited by Wolf-Dietrich Löhr und Stefan Weppelmann, 201–23. Munich: Hirmer.

Schwarz, Michael Viktor. 2012. "The Gold Ground in the Middle Ages: 'Don't Ask for the Meaning, Ask for the Use!'" In *Gold: Artists in Gold; Tradition and Today*, edited by Agnes Husslein-Arco and Thomas Zaunschirm, 28–37. Vienna: Belvedere.

Scribner, Charles, III. 1977. "*In Alia Effigie*: Caravaggio's London *Supper at Emmaus*." *Art Bulletin* 59: 375–82.

Seifertova, Hana. 2007. *Malby na kameni: Umělecký experiment v 16. a na začátku 17. století / Painting on Stone: An Artistic Experiment in the 16th and Early 17th Centuries*. Prague: National Gallery Prague.

Serlio, Sebastiano. 2001. *Books VI and VII of 'Tutte l'opere d'architettura et prospetiva' with 'Castrametation of the Romans' and 'The Extraordinary Book of Doors' by Sebastiano Serlio*. Vol. 2 of *Sebastiano Serlio on Architecture*, edited and translated by Vaughan Hart and Peter Hicks. New Haven: Yale University Press.

———. 1996. *Books I–V of 'Tutte l'opere d'architettura e prospetiva' by Sebastiano Serlio*. Vol. 1 of *Sebastiano Serlio on Architecture*. Edited and translated by Vaughan Hart and Peter Hicks. New Haven and London: Yale University Press.

Serres, Michel. 1991. *Rome: The Book of Foundations*. Stanford: Stanford University Press.

Sframeli, Maria, Valentina Conticelli, Riccardo Gennaioli, and Gian Carlo Parodi, eds. 2015. *Lapislazzuli: Magia del blu*. Livorno: Sillabe.

Shearman, John. 2003. *Raphael in Early Modern Sources, 1483–1602*. 2 vols. New Haven: Yale University Press.

———. 1995. "Refraction, and Reflection." *Studies in the History of Art* 48: 212–21.

———. 1992. *Only Connect: Art and the Spectator in the Italian Renaissance*. Princeton: Princeton University Press.

———. 1984. "A Functional Interpretation of Villa Madama." *Römisches Jahrbuch für Kunstgeschichte* 20: 313–27.

———. 1972. *Raphael's Cartoons in the Collection of Her Majesty the Queen, and the Tapestries for the Sistine Chapel*. London: Phaidon.

Shildrick, Margrit. 2015. "'Why Should Our Bodies End at the Skin?': Embodiment, Boundaries, and Somatechnics." *Hypatia* 30: 13–29.

Silver, Nathaniel E. 2018. *Fra Angelico: Heaven on Earth*. London: Paul Holberton.

———, ed. 2013. *Piero della Francesca in America: From Sansepolcro to the East Coast*. New York: Frick Collection.

Silverman, Kaja. 2010. *Flesh of My Flesh*. Stanford: Stanford University Press.

———. Forthcoming. *The Three-Personed Picture, or the History of Photography, Part 2*.

Skaug, Erling S. 2008a. "Not Just Panel and Gound." In *Preparation for Painting: The Artist's Choice and its Consequences*, edited by Joyce H. Townsend, Tiarna Doherty, Gunnar Heydenreich, and Jacqueline Ridge, 22–29. London: Archetype.

———. 2008b. "Painters, Punchers, Gilders or Goldbeaters? A Critical Survey Report of Discussions in Recent Literature about Early Italian Painting." *Zeitschrift für Kunstgeschichte* 71: 571–82.

Sohm, Philip. 2014. "Interactive Painting and the Empathic Viewer." Paper presented at the Annual Meeting of the Renaissance Society of America, New York, March 27.

———. 2002. "Caravaggio's Deaths." *Art Bulletin* 84: 449–68.

———. 1991. *Pittoresco: Marco Boschini, His Critics, and Their Critiques of Painterly Brushwork in Seventeenth- and Eighteenth-Century Italy*. Cambridge: Cambridge University Press.

Soria Mesa, Enrique. 1997. *La biblioteca genealógica de don Luis de Salazar y Castro*. Córdoba: University of Córdoba.

Sorrell, Roger D. 1988. *St. Francis of Assisi and Nature: Tradition and Innovation in Western Christian Attitudes toward the Environment*. Oxford: Oxford University Press.

Sorte, Cristoforo. 1960. "Osservazioni nella pittura." In *Trattati d'arte del Cinquecento*, edited by Paola Barocchi, 273–301. Bari: Laterza.

Spallanzani, Marco. 2010. *Metalli islamici a Firenze nel Rinascimento*. Florence: S.P.E.S.

———. 2007. *Oriental Rugs in Renaissance Florence*. Translated by Anna Moore Valeri. Florence: S.P.E.S.

Sparti, Donatella Livia. 2008. "Novità su Giulio Mancini: Medicina, arte e presunta 'Connoisseurship'." *Mitteilungen des Kunsthistorischen Institutes in Florenz* 52: 53–72.

Spencer, John R. 1970. "The *Cà del Duca* in Venice and Benedetto Ferrini." *Journal of the Society of Architectural Historians* 29: 3–8.

Spengler, Oswald. 1926. *Form and Actuality*. Vol. 1 of Spengler, *The Decline of the West*. Translated by Charles Francis Atkinson. New York: A. A. Knopf.

Speroni, Sperone. 1560. *Dialoghi: Nuovamente ristampati, & con molta diligenza riveduti, & corretti*. Venice: Francesco Lorenzini da Turino.

Spezzaferro, Luigi. 2000. "Caravaggio." In *L'idea del bello: Viaggio per Roma nel Seicento con Giovan Pietro Bellori*, edited by Carlo Gasparri and Evelina Borea, 271–82. Rome: De Luca.

———. 1983. "Ferrara–Roma, 1598–1621: Un rapporto di indirette coincidenze." In *Frescobaldi e il suo tempo nel quarto centenario della nascita*, edited by Jadranka Bentini, 113–28. Venice: Marsilio.

———. 1974. "La Pala dei Palafrenieri." In *Colloquio sul tema: Caravaggio e i caravaggeschi*, 125–37. Rome: Accademia Nazionale dei Lincei.

Steinberg, Leo. 1996. *The Sexuality of Christ in Renaissance Art and in Modern Oblivion*. 2nd ed. Chicago: University of Chicago Press.

Steingräber, Erich. 1969. "Nachträger und Marginalien zur französisch-niederländische Goldschmiedekunst des frühen 15. Jahrhunderts." *Anzeiger des Germanischen Nationalmuseums*: 30–35.

Stockinger, Claudia. 2010. *Das 19. Jahrhundert: Zeitalter des Realismus*. Berlin: De Gruyter.

Stoichita, Victor I. 2016. "The Perfectible Body: Splendour and Misery of Renaissance Armor." In *Iconologie: Studi in onore di Claudia Cieri Via*, edited by Ilaria Miarelli Mariani, Stefano Pierguidi, and Marco Ruffini, 231–40. Rome: Campisano Editore.

———. 2015. *The Self-Aware Image: An Insight into Early Modern Metapainting*. Edited by Lorenzo Pericolo. Translated by Anne-Marie Glasheen. London: Harvey Miller.

———. 2012. "'La seconde peau': Quelques considérations sur le symbolisme des armures au XVIe siècle." *Micrologus* 20: 451–63.

———. 1997. *A Short History of the Shadow*. Translated by Anne-Marie Glasheen. London: Reaktion Books.

Stolfi, Giuseppe. 2005. "Riflessioni sulla cappella Trivulzio in San Nazaro a Milano." In *Aspetti dell'abitare e del costruire a Roma e in Lombardia tra XV e XIX secolo*, edited by Augusto Rossari and Aurora Scotti, 279–95.

Stols-Witlox, Maartje. 2018. *A Perfect Ground: Preparatory Layers for Oil Paintings 1550–1900*. London: Archetype.

Stone, David M. 2012. "Signature Killer: Caravaggio and the Poetics of Blood." *Art Bulletin* 94: 572–93.

Stone, David M., and Lorenzo Pericolo. 2014. *Caravaggio: Reflections and Refractions*. Burlington: Ashgate.

Strehlke, Carl Brandon. 2004. *Italian Paintings, 1250–1450, in the John G. Johnson Collection and the Philadelphia Museum of Art*. Philadelphia: Philadelphia Museum of Art.

Strehlke, Carl Brandon, and Machtelt Brüggen Israëls, eds. 2015. *The Bernard and Mary Berenson Collection of European Paintings at I Tatti*. Florence: Villa I Tatti.

Stumpel, Jeroen. 1990. "The Province of Painting: Theories of Italian Renaissance Art." PhD diss., Utrecht University.

———. 1988. "On Grounds and Backgrounds: Some Remarks about Composition in Renaissance Painting." *Simiolus: Netherlands Quarterly for the History of Art* 18: 219–43.

Summers, David. 2018. "Emphasis: On Light, Dark, and Distance." In *Chiaroscuro als aesthetisches Prinzip: Kunst und Theorie des Helldunkels 1300–1550*, edited by Claudia Lehmann, Norberto Gramaccini, Johannes Rössler, and Thomas Dittelbach, 165–88. Berlin: De Gruyter.

———. 2003. *Real Spaces: World Art History and the Rise of Western Modernism*. London: Phaidon.

Susenbrotus, Johann. 1608. *Epitome troporum ac schematum, et grammaticorum et rhetoricorum*. London: Societatis Stationariorum.

Sutcliffe, John. 2013. *The Colours of Rome: An Examination of the Use of Colour on the Façades of Today's Rome, with Historical and Other Notes, and a Selection of Colours Copied on Site*. Bath: Old School Press.

Suthor, Nicola. 2018. *Rembrandt's Roughness*. Princeton: Princeton University Press.

———. 2010. *Bravura: Virtuosität und Mutwilligkeit in der Malerei der frühen Neuzeit*. Paderborn: Wilhelm Fink.

Syson, Luke. 1999. "Ercole de' Roberti: The Making of a Court Artist." *Burlington Magazine* 141: v–xiv.

Szafran, Yvonne. 1995. "Carpaccio's *Hunting on the Lagoon*: A New Perspective." *Burlington Magazine* 137: 148–58.

Tardito, Rosalba. 1990. *Ritrovamento del corpo di San Marco del Tintoretto: Vicende e restauri*. Florence: Cantini.

Tassi, Francesco Maria. 1793. *Vite de' pittori, scultori e architetti Bergamaschi*. 2 vols. Bergamo: Locatelli.

Taygetus, Johannes Antonius, ed. 1566. *Carmina praestantium poetarum, Io. Antonij Taygeti academici occulti studio ex quamplurimis selecta*. Brescia: Apud Io. Baptistam Bozolam.

Taylor, Paul. 2015. *Condition: The Ageing of Art*. London: Paul Holberton.

Terraroli, Valerio, ed. 2011. *Scultura in Lombardia: Arti plastiche a Brescia e nel Bresciano dal XV al XX secolo*. Milan: Skira.

Theoderich of Würzburg. 2016. "Guide to the Holy Land." In *The Holy Land in the Middle Ages: Six Travelers' Accounts*, 127–215. New York: Italica Press.

Thimann, Michael. 2006. "'Fece senza ritrarlo l'imagine sua': Mimesis, *capriccio* und *invenzione* in Parmigianinos Portraets." In *Parmigianino: Zitat, Porträt, Mythos*, edited by Alessandro Nova, 65–77. Perugia: Guerra.

Thissen-Lorenz, Rebekka. 2014. "Space, Power, Chart: The Catalan Atlas (ca. 1375)." In *Representations of Power at the Mediterranean Borders of Europe (12th–14th Centuries)*, edited by Ingrid Baumgärtner, Mirko Vagnoni, and Megan Welton, 103–17. Florence: SISMEL.

Thornton, Peter. 1991. *The Italian Renaissance Interior, 1400–1600*. New York: H. N. Abrams.

Tilghman, Benjamin C. 2016. "Ornament and Incarnation in Insular Art." *Gesta* 55: 157–77.

Tiraboschi, Giampiero. 2016. *Giovan Battista Moroni: L'uomo e l'artista*. Bergamo: Tera Mata.

Tizio, Sigismondo. 1998. *Historiae senenses*. Edited by Petra Pertici. Vol. 3. Rome: Istituto storico italiano per l'età moderna e contemporanea.

Tomassetti, Luigi, ed. 1862. *Bullarum, diplomatum et*

privilegiorum sanctorum Romanorum pontificum. Vol. 7. Turin: Franco & Dalmazzo.

Tomìo, Luca. 2002. "Bramantino e gli arazzi dei mesi Trivulzio: Dalla rustica classicità alla maniera moderna." *Rassegna di studi e di notizie* 26: 299–350.

Torre, Carlo. 1674. *Il ritratto di Milano diviso in tre libri*. Milan: Agnelli.

Trachtenberg, Marvin. 2005. "Building Outside Time in Alberti's *De re aedificatoria*." *RES: Anthropology and Aesthetics* 48: 123–34.

Tripps, Johannes. 2008. "'Nimm Steine, rauh und nicht gereinigt': Cennino Cennini und das Gebirge als kunsttheoretisches Studienobjekt in der Malerei des Trecento." In *Fantasie und Handwerk: Cennino Cennini und die Tradition der toskanischen Malerei von Giotto bis Lorenzo Monaco*, edited by Wolf-Dietrich Löhr and Stefan Weppelmann, 109–19. Munich: Hirmer.

Tucker, Elizabeth. Forthcoming. "Translator's Introduction." In *The Selected Essays of Henry van de Velde*. Los Angeles: Getty Publications.

Ubertino da Casale. 2001. "The Tree of the Crucified Life of Jesus: Book Five." In *Francis of Assisi: Early Documents*, edited by Regis J. Armstrong, J. A. Wayne Hellmann, and William J. Short, 141–206. Vol. 3. New York: New City Press.

UNESCO. 1960. "The Care of Paintings: Fabric Paint Supports." *Museum* 13: 135–71.

———. 1955. "The Care of Paintings: The Care of Wood Panels." *Museum* 8: 139–94.

Vaccaro, Mary. 2002. *Parmigianino: The Paintings*. Turin: U. Allemandi.

Valseriati, Enrico. 2016. "Cultura e politica a Brescia nella prima età moderna: Il ruolo delle *laudes urbium*." *Archivio storico italiano* 174: 483–98.

Varriano, John. 2006. *Caravaggio: The Art of Realism*. University Park: Pennsylvania State University Press.

Vasari, Giorgio. 1996. *Lives of the Painters, Sculptors, and Architects*. Edited by David Ekserdjian. Translated by Gaston du C. de Vere. 2 vols. New York: Alfred A. Knopf.

———. 1991. *Le vite de' più eccellenti architetti, pittori, et scultori italiani, da Cimabue insino a' tempi nostri, nell'edizione per i tipi di Lorenzo Torrentino, Firenze 1550*. Edited by Luciano Bellosi and Aldo Rossi. 2 vols. Turin: Einaudi.

———. 1907. *Vasari on Technique*. Edited by G. Baldwin Brown. Translated by Louisa S. Maclehose. London: J. M. Dent & Company.

———. 1588. *Ragionamenti del Sig. cavaliere Giorgio Vasari, pittore et architetto aretino, sopra le inuentioni da lui dipinte in Firenze nel palazzo di Loro Altezze Serenissime*. Florence: F. Giunti.

———. 1568. *Le vite de' piv eccellenti pittori, scvltori, e architettori, scritte da M. Giorgio Vasari, pittore et architetto aretino. Di nuouo dal medesimo riuiste et ampliate con i ritratti loro et con l'aggiunta dell evite de' viui, & de' morti dall'anno 1550 insino al 1567*. 3 vols. Florence: Giunti.

——— 1550. *Le vite de piv eccellenti architetti, pittori, et scvltori italiani, da Cimabve insino a' tempi nostri, descritte in lingua toscana, da Giorgio Vasari, pittore aretino; con vna sua vtile & necessaria introduzzione a le arti loro*. 2 vols. Florence: Lorenzo Torrentino.

Verougstraete, Hélène. 2006. "Diptychs with Instructions for Use." In *Essays in Context: Unfolding the Netherlandish Diptych*, edited by John Oliver Hand and Ron Spronk, 161–62. New Haven: Yale University Press.

Vesalius, Andreas. 1998. *Book 1: The Bones and Cartilages; A Translation of* De humani corporis fabrica libri septem. Vol. 1 of *On the Fabric of the Human Body*, translated by William Frank Richardson and John Burd Carman. San Francisco: Norman Publishing.

Vesely, Dalibor. 2002. "The Architectonics of Embodiment." In *Body and Building: Essays on the Changing Relation of Body and Architecture*, edited by George Dodds and Robert Tavernor, 28–43. Cambridge, MA: MIT Press.

Villa, Giovanni C. F. 2013. "Il paesaggio di Cima, e il nostro." In *Il paesaggio di Cima: Da Conegliano ai monti di Endimione*, edited by Michele Potočnik and Giovanni Carlo Federico Villa, 24–63. Crocetta del Montello: Antiga, 2013

———, ed. 2010. *Cima da Conegliano: Poeta del paesaggio*. Venice: Marsilio.

Vitale-Brovarone, Alessandro. 1987. *Il Codice varia 124 della Biblioteca reale di Torino, miniato da Cristoforo De Predis (Milano, 1476)*. 2 vols. Turin: U. Allemandi.

Vitruvius, Pollio. 1983. *De architectura / On Architecture*. Translated by F. Granger. 2 vols. Cambridge, MA: Harvard University Press.

Vodret, Rossella. 2016. "Introductory Notes on Caravaggio's Technique of Execution." In *Caravaggio, opere a Roma: Tecnica e stile / Works in Rome: Technique and Style*, edited by Rossella Vodret, Giorgio Leone, Marco Cardinali, Maria Beatrice De Ruggieri, and Giulia Silvia Ghia, vol. 1 (*Saggi / Entries*), 17–51. Milan: Silvana.

———. 1998. "Catalogue of Exhibited Works." In *Caravaggio and His Italian Followers from the Collections of the Galleria Nazionale d'Arte Antica di Roma*, edited by Rossella Vodret and Claudio Strinati, 59–123. Venice: Marsilio.

———. 1995. *Caravaggio e la collezione Mattei*. Milan: Electa.

Vodret Adamo, Rossella. 2010. *Caravaggio e Roma*. Cinisello Balsamo, Milan: Silvana.

Volpin, Stefano, and Lorenzo Lazzarini. 1994. "Il colore e la tecnica pittorica della Pala di San Giobbe di Giovanni

Bellini." *Quaderni della Soprintendenza ai beni artistici e storici di Venezia* 19: 29–37.

Volta, Valentino. 2014. *Intorno alle mura: Brescia medievale*. Rome: Studium.

Wagner, Monika. 2013. "Notes from the Field: Materiality." *Art Bulletin* 95: 28–31.

Warburg, Aby. 1999. *The Renewal of Pagan Antiquity: Contributions to the Cultural History of the European Renaissance*. Edited by Kurt Walter Forster. Los Angeles: Getty Research Institute.

Ward, R. M. 1993. *Islamic Metalwork*. London: British Museum Press.

Wardropper, Ian. 2011. *European Sculpture, 1400–1900, in the Metropolitan Museum of Art*. New York: Metropolitan Museum of Art.

Warwick, Genevieve. 2006. *Caravaggio: Realism, Rebellion, Reception*. Newark: University of Delaware Press.

Ważbiński, Zygmunt. 1963. "Le 'cartellino': Origine et avatars d'une etiquette." *Pantheon* 21: 278–83.

Weber, Karl Heinz. 1984. "Die Sixtinische Madonna." *Maltechnik, Restauro* 90: 9–28.

Weddigen, Tristan. 2015. "Weaving the Face of Christ: On the Textile Origins of the Christian Image." In *Senses of Sight: Towards a Multisensorial Approach of the Image; Essays in Honor of Victor I. Stoichita*, edited by Henri de Riedmatten, Nicolas Galley, Jean-François Corpataux, and Valentin Nussbaum, 83–110. Rome: "L'Erma" di Bretschneider.

———. 2013. "Unfolding Textile Spaces: Antiquity/Modern Period." In *Art and Textiles: Fabric as Material and Concept in Modern Art from Klimt to the Present*, edited by Markus Brüderlin, 88–102. Ostfildern: Hatje Cantz.

———. 2006. *Raffaels Papageienzimmer: Ritual, Raumfunktion und Dekoration im Vatikanpalast der Renaissance*. Edited by Raphael. Emsdetten: Edition Imorde.

Weddigen, Tristan and Gregor J. M. Weber. 2010. "Alchemie der Farben. Tizian porträtiert seinen Farbenhändler Alvise 'dai colori' dalla Scala." In *Tizian:* Die Dame in Weiß, edited by Andreas Henning and Günter Ohlhoff, 47–59. Dresden: Sandstein Verlag.

Weigel, Sigrid. 2001. "Die Richtung des Bildes: Zum Links–Rechts von Bilderzählungen und Bildbeschreibungen in kultur- und mediengeschichtlicher Perspektive." *Zeitschrift für Kunstgeschichte* 64: 449–74.

Weinstein, Donald. 2011. *Savonarola: The Rise and Fall of a Renaissance Prophet*. New Haven: Yale University Press.

Wenderholm, Iris. 2005. "Aura, Licht und schöner Schein: Wertungen und Umwertungen des Goldgrunds." In *Geschichten auf Gold: Bilderzählungen in der frühen italienischen Malerei*, edited by Stefan Weppelmann, 100–113. Berlin: SMB-DuMont.

Weppelmann, Stefan. 2008. "'Storia o ffighura': Objektstatus und Kontext der Berliner Tafeln Cenninis und Überlegungen zur Werkstatt des Agnolo Gaddi." In *Fantasie und Handwerk: Cennino Cennini und die Tradition der toskanischen Malerei von Giotto bis Lorenzo Monaco*, edited by Wolf-Dietrich Löhr and Stefan Weppelmann, 57–79. Munich: Hirmer.

Wetering, Ernst van de. 2009. *Rembrandt: The Painter at Work*. Amsterdam: Amsterdam University Press.

Wharton, Edith. 1905. *Italian Backgrounds*. New York: Charles Scribner's Sons.

Wiemers, Michael. 1996. *Bildform und Werkgenese: Studien zur zeichnerischen Bildvorbereitung in der italienischen Malerei zwischen 1450 und 1490*. Berlin: Deutscher Kunstverlag.

Wilkinson, John. 1977. *Jerusalem Pilgrims before the Crusades*. Jerusalem: Ariel.

Williams, Gareth D. 2017. *Pietro Bembo on Etna: The Ascent of a Venetian Humanist*. Oxford: Oxford University Press.

Williams, Robert. 2017. *Raphael and the Redefinition of Art in Renaissance Italy*. Cambridge: Cambridge University Press.

———. 1997. *Art, Theory, and Culture in Sixteenth-Century Italy: From Techne to Metatechne*. Cambridge: Cambridge University Press.

Wilson, Bronwen. 2016. "Giovanni Battista Moroni, Portraiture, and the Ethics of Early Modern Conversation." In *Heidegger and the Work of Art History*, edited by Amanda Boetzkes and Aron Vinegar, 79–100. New York and London: Routledge.

Wilson, Carolyn C. 2019. "Moving Forward: Bellini's Pesaro Altarpiece in View of New Advances." In *Giovanni Bellini: ". . . il migliore nella pittura,"* edited by Peter Humfrey, Vincenzo Mancini, Anchise Tempestini, and Giovanni Carlo Federico Villa, 89–102. Venice: Fondazione Giorgio Cini.

———. 1977. "Giovanni Bellini's Pesaro Altarpiece: Studies in Its Context and Meaning." PhD diss., New York University.

Wipfler, Esther P. 2017. "'Mit solchen Farbschattierungen hat der Schoepfer seines Ebenbildes unsere Natur gekennzeichnet.' (Gregor von Nyssa): Schriften zur Theologie des Bildes als Quellen zur Kunsttechnik." In *Inkarnat und Signifi kanz: Das menschliche Abbild in der Tafelmalerei von 200 bis 1250 im Mittelmeerraum*, edited by Yvonne Schmuhl and Esther P. Wipfler, 42–50. Munich: Zentralinstitut für Kunstgeschichte.

Wittekind, Susanne. 1996. "Vom Schriftband zum Spruchband: Zum Funktionswandel von Spruchbändern in Illustrationen biblischer Stoffe." *Frühmittelalterliche Studien* 30: 343–67.

Wittkower, Rudolf. 1999. *Art and Architecture in Italy, 1600–1750*. New Haven: Yale University Press.

Wolf, Gerhard. 1999. "The Origins of Painting." *RES: Anthropology and Aesthetics* 36: 60–78.

———. 1998. "'Arte superficiem illam fontis amplecti': Alberti, Narziß und die Erfindung der Malerei." In *Diletto e Maraviglia*, edited by Christine Göttler and Ulrike Müller Hofstede, 10–39. Emsdetten: Edition Imorde.

Wölfflin, Heinrich. 2015. *Principles of Art History: The Problem of the Development of Style in Early Modern Art*. Edited by Evonne Levy and Tristan Weddigen. Translated by Jonathan Blower. Los Angeles: Getty Research Institute.

Wollheim, Richard. 1987. *Painting as an Art*. London: Thames & Hudson.

Wolters, Wolfgang. 1983. *Der Bilderschmuck des Dogenpalastes: Untersuchungen zur Selbstdarstellung der Republik Venedig im 16. Jahrhundert*. Wiesbaden: Steiner.

Wood, Christopher S. 2019. *A History of Art History*. Princeton: Princeton University Press.

———. 1993. *Albrecht Altdorfer and the Origins of Landscape*. London: Reaktion Books.

Wright, Alison. 2019. *Frame Work: Honour and Ornament in Italian Renaissance Art*. New Haven: Yale University Press.

———. 2015. "Crivelli's Divine Materials." In *Ornament and Illusion: Carlo Crivelli of Venice*, edited by Stephen Campbell, 57–77. London: Paul Holberton.

Wulfram, Hartmut 2001. *Literarische Vitruvrezeption in Leon Battista Albertis* De re aedificatoria. Munich: K. G. Saur.

Zani, Carlo. 1988. "Moretto e l'architettura." In *Alessandro Bonvicino, il Moretto*, 287–90. Brescia: Nuova Alfa.

Zani, Vito. 2010. *Gasparo Cairano e la scultura monumentale del Rinascimento a Brescia (1489–1517 ca.)*. Roccafranca: Compagnia della Stampa.

Zaunschirm, Thomas. 2012. "Die Erfindung des Goldgrundes." In *Gold: Artists in Gold; Tradition and Today*, edited by Agnes Husslein-Arco and Thomas Zaunschirm, 10–27. Vienna: Belvedere.

Zieke, Lars. 2020. *Natur und Mimesis: Visualisierungen des Atmosphärischen in der religiösen Malerei Venedigs und Mailands um 1500*. Regensburg: Schnell & Steiner.

Ziff, Jerrold. 1963. "'Backgrounds, Introduction of Architecture and Landscape': A Lecture by J.M.W. Turner." *Journal of the Warburg and Courtauld Institutes* 26: 124–47.

Zorach, Rebecca. 2011. *The Passionate Triangle*. Chicago: University of Chicago Press.

———. 2008. "Renaissance Theory: A Selective Introduction." In *Renaissance Theory*, edited by James Elkins and Robert Williams, 3–36. New York and London: Routledge.

Zorzi, Giangiorgio. 1961. "Notizie di arte e di artisti nei diari di Marino Sanudo." *Atti dell'Istituto veneto di scienze, lettere ed arti, classe di scienze morali e lettere* 119: 471–604.

Index

Note: Page numbers in italics indicate illustrations.

Credits

Erich Lessing / Art Resource, New York (fig. I.1.); Photo Scala, Florence, courtesy of the Ministero per i beni e le attività culturali e per il turismo (fig. I.2.); Photo Scala / Art Resource, New York (fig. I.3.); Photo Scala, Florence / Art Resource, New York (fig. I.4.); © Fitzwilliam Museum, Cambridge / Art Resource, New York (fig. I.8.); © 2008. Kunsthistorisches Institut in Florenz, Max-Planck-Institut, Florence (Fig. 1.1.); © National Gallery, London / Art Resource, New York (Fig. 1.2.); Erich Lessing / Art Resource, New York (Fig. 1.3.); © National Gallery, London / Art Resource, New York (Fig. 1.4.); Photo Scala, Florence / Art Resource, New York (Fig. 1.5.); Photo Scala, Florence, courtesy of the Ministero per i beni e le attività culturali e per il turismo / Art Resource, New York (Fig. 1.6.); Photo Scala, Florence, courtesy of the Ministero per i beni e le attività culturali e per il turismo / Art Resource, New York (Fig. 1.7.); Photo Scala, Florence, courtesy of the Ministero per i beni e le attività culturali e per il turismo / Art Resource, New York (Fig. 1.8.); Erich Lessing / Art Resource, New York (Fig. 1.9.); © Metropolitan Museum of Art, New York / Art Resource, New York (Fig. 1.10.); © National Gallery, London / Art Resource, New York (Fig. 1.11.); © BnF, Dist. RMN-Grand Palais / Art Resource, New York (Fig. 1.12.); National Gallery of Art, Washington, DC. (Fig. 1.13.); © National Gallery, London / Art Resource, New York (Fig. 1.14.); Photo Scala, Florence / Art Resource, New York (Fig. 1.15.); Photo Scala, Florence / Art Resource, New York (Fig. 1.16.); Photo Scala, Florence / Art Resource, New York (Fig. 1.17.); Photo Scala, Florence, courtesy of the Ministero per i beni e le attività culturali e per il turismo / Art Resource, New York (Fig. 1.18.); J. Paul Getty Museum, Los Angeles (Fig. 1.19.); Photo Scala, Florence / Art Resource, New York (fig. 2.1.); Photo Scala, Florence / bpk-Bildagentur für Kunst, Kultur und Geschichte / State Hermitage Museum, St. Petersburg / Roman Beniaminson / Art Resource, New York (fig. 2.2.); British Museum, London (fig. 2.4.); bpk-Bildagentur für Kunst, Kultur und Geschichte / Gemäldegalerie der Staatliche Museen zu Berlin (fig. 2.5.); Erich Lessing / Art Resource, New York (fig. 2.6.); J. Paul Getty Museum, Los Angeles (fig.2.7.); Photo Scala, Florence, courtesy of the Ministero per i beni e le attività culturali e per il turismo / Art Resource, New York (fig. 2.8.); Photo Scala, Florence, courtesy of the Ministero per i beni e le attività culturali e per il turismo / Art Resource, New York (fig. 2.9.); Photo Scala, Florence, courtesy of the Ministero per i beni e le attività culturali e per il turismo / Art Resource, New York (fig. 2.10.); © Metropolitan Museum of Art, New York / Art Resource, New York (fig. 2.11.); © Metropolitan Museum of Art, New York / Art Resource, New York (fig. 2.12.); Photo Scala, Florence / Art Resource, New York (fig. 2.13.); Photo Scala, Florence, courtesy of the Ministero per i beni e le attività culturali e per il turismo / Art Resource, New York (fig. 2.14.); British Museum, London (fig. 2.15.); HIP / Art Resource, New York (fig. 3.1.); Photo Scala, Florence / Art Resource, New York (fig. 3.2.); Photo Scala, Florence / bpk-Bildagentur für Kunst, Kultur und Geschichte / Gemäldegalerie der Staatliche Museen zu Berlin / Jörg P. Anders / Art Resource, New York (fig. 3.3.); HIP / Art Resource, New York (fig. 3.4.); Cameraphoto Arte Venice / Art Resource, New York (fig. 3.5.); HIP / Art Resource, New York (fig. 3.6.); Art Resource, New York (fig. 3.7.); HIP / Art Resource, New York (fig. 3.9.); Photo Scala, Florence, courtesy of the Ministero per i beni e le attività culturali e per il turismo / Art Resource, New York (fig. 3.10.); Photo Scala, Florence, courtesy of the Ministero per i beni e le attività culturali e per il turismo / Art Resource, New York (fig. 3.11.); Photo Scala, Florence, courtesy of the Ministero per i beni e le attività culturali e per il turismo / Art Resource, NY (fig. 3.12.); HIP / Art Resource, New York (fig. 3.13.); HIP / Art Resource, New York (fig. 3.14.); © Sarah Quill (fig. 3.15.); HIP / Art Resource, New York (fig. 3.16.); Warburg Institute Library, London (fig. 3.17.); Gianni dagli Orti / Art Resource, New York (fig. 3.18.); © Alinari Archives / Art Resource, New York (fig. 3.19.); HIP / Art Resource, New York (fig. 3.20.); National Gallery of Art, Washington, DC. (fig. 3.21.); Walters Art Museum, Baltimore (fig. 3.22.); HIP / Art Resource, New York (fig. 3.23.); Photo Scala, Florence/ bpk-Bildagentur für Kunst, Kultur und Geschichte / Gemäldegalerie der Staatliche Museen zu Berlin / Joerg P. Anders / Art Resource, New York (fig. 3.24.); HIP / Art Resource, New York (fig. 3.25.); HIP / Art Resource, New York (fig. 3.26.); J. Paul Getty Museum, Los Angeles (fig. 3.27.); HIP / Art Resource, New York (fig. 3.28.); Photo Scala, Florence / Art Resource, New York (fig. 4.1.); Warburg Institute Library, London (fig. 4.2.); © Biblioteca Nazionale Centrale, Florence (fig. 4.3.); Warburg Institute Library, London (fig. 4.4.); © National Gallery, London / Art Resource, New York. (fig. 4.5.); © National Gallery, London / Art Resource, New York (fig. 4.6.); © National Gallery, London / Art Resource, New York (fig. 4.7.); © BnF, Dist. RMN-Grand Palais / Art Resource, New York (fig. 4.8.); © BnF, Dist. RMN-Grand

Palais / Art Resource, New York (fig. 4.9.); © National Gallery, London / Art Resource, New York (fig. 4.11.); © National Gallery, London / Art Resource, New York (fig. 4.12.); Photo Scala, Florence / Art Resource, New York (fig. 4.13.); Erich Lessing / Art Resource, New York (fig. 4.14.); Photo Scala, Florence / Art Resource, New York (fig. 4.15.); Photo Scala, Florence / bpk-Bildagentur für Kunst, Kultur und Geschichte / Gemäldegalerie der Staatliche Museen zu Berlin / Jörg P. Anders / Art Resource, New York (fig. 4.16.); Art Resource, New York (fig. 4.17.); Mario Bonotto / Photo Scala, Florence / Art Resource, New York (fig. 4. 18); © National Gallery, London / Art Resource, New York (fig. 4.20.); Arsenal Library, Bibliothèque nationale de France, Paris (fig. 4.21.); Photo Scala, Florence / Art Resource, New York (fig. 4.22.); Photo Scala, Florence / Art Resource, New York (fig. 4.23.); Photo Scala, Florence / Art Resource, New York (fig. 4.25.); Photo Scala, Florence / Art Resource, New York (fig. 4.26.); Photo Scala, Florence, courtesy of the Ministero per i beni e le attività culturali e per il turismo / Art Resource, New York (fig. 5.1.); © Metropolitan Museum of Art, New York / Art Resource, New York (fig. 5.2.); © Museu Nacional d'Art de Catalunya, Barcelona (fig. 5.3.); © National Gallery, London / Art Resource, New York (fig. 5.4.); © National Gallery, London / Art Resource, New York (fig. 5.5.); © National Gallery, London / Art Resource, New York (fig. 5.6.); © National Gallery, London / Art Resource, New York (fig. 5.7.); © Alinari Archives / Art Resource, New York (fig. 5.8.); Photo Scala, Florence / Art Resource, New York (fig. 5.9.); Photo Scala, Florence / Art Resource, New York (fig. 5.10.); © British Museum, London (fig. 5.11.); Photo Scala, Florence / Art Resource, New York (fig. 5.12.); Photo Scala, Florence / Art Resource, New York (fig. 5.13.); Photo Scala, Florence / Art Resource, New York (fig. 5.14.)

Printed by Conti Tipocolor, Italy
Designed by Jeff Wincapaw
Coordinated by Steven Sears

A NOTE ON THE TYPE

The text face is Dante, a mid-20th-century old-style serif typeface designed by Giovanni Mardersteig. Mardersteig started work on Dante after the Second World War when printing at the Officina Bodoni returned to full production. Dante was redrawn for digital use by Monotype's Ron Carpenter in 1993.

The display face is Epicene, a contemporary typeface designed by Kris Sowersby and released in 2021. It is a Baroque typeface inspired by 18th century typographers J-F. Rosart and J.M. Fleischmann. Epicene's exaggerated details add rigour and style.